# Pouldine School
# ⸗ Inné agus Inniu

*A History of*
*Moycarkey National School*

*1847 – 2009*

Liam Ó Donnchú

First published in 2009

by

Moycarkey National School,
Pouldine,
Thurles,
Co. Tipperary.

## Pouldine School - Inné agus Inniu

*A History of Moycarkey National School*
*1847 – 2009*

Compiled and edited by Liam Ó Donnchú

© 2009

ISBN 978-0-9560755-1-2

*Design and layout:* Tom Beirne

*Printed in Ireland by:*
Walsh Colour Print, Castleisland, Co. Kerry.

*. . . cherishing all the children*
*of the nation equally . . .*

1916 Proclamation

*Míle Buíochas Fr. George*

*Liam ó Donnchú*

This book is dedicated
to the school community, past and present,
of Moycarkey N.S., Pouldine.

*Mol an óige agus tiocfaidh sí.*

# Contents

# Parochial Map
# of Co. Tipperary

UACHTARÁN NA hÉIREANN
PRESIDENT OF IRELAND

## MESSAGE FROM PRESIDENT McALEESE

It gives me great pleasure to send my best wishes to all those involved in the publication of a book on the history of Moycarkey National School. For over one hundred and sixty years, the school has been a focal point of the local area and it is marvellous to see its history carefully documented and recorded. The book will no doubt be of huge interest to pupils past and present, as well as an important source for future historians. I would like to congratulate all those who contributed to the book and I wish Moycarkey National School many more years of continued academic and sporting success in the future.

*Mary McAleese*

MARY McALEESE
PRESIDENT OF IRELAND

August 2009

ARCHBISHOP'S HOUSE,
THURLES,
CO. TIPPERARY.

Tel.:  0504-21512
Fax:  0504 - 22680
e-mail: office @cashel-emly.ie

## Foreword by
## *His Grace, Most Rev. Dermot Clifford, DD,*
## *Archbishop of Cashel & Emly*

During my first years in the National School, I was regularly questioned by old men with moustaches and walking sticks;

> *Are you going to school? Yes Sir.*
> *Are you a good scholar? I am.*
> *What book are you in? The Roll Book.*

After a time I found out it was the class I was in they were enquiring about.

They would then say sagely, *"Remember, your schooldays are the happiest days in your life"*. They would go on to describe how they each carried a sod of turf with them every morning during the winter. But the problem was that the *"Missus"*, their teacher, was *"fine stump of a woman"* and she stood in front of the fire all day preventing the possibility of any heat ever getting to them by conduction, convection or radiation!

The older generation of grandparents retained an active interest in their old school and liked to talk about their experiences there. The grandchildren liked to listen to their stories. Alice Taylor's, *"To School Through the Fields"* was a best seller when first published in 1988. Alice did not like to be sitting down in a desk all day learning everything by rote in a rundown two-roomed building. Coming home through the fields in the evening was what she mainly enjoyed about the school day.

But, go back a hundred years again to the *Big Sycamore* by Joseph Brady and you will find Maurice Fitzgerald teaching in a one-roomed school in Grangemockler in 1869 where only half the pupils could sit down. The other half had to stand while the babies sat on the mud floor with their slates and chalk. It was a far cry from the *interactive white board* and en-suite toilet of the present day! Maurice's father had attended a hedge-school and he, himself, knew the last surviving hedge schoolmaster who then acted as sacristan.

Our ancestors in Moycarkey came through similar changes in the educational system. There were ten small Catholic schools in the parish before the 1838 National Schools Act. They were held in thatched cabins and hay barns. But, one thing never changed throughout the centuries. It was the desire of parents to give a good schooling to their children. They had great respect for teachers. The local people gave sites for schools and they contributed very scarce money for school building. The main criticism of a teacher in those days was that he or she was too easygoing and did not push or punish their children enough to make good scholars of them! "Don't spare him, Master", was a regular mantra.

The first school in Pouldine was built in 1847, *"Black Forty Seven"*, the worst year of the Famine. The site was *"donated for nothing"* as they say hereabouts by Miss Emma Stanwix, a very generous local Protestant lady who also founded the Stanwix Home for Widows in Thurles. Fr. Robert Grace PP was the manager. There were fifty-one pupils at that time.

This "old school" lasted until 1970 when the new school was built. This now houses one hundred and fifty-eight children – eighty-two boys and seventy-six girls. There are six class teachers, three support teachers, a secretary and a caretaker. Mr. Liam Ó Donnchú is the Principal and Fr. George Bourke PP, is the Chairman of a very active Board of Management.

The school community reflects the values and the interests of the Moycarkey people, their love of learning, sport, especially hurling, and the tradition of music, singing and dancing. Religion plays a central role, the Catholic ethos or spirit contributes to the overall atmosphere of joyful caring and sharing. The children are taught their religious knowledge; they are prepared for the sacraments of First Confession and First Communion. I am privileged to have conferred Confirmation on twenty-one classes since 1988 and to convey my heartfelt thanks to the teachers on every occasion.

Liam Ó Donnchú has made a magnificent contribution to Pouldine National School for many years as Principal. He has now again used his talent as an Editor to produce this marvellous history of the school. For him, it is a labour of love. He has assembled the facts and he has long experience as Editor of the Tipperary GAA Yearbook. It always *"flew off the shelves"* the newsagents tell me. It won national awards while he was Editor.

In this history, Liam includes the personal memories of the older generation, photographs of pupils, past and present, together with an up-to-date picture of an exceptionally run school in the twenty-first century. I know that this book will be eagerly read by old and young alike. What is more, it will be a treasured possession in the homes of Moycarkey and in whatever part of the world the past pupils of Pouldine now live. They have always been proud of their school but they can be even more proud now.

Go mbhainfidh sibh go léir árd taithneamh as an saothar máistriúl seo.

+ Dermot Clifford,
Archbishop of Cashel & Emly.

# Milestones and Memories

T HE VISITOR is sometimes surprised to find a relatively large National School at a country crossroads. Officially known as Moycarkey National School, it is often, of course, locally known as Pouldine School, taking its name from the now very busy junction, and as these pages will recount, this intersection has been the location of a parish school since 1847.

It is timely that the history of education here should be recorded, and that memories should be put in print. While the school is located a distance away from the parish Church in Moycarkey, it is and has proved to be in so many ways an apt setting for a centre of education. The crossroads is very evocative as a place of assembly, a meeting place, and over the

*Fr George Bourke P.P.*

years the pupils have come – on foot, by road, and across the fields, on bicycles, on horse carts, and then of course in the latter years almost exclusively in cars, and a small number by bus. The catchment area sees the pupils coming in from all the surrounding districts.

It is just speculation, but Pouldine Cross may have been the location of a milestone, indicating the distance from Thurles, but the School History certainly will recall some of the milestones of life for the past pupils – the first day in school, the final or graduation day, and most importantly all the days, months and years in between, where the work of education and formation progressed. For many there will be the happy memories, class-mates working together, friendships formed, teachers bringing out the best in the young children, growth, and development in human and Christian values. For some the experience will have been less positive, and the hurts may have lived on, and healing may be needed.

On behalf of the Board of Management, I wish to express sincere thanks to all the Teachers, Pupils and Parents with whom we have worked. As priests of the parish our principal role must always be in the area of chaplaincy and Pastoral Care, and I must here acknowledge the outstanding contribution made by our teachers in teaching religion, preparation for the sacraments and handing on the faith.

I compliment Liam Ó Donnchú on undertaking this mammoth task of organising, editing and writing so much of this historical record of our school, and he in turn would wish to acknowledge the work of all contributors. Tréaslaím leis thar an gníomhaíocht oll-mhór, agus mar gheall ar an cnuasach eolais fíorluachmhar atá bailithe aige tríd na blianta a thabhairt dúinn. Tá ár mbuíochas tuillte ag Liam as a shár-obair leis an foilseachán seo. Agus tá buíochas glúinte na hiar-daltaí, na tuismitheóirí, agus an phobail i gcoitinne gnóthaithe aige mar Phríomh-Oide Scoil Má Chorca Éile. 'Give them roots to grow and wings to fly,' I once heard Liam say, citing this as part of his mission as a teacher – opening up young minds through literature, poetry, all the school subjects, and enabling them to broaden their horizons through initiave and imagination. Guíom sláinte agus fad-saol dó tar éis seirbhís na mblianta mar mhúinteoir bríomhar díoghraiseach.

May Moycarkey National School, now under the leadership of Múinteoir Robert White with his team of committed and dedicated teachers and staff continue the good work tríd na blianta atá rómhainn.

Beannacht Dé ar an obair,

*Fr. George Burke*

Board of Management Chairman

# Buíochas
## agus Beannacht

*'No man will love his land and race,*
*Who has no pride in his native place.'*

ONE HUNDRED and sixty two years have passed since Fr. Robert Grace initiated the building of a school at Pouldine. Jubilee years, centenary year etc. have come and gone without any celebration of our existence as a school community. I suppose it was this that prompted me to put pen to paper, because I firmly believe we have so much to celebrate.

Thousands of pupils, both boys and girls, have passed through the doors of Pouldine School and have made and are making a vital contribution to the communities in which they now live. Past pupils have made their homes not alone throughout Ireland but worldwide in a multiplicity of disciplines and occupations.

*Liam Ó Donnchú*

Parents, teachers and school managers have played their part and are an integral element of the story of the success of the school and its pupils. In more recent times Boards of Management and Parents' Councils have ensured that the organisation and support is there for pupils and teachers.

Having knowledge of and an interest in the locality gives us a greater appreciation of the place and the people who reside there. It improves the quality of our lives by giving us a greater sense of belonging. It nurtures a caring and respectful attitude to life and the environment, which makes one's own life more complete. I feel it is important to record the past and the story of our predecessors. The story of our school has its beginning in Famine times and has progressed through all the 'joys and sorrows' of Irish life since. Our ancestors handed on a rich heritage to this generation – a great legacy, which is entrusted to us in our day.

I want to acknowledge with gratitude the help, support and encouragement I got, when compiling this book. A special word of appreciation to Fr. George Bourke, to the Board of Management, School Staff, Parents Council and to all who contributed articles and photographs. Thanks to school secretary, Mrs. Catherine Walsh, who typed many of the articles. Thanks to Peggy Morris and her daughter Melissa (Curraheen) for their help with interviewing some past pupils and naming the old photographs. I got great co-operation from the staff at the Local Studies section of Tipperary Libraries in Thurles, thanks to Mary Guinan-Darmody and John O'Gorman. The help and advice of Tom Beirne (Kilkenny) with the printing process was invaluable.

The dedicated Finance Committee ensured the success of the project and deserves a special mention:- Christopher Mooney (Ashfield), Michelle Donnelly (Aughnagomaun) and Joseph Byrne (Moycarkey). Thanks to those who agreed to sponsor the book. Your help and generosity, particularly in recession times, was vital.

Many of those named in this book have gone to their eternal reward. Sadly for some, it was long before their prime. Suaimhneas síoraí dóibh go léir.

A sincere thanks to the people of Moycarkey for their support and friendship through the many pleasant years I spent as Principal Teacher in Pouldine. Best wishes to Robert White who is now in that role.

I hope this book will recall pleasant memories of family, home, youth, friendships, native place and of course, schooldays in Pouldine.

Mo bheannacht leat a scríbhinn.

*Liam ó Donnchú*

*Samhain 2009*

Townlands of
Moycarkey / Borris

# Scoileanna Scairte
# – Hedge Schools

*'Still crouching 'neath the sheltering hedge,*
*Or stretched on mountain fern,*
*The teacher and his pupils met feloniously to learn.'*

The Penal Laws, introduced by the British Government at the end of the 17th century prohibited Irish Catholics from receiving an education or establishing their own schools.

"That no person whatever of the popish religion shall publicly or in private houses teach school, or instruct youth in learning within this realm, under pain of twenty pounds, and of being committed to prison for the space of three months for every such offence..."

As a result, illegal schools, where schoolmasters and pupils congregated in remote areas, sometimes under hedges, began to emerge. Later, when the Penal Laws were relaxed, "schools" or "pay schools" were sometimes held in the schoolmaster's house, or usually in some rough building, barn, cabin, cow-house or outhouse provided by the parents. These schools were called "Hedge Schools", a name that lasted until the 19th century.

Conditions within the Hedge Schools were primitive in the extreme. The schoolhouses of the period were no better than the wretched hovels of the people. Heating arrangements were haphazard; pupils were expected to bring a few sods of turf with them to supplement any fuel provided.

In the great majority, the three R's (Reading, Writing and Arithmetic) were the only subjects taught. For most of the children who attended, this was about all they needed. Parents who could afford the hedgemaster's fee sent their children to these schools. In some schools, both Latin and Greek were part of the curriculum. Reading was generally based on chapbooks, sold at fairs or by travelling salesmen, typically with exciting stories of well-known adventurers and outlaws.

*Moycarkey N.S., Pouldine – c. 1910*

Back row: Martin O'Grady, Mary Fitzgerald, Sarah Moloney, Molly O'Grady, W. Fanning, Neddy Shanahan, Mick O'Grady. 4th row: Josie O'Grady, M. Shanahan, M. Brien, N. Shanahan, Nan O'Grady, Joe Ryan, Josie O'Grady. 3rd row: Maggie Moloney, Nan Brien, Nora O'Grady, M. Hogan, N. HOgan, M. O'Grady, Alice O'Grady, Kitty Fanning. 2nd row: Ned O'Grady, Jimmy Fitzgerald, John Fanning, D. Coman, Jimmy Brien, Jim O'Grady, Jack Shanahan. Front row: John Fitzgerald, M. Coman, Larry Coman, Mick Moloney, Phil Fitzgerald, J. Benson.

Back row at the window (l.-r.): Jack Costello, Parkstown; Jack O'Keeffe, Parkstown. Second row from back (l.-r.): Kieran Costello, Parkstown; Jimmy Heffernan, Ballymoreen; Jimmy Maher, Graigue; —; Andy O'Keeffe, Parkstown; Harry O'Keeffe, Parkstown; —; John Joe O'Keeffe, Horse & Jockey; Kitty Buckley, Cloughmartin; Peg

O'Keeffe, Parkstown; Billy Skehan, Knockroe; Mary Harris, Kitty Whelan, Galboola. Front row (l.-r.): —; Jerry Butler; —; Josie Donnelly, Moycarkey; Judy Harris, Kylnoe; Rosie Kennedy, Galboola; —; —; Nial Heffernan, Galboola; Kitty Buckley, Pouldine.

*An Scoil Scairte – Hedge School*

Padraic Colum, in his poem, 'A Poor Scholar of the Forties' aptly described a hedge school of the 1840s:

*My eyelids red and heavy are*
*From bending o'er the smouldering peat.*
*I know the Aeneid now by heart,*
*My Virgil read in cold and heat,*
*In loneliness and hunger smart;*
*And I know Homer too, I ween,*
*As Munster poets know Ossian.*

Hedgeschool Teachers were poorly paid. Payment to the schoolmaster was generally made per subject, and brighter pupils would often compete locally with their teachers. The number of pupils in a school was, on average, about forty. Fees were charged quarterly and on many occasions turf, butter, eggs, etc. were taken as part payment. The schoolmaster frequently stayed free of charge in a parent's house or at a number of houses in rotation.

These schools were best attended in summer, less well attended in springtime and harvest, as the pupils were needed to work on the farms or in the bog. Wintertime attendance often depended on the condition of the schoolhouse and on the distance pupils had to walk to school.

The Hedge School Master was proud of the extent of his own knowledge. His income and the very existence of the school depended on what he could teach and his confidence in teaching it. Any young man with ambitions to be a schoolmaster first learned all he could at his local school and then travelled to other schools, which had gained reputations for their teaching.

Although the Hedge Schoolmaster's monetary income was small, his social prestige was immense. The Hedge Schoolmaster not alone taught the children who came to his school, but was often their parent's letter- writer and reader, lawyer and general adviser. Next to the Protestant Minister and the Priest, he was the most important person in the parish. No function of consequence, wedding, christening or local meeting took place at which he was not a prominent figure. Oliver Goldsmith, the renowned Irish Poet of the 18th century remembered with awe and reverence, his old village schoolmaster:

*Beside yon straggling fence, that skirts the way*
*With blossomed furze unprofitably gay,*
*There, in his noisy mansion, skilled to rule,*
*The village master taught his little school;*
*A man severe he was, and stern to view;*
*I knew him well, and every truant knew;*
*Well had the boding tremblers learned to trace*
*The day's disasters in his morning face;*
*Full well they laughed, with counterfeited glee,*
*At all his jokes, for many a joke had he;*
*Full well the busy whisper, circling round,*
*Conveyed the dismal tidings when he frowned;*
*Yet he was kind; or if severe in aught,*
*The love he bore to learning was at fault.*
*The village all declared how much he knew;*
*'Twas certain he could write, and cipher too;*
*Lands he could measure, terms and tides presage,*
*And even the story ran that he could gauge.*
(Lines from:- The Deserted Village.)

With the advent of the National School System in Ireland in the 1830s most of the old Hedge Schools went into decline. Parents began sending their children to the new National Schools because fees were lower. Teachers began taking up posts in them because of the regular salary, however small. Faced with an acute shortage of pupils the Hedge Schools and other "pay schools" gradually began to disappear.

## LOCAL SCHOOLMASTERS AND MISTRESSES IN 1826 –'27

| | | |
|---|---|---|
| Patrick Archer | Roman Catholic | Moycarkey |
| James Belser | Protestant | Littleton |
| Thomas Coonan | Roman Catholic | Grallagh |
| James Hackett | Roman Catholic | Ballymurreen |
| Anne Lamphier | Roman Catholic | Parkstown |
| Patrick Ryan | Roman Catholic | Turtulla |
| Patrick Smith | Roman Catholic | Parkstown |

## LOCAL SCHOOLS IN THE DAYS BEFORE NATIONAL EDUCATION

When Archbishop James Butler visited the parish of Moycarkey –Borris on July 26th 1759 he reported on the Catholic elementary school system then in operation in the parish. Two Catholic shoolmasters in Two-Mile-Borris are named, Henry Fox and Cornelius Ryan. The schoolmaster in Moycarkey, James Bell, "exhibited a list of 32 boys perfected in the Christian doctrine."

In 1824, on the eve of the introduction of the National School system, the parish had ten private Catholic schools. These were mostly in thatched cabins. One was described as "a thatched barn", another as a "stable".Annual income for these schools varied from a maximum of £25 to as low as £5. The overall enrolment of Catholics was 378 while 22 Protestant children attended at these schools. The only school to receive outside funding was the one at Ballymoreen, which rejoiced in a £2 annual donation from the Protestant Rector and £1 from the curate.

In the 1840's, Tom Fogarty had a Hedge School at Moycarkey with 40 pupils attending. About the same time, Pat Doyle had a Hedge School at Graigue with 30 pupils. This school moved later to Ballytarsna. In 1837 there was a 'pay school' at Galboola for 100 children. Closer to Littleton Master Holmes had a Hedge School at Ballyvinane.

The changeover to the National School system occurred rather slowly in Moycarkey, as elsewhere. There was still no national school in the parish in 1844, though in an application for a grant that year it was stated that "the Catholic parish priest will co-operate".

*Acknowledgment*

*Geographical*

*Thoughtfully*

*Included in this photo are: Jack Callanan, Paddy Maher, Rodge Callanan, Jack Maher, – Twomey, Jack Harris, Michael Skehan, Paddy Leahy, Paddy Ryan, Tom Ryan, Danny Maher, Tommy Molloy, Jack Heffernan, Dick Buckley, Sam Melbourne, Paddy Dwyer, Jack Butler, Harry O'Keeffe, Tom Fitzgerald, Billy Skehan, Bill Lamphier, Rodge Molloy.*

*Back row (l.-r.): – Lamphier, Tom Fitzgerald, J Butler, Patrick Purcell, John Brien, Dan Maher, Nell Maher, Josie Donnelly, Mary Donnelly, Catherine Maher, Patricia Maher, Mary Brien, Mary Hogan. Middle row (l.-r.): J.J. O' Keeffe, M. Heffernan, Mick Brien, Bill Brien, Dan Taylor, —, Mary Maher, M. Fitzpatrick, Sarah Bourke. Front row (l.-r.): –, Paddy Molloy, Joe Murphy, Pat Dwyer, Tom Taylor, James Ryan, D. Maher,–, Sarah Delaney, Mary Maher, Rita Maher, Statia Donnelly, Peg Taylor, Josie Buckley.*

# National School System

THE Commissioners for National Education (National Education Board) were established in 1831 for the purpose of administering a fund of £30,000 placed at the disposal of the Lord Lieutenant for the education of the poor in Ireland. Their powers were based on a set of instructions drawn up by Chief Secretary Stanley, and were not defined in any enactment. They were empowered to make grants to existing schools for the payment of teachers and the provision of equipment and also to provide for the building of new schools, to appoint and pay inspectors, and to establish a model school for the training of teachers. They were granted a charter in 1845.

## MOYCARKEY NATIONAL SCHOOL, POULDINE.

## THE OLD SCHOOL, AN SEAN SCOIL, FACTS AND FIGURES

1844 – May12th, Rev. Robert Grace P.P. made an application to the Commissioners of Education for aid towards the building of a school to be called Moycarkey National School. Roll Number: 4005.

1844 – July 16th, an inspector from the Commissioners submitted a favourable report on the application. This included that a one-acre site, at Knockroe, was available on lease at a nominal rent from Emma Sloughter Stanwix of Versailles, in the kingdom of France. The length of this lease would be forever, if required. The schoolhouse and grounds would be enclosed and the Trustees of the proposed school would be Rev. Robert Grace P.P., Nicholas Maher Esq. M.P.,Turtulla House and William Max Esq.of Maxfort. One hundred and fifty pupils, 80 male and 70 female were expected and a local contribution of one-third of the cost was available. The inspector also stated that there was no Protestant clergyman in the parish but included that the Catholic parish priest would co-operate. He also reported that the only education in the parish, within three miles of the proposed school, was 'none save a hedge school or two'. Patrick Quinlan, the

Superintendent of National Schools, concluded his report as follows – 'I beg to recommend to the favourable notice of the Commissioners, there being no school properly so called in this wide, extensive and populous parish'.

Permission was granted for a school containing a single room 34ft. by 18ft. to cater for 100 children. The commissioners agreed to pay – sixty six pounds, thirteen shillings and four pence towards building costs and seven pounds and ten shillings towards furniture expenses. The furniture would consist of eight desks. The total expense in providing the school amounted to one hundred and eleven pounds and five shillings.

The local contribution amounted to thirty seven pounds one shilling and eight pence.

1846 – Dec. 31st. Inspector stated that having visited the school, he found that the foundations were only fifteen inches deep, under the ground line. He also noted that the mortar used had not a sufficient proportion of sand. The Manager of the school was informed that until the building was executed according to specifications that the commissioners would not feel themselves bound to pay the grants.

1847 – Oct. 1st Moycarkey School opened. The first schoolmaster was Thomas Fogarty. £10 was granted as salary. He was described as being twenty five years of age and as having 'no experience'.

1847 – 331 children from the parish received the sacrament of Confirmation

1850 – The average school attendance for all the schools in the parish of Moycarkey Borris was 267.

1852 - 494 children from the parish received the sacrament of Confirmation. The parish now had three National Schools, while one Hedge School still survived.

1852 – The salary was withdrawn from Thomas Fogarty due to his excessive absences in the last three years.

1853 - Very Rev. John Bourke appointed Parish Priest and School Manager. He is said to have built a new school at Pouldine. (W. Skehan)

1857 – Teacher, James Walsh, fined one pound for the retrograde and most unsatisfactory state of the school. His annual salary was £13.

1858 – Nov.26th. School closed early. Teacher, John Robinson, was ordered by the inspectors to guard against this and to improve his punctuality in the mornings.

1861 – January 19th, Rev. John Bourke P.P. applied successfully for aid towards the payment of the salary of a work-mistress named Mary Jane Robinson. She was

## POULDINE SCHOOL, HORSE & JOCKEY, THURLES

### FOR SALE BY PRIVATE TREATY

We have received instructions from Very Rev. Fr. J. Moynihan, P.P., to sell by Private Treaty.

The school at Pouldine and plot of ground. Held, free of rent. This single storey slated structure comprises five rooms, 28' x 24', 28' x 28', 30' x 27', 27' x 10' and two cloakrooms with two w.h.b. in each, two play sheds 34' x 12' each and five outside toilets.

The Auctioneers wish to draw special attention to the sale of this property, which is in good repair, ideally situated, convenient to Thurles and Horse and Jockey and would make a most comfortable dwelling or business premises.

For further details apply to:—

**PATRICK J. O'MEARA, Esq.,** Solicitor, Thurles, or the Auctioneers.

aged 18 and according to the inspector's report taught; Knitting, Embroidery and Crochet and also assisted in 'the Literary Department'. She worked from 10.00 a.m. to 3.00 p.m. Monday to Friday and from 10.00 to 12.00 noon on Saturday. Eight pounds salary was granted to Miss Robinson.

The only other teacher in the school, at this time, was John Robinson.

1861 – Even though there were 151 pupils on roll, 62 male and 89 female, the average attendance, in a four-month period was only 58, 26 male and 32 female. This was probably due to the fact that schoolchildren were expected to take part in farm work and work on the bog during the busy spring and autumn seasons.

1865 – Average daily attendance for this year was 64 even though the number on roll was 123. Average age of pupils was 8.9. Of those examined, only one had reached the highest level of achievement with all others on the First Book.

1880 – Nov.4th. The inspector reported that the attendance for that day was not to be recorded, as the pupils went to the Thurles Races after their morning tasks.

1889 – Teachers' salary per quarter, £10 and 16 shillings while the monitress was paid £1 and 10 shillings.

1891 - Very Rev. Thomas Fennelly appointed Parish Priest and School Manager. He wrote to the commissioners regarding overcrowding in the school and the need for an extra classroom for 30 pupils, along with the enclosing of the grounds.

1891 – Feb.2nd. Miss Mary Ryan appointed assistant teacher. Her salary was £27 per year plus a share of the results fees.

1891 – A grant of £119...10 shillings was agreed, towards the building of a classroom (18 feet by 12 feet) and construction of enclosing walls, piers and gate...

1892 - Feb. 23rd. Only 8 pupils present due to snow

*Pouldine 1921*

*Back row (l.-r.): – Grant, Turtulla; Jim Hayes, Ballymoreen; T. O'Keeffe, Horse & Jockey; M. Callanan, Coolkip; – Costello, Parkstown; – Costello; Parkstown; –; B. Connors, Grallagh. Second row from back (l.-r.): J. O'Keeffe, Horse & Jockey; M. Hogan, Coolkip; C. Heffernan, Ashill; M. Furlong, Horse & Jockey; C. Heffernan, Ashill; B. Twomey, Forgestown; C. Hayes, Ballymoreen; M.Bourke, Graigue; M. Hackett, Liskiveen; M. Manning, Ballymoreen. Third row from back (l.-r.): M. A. O'Keeffe, Horse & Jockey; – Bourke, Graigue; M. Mc arthy, Horse & Jockey; H. O'Keeffe, Horse & Jockey; Kitty Ryan, Maxfort or H & J.; May Manning, Ballymoreen; E. Maher, Forgestown; Moll Bourke Hewitt, Knockroe; – Hanley, Liskiveen; – Hanley, Liskiveen; Mary "Dolly" Hayes, Ballymoreen. Front row (l.-r.): Sarah Dwyer, Kylnoe; B. O'Keeffe, Horse & Jockey; – Burke, Knockroe; – Foley, Liskiveen; – Foley, Liskiveen; T. O'Keeffe, Parkstown; M. O'Keeffe, Parkstown.*

*Pouldine school photograph from the early 20th century. We have been unable to name the pupils and exact year.*

1892 – Monitor was paid 5 shillings for two months work

1892 – Local contribution towards improvements at the School (Estimated at one third of the Total Cost) £59...15s...0 Building Classroom and enclosing Wall.

1893 - £15...7s...4 d, Local contribution towards the cost of raising the floor level by eight inches and Wainscoting Schoolroom,£18..5s..0. Erection of Porch, Removal of Privies and putting dividing wall through playground. The state grant was £36...10shillings. There were now four schoolrooms in the school, the dimensions of which were 34 x 18, 12 x 18, 34 x 22 and 14 x 22. There were seven desks with forms, each twelve feet long.

1893 – June 12th, Parish priest, Rev. Thomas Fennelly, visited the school and examined the pupils in reading and spelling. Fr. Fennelly would later succeed Archbishop Thomas Croke as Archbishop of Cashel and Emly.

1893 – Rev. Thomas Fennelly sought a loan from the Commissioners towards the erection of accommodation for the teachers.

The summer vacation in 1893 commenced on July 3rd and ended on July 28th.

1894 – March 3rd - The Manager, Rev. Thomas Fennelly P.P. applied for a supply of new furniture for the school. He stated that no new furniture had been supplied since the school opened in 1847. Following an inspection of the school, the district inspector wrote that:' the present desks are old and much the worse for wear. Besides, they were originally of bad construction, being narrow and of too great incline'. The application was successful and furniture valued twenty two pounds and eighteen shillings was purchased. The furniture consisted of six new desks (each nine feet in length), one new press, a new table, three forms and two chairs.

1895 – A loan of £250 was granted towards the erection of a residence at Pouldine for the Principal Teacher.

1896 – The school was whitewashed, repaired and furniture varnished. Total cost - £7 and 9 shillings.

1900 – New Teacher, Margaret Carroll.

1901 - Very Rev. Nicholas Duggan appointed Parish Priest and School Manager.

1901 – Teachers were paid per quarter year as follows: - Jerry Coman (Principal) £27, Ellen Coman (First Assistant) £12 and 12 shillings, Bridget Quinn (Second Assistant) £7 and 8 shillings. The monitress received £4.

1903 – New Trustees appointed: - Most Rev. Thomas Fennelly D.D., Archbishop of Cashel and Emly, Mr. Daniel B. Hayes, Ballyerk, Moycarkey and Mr. Philip Byrne, Ballymoreen, Moycarkey.

1908 – Jeremiah O'Reilly, an extern teacher, was paid £6...10s...0 for one year's instruction given in the Irish language, as an extra subject.

1909 – New Science Press purchased for the school, costing £6.

1912 – Rev. Fr. Nicholas Duggan wrote to the Commissioners seeking a grant towards additional accommodation due to the congested conditions in the school. Average on Roll was 180.4 with 144 being the average attendance. An extra classroom was required and the estimated cost of the work was £380. He was anxious to proceed and the local contribution was available but is awaiting the grant.

1913 – Rev. Fr. Duggan is losing patience with the Commissioners. He wrote: - 'For goodness sake hurry up with it and let us have it finished before I die'. His appeal was successful and permission to proceed arrived on Oct.11th. He immediately set to work and the contractor was Matthew Purcell of Ballydavid, Littleton who had agreed to complete the work for the sum of £370. So anxious was Fr. Duggan to have the work completed by the following April 1st that he insisted on the inclusion of a penalty clause in the agreement which stated that £2 would be paid for each week following that date that the work was not completed to the satisfaction of the engineer.

1914 – '18 During World War One a war bonus was paid to Teachers.

1915 – Rev. N. Duggan P.P. applied for a new stove and fireguard for the school. The Principal Teacher was Jeremiah Coman and three assistant teachers were employed in the school at the time. The inspector, J. Dickie, called to the school and supported the application for a new cooker. This was successful and a Stanley No.8 Range was purchased and installed. The total cost, including a fender and fireguard, was £14. By October 1916, with winter approaching, the fire in the range could not be lit, as it had to be inspected by the Department inspector. Fr. Duggan again wrote, 'so that we can start the fire as the weather is getting cold now'.

1922 – Letter from Jeremiah Coman (Principal) requesting a new Roll Book and a Daily Report refers to the 'disturbed state of Clonmel' due to the Civil War.

*An sean scoil – the old school.*

1922 – Nine pupils in seventh class

1923 – '25 Teachers attend Irish courses during these years.

1926 - Very Rev. Daniel Moloney appointed Parish Priest and School Manager

1928 – April - Names of pupils are in the Irish language from now on.

1935 - Very Rev. John McGrath appointed Parish Priest and School Manager.

1954 – Annual Rent on Teachers' Residence was £6 plus rates.

1955 - Very Rev. William Breen appointed Parish Priest and School Manager.

1958 - Fuel store added and toilets upgraded.

1965 – Summer holidays commence on July 17th and end on Sept. 6th.

1966 – The need for a new school was recognised by Rev. Fr. Willie Breen who sought and received permission from the Department of Education to enter into negotiations regarding a new school. As the existing site was deemed unsuitable, a more suitable and extensive site was purchased, across the road, from the Quinlan family. The architect appointed by the Department was Basil Boyd-Barrett and the new school would include four classrooms, toilets and cloakrooms, teachers' room, general purpose room, kitchen and staff toilet. Bicycle shed, boiler house, pump house, a large concrete yard and playground would also be supplied.

1968 – March 12th, School closed due to the death of Donagh O'Malley, Minister for Education.

1968 – Very Rev. James M. Moynihan appointed Parish Priest and School Manager. New School under construction – Building Contractor was Tommy O'Keeffe from Gortnahoe.

1969 – Jan. 11th, Tipperary Star carried an advertisement announcing the sale of the school. It was purchased by the Walsh family.

Moycarkey *NATIONAL SCHOOL.*

## ORGANISERS'
## OBSERVATION BOOK.

*Pouldine 1930*

Back row: Mary Fogarty, Graigue; Bridie Dempsey, Ballytarsna; —; Nellie Heffernan, Galboola; Josie Donnell, Forgestown; Eileen O'Keeffe, Horse & Jockey; Mary Maher, Horse & Jockey. Second row from back: Agnes Manning, Pouldine; Mary Heffernan; Mary Ann O'Keeffe, Horse & Jockey; Nell O'Keeffe, Horse & Jockey; Josie McCarthy, Maxfort; Maggie Skehan, Graigue; Alice Dempsy, Ballytarsna; Nell Cantwell, Pouldine; Katie Ryan, Moycarkey; Josie Buckley, Graigue. Third row from back: Kitty Buckley, Graigue; Peg Taylor, Graigue; Mary Ryan, Maxfort; Mary Quirke, Heathview; Josie Dwyer, Pouldine; Nellie Gleeson; Biddy O'Keeffe, Horse & Jockey; Ciss Melbourne, Curraheen; Kitty Cantwell, Pouldine; Josie Ryan, Moycarkey; M. Fitzpatrick; Peg O'Keeffe, Horse & Jockey. Front row: Statia Donnelly, Forgestown; Annie Maher, Maxfort; Kitty O'Keeffe, Horse & Jockey; Kate Dunne, Graigue; Sarah Regan, Knockroe; Nancy Molloy, Moycarkey; – Buckley.

Back row: —, —, Paddy Flanagan, Tony Ryan, Andy Moloney, Andy Maher, Mick Moloney, Jack Maher, Paddy Moloney. Third row: —, Paddy Ryan, Jack Dwyer, Laurence Coman, Rody Lambe, James O'Grady, Dan Coman, Paddy Hogan, —, Larry Hogan. Second row: Nell Cantwell, —, Bridie O'Grady, Ellie O'Grady, – Dwyer, —, Mary Flanagan, —, —, Mary Hogan, Mary Moloney, Rita Maher, May Maher. Front row: Thady Flanagan, Neddy Flanagan, James Maher, Willie Maher.

# Jeremiah Coman

JEREMIAH COMAN, born 1870, was a native of Clareen in the parish of Boherlahan - Dualla. He became principal of Moycarkey N.S., Pouldine in the 1890s.

The school in those years was much in need of refurbishment and Jerry along with the school manager worked ceaselessly to improve the conditions for both pupils and staff. An extra classroom was provided in an effort to ease the overcrowded conditions, new furniture was purchased– the first since the opening of the school in 1847, and a new range was installed to help heat the building.

The numbers of pupils attending Pouldine during his time were among the highest ever to attend the school, peaking in 1909 with 189 on roll. It was also a troubled time in Ireland and abroad. The Easter Rebellion, First World War, War of Independence and Civil War all occurred during his time as principal.

When construction of the teacher's residence at Pouldine was completed in 1896, Jerry Coman, his wife Ellen and family were the first occupants. They had four children:- Margaret Mary, Úna, Daniel and Lawrence.

His wife Ellen (nee Maher) predeceased Jerry on January

I. O. [60.]

District No. 43.

Moycarkey National School    Roll No. 4005.

EDUCATION OFFICE,
Dublin, 19th May 1892

Rev SIR,

We have to inform you that, on the recommendation of the District Inspector, the Commissioners of National Education have sanctioned the *promotion* of Mr.

*Jeremiah Coman*

Teacher in the above named National School, from the lower to the higher division of Third class

This promotion dates from 1st April, 1892.

We have the honor to be,
Rev SIR,
Your obedient Servants,

JOHN E. SHERIDAN,  } Secretaries.
J. C. TAYLOR,
W. R. Molloy.

23rd 1916. Her death, at the age of 38 years, was described as untimely and as having occurred at the teacher's residence in Pouldine. This kind and gentle lady had been in delicate health for some months. She had also taught in the school at Pouldine.

Jeremiah Coman resigned the principalship of Moycarkey N.S., Pouldine in October 1923. This was due to failing health. He had been principal for over thirty years, a position which brought distinction to himself and great benefit to the parish.

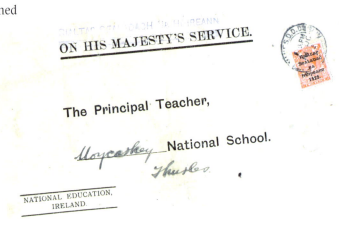

His popularity can be seen in the fact that following his resignation, past pupils and friends met and decided to present Jerry with a Testimonial, as a mark of the esteem and friendship in which he had been so long held and as a small token of gratitude for the many services he had rendered to the people of the parish, during his time among them. A committee, with the following officers, was appointed to organise the Testimonial: - Chairman- Very Rev. Cannon Duggan P.P., Treasurer – James O'Brien, Moycarkey, Hon. Sec. Patrick Maher, Pouldine and Nicholas Hogan, Coolkip.

Sadly, within a month, and before the proposed testimonial could be presented, Jeremiah Coman was dead, passing to his eternal reward on November 22nd 1923, aged 53 years. He was buried in the family plot in Ardmayle churchyard.

At a general meeting of the Moycarkey branch of the Farmers' Association, presided over by James O'Keeffe, the following motion of condolence, proposed by Thomas Cantwell and seconded by Mtn. P. Hogan, was passed.

'With sincere and profound regret we, the farmers of Moycarkey, deplore the death of Jeremiah Coman, principal teacher of Moycarkey N.S. He was loved and liked by young and old with whom he came in contact, and we tender our deepest sympathy to his dear family and relatives in their sad affliction.'

Similar expressions of sympathy were offered by other local organisations.

# Teacher Training

## MONITORS

MOST STUDENTS entering teacher-training colleges, prior to 1926, were ex-monitors. Monitors could be appointed in any suitable national school. They were in reality apprentice teachers. They were selected from promising pupils in the higher classes in the national school and appointed by the manager, on the recommendation of the inspector for the district. The age range for appointment as a monitor was 12 to 16 years. Monitors spent a certain number of hours teaching each day, under the supervision of the school principal and received special instruction for which the teacher was paid a small fee. Monitors were paid a salary varying from five pounds in the first year to eighteen pounds in the final year.

This system prevailed in Moycarkey N.S. Pouldine from 1860. Jim Robinson was first reported to have been granted a gratuity of 34 shillings - "for instructing unpaid monitor for period ended 31/12/1859". By February of 1861 this gratuity increased to £4. Denis Commins, in 1865 and 1866, was paid £2/10 and £4 respectively for his instruction to D. Shanahan, who was appointed Junior Monitor on 1/11/1865, and to Margaret Shanahan who was appointed Junior Monitor on 1/4/1868.

Monitors, who passed a competitive examination, were eligible for entry to a teacher-training college. The normal training period was two years. This system prevailed until the opening of the Preparatory Colleges in 1926.

## THE PREPARATORY COLLEGES

These colleges were established in 1926 to provide a four year secondary school course for students who desired to prepare themselves for admission to a training college, to become primary teachers. It was also a significant attempt by the state to remedy the shortage of student teachers with a fluent knowledge of the Irish language. Age range for entry was 14 to 16 years. Compulsory subjects for the entrance examination to these colleges were Irish, English, Arithmetic, History and Geography while Algebra, Geometry, Drawing, Nature Study and Vocal Music were additional subjects. The examination was both oral and written. To qualify for entrance the candidate should obtain 50% in Irish and 40% in the other compulsory subjects, with an overall percentage of 50% - the standard was that for seventh class in a national school. Irish was to be the ordinary language of these colleges.

Students from ordinary Secondary Schools, who obtained the Leaving Certificate and had obtained such marks in Irish as were regarded as satisfactory by the Department of Education and had passed a special oral test in Irish, were also eligible for entrance to a teacher training college. However, in filling vacancies in the training colleges, priority was given to preparatory college students.

The Catholic preparatory colleges remained in existence until 1961. From that year forward there was open entry to teacher training colleges through competitive examination i.e. The Leaving Certificate.

## COLLEGES OF EDUCATION

Today there are five Colleges of Education for primary teachers, which offer three year full-time courses leading to a Bachelor of Education (B.Ed.) degree, which is the recognised qualification for primary teaching.

*The Colleges are:*

The Church of Ireland College of Education, Upper Rathmines Road, Dublin .
St. Patrick's College, Drumcondra, Dublin .
Mary Immaculate College, South Circular Road, Limerick
Froebel College of Education, Sion Hill, Blackrock, Co. Dublin.
Coláiste Mhuire, Marino Institute of Education, Griffith Avenue, Dublin 9.

# Teachers' Residence
# at Pouldine

UNDER THE National School Teachers Residences (Ireland) Act, 1875, provision was made for the purchase or erection of residences for national teachers. A grant of half the estimated cost up to a maximum of £100 was made available for the erection, improvement or purchase of a house for the principal teacher. The site was to be free of rent and have a lease of 61 years or more. This Act also enabled the State to make a loan up to a maximum of £250, repayable over 35 years at 5%, for the erection of a teacher's residence. The loan was made to the manager, who became the owner of the house, subject to the repayment of the annual interest charge. In practice the manager's liability was usually discharged by the teacher, whose legal position was that of a caretaker. All the arrangements regarding the building of the residence were made by the Board of Works. Loans for teacher's residences were discontinued shortly after the outbreak of World War 1 in 1914.

On Nov. 30th 1893 the Manager of Moycarkey National School, Rev. Thomas Fennelly

*Former teacher's residence at Pouldine. This photograph taken in 2009 is of the extended building.*

wrote to the Commissioners of Education seeking a loan of £250 for the erection of a residence for the Principal Teacher, beside the school at Pouldine. He was anxious that the work on this project would start during the following spring. He stated that a suitable site, half acre in area, was available just outside the enclosure of the school. The land would be leased by the Governors of the Stanwix Charity, of whom Rev. T. Fennelly was one. The rent was seven shillings per year and this would be paid by the school trustees. The Commissioners recommended that, before proceeding any further, an inspectors report be sought on the viability of the school. The District Inspector was charged with this responsibility and following a visit to the school he reported: - 'the past character of the pupils' attendance and the circumstances of the locality warrant the conclusion that the school will be a permanent institution'.

**Instructions in regard to the Infliction of Corporal Punishment in National Schools.**

(1.) Corporal punishment should be administered only for grave transgression— never for failure in lessons.

(2.) The Principal Teacher only should inflict the corporal punishment. An interval of at least ten minutes should elapse between the offence and the punishment.

(3.) Only a light cane or rod may be used for the purpose of inflicting the corporal punishment. The boxing of children's ears, the pulling of their hair, and similar ill-treatment are absolutely forbidden, and will be visited with severe penalties.

(4.) No Teacher should carry about a cane or other instrument of punishment.

(5.) Frequent recourse to corporal punishment will be considered by the Commissioners as indicating bad tone and ineffective discipline.

(6.) The particulars required by the headings should be entered in this Book before the infliction of the punishment.

(7.) The Principal Teacher must submit the Book to the Manager on the occasion of his first visit to the school after every case of punishment.

P. E. LEMASS,  
W. J. DILWORTH. } *Secretaries.*

OFFICE OF NATIONAL EDUCATION.  
MARLBORO' STREET, DUBLIN.

In 1895 the loan of £250 was granted and the Manager proceeded with supervising the erection of the building. It was a slate roofed two-storey stone structure; four bedrooms upstairs (two with fireplaces) while downstairs contained a parlour with fireplace, large kitchen with range, scullery and pantry. Instalments on the loan were due on April 5th and October 10th each year. The final payment was made in the spring of 1931.

In 1915 the annual rent paid by the principal teacher was six pounds and five shillings. The teacher was also expected to pay insurance on the property. This amounted to one shilling and six pence in 1915.

Mr. Jerry Coman was the first principal teacher to occupy the residence. The Myers family resided there from the 1920s and they were succeeded by the Maher family in the 1940s.

# Michael Myers

**M**ICHAEL MYERS was the seventh and youngest child of James and Elizabeth Myers (nee Devane) of Nodstown in the Parish of Boherlahan- Dualla. In all, he had three sisters, Anne, Bridget and Mary and three brothers, Edmond, John and James. He was baptised in Boherlahan on 19th August 1879 and educated in Nodstown N.S.

*Michael and Kathleen Myers*

Michael had a deep interest in the G.A.A. and was an officer of the fledging Boherlahan G.A.A. Club, having been previously Treasurer of the famed Tubberadora Club. He was a regular at all the venues whenever the Tubberadora men crossed camáns. At the time of his death, Michael was President of the Boherlahan Hurling Club.

He trained as a national teacher in Marlborough Street, Dublin, between 1897 and 1899, receiving his Diploma in March 1904. He was appointed as the first principal teacher of Gaile N.S. on 1st September 1900, at the age of 21. Although the school was built as a two-teacher school, Michael was sole teacher on opening day and a letter from the Commissioners of National Education to the manager, Fr. Thomas Fennelly P.P., in November 1900 advised "that the appointment of a lady teacher cannot be sanctioned until an annual average of 20 girls be secured".

On appointment, his salary was £52 per annum, with just over five shillings "pension stoppage", per quarter. According to the salary book, his salary for the quarter ending March 31st 1901 was twelve pounds twelve shillings and nine pence. For each quarter until the end of 1902, he received thirteen pounds twelve shillings and nine pence. By April 1911, his annual salary was £107.

Although Gaile School opened in September 1900, the adjoining residence was not completed until the summer of 1903. As a result, Michael Myers was forced to walk from Nodstown each day. In the 1901 census, he still shared his parents' house with sisters, Annie and Bridget and older brother, James.

Michael was considered an excellent teacher and people were disappointed when he transferred to Moycarkey N.S. in 1923. He was presented with a silver tea service and an address signed by Dr. T.P.

Lyons, P.S.M; Mrs J. Lyons N.T.; Michael Shanahan; Michael Tuohy; Edmond Dunne and Philip Fogarty D.C. on behalf of his past pupils.

The civil war ended in the months before his appointment to Moycarkey National School, Pouldine. The economic war of the 1930's and the Emergency during World War Two were testing times for Irish people everywhere. Michael Myres performed his duties during these years with fervent dedication even though greatly under-resourced. Michael taught in a time of great turbulence and upheaval in Ireland. He was Irish and National in the highest meaning of the term and like many teachers of his era, he instilled in his pupils a pride in their native land.

He was to remain in Moycarkey N.S., Pouldine until his retirement on June 30th 1944.

Gardening was one of Michael's passions and his garden at the teacher's residence in Pouldine was a tribute to him and much admired.

He and his wife, Kathleen had one daughter, Maura (Scully). Maura followed her father's career and taught for many years in the Ursuline Secondary School in Thurles. She was also a member of Thurles Urban District Council. The Myers family spent their later life in Thurles. Michael died at Laurel Lodge, Thurles, on January 4th 1951 and is buried in St. Patrick's Cemetery in the town.

Suaibhneas síoraí dá anam.

# Teachers and Monitors in the Old School

1847 – Thomas Fogarty – School Principal

1855 – John E. Larkin – School Principal (Salary £20)

1856 – James Walsh – School Principal

1858 – Denis Commins – Assistant Teacher

1861 – John Robinson, - School Principal, J. Molumby – Assistant, Mary Jane Robinson (Work Mistress)

1865 – Catherine Molloy - Assistant Teacher, Margaret Shanahan – Junior Monitor

1868 – Margaret Shanahan – Assistant Teacher

1869 – John Manning - Monitor

1872 – John Manning – Assistant Teacher

1878 – Denis Commins – School Principal

1880 – Johanna Molumby – Assistant Teacher

1891 – Mary Ryan (Assistant), James Commins (Monitor) James was appointed Principal Teacher in Littleton N.S. in 1898.

1894 – Jeremiah Coman – School Principal, Margaret M. Skally. Monitress: Ellen Coman, Mary A. Costello

1898 – Jeremiah Coman, Margaret M. Scally. Margaret also taught in Littleton N.S. in later years.

1900 – Margaret Carroll – Second Assistant

1904 – Jeremiah Coman, Ellen Coman, Eleanor Mary Mulcahy, Bridget Baker

1905 – Jeremiah Coman, Ellen Coman, Mary Coyle

1907 – Jeremiah Coman, Ellen Coman, Mary Coyle, Bridget Baker

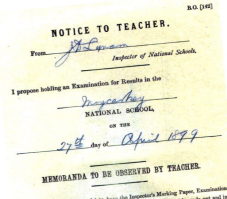

B.O. [142]

**NOTICE TO TEACHER.**

From _____ Inspector of National Schools.

I propose holding an Examination for Results in the

_Moycarkey_ NATIONAL SCHOOL,

ON THE

27th day of April 1879

**MEMORANDA TO BE OBSERVED BY TEACHER.**

1. Teacher will be careful to have the Inspector's Marking Paper, Examination Roll, and Results Report, Parts II. and III., accurately and neatly made out and in strict accordance with the instructions. This should be done on last day of the Results Year, and the names of all pupils who made 100 attendances or more during the period, and whose names are legitimately on the Rolls on that day, are to be included, and those only.

2. Any informality or inaccuracy must be productive of great inconvenience, and, if at all serious, may invalidate the Examination, and lead to the forfeiture of the Results Fees.

3. The Pupils should be trained for some time previous to the day fixed for holding the Examination to take their places in class according to the position of their names on the Examination Roll.

4. The Copy books of all pupils who have attended the required 100 days should be arranged in the order of the names on the Roll, so that no delay may occur in examining them.

5. A sufficient supply of pens and ink (and in the case of Girls or Mixed Schools where needlework is taught, materials for executing a specimen in this branch) should be ready for the use of the senior classes. Drawing materials to be ready when pupils are to be examined in this branch, and every preparation should be made that would be calculated to facilitate the conduct of the Examination.

1908 – As above except that Sarah Delaney is in place of Mary Coyle

1909 – 1912 Jeremiah Coman, Ellen Coman, Sarah Delaney, Mary Agnes Commins

1913 – Jeremiah Coman, Ellen Coman, Kathleen Commins, Leanne Kehoe, Ellen Callanan

1916 – Jeremiah Coman, Kathleen Commins, Ellen Callanan, Margaret Fitzgibbon

1917 – Mrs. Ellen Maher is listed as Assistant No.2

1920 – Jeremiah Coman, Kathleen Commins, Ellen Maher. Annie Maher (Substitute for Ellen Maher)

1922 – As above but Mary Sheahan as substitute for Ellen Maher

1923 – James F. Feehan as sub for Jeremiah Coman

*Mrs. Ellen Maher with her son Jack.*

1923 – July 1st, Michael Myers appointed Principal Teacher following the retirement of Jeremiah Coman. The assistant teachers were: - Miss. Commins and Mrs. Maher. Both attended Irish courses during this year.

1925 – Mrs. Myers is listed as first assistant teacher.

1944 – July 1st, Tadhg Ó Meachair appointed Principal Teacher, replacing Mr. Michael Myers who retired June 30th 1944. Michael Myers died in January 1951.

1945 – 1954 Tadhg Ó Meachair, Eibhlín Ní Mheachair, Pádraig Ó Lachtnáin

1951 – 1954 Máire Bn. Uí Chearbhaill replaced Pádraig Ó Lachtnáin

1956 – Póilín Ní Threasaigh replaced Eilín Bn. Uí Mheachair (Jan. 7th 1955), Máire Ní Chondúin replaced Nóra S. Ní Chonchradha

1957 – Bríd Bn. Uí Chinnéide replaced Máire Ní Chondúin

1957 – July 1st, Ms. Bríd Ryan, Reiska, Kilcommon, appointed assistant teacher. Retired August 31st 1998

1959 – Mrs. Maura Butler appointed assistant teacher.

*Paddy Loughnane (1926)*

*Mrs. Maura Butler*    *Ms. Pauline Treacy*    *Ms. Bríd Ryan*    *Tadhg Ó Meachair*

Look at the dog.
His name is Sam.
He is a good dog.
Tom is fond of him.

Look at Mary.
She has a rag doll.
Her name is Nan.
Mary is fond of her rag doll.

*Standard Two 1957*

*Mrs. Mary Condon-Quinn*

*Pouldine National School 1938*

*Back row (l.-r.): Joe Carthy, Philly Carroll, Michael Carroll, Josephine Stapleton, Billy Harris, Jimmy Normoyle, Jimmy Noonan, Willie Tynan, Jimmy Jobin, Jimmy Stapleton, Martin Fitzpatrick, – Fitzgerald, Leo Ryan, —. Second row (l.-r.): Alice Carroll, Margaret Meehan, Mary Shanahan, Peggy Boylson, May Heffernan, Maura Myres, Kitty O'Keeffe, Tess Buckley, Greta Harte, Bridie Ryan. Third row (l.-r.): Joby Buckley, Dan Ryan, Johnny Ryan, Mary Gooney, Rita Kinnane (Guinanne), Lizzy Noonan, Rita Costello, Kitty Gooney, Winnie Carroll, Teresa Armstrong. Fourth row (l.-r.): Billy Scott, Statia Harris, Dick Maher, Jim Fanning, Tom Costello, Larry Buckley, Maurice Noonan, Andy Dwyer, Andy Fitzpatrick, Joe Callahan, Tommy Tynan, Jimmy Boylson, Tom Regan, Kitty Ryan, Nellie Tynan. Front row (l.-r.): Betty Callahan, Paddy Murphy, Jackie Armstrong, Paddy Molloy, Thos Boylson, Nicholas Stokes, Jimmy Kinnane, Ronnie O'Connor, Jack Murphy, Thomas McGrath, Sarah Burke, Ann Leahy, Aggie Hayes.*

*Back row (l.-r.): Timmy Maher (Headmaster), Pouldine; Pat Buckley, Cloughmartin; Michael O'Connell, Ashill; Fintan Stapleton, Horse & Jockey; Philip O'Dwyer, Graigue; James Fitzgerald, Forgestown; Michael Lambe, Grallagh; Bobby Gleesone, Kylnoe; Jimmy Butler, Parkstown; Charlie Ryan, Pouldine; Johnny Maher, Pouldine (Master's son); Kieran Phillips, Grallagh; Paul Boylson, Kylnoe; Pat Barry, Grallagh. Second row from back (l.-r.): Kathleen Shanahan, Maxfort; Ann Scott, Kylnoe; Kathleen Kavanagh, Graigue; Kathleen O'Connell, Ashill; Kathleen O'Meara, Graigue; Biddy Ann Lanphier, Curraheen; Phyllis Tynan, Curraheen; Flora Wilson, Ballymoreen; Kitty Wilson, Ballymoreen; Kathleen Fanning, Cloughmartin. Third row from back (l.-r.): Eileen Lamphier, Curraheen; May Britton, Moycarkey; Mary Dwyer, Graigue; Sean Gleeson, Kylnoe; John McGrath, Moycarkey; Pat Flanagan, Graigue. Front row (l.-r.): Mary Shanahan, Pouldine; Madeline Shanahan, Drumboe; Tommy Britton, Moycarkey; John or Willie Meaney, Kylnoe; Christy Phillips, Grallagh; Mary Maher, Coolkennedy; Brendan Hogan, Coolkip.*

# Occupations of Parents/Guardians

**W**HEN A PUPIL is being enrolled in a National/Primary School, one of the items of information sought by the Department of Education is the position, occupation or 'means of living' of the parent or guardian. A survey of the occupations, named in the period 1866 to 1960 in this school shows, as expected, a large majority listed as **Farmers**. The second largest group described themselves as **Labourers**. The remaining group displays an interesting mix of crafts, trades and professions, reflecting the demands of the period surveyed and the varied list of services provided in a rural Tipperary parish, such as Moycarkey.

As farming was the predominant occupation, many other occupations associated with agriculture are listed. These include: – **Farm Labourer, Blacksmith, Herdsman, Shepherd, Farm Steward, Miller** and **Ploughman**.

*Mr. Daniel O'Regan, Coolkennedy, returning from the Creamery in Thurles.*

Occupations linked to building and house maintenance were common such as: - **Mason, Thatcher, Carpenter, Tradesman** and **Plasterer**.

The provision of clothing and footwear provided an income for many families with "means of living" listed as: - **Weaver, Tailor, Bootmaker, Shoemaker, Dressmaker** and **Draper**.

The local railway line with its station at Horse and Jockey also provided employment, such as: - **Station Master, Railway Employee, Railway Gate Keeper, Engine Driver** and **C.I.E. worker**.

**Shopkeeper, Grocer, Hostler, Publican, Hotel Proprietor** and **Merchant** are all mentioned. In the early years we find the entry **Policeman**, in later years this has changed to **Garda Síochána. Teacher** and **Postman** appear on the list from the early days, while **Mechanic, Lorry Driver** and **Garage Owner** are first mentioned in the 1950s.

Listed, but only rarely, are the following: - **Coachman, Gardener, Insurance Agent, Road Steward, Telegraph Clerk** and **Dog Slipper**.

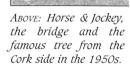

*ABOVE: Horse & Jockey, the bridge and the famous tree from the Cork side in the 1950s.*

*RIGHT: Horse & Jockey Station as it looked in April 1955.*

# The Best of Times, the Worst of Times

*By: MARY TOBIN (née Shanahan)*

MY FORMAL education began in the month of September 1931 when my name was added to the roll of Moycarkey National School. Previous to that however, I had learned quite a lot as I sat round the hearth on winter evenings, listening to my parents and neighbours reminiscing about times past or discussing the events of the day. A frequent visitor to our house at that time was Tommy Tobin the tailor's son, who always had a tall tale or a riddle for us children before the adults settled down for their chat.

Although nearly eighty years have passed by since I started school, many of the details of that first day remain firmly fixed in my mind. I was up bright and early and after a breakfast of porridge, tea and home made brown bread- baked in the oven pot, I joined my older sister on the short walk over to Danny Maher the teacher's house. Danny's wife was teaching in Pouldine and travelled to and from work each day by pony and trap, accompanied by her own children and my sister Josie. Mrs Maher was glad to have an extra passenger on board as the teacher's job depended on the number of children on the roll book.

When classes began at 9.30, I was sent to Mrs Myers, the Master's wife, who taught junior infants, senior infants and first class all in the same room. We had just sat in to our benches when Mr. Myers came in to welcome the new pupils. In addition to running the school, the Master also taught 2nd, 5th, 6th and 7th classes. Our neighbour Mrs. Maher was in charge of 3rd. and 4th years. All the rooms were heated by open fires, with the exception of the Master's, which contained a cast iron stove. Parents were required to contribute five shillings a year towards the fuel bill or supply a load of turf or coal. My father had a turf bank in nearby Liskeveen, so he used drop a cartful off at the school on his way home from the bog. We were let out to the yard for a ten minute break (Sos, as it was called) at eleven o'clock, I was so hungry that I ate some of my brown bread and butter and washed it down with a drink of water from the tap, a decision much regretted at lunch time (12.30-1 o'clock) when I discovered to my dismay that I hadn't sufficient supplies for the main break of the day! Food was consumed in the yard, although in bad weather we were allowed to use the "idle room". Sometimes Mrs. Maher would make tea

*School Tour to Dublin – June 23rd 1959. Photo taken at Independent House*

*Back row (l.-r.): Paddy Lambe, Curraheen; Brid Ryan, (Teacher), Thurles; Neddie Shanahan, Drumboe; —; Dan Fitzpatrick, Pouldine; —; Andy Moloney, Graigue; Chriss Gleeson, Kylnoe; —; Dick Fitzgerald, Forgestown; Noel Walsh, Graigue; Joe Felle, Knockroe; Mary Fitzferald, Forgestown; Mai Heffernan, Ballymoreen. Second row from back (l.-r.): Pauline Treacy (Teacher), Thurles; Eddie Buckley, Pouldine; Donal Regan, Coolkennedy; John McCormack, Curraheen; John Fitzgerald, Forgestown; Lena O'Meara, Galbertstown; —; —; Maura Walsh, Graigue; Carmel Heffernan, Ballymoreen; J.J. Cummins, Moycarkey; Paddy Ryan, Pouldine; —; Seamus Graydon, Knockroe; Statia Moloney, Graigue; Dolorus Cahill, Maxfort; Bridie Dwyer; Ambrose Sheehy, Graigue; Martin Ryan; Joe O'Meara, Galbertstown; Seanie Sheehy, Graigue; Timmy Maher (Headmaster); Mrs. Timmy Maher, Pouldine. Third row from back (l.-r.): —; —; — possibly Meaney; Joe Moloney, Graigue; —; —; Dolly Hewitt, Moycarkey; Mary Skehan, Knockroe. Front row (l.-r.): Donal Cummins, Moycarkey; Tommy Ryan, Pouldine; Alice Shanahan, Maxfort; Tessie O'Keeffe, Horse & Jockey; Mary McCormack; Margaret O'Hea, Maxfort; Peggy Skehan, Knockroe; Teresa Britton, Moycarkey; Maura O'Connell, Grallagh; Mary O'Keeffe, Horse & Jockey; Ann Heffernan, Ballymoreen; Noreen Fell, Knockroe; —; Teresa Fell, Knockroe; Mary Heffernan; Peggy Moloney, Graigue; —; —.*

*Third and Fourth Class 1964*

*Back row (l.-r.): Benny Coen, Knockroe; David O'Hea, Maxfort; Billy Carrie, Knockroe; Phonsey Croke, Curraheen; Seamus Maher, Aughnagamon; Jerry Fogarty, Graigue; Michael Ryan, Ballymoreen; Pat Skehan, Graigue; Billy Skehan, Knockroe. Third row (l.-r.): Christy Meaney, Kylnoe; Paul Cummins, Littleton; Brendan O'Meara, Galbertstown; Seamus Fell, Knockroe; Pat Leahy, Kylnoe; John Dee, Pouldine; Joe Coen, Knockroe; Paul Murphy, Horse & Jockey; Sylvie Stapleton, Horse & Jockey; Patsy Meaney; Kylnoe. Second row (l.-r.): Breda Ryan, Moycarkey; Helen Cormack, Curraheen; Mary Moloney, Graigue; Biddy Heffernan, Curraheen; Mary Butler, Parkstown; Kathleen Gleeson, Curraheen; Angela Maher, Coolkennedy; Kathleen Morris, Ashill; Mary Sheehy, Graigue; Nellie Shaw, Ashill. Front row (l.-r.): Eddie Flanagan, Graigue; Josephine Regan, Knockroe; Phyllis Graydon, Knockroe; Margaret O'Brien, Moycarkey; Peggy Costello, Shanbally; Francis Skehan, Graigue; Breda Ryan, Pouldine; Maura Costello, Parkstown; Margaret Leahy, Kylnoe; Francis Leahy, Kylnoe.*

for us, especially if the weather was very cold, being on friendly terms with the teacher certainly had its advantages! As I was unfamiliar with my surroundings I didn't play a lot on the first day, but as time went by we used to have great fun running races from one end of the yard to the other, skipping, spinning tops, playing marbles and doing the high jump. (Two people would hold up a stick for the others to jump over) We also played games such as "High Gates" and "Dan, Dan Thread the Needle". Classes finished for the junior infants at 2.30, but since I was too small to walk home on my own I waited in the yard until 3.30 when Mrs Maher and her passengers were ready for the return journey to Turtulla. My first few years at Pouldine passed by happily, I enjoyed the lessons and loved the new books, especially the history books which were illustrated with nice drawings and some coloured pictures. Although Irish eventually became one of my favourite subjects I found it hard enough at first, my father had never learned the language at school so I depended on my mother for help whenever I got stuck.

Unfortunately the good times came to an abrupt end when Mrs. Maher decided that she would cycle to school instead of struggling with the pony which had become difficult to manage, the Maher children and the Shanahan sisters would have to make do with "shanks mare" from then on! The journey up Knockroe hill was a lot tougher now especially on cold frosty mornings while the return trip often tested our endurance on a dark, wet, winter's evening. On the other hand, the walk to and from Pouldine had some benefits, as it gave us the opportunity to explore the countryside and to make new friends along the way. At that time children were very friendly, the Regans of Knockroe in particular, would often wait for us in the mornings if they saw us coming along behind them on the road. Sometimes we would get a lift in a passing horse and trap or on one of Skehan's lorrys. (Jim Skehan was originally from Parkstown and had a building contracting business in Thurles) The Shanahan brothers from Pouldine were always good for a lift in the evening if they were drawing grain or timber to Brady's mill in Archerstown, although they were big, strong, hardy looking, men they were very gentle and would carefully lift us up on the dray car. More often than not we made our way home on foot, filling our empty stomachs with hazel nuts, haws sloes, blackberries, crab apples or pieces of turnip.

On our way to school we came into contact with the many little local industries that existed at the time. At the top of our lane were two quarries one owned and operated by the Lyons family the other by the County Council. The men working in the Council quarry lived in tractor drawn vans and returned home to their families at weekends. Occasionally some of these men would sit by our fire at night and pass the time "tracing" with my father in an effort to relieve the monotony of their existence. Just over the road from our house were Brady's and Byrne's mills where corn was ground into meal and logs sawn into planks. Maher's forge was located at the cross of Turtulla where the smith, Jim Caulfield, shod horses, banded wheels and repaired implements and agricultural machinery. Turtulla cross was a well known meeting place on summer evenings, a lot of young men would walk out from Thurles to play pitch and toss or skittles, others would

*A day in the meadow – Mary Shanahan, Turtulla and Kitty Lyons, Galbooly.*

join in the jumping competitions or games of hurling in Dr. Barry's field. Maher's house presided over by Nora and her brother Phil. was also a great venue for card playing especially in the months leading up to Christmas. As we turned into Danny Maher's entrance, we passed by John Burke the coach painter's house on our right. John was a highly skilled craftsman, who worked at John Donaghy's coach building yard in Hall St. Thurles. The next house on the road was Tobin's, old Tommy Tobin was a master tailor, who employed journeymen for a few months at a time, before they moved on to exercise their skills at some other premises. Tommy was also a competent stone mason although he rarely worked at that trade. The two best known builders from the townland, Bernard Lyons and Tom" the Gaffer" Kenna had moved away from the locality before I was born. Tom Kenna won all-Ireland hurling honours with the Thurles Blues in 1906 and 1908, while Bernard Lyons was a very good athlete and uncle of my school friend John Lyons. One of Bernard's brothers, Joe, was a professor of dairy science at U.C.C. The Kennas lived down the lane behind Tobin's house, while the Lyons family occupied the substantial farmhouse that stood at the junction of the lane and main road. Further down the road on the right hand side, Bill Brereton conducted a successful trade as a wheelwright and cart maker, ably assisted by his daughter Kitty who would paint the finished products with red lead to protect them from the elements. Brereton's field was often the scene of a spirited hurling match on a Sunday evening, Mrs. Brereton, ash plant in hand, directed operations, and those foolish enough to engage in rough play were unceremoniously punished with a hefty wallop of the stick! Two future county senior medal winners, Dick Grant and Tom Tobin, served their apprenticeship under Mrs. Brereton's watchful eye. After match refreshments consisted of spring water from the pump in the yard and pieces of turnip from the slicer in the haggard.

The road to Pouldine also reinforced in our minds the harsh economic realities of the 1930's. One of my saddest memories is the sight of men sitting along the side of the road, breaking heaps of stones. In wet weather they would continue working with sacks draped across their shoulders, since they were paid by the load rather than by the day. With the exception of the larger farmers and the professional groups, very few people were immune to financial hardship. My own father had grown up on a comfortable farm in the Borrisoleigh area, yet within a few years he found himself down on his luck and renting a small property in Turtulla. When the weather got good a lot of children went to school barefooted, some by choice, a considerable number out of necessity. Boys generally, had to work harder than girls; many had to help out at home in the mornings and again in the evenings when they returned. I can still vividly remember Danny Fanning bringing the milk from Ballytarsna to Littleton creamery and getting back in time for school at Pouldine, where he would tie up the reins around the donkey's collar and allow the animal wander off home on its own. One man who took little notice of the recession was J.J. Shine of Thurles who proceeded to build a large modern shop opposite the school sometime in the early 1930's. The building work itself caused great excitement for a time, but it was the goods on display in the window that most aroused our curiosity. If money was plentiful at home or if Mrs.Maher was in a generous mood, ten NKM toffee sweets or two small bars of chocolate could be purchased for the princely sum of one penny. There was better chewing in the NKMs, but they tended to be tough and not very palatable.

As the years passed by and we moved into the senior classes, the lessons became more difficult and the homework much longer. I still have memories of long nights spent sitting at the kitchen table, writing Irish and English compositions, by candle light. As far as I can recall, the full list of subjects on the curriculum was; Irish, English, History, Geography, Maths, Singing, Christian Doctrine, Knitting and Sewing. The Master was often so engrossed in his task, that we would have gone a half hour over time, before he looked up at the clock to let us home. His zeal and demeanour often reminded me of Goldsmith's village schoolmaster "Full well the busy whisper circling round / Conveyed the dismal tidings when he frowned / Yet he was kind, or, if severe in aught, / The love he bore to learning was in fault;"

Towards the end of the 1930's the Irish Folklore Commission undertook a nationwide scheme to collect the folklore of the countryside, before it disappeared from memory. Mr. Myers, a lover of all things Irish, was an enthusiastic supporter of the initiative. We spent many weeks gathering information from elderly neighbours and then recorded our findings with pen and ink at school, as directed by the commission. The results of our endeavours are preserved in the Department of Irish Folklore U.C.D. Strangely enough many years later I would get the opportunity to contribute some additional information to the U.C.D. archive. The departmental head Dr. Bo Almqvist was delighted with my efforts; the Master would have been pleased, but not as easily impressed!

### First and Second Class 1965

*Front row (l.-r.): Billy Fogarty, Graigue; Pat Skehan, Graigue; Joe Cullagh, Littleton; Tom Morris, Ashill; Brendan Meaney, Kylnoe; Liam Croke, Kylnoe; Timmy Regan, Coolkennedy. Second row (l.-r.): Josephine Halloran, Graigue; Mary Carrie, Knockroe; Bernadette Sheehy, Graigue; Ann Ryan, Maxfort; Therese Lanphier, Curraheen; Catherine Shaw, Ashill; Mary O'Connell, Cloughmartin; Joan Cummins, Littleton; Bernadette Lanphier, Curraheen. Third row (l.-r.): Geraldine O'Brien, Moycarkey; Ann Callanan, Parkstown; Antoinette Lanphier, Curraheen; Alice Regan, Ballymoreen; Helen Regan, Ballymoreen; Rita Dee, Pouldine; Bridget Shaw, Ashill. Back row (l.-r.): Seamus O'Halloran, Graigue; Monica McLoughney, Coolkennedy; Paddy Butler, Parkstown; Martin Heffernan, Curraheen; John Ryan, Pouldine; Tom Hogan, Coolkip; Pat Morris, Ashill; J.J. Cummins, Moycarkey.*

### Fifth and Sixth Class 1965

*Back row (l.-r.): Johnny Coen, Knockroe; David Dee, Pouldine; Jim O'Hea, Maxfort; John Ryan, Moycarkey; John Shanahan, Maxfort; P. J. Lamphier, Curraheen; Dick O'Keeffe, Horse & Jockey; Joseph Cormack, Curraheen. Second row from back (l.-r.): Marie Dee, Pouldine; Margaret Fitzgerald, Forgestown; Mary O'Dwyer, Kylnoe; Catherine Ryan, Graigue; Gerry Coen, Knockroe; Philip Croke, Kylnoe; Joseph Coman, Littleton. Third row from back (l.-r.): Helen O'Regan, Coolkennedy; Mary Ryan; Mary Maher, Forgestown; Mary Skehan, Graigue; Margaret Buckley, Cloughmartin; Ann Sheehy, Graigue; Marie Morris, Ashill; Kathleen O'Meara, Galbertstown. Front row (l.-r.): Hannah Murphy, Horse & Jockey; Pauline Murphy, Horse & Jockey; Marie Lamphier, Curraheen; Catherine Heffernan, Curraheen; Lilly Graydon, Knockroe; Ann O'Regan, Coolkennedy; Helen Cummins, Moycarkey.*

# Peggy Morris
# Interviews

## AGGIE HAYES COSTELLO,
PARKSTOWN,
BALLYMOREEN AND LISKEVEEN.
*(Aged 84)*

I started school in Pouldine at the age of five. At that time school hours were from 9.00 a.m. to 3.30 p.m. There were three teachers in the school, Mr. and Mrs. Myers and Mrs. Maher. I remember the teachers being very cross and they used the stick freely. It was very hard to learn from them because they were so cross. Mrs. Myers was a sister of Jerry Coman who also taught in the school in earlier years. Mr. Myers brought in two new sticks every morning (under his arm) and usually broke at least one of them during the day.

In the early years, I lived in Ballymoreen and got a lift to school with a man bringing home his churn from the creamery in Littleton. I later lived in Parkstown and remember walking to school through the fields with my friends Rita and Tom. Tom used to tie a rope around us and pretend we were horses and 'drive' us to school turning right and left along the way.

'Tig' and Marbles were some of the games we played. We also played a game called 'Rise Sally Water'! In this game a group of children would form a circle and someone would stand in the middle, those in the circle would keep going round with their eyes closed reciting the rhyme 'Rise Sally Water' until they stopped and touched someone which would be "your young man". Then the game began again with that person now in the centre.

On our way to and from school we sometimes robbed the orchard at Boylson's and

Michael Shanahan's, where we would get turnips and would throw them at a wall to break them and then eat them. We also 'got' apples at Jack Dwyer's, which we would bring into school the following morning and swap around. An apple was a big treat then.

One day my friend Rita and myself took off our shoes and left them in the ditch, went across the fields barefoot but when we got to school we were not allowed to play in the yard during breaks in case we got hurt on the stones. It was normal from the 1st of May onwards for children to leave off their shoes going to school and return with new ones in September.

Shine's Shop is a fond memory also. The shop stood on the corner of the crossroads turning left from Thurles going to Ballymoreen. Before and after school we would go to the shop for a halfpenny bar, Peggy's Leg or Fat Meat (pink and white mallow type sweet), if we had money, which was very scarce at the time.

In school there were two stoves, one in the Master's room and one in Mrs. Maher's room. Every family in the school would donate an ass and car load of turf to the school to provide heat for the year.

Two of the older children were responsible for lighting the fires in the morning. Fifth and sixth class were also responsible for sweeping and cleaning the school every Friday evening.

Though they were tough times, they were happy times and everybody looked out for each other. I have great memories of my school days. We had great friends, always had great fun and entertained ourselves.

*(Aggie was interviewed by Peggy Morris, Curraheen. July, 2009)*

**JACK HARRIS**
LISKEVEEN,
HORSE AND JOCKEY
AND GRALLAGH
*(Aged 90)*

Jack walked to school in Pouldine from Liskeveen with his two sisters Mary and Judy. He recalls school days being tough and memories are far from pleasant. Corporal punishment and verbal criticism was very common in his school days in Pouldine.

Jack recalled when his father was in school, girls used to wear their hair very long and in two plaits. If one of the girls was bold, The Master would sit one of the boys down in front of the girl, grab the girl's plaits, tie them around the boy's neck and hit the girl with his stick. Jack recalls that this type of punishment was given to working-class children. The teacher would never hit a 'well-to-do' child.

Jack added that the pupils of fourth, fifth and sixth class cleaned the class rooms everyday.

*(Jack was interviewed by Peggy Morris, Curraheen. August, 2009)*

## MAY HEFFERNAN GLEESON
CURRAHEEN
HORSE & JOCKEY
*(Aged 81)*

I started school at the age of six. I was brought to school by my eldest brother Sean. My first teacher was Mrs. Myers who taught infant class and first class. Mrs. Maher taught third and fourth class and Mr. Michael Myers (the Master) taught second class, fifth and sixth in his room. We carried our schoolbags on our backs and had no lunch boxes. We said the Angelus in school every day at 12.00 noon. We had a half hour lunch break and two five minute breaks in the school yard. There were two school yards – one for the boys and one for the girls with a high dividing wall. The boys usually played ball and the girls played games such as: 'Tig', and Die-Die-Ducks under the Water.

We were not allowed out on the road, so Shine's shop which was a great attraction was out of bounds until after school (if we were lucky enough to have money). It was a sweet and grocery shop.

I walked the three miles to school from Curraheen, hail rain or snow. In the Jockey I would meet up with my friends, Gretta Harte, Kitty Fitzpatrick, Kitty O'Keeffe, Joan O'Keeffe, Eileen Scott, Peggy and Jimmy Boylson.

In school, religion was very hard. There was a religious exam every year and if you missed a question, you would be in trouble. When the Inspector called to the school, he spent his time with fifth and sixth class pupils. Mrs. Maher taught knitting and sewing to third and fourth class girls. We always got a day off school for the June races in Thurles and always looked forward to it. For lunch we had homemade bread and butter, sometimes homemade jam. The lunch was wrapped up in paper. After lunch one of the older boys would collect any papers left lying around the yard and take them to the end of the yard and burn them in the corner.

For 'Lessons' we were sometimes given a composition to write, spellings and religion. Sometimes, a so called 'Scholar' would be called up in class to read a paragraph and while doing so would indicate where the comma and full stop should go. If someone reading a passage didn't indicate where the comma or full stop should go, everyone in the class got slapped.

Preparing for First Communion was very hard. Fr. Fitzgerald examined us. Confirmation took place every three years at the age of eleven. In my time Bishop Harty from Thurles was in very poor health and Confirmation was postponed for a year. Before Easter, we were allowed out of school to walk to Moycarkey for confession.

There was an idle room in the school between the class rooms, which was used to store fuel and where we sometimes had our lunch, maybe on a wet day. I remember a magician having a show in that room at one time for which we paid two or three old pence.

Sometimes on our way home from school, the odd fight broke out but was never very serious. I usually walked home with my friends.

*(Aggie was interviewed by Peggy Morris, Curraheen. August, 2009)*

*Peggy Costello-Morris*

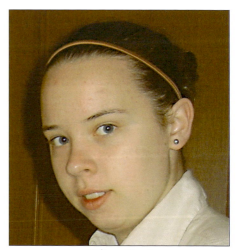

*Melissa Morris*

# An Bun Teastas
# – The Primary Certificate

THE PRIMARY Certificate Examination was introduced as an optional examination in 1929 and became compulsory in 1943. The "Primary Cert" as it became known, consisted of written tests in English, Irish and Mathematics. The Maths exam was divided into two sections. The first section usually contained about five long questions and the second section consisted of thirty short questions entitled "Mental Arithmetic" – this latter section had to be completed in thirty minutes. One Maths question remembered was on how to calculate the wallpaper needed to paper the four walls of a room. English and Irish consisted of essays, comprehension and grammar. One and a half hours were given to each subject.

Preparation for the examination was intense, with papers from previous years being studied. The examination was held in June, with the Príomhoide from a neighbouring school acting as superintendent for the day.

The results of the examination were delivered to the schools in September and the Certificate was a coveted award for any student. As free second-level education had not yet arrived, these results were extremely important, as they allowed access to further education, or into employment such as the Gardaí or Civil Service.

1951.

EXAMINATION FOR PRIMARY SCHOOL CERTIFICATE.

ARITHMETIC—B.—100 marks.

Time—1 hour.

Work *any three* questions.

$1\frac{1}{2} + 2\frac{1}{4} \times \frac{3}{8}$

$\frac{7}{11} \cdot \frac{7}{11} \cdot \frac{1}{11}$

9 tons 12 cwt. 2 qrs. of coal at £

1959.

Scrúdú faoi Teastas bunscoile.

Gaeilge.—200 marc.

Am—Uair go leit.

Moltar timpeall 50 nóiméad a cabairt do Ceist 1, agus timpeall 40 nóiméad do Ceist 2.

1. Scríob aiste (gan dul tar leataṅac) ar ceann amáin de na hábair seo:

(a) Na péiríní a fuair tú i Scornair do lá breice.

(b) Na fáinleoga.

(c) Cuairt a cug tú ar cara leat a bí tinn.

(d) Fear an poist nó fear an bainne.

(e) Cáit tú lá saoire faom dtuaiṫ (nó cois farraige) le do companaig. Scríob litir cuig d'uncait (nó d'aintín) ag cur síos ar an spórt a bí agaib.

2. Léig go cúramac an píosa atá ar leataṅac 2 agus ansin freagair na ceisteanna atá in a ṫiaid.

1958.

EXAMINATION FOR PRIMARY SCHOOL CERTIFICATE

ENGLISH.—200 marks.

Time—One hour and a half.

Candidates are advised to give about 50 minutes to Question 1, and about 40 minutes to Question 2.

1. Write on *one* of the following subjects; not more than a page is expected:—

(a) Wild birds.

(b) A dream you had.

(c) You fell into the river and after much difficulty reached safety unaided. Write a letter to your friend telling him (her) all about it.

(d) Railways.

(e) You fought with Brian Boru at Clontarf or with Sarsfield at Ballyneety. Describe your adventures and feelings on that occasion.

2. Read carefully the passage on page 2, and then answer the questions which follow it.

NOTE.—It is not necessary to write out the questions. Write the number of each question before your answer. The answers may be short.

With the introduction of free second-level education in 1967, the Primary Certificate was abolished and replaced by an assessment system based on a personal record card for each pupil in Fifth and Sixth classes.

## PREPARING FOR THE PRIMARY – A FORMER PUPIL REMEMBERS

It began after the Christmas holidays. The teacher produced a small sheaf of coloured papers and summoned sixth class to come up and stand at the table where he sat at the front of the classroom. Sixth class duly did as they were told. Teacher explained that this was our Primary Cert year. We would have to sit the exam in June, and we would have to pass it to get the actual certificate. The coloured papers were a varied, dog-eared selection of papers from past years, and we would have to study and work on these papers from now on. There were just three subjects – Irish, English and Arithmetic. The Arithmetic or "sums" was divided into two sections, mental arithmetic and problem solving.

Week by week we worked with the papers. Teacher always seemed to be available to correct, admonish, scold and dole out plenty more papers, and a few "slaps" with a "sally rod". First thing in the morning, before and after lunch, and last thing before we went home, we were burdened with loads of "lessons".

I struggled with the problem solving sums, worked manfully through the Irish, and actually enjoyed the English.

Though the English grammar was a bit tricky, I could, at the end, parse a sentence, write a list of adjectives and distinguish between nouns and verbs. The pressure was on. Homework was taking longer, help had to be sought from parents, and the fear of the consequences of not having it all done, much less done correctly, drove me to late hours and a few tears and envy of my brothers and sisters out playing or just sitting around making fun.

Sixth class were given homework for Saturday and Sunday to make sure we passed our Primary Cert.

We were told in May that June 13th was the "big day" and now the pressure was really on to perform. When the dreaded day came, we were ready and survived the ordeal with flying colours. Indeed, I have faced many of the challenges of life since, but I will never forget those days, now long past, when the 'Primary' was the biggest decade on my beads.

# Athletes from 'The Jockey' and Pouldine ...A Proud Tradition

*By: JOE TOBIN, Turtulla*

*Joe Tobin*

IT WOULD appear from the evidence available that hurling began to decline in popularity from the end of the 18th century, to reach a low point in the early 1870's, when the game was struggling for survival, even in traditional strongholds such as Moycarkey-Borris. On the other hand modern codified sports such as, rowing, rugby, association football, cricket and tennis were steadily being diffused across the country. The game of cricket in particular was quite popular in the Moycarkey-Borris and Thurles areas from the 1870s until the early years of the 20th century. When the modern athletics revival began in the 1860s many of the meetings were conducted by clubs associated with the above mentioned sports – the Nenagh Cricket Club organised a number of successful gatherings, while the Clonmel Rowing Club promoted one of the most prestigious fixtures in Munster for many years.

One of the first modern athletics meetings in Ireland took place in 1857, at Trinity College Dublin, under the auspices of the football club. It wasn't long before Moycarkey men began to take an interest in the revival of this ancient pastime and as early as 1866, we read of a well attended foot-racing competition at Coolkennedy, organised by Charles Langley. By the 1870's some of our athletes were seeking challenges further afield, most notably Martin Grady of Archerstown, who was good enough to win the long jump at Drangan in 1875. His brother Tom, ("The Captain") was a capable weight thrower and sprinter, who won a number of events at the inaugural Littleton sports meeting. Martin Grady later emigrated, to Australia and prior to his departure is said to have jumped across a siding at Thurles railway station, declaring that nobody would repeat the feat until his return! By 1876 interest in athletics was so strong in the district that a successful sports was organised at Littleton and was followed a year later by an even more elaborate fixture. In 1878, the parish was celebrating its first all-Ireland victory when T.K. Dwyer, won the Irish one mile championship in Dublin and set a standard for athletics in the parish which has endured to the present day

The sport of athletics grew so rapidly during the last quarter of the 19th century, that small communities such as the Horse-and-Jockey were capable of producing a number of good athletes. Tom Gleeson was the first man from the village to come to prominence when he won the parish half-mile at Littleton sports in September 1877. His brother Mick came home first in the boys' race over the same distance, from a large field. The following July at Thurles, Tom was second in the half-mile, one mile and 440 yds. hurdles. He returned to Thurles in June, 1879 to win the half-mile and later that summer recorded a middle distance double at Mullinahone. In 1880 he won the mile at the Armitage estate in Noan, Ballinure and went on the following season to record second places in the mile, 1,000 yds. and steeplechase, at Carrick-on-Suir. Gleeson was still in top form in 1882 winning over the mile distance at Cashel and Carrick-on-Suir. He had an unhappy outing at Clonmel in August of the next year placing third in the half-mile and breaking the tape first in the mile only to be disqualified for jostling. Tom subsequently settled in Australia where he is reputed to have enjoyed a successful athletics career.

Pat Shanahan's victory in the mile race at Cashel sports in June 1890 heralded the emergence of some new local talent. Two months later Shanahan was unplaced in the half-mile at Clonmel. This was probably Patsy Shanahan of Pouldine who won a county championship with the hurlers in 1889 and whose son Paddy ran with Templemore, Thurles and Galteemore athletic clubs in the 1920's and 1930's. There was still no luck for our athletes at the Clonmel meeting the following year when Danny Mullins was unplaced in both the 120 yds. and 220 yds. races. Tom Gleeson's brother Mick also failed to live up to expectations in the mile. In July, 1894 at Moyne, M. Maher and M. Coady, Moycarkey finished 1st and 2nd in both the 100 yds. and the high jump. Maher also won the 440 yds ( M. Coady was probably Ned Caudy, as at the Clonmel sports of the previous year" E. Caudy, Horse-and-Jockey" was listed among the unsuccessful competitors in the 220 yds. event. Caudy's brother, Mick, was a member of the Moycarkey hurling team in 1906)  A sports meeting was held at Two-Mile-Borris the following month where P. Shanahan finished second over the 440 yds distance. Danny Mullins finished out of the prizes in the same race while both he and "E. Candy" were also unsuccessful in the 100 yds. event. Caudy travelled to Clonmel the next day where it was recorded that "Candy, Horse-and-Jockey" was unplaced in the long jump. Towards the end of August some events which had been postponed at Two-Mile-Borris were run off at a sports meeting in Thurles. Danny Mullins was in fine form to win the half-mile from scratch beating a field of ten which included P. Shanahan and "T. Simple". Mullins also finished second in the 440 yds. July 1895 saw Ned Caudy finish 3rd in the long jump at Nenagh behind the future world and Olympic champion Tom Kiely, while a month later at Templemore, he placed second at the high jump and finished third in the 100 yds. and 440 yds. races. Three years later Danny Mullins was still running well and ran one of the best races of his career to take second place in the mile at the Rowing Club sports in Clonmel, on August 1st 1898. Mullins did much of his running in Dublin where he worked from a young age. He was a member of the Grocers Gaelic Athletic Club and began winning prizes as early as 1887 when still only a teenager.

| Mikey Condon | Jack Gleeson | Bill Gleeson | Danny Mullins |

About this time, Dan Gleeson began to make sporting headlines by taking third place in the mile at the Clonmel Cycling Club sports. (Some weeks previously the winner of the mile at Cashel sports was reported as Con Gleeson, Curraheen – was "Con" a misprint for Dan or was it his first cousin Con, the hurler?) In September 1898, Dan established himself as one of the best middle distance men in the country, when winning the silver medal in the mile race, at the Irish Championships in Thurles. He also placed 3rd in a half-mile handicap, which was run in conjunction with the main programme. The following August he emulated the 1883 achievement of his brother Tom, by winning the mile at the Clonmel Rowing Club sports – there was no jostling on this occasion! Unfortunately, he was run out of the medals, at the National Championship in Thurles, some weeks later. However, Dan was back in winning form by October when he won the mile at Ballylusky. He finished second in the half-mile and third in the mile at Clonmel in August, 1900 and won at Cashel over the longer distance where he was also third in the half-mile. The following month, at Crohane, he emerged victorious at both the quarter and half-mile events. A strong Horse-and-Jockey contingent travelled to this venue and a new name appeared on the prize list when J. Tobin (probably Jack Tobin of Curraheen) finished 3rd in the 100 yds. Jack and Bill Gleeson were unplaced in the high jump as was the former in the 28 lbs. shot.

Around the turn of the century Jack Gleeson, the fourth member of that great sporting family, also began to demonstrate his prowess as a runner. An account of the inter-county athletics contest between Cork and Tipperary at Dungarvan, published in "The Nationalist" on September 26th. 1900, reveals that Jack Gleeson finished second behind J.C. Hayes in the 4 miles, while his brother Dan was unplaced in the mile. In 1901, Jack won a mile race in Shepherd's Bush, London at the August bank holiday sports. That same weekend he also lined out with the Tipperary hurling team which defeated London by 3-15 to 1-3. The family running tradition was continued by Jack's son Connie who competed with Coolcroo A.C. in the 1940's.

Mikey Condon of Ballinure was another local athlete to enjoy a long and successful career. Condon who was a member of the victorious All-Ireland hurling panel of 1899 was still agile enough to win prizes in jumping competitions some fifteen years later. He

*Dan Gleeson*

*Jim Skehan*

tied for first place in the high jump with Bernard Lyons of Turtulla at Fethard in July 1909 while a month later he had a great win at Kilmoyler before taking second to Lyons in Mullinahone. At Ardfinnan in September he was runner-up in the high jump and 3rd in the horizontal event. Later that month he again had to give way to Lyons over the lath at Tipperary but went on to win at the Milestone in October. The Ballinure man had a very successful season in 1910 with wins in Mullinahone and Borrisoleigh and a second at Fethard. The following year in Tincurry he placed third at the long jump and the 120 yds. hurdles, while he concluded the season with a victory in the high jump at Fethard and a second place at Cashel. In June 1912, he again won at this event in Thurles, where he overcame his old rival, Bernard Lyons, however Lyons and he reversed places at Mullinahone some weeks later. Condon finished the year strongly with a win at Cashel. Mikey was in fine form the following year and recorded successes at Nenagh and Golden thereby ensuring selection on the Tipperary team to meet Cork in an athletics contest. Condon's remarkable career stretched on into 1914 when he was once more supreme over the lath at Nenagh and went on to record a number of minor successes at a variety of locations around the county. Mikey's son, Neil, won a Munster senior hurling championship medal in 1941 and was also an accomplished high jumper. Neil competed with Coolcroo A.C. and with both Croke and St. Joseph's A.C. of Thurles – winning Tipperary high jump titles in 1944, 1952 and 1953.

The final character in this brief sketch of athletics in the Horse-and-Jockey district is the Parkstown native Jim Skehan, who specialised in weight throwing. (Jim also won a Mid. Junior hurling title with a Horse-and-Jockey, Two-Mile-Borris combination in 1909). One of Skehan's first successes was at Donaskeigh in July 1909 when he won the 56 lbs. with follow and took third place in the 28 lbs. shot. The following month at Kilmoyler he again won the 56 lbs. with another mighty heave and completed the afternoon with a victory in the quarter-mile. A second place at Anacarthy a few weeks later brought the season to a successful conclusion. Jim was off to a quick start in 1910 taking two second places with the 56 lbs. and 28 lbs. weights at Donohill, in early May. The following year the big Parkstown man came to national prominence with a great win at the prestigious Dublin Drapers sports in June, when he won the 56 lbs. over the bar competition, with a throw of thirteen feet. However his performance at the G.A.A. National Championships a month later was to be the highlight of his career when he slung the heavy implement out to 22'10" for a commendable third place finish. By August he was back on the local circuit to win the 56 lbs. for distance competition at Thurles and finish third in the 28 lbs. shot. Later that month he was successful with the heavier weight at Mullinahone, beating the opposition with a fine throw. It would appear that Skehan's career began to go into decline during 1912, yet he was still considered to be of inter-county standard in 1913,

*Three athletes from the 19th century (l.-r.): Tom Gleeson, Curraheen (miler); Billy Gleeson, Curraheen (hurler) and Willie Joe Delaney, Ballybeg (weight thrower).*

when the Tipperary selection to meet Cork was published in the local press. Following his retirement from competition, Jim continued to make a significant contribution to the sport in an administrative capacity and was elected vice-chairman of the county board N.A.C.A. in 1938. The family interest in athletics was maintained by his son Liam who won the 56 lbs. for distance at a sports meeting held on his own lands at Ballycurrane, in 1950.

As the old Horse-and-Jockey stars faded from the arena, the focus of athletics moved towards the other end of the parish, where a new and highly successful era was about to dawn.

Ach sin scéal do lá eile !

**Third and Fourth Class 1969**

*Back row (l.-r.): Malachy Cullagh, Littleton; Maurice Sheehy, Graigue; Johnny O'Halloran, Graigue; Tom Kirwan, Moycarkey; Thomas Kirwan; Pat Flanagan, Graigue; John Shaw, Ashill. Second row from back (l.-r.): Anthony Gooney, Galboola; Geraldine Dee, Pouldine; Theresa Costello, Paskstown; Ann Shaw, Ashill; Mary Hogan; Noreen Fogarty, Graigue; Bernadette Mc Loughlin, Coolkennedy. Third row from back (l.-r.): Una Coman, Littleton; —; Theresa Dee, Pouldine; Breda Ryan; Paddy Fogarty, Graigue; Marie Callanan, Parkstown; Denise Lanphier, Curraheen; Concepta O'Keeffe, Horse & Jockey. Front row (l.-r.): Noel Croke, Kylnoe; Tom Skehan; Gregory Cullagh, Littleton; Denis McLoughlin, Coolkennedy; —; John Costello, Parkstown; Tom Leahy, Kylnoe; Eddie McCormack, Curraheen.*

GAELIC ATHLETIC ASSOCIATION, MOYCARKEY.

A meeting of the young men of this parish was held on Sunday evening, 1st inst., for the purpose of forming a Branch of the G.A.A.— The following gentlemen were unanimously adopted :—Rev. J. Murphy, C.C., President ; Mr. William Fogarty, Vice-president ; Mr. John Molumby, Hon. Sec. Committee— Messrs. Thomas O'Grady, John O'Brien, Patrick Molloy, James O'Grady (Graigue), Michael Shanahan, James Cahill, and Daniel Wilson.

The resolutions were passed with acclamation :—

" That we tender our sincere gratitude to our patriotic Archbishop Croke the Most Rev. Dr. Croke, Charles S. Parnell, M.P., and Michael Davitt in patronising the ancient and historic pastimes of our people, whose only enjoyment was an everlasting pound of labour."

" That we hail with delight the revival of our ancient games. Although we have suffered from emigration and oppression in this parish yet Moycarkey can boast they have never given up the ancient game of hurling."

Mr. John O'Brien proposed Mr. Thomas O'Grady as Captain of their clubs. The proposition was seconded by Mr. Michael Shanahan and was passed unanimously.

*Moycarkey GAA Club was founded on November 1st 1885. This is how the 'Cashel Sentinel' reported the event on November 14th of that year.*

*Sr. Marie Goretti (Maureen Kelly), Maxfort. Maureen started Primary School in Pouldine but returned in 1953 to Commonaline, Hollyford. She entered the Presentation Order and now teaches at their foundation in California, USA.*

# Placenames around Pouldine

## Logainmneacha

| PLACE-NAME | LOGAINM | ORIGIN |
|---|---|---|
| Ashill | Cnoc na Fuinseoige | The hill where ash trees grow. Area 304 acres |
| Aughnagomaun | Achadh na gCamán | The field of the hurleys. – The hurling field. Area 1081 acres |
| Ballybeg | Baile Beag | Little town or homestead – Littleton Area 1691 acres. |
| Ballymoreen | Baile Uí Mhuirthin or Baile Muirín | O'Morris's homestead Little Mary's town –Area 367 acres. |
| Cloughmartin | Cloch Mháirtín | Martin's Stone or Stone Castle Area 391 acres. |
| Coolkennedy | Cúl Uí Chinnéide | Kennedy's Corner or Behind Kennedy's Area 187 acres. |
| Coolkip | Cúl Cip | Corner of a tree trunk Area 216 acres |
| Curraheen | Curraichín | Little marsh Area 895 acres |
| Dromgower | Drom Geabhair | The ridge of young corn – Area 113 acres |
| Forgestown | Baile Mhic Fheorais | Old maps show this place as Foulcherstown, named after the Anglo-Norman family Foulcher. Area 291 acres. There are other local townlands named after Anglo Norman colonisers:- Galbertstown, Gracetown, Archerstown. |

| | | |
|---|---|---|
| Galboola *(Galbooly)* | Gall Bhuaile | Milking place of the foreigner. Area 433 acres. |
| Graigue | Gráig | Village or hamlet of Anglo-Norman origin – Area 970 acres. |
| Grallagh | Greallach | A mire or marshy place Area 908 acres. |
| Horse and Jockey | An Marcach | Situated on the Dublin Cork road. In the mid eighteenth century there was an inn here, where mail cars, later Bianconi cars, would stop to feed, water, and exchange horses. The needs of passengers would also be satisfied. |
| Kylenoe | Coill Nua | New wood Area 160 acres |
| Kilmelan | Cill Maoláin | St. Maelan's Church. Area 44 acres. |
| Clohoge | Clochóg | A corruption of Clémochaomhóg. St. Mochaomhóg's ditch. He was founder and Patron of the monastery at Leigh, Two-Mile-Borris. Area 316 acres. |
| Knocknanuss | Cnoc na n-Os | Hill of the fawns (deer) Area 365 acres. |
| Knockroe | Cnoc Rua | Site of Battle against the Vikings or - The red hill (red soil seen after ploughing). Area 362 acres. |
| Liskeveen | Lios Caoimhín | Kevin's Fort – St. Mochaomhóg was founder and Patron of the Monastery at Leigh, Two-Mile-Borris. Area 1453 acres. |
| Maxfort | | Max family were major landowners here in the past. |
| Moycarkey | Má Chorcu Éile | The plain of the tribe of Éile. These were the people who settled in the Ely area of mid Tipperary Area 518 acres. |
| Newtown | Baile Nua | The new town or settlement. Area 160 acres. |
| Parkstown | Baile na Páirce | Parkland – The good level land around here was laid out in open parkland. Area 624 acres. |

| Pouldine | Poll Doimhin | The deep hole (maybe a slugga in this limestone area). Area 120 acres. |
| Rathinch | Rath Inis | The fort near the river on marshy land. Area 183 acres. |
| Sallsquarter | | Portion of land given to the Sall family. They were friends of the Cantwells of Moycarkey Castle. Sall family also in Thurles. Area 116 acres. |
| Shanacloon | Sean Chluain | The old meadow. Area 176 acres |
| Shanbally | Sean Bhaile Sean Bhealach Sean Bhuaile | Old Town Old Road Old Milking Place. Area 107 acres |
| Turtulla | Turtullach | The bushy hill Area 824 acres. |
| Thurles | Dúrlas Éile | Strong fort in the territory of Éile. Associated with the O'Fogarty family. |
| Tipperary | Tiobraid Árann | The well of Arra. The river Arra is associated with Tipperary Town. |

*The magnificent stone-cut double-arched railway bridge which stood at the Horse & Jockey. Ironically, a CIE lorry crosses the bridge.*

*Roadworks at the Horse & Jockey in the 1960s.*

*ABOVE: Jerry Fogarty with Jimmy Bracken.*

*RIGHT: Jimmy Bracken and Jimmy Foley (both Liskeveen).*

*Horse & Jockey 1960s – looking towards Cork.*

# Fond Memories from over the Ocean

IN SEPTEMBER 1936, I started in Pouldine School in Junior Infants. My cousins Terry and Ronnie O'Connor were already attending. Terry accompanied me from our home in Ballymoreen. Our walk to the school took us past Dan Mulcahy's Cross, Meara's Hollow, past Jimmy Hayes's house and Quinlan's old home where the leonine and foreboding structure of the school came into view. The school was built in the early 1800s under an Education Act, which introduced formal primary education to Ireland. The Irish language and culture was not allowed to be taught in the schools and speaking it was discouraged. Subsequently this had dire consequences for the language in later years. The school had four rooms and three teachers, Mrs. Myers, who taught the infants and first class, Mr. Myers who taught second, fourth, fifth and sixth classes

*Jimmy Normoyle*

and Mrs. Maher who taught catchecism and the third class. The fourth room was called "the idle room" and was used during wet days for the lunch period. As I recall, there was a total of eighty-four students in the school and every morning the "master" updated a small blackboard in his room to reflect that day's attendance.

In the infant class, Philly Carroll and myself sat in the same desk. Philly lived in Graigue near Taylor's Quarry and talked about all the abandoned cars in the quarry. Mrs. Myers had play clay for the class but I am afraid our interest was in the items from the quarry, which Philly had in his pocket.

In the First Class Mrs. Myers introduced us to the Irish Language. Irish had been introduced into the schools in 1922 after Ireland had attained "Free State" status. It was difficult for the teachers, Mrs. Myers situation was no exception, and she used to have to consult with Mr. Myers on the various intricacies of the language. Mrs. Maher taught us catechism and prepared us for our First Communion. Religion was an important part of the curriculum and Father (later Canon) McGrath and Father Fitzgerald visited the school regularly during religious instruction. Aside from the religious aspect, First Communion Day in Moycarkey Church meant getting a new suit and a ride to the church in Danny Tierney's motorcar.

*Jimmy Normoyle photograhed in the late '30s.*

Mr. Myers put a lot of emphasis on Arithmetic and Irish in the second class. Every morning "sums" were put on the blackboard and after we completed the exercise, the Master collected the papers for correction. One day I remember he put the sums to be done as usual on the board but used the same sums as he had the previous day except that he changed the last line of figures. Assuming that the master had forgotten and that the sums were the same as the previous day I copied all the answers from the previous day's exercise and of course got them all wrong. My punishment was a slap on the hand from the ever-ready ash switch. The lesson that I learned that day and to which I still adhere was "never assume anything until you have checked all the details"

Organized sports and activities within the school were pretty much non-existent. In the morning, the boys who had brought a hurley or "bunnán" with them to school would hurl in Shanahan's field near the "little bridge". Another activity was "scrooging" which involved hurling on the road using a tin can for a sliotar (ball). This lasted until we heard the ringing of the bell indicating the start of the school day. In the summer of 1937, there was excitement in the air. Tipperary were in the All-Ireland and Paddy Ryan (Sweeper) and his brother Johnny (Cusack) were on the team. Needless to say, they were our heroes.

Mrs. Shine had a shop across from the school and when we had a penny or two was a source for sweets. However, during lunch break we were confined to the schoolyard. My years at Pouldine were happy ones. In September 1939, I transferred to Littleton School but fond and positive memories of my early formative years at Pouldine will always remain with me.

JIMMY NORMOYLE
Stony Point,
New York.


*(Jimmy Normoyle – pupil at Pouldine School 1936 – '39)*

# Daniel O'Connell and the Monster Meeting at Knockroe

*Daniel O'Connell*

ONCE Catholic Emancipation was achieved in 1829, The Liberator – Daniel O'Connell campaigned for Repeal of the Act of Union. To push for this, he held a series of Monster Meetings throughout Ireland. They were so called because each was attended by around 100,000 people. Here is a newspaper report of one such meeting held at Knockroe, in the parish of Moycarkey.

### Monster Demonstration at Thurles on Friday, Sept. 26.

*Mr. O'Connell (the Liberator) addressed the crowd of between 90,000 and 100,000 people. "England has given us ignorance, bigotry, starvation, rags, wretchedness, cabins without beds or night clothing. There is no employment, no trade, no commerce – is this good government? Does this not call for Repeal?"*

*The men were all very well clad. The women were decked out in their Sunday best.... The eternal temperance bands (composed of performers, who, however temperate in other thing, spare neither breath nor muscle to brass and sheepskin) paraded the town, making the most horrible musical caricature of such airs as "Love Not", "The Days we went Gipsying", and "The Night Before Larry was Stretched"....*

*Among the attendees were Mr. Maher, M.P., Mr. W. McDonnell, of Carrick-on-Suir, the very Rev. Dean McDonnell, Mr. R. Keating of Garranlee, Rev. Mr. Morris, parish priest, Borrisoleigh, the Mayor of Clonmel, Mr. J. Lanigan, Mr. Doheny, Rev. Dr. Bourke, Patrick Fogarty of Cabra Castle, and Mr. Joseph Rivers.*

## O'CONNELL'S GREAT MEETING AT KNOCKROE 1845

Local historian – Daniel Maher, Turtulla, wrote the following account in the 1940s:

*One of the Emancipator's monster meetings, held in Knockroe, in parish of Moycarkey so aroused the patriotic ardour of the Mid-Tipperary plain that when the great Dan mounted the platform, he had around him a throng surging in like a mighty sea, but thousands were unable to hear the faintest echo of the voice they loved so well. Over 100,000 people are said to have been present, the place of the meeting was in the field behind Mr. Smith's house, once the property of the Kirwans of Thurles. The table at which the Liberator sat is still preserved as a "Memento" by the Meagher family at the cross of Turtulla.*

*People set out at early morning and when tired and hungry they went into any house they liked for a free meal of boiled potatoes. O'Connell stayed the night at Mahers of Turtulla House – now Thurles Golf Clubhouse.*

## KICKHAM WAS THERE

Seventeen-year-old Charles J. Kickham who travelled from Mullinahone that morning wrote:

*It was one of those September mornings which gladden the farmer's heart . . . But no hand touched sheaf or reaping hook that glorious harvest day . . . For Tipperary's sons and daughters were trooping in thousands and tens of thousands to the great Repeal meeting in Thurles . . . The cornfields of Slieveardagh and Middlethird were laden with glorious grain. Yet the inhabitants of this land were the worst fed the worst clad and the worst housed people in Europe. The abundant harvest was not for them. There was nothing between hundreds of thousands of them and starvation but the diseased tubers rotting at the roots of those blighted and dropping stalks . . . The parish priest on horseback at the head of his parishioners . . . the trades respectably dressed, earnest looking and disciplined; the tall frieze-coated peasantry on foot and the farmers on horseback . . . As I approached the town of Thurles I became nervous with excitement and had a vague fear lest the immense crowds on foot and on horseback and in vehicles of all kinds might surround the Liberator like a sea and prevent me from catching even a glimpse of him.*

*Later in the evening two thousand of the Catholic middle classes of the county had O'Connell and his entourage to themselves at a banquet in Thurles, costing half-sovereign a head, when the 'frieze-coated peasantry' and the lower orders generally, had scattered. The banquet was held in a temporary wooden building erected for the occasion.*

## SOME LOCAL KNOWLEDGE FROM TOM

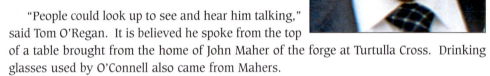

Tom O'Regan, Coolkennedy, now in his eighties, and a past-pupil of Pouldine School. knew the precise location of the famous 'Monster Meeting'. "T'was on Knockroe Hill in a 52 acre field, which we always called the 'Kill' (Kiln) field. 'Tis O'Regan property now. My father Dan bought it from Richard Kirwan in the early 1920s."

Tom said thousands attended the 'Monster Meeting'. Such was the magnetic attraction of Daniel O'Connell who spoke from the top of the 'red hill' at Knockroe, reputed to have been the same height as Killough Hill.

"People could look up to see and hear him talking," said Tom O'Regan. It is believed he spoke from the top of a table brought from the home of John Maher of the forge at Turtulla Cross. Drinking glasses used by O'Connell also came from Mahers.

"Mahers were highly skilled metal-workers and their craftsmanship is still to be seen. The gates of the Cathedral of the Assumption, Thurles and the railings were made at that forge," Tom O'Regan stated. " In that same year, they started the Thurles – Clonmel Railway Line, now out of operation. In the days of the old steam engines, it was common for local children to place a penny on the tracks near the bridge at Leahy's field to see what would happen when the trains went over it. It they had a penny to spare that is!"

Tom also recalled Fr. Robert Grace, whose house, a two storey thatched house, was in Coolkennedy. This townsland is also noted for its wells and springs. Toberavocky and the Holy Well are there as well as the famous spring Poulaneigh. In the past, Tom reminded me that it was the custom to baptise children at the Holy Wells.

The water gushing from Poulaneigh was the power supply for mills in years gone by, such as the ancient one at Archerstown and the more recently used Brady's Mill on the Mill Road. The site of the Archerstown Mill was lost for years but was uncovered, due to drainage work in 1968. Archaeologists from the National Museum in Dublin examined its quern stones, its remains of mud covered hazel huts and oak beams and concluded that it was among the oldest such mill sites they had examined.

Tom also stated that the water in Poulaneigh was so cold, even on a summer's day, that you could not finish a cupfull. He recalled that two divers from Australia explored its depths in the 1970s and concluded that it was at least twenty feet deep, making it one of the deepest such wells in Tipperary.

Tom also mentioned the 'Churchfield' at Turtulla. Some of the ruins are still there today on the farm, now the property of the Pallotine Fathers. There was a tunnel from the 'Churchfield' to Holycross Abbey. This was needed during times of religious persecution in Ireland.

We finished our chat with a prayer, that has been in the O' Regan family for over 300 years.

As Tom said – "This is to be said when you put your foot on the floor in the morning".

*Good morning, fair morning,*
*My soul from sin,*
*My body from shame,*
*Here I am, I bless you,*
*In my Lord's name.*
*Amen.*

*'I will go with my father a ploughing' . . .*

*Tom O'Regan, Coolkennedy and son Jerry in July 1962.*

# Miracle at Pouldine – Holocaust at Drumcollogher

IN THE midst of our own Election results, the media told us of grieving parents who began burying their children, all under the ago of six, after a fire in a nursery in Mexico killed 38 toddlers in a tragedy that stunned the country. The fire initially spread from an adjoining tyre warehouse to the roof of the day centre and sent flames raining down on the young children. Fire officials still do not know how the blaze started. Pope Benedict XV1 sent a telegram of sympathy to those killed or injured in the fire.

These scattered facts may help us better to understand another fire in another age, in another place, later to become known as the Drumcollogher 'Holocaust'. Drumcollogher lies on the border of the counties of Limerick and Cork, thirty-six miles from the city of Limerick, at the time so removed from the amenities of civilisation, that twenty years before the fire, Percy French made it the subject of a jesting song.

*Rev. James Feehan*

On Sunday night, September the 5th, 1926, a cinematograph performance was given in the upper hall of a store in the village. The store underneath was used as a garage. The hall was approached through a narrow door 3.5 feet in width by a staircase or ladder and the only other means of exit were two barred windows at the back of the hall. There were about 150 people in the hall at the time. Many of the victims were women and of the twenty children, only five escaped. It is thought that the fire was caused by a lighted candle on a table where several films were exposed. The flames which spread with great rapidity cut off the only means of escape. In the stampede, which followed, Jeremiah Buckley the village schoolmaster dis-played great heroism in the number of people whom he steered to safety. But

*Thomas Feehan with his car.*

then in the intense heat the wooden floor of the hall crumbled and there was an avalanche of burning bodies, amongst them Jeremiah Buckley and his entire family consigned in horrific heaps to the garage underneath. Only seven of those who fell to their deaths in this manner were later identified. These included Jeremiah Buckley and his brother Thomas Buckley also a teacher. Another teacher who travelled from England as the guest of the Buckley family was Kate Wall. She too perished in the fire.

A pathetic little incident which served to emphasise the poignancy of the tragedy was seen in an attempt to coax away from the house of gloom, where Jeremiah Buckley and his family lived, was a red setter dog. His master and mistress and Bridie his little girl playmate had all perished, but with that faithfulness characteristic of dogs, the poor animal declined to leave. He was brought to a neighbouring house and given some food, but slipped away again and lay at the door of the empty house refusing to be coaxed or consoled.

## EPILOGUE

My father Thomas Feehan and his wife Ellen should have been in Drumcollogher on the night of the 'Holocaust' as the guests of Jeremiah Buckley. Time and again down through the years my father had regaled me with the events of that fateful weekend. He would begin by telling me of this friendship with Jeremiah Buckley which began in the De La Salle College in Waterford where they were both trained as teachers under the British regime. Storytelling was the bond, which drew them together as it did with two of their contemporaries, Michael Myres of Pouldine and Andrew Finn of Dualla.

The Ten Commandments: Jeremiah Buckley telegraphed my father to come and see a lavish biblical spectacle created by Cecil B. de Mille in 1923 in the black and white and to be screened in the hall in Drumcollogher on Sunday night, September 5th. My parents were to be the guests of Jeremiah Buckley and his wife in their home at Woodfield, Drumcollogher after the show. Needless to say, Thomas Feehan responded to Jeremiah Buckley's invitation with alacrity and telegraphed his host that he and Ellen would travel to Drumcollogher after Mass on Sunday and stay overnight in the Buckley household after the screening of the film.

On the Saturday, he took his car into Franklin's Garage in Thurles to be serviced, got a box of chocolates for little Bridie and here is how he told what happened on the way home.

The Accident: 'As I approached the Crossroads at Pouldine the school house was on my right and leaning against the school wall was a pack of yahoos (sic) who gave no sign or indication that there was another vehicle coming at speed from Moycarkey.' It was a cartload of travellers and they galloped straight into my car. Such was the damage that the trip to Drumcollogher had to be called off. I can't tell how mad I was with the yahoos who caused the accident.'

'But then, 'he mused, 'when I read about the death toll in Drumcollogher on Sunday night and how your mother and I could have perished with them, all I can say is that God was looking after us! '

'O felix culpa!' I reminded him of the Easter Hymn, the Exultet, on the Saturday night of Holy Week, and how good can so often come out of evil!

*Rev. James Feehan*

*Archbishop Thomas Morris on Confirmation Day in Moycarkey in the 1960s.*

## Pouldine Fundraiser for Bóthar

Proceeds of the fundraising are presented to Mr. T.J. Maher. Lent 2000

## Tipperary's Triple Crown All-Ireland Hurling Captains visit Moycarkey N.S.

Autumn 1989 – Tipperary's Triple Crown All-Ireland Hurling Captains visit Moycarkey N.S.
Captains: Senior – Bobby Ryan, Junior – Kevin Laffan, Under 21 – Declan Ryan.

# The Old School Yard

WHEN I HEAR the song "The Old School Yard" sung by Mick Flavin, I always recall my childhood memories at Pouldine National School. I commenced my education there in 1949 and completed the Primary Cert in 1957. My sister Maura was two years younger than I was and she also completed her Primary Education at the school. We lived at Graigue Bridge about a mile from the school.

*Noel Walsh*

My first teacher was Mrs. Maher. She taught the infants and first class. I recall her as a very kind person who prepared us very well for the long road ahead, and prepared the class for our first Holy Communion. My mother was (Ellen Walsh nee Wilson) died at a young age, a short time before I began school and I think that Mrs. Maher was conscious of that and kept a special eye out for me. Her husband Danny Maher was a well-known teacher in Thurles. Her two sons Jack (English) and Kevin (Latin) later taught me in Thurles C.B.S. secondary school.

We got a rude awakening when we went from Mrs. Maher's room into the next room for second and third class. The teacher there was Paddy Loughnane, a native of Borrisoleigh. He was a bachelor and stayed in lodgings at the residence of Jimmy and Mrs. Hayes near Galboola Cross, as you go towards Ballymoreen. He arrived at school each morning astride the old-fashioned high bicycle. He adopted a rather robust method of teaching. I must be circumspect in my comments but it would be fair to say that he did not believe in the philosophy of "spare the rod and spoil the child". He took a large bottle of Guinness and sandwiches each day for his lunch and as we peeped in the window at him, his demeanour would remind one of the grumpy Mister Squeers, in the novel, Nicholas Nickleby by Charles Dickens.

We eventually got away, when we went to our last room in the school for fourth, fifth and sixth class. The School Principal taught these classes. Timmy Maher, or the Master as he was known. Timmy was one of nature's gentlemen and a fine teacher. He had a great habit of coaxing the best out of his pupils by persuasion and praise rather than by robust tactics. The main subjects were Irish, English, Arithmetic and Religion. However, Timmy was fond of the arts. We had singing lessons. He taught us "Slievenamon", The Croppy Boy, Kelly the Boy from Killane to note but a few and explained the origin of each to us. He had a large map of Europe on the wall and we got acquainted with all the capital cities on the continent. He treated us all with respect and courtesy. I will always remember him for that. He was a friend of mine until his death in 1986.

I always looked forward to the visitors who came to the school during class to speak with the Master. The School Inspector called at least twice a year so we all had to be up to speed with our programme in case he would ask us any questions. The Parish Priest, Father Breen and curate Father O'Meara were also regular visitors. Confirmation was in Moycarkey Church every three years with the result that I was in second year in Thurles C.B.S. when I received the sacrament with my sister Maura on 11th May 1958. That date is significant as it was the 100th anniversary of the execution of the Cormack Brothers from Loughmore, in Nenagh Jail. Garda Mick O'Meara, Littleton was another regular visitor to check the school attendance register. Mick was a great man and a highly respected member of the force. A native of Kerry, he requested that on his death he be buried in Ballymoreen.

I remember one occasion when we went on a school tour to Dublin. We visited, Dáil Eireann and were welcomed there by our local T.D. John Fanning from Two-Mile-Borris. I found it very educational seeing the parliamentary debates in reality for the first time.

During my time in Pouldine Mrs. Maher and Paddy Loughnane retired and were replaced by Pauline Treacy from Thurles and Mary Condon from Ballinure. Mary played the church organ and recruited many of us into it. Indeed, by the time we left I had the sung version of the Latin Mass off to perfection. Mary later married the famous Tipperary hurler Billy Quinn, their son Niall was one of our great international soccer players.

I left Pouldine in 1957 after the Primary Cert and went on to Thurles C.B.S. The other attraction at Pouldine was Mrs Shine and Jack Shanahan's shops where we got our sweets, when we could afford them. The Sean Treacy Pipe Band had a room adjacent to Shine's shop and had all their practice sessions there. The railway line from Waterford to Thurles was located in the area with a station at the Horse & Jockey. It provided a very valuable service, including the carriage of beet to the Sugar Factory in Thurles as well as the large crowds who travelled from Waterford to the many hurling matches in Thurles. The government in its wisdom decided to close this line and others. It was a retrograde step and it is only now that they are seeing the folly of their ways and some of those lines are now likely to be re-opened again.

My late father Dick Walsh was a native of Boherlahan, and we agreed to differ when Moycarkey provided the opposition at the hurling matches.

I left the area on 16th September 1964 to join An Garda Síochana, spending all my service in the midlands, in Edgeworthstown, Co. Longford, retiring on 23rd November 2001. My old friend from Horse & Jockey and Pouldine School-Bobby Gleeson, together with his son, Tipperary hurler Conor Gleeson came to my retirement party, bringing with them the Liam McCarthy Cup. It was great to have a fellow pupil of Pouldine present on the night; other people present included the late Séamus Cooney and his wife Kathleen from Littleton.

There are many other memories I could recall during my period in Pouldine but I will leave it to others more gifted in the use of the pen than myself to relate them. Suffice to say that I enjoyed my stay in the school and I treasure the education I got there. I am sure that the present members of the teaching profession there will continue to uphold the high standard of those who went before them.

I wish all involved continued success in the years ahead.

*(Noel Walsh was a pupil at Pouldine from 1949 until 1957)*

# First Communion Day in Moycarkey

*Above –*
*Back: Geraldine*
*Lanphier, Mary*
*Scott, Mary*
*Paula O'Keeffe,*
*Martha Kirwan.*
*Front: John*
*Kirwan, John*
*O'Keeffe – 1970.*

*ABOVE – Back: Mrs. Ann Kirwan,*
*Miss Pauline Treacy, Mrs. Joan O'Keeffe.*
*Front: Bridget and Brima Kirwan,*
*Lucy O'Keeffe – 1968.*

*LEFT – Mary and Tessie O'Keeffe – 1957.*

**School Year:-
1976-'77 Sixth Class**
Back row: Denis
O'Halloran, Pat Fahy,
Seamus Morris, Tadhg
Maher, Tom Ryan, Liam
Lahart, Michael
McCormack, Michael
Croke, Liam Cawley,
Thomas Abbott. Front
row: Elizabeth Sheehy,
Mary Cooney, Esther
Kirwan, Mary
Cummins, Kathleen
Leahy. Absent from
photo – Mark Shaw.

**School Year:- 1977-'78
Sixth Class**
Back row: Maurice Shaw,
John Cooney, Noel Sweeney,
Seamus McCormack,
Brendan Kirwan, John
Fahy, Declan Kirwan, Liam
Ó Donnchú (Principal).
Front row: Christina Croke,
Niamh Cassidy, Angela
Lanphier, Eileen Lanphier,
Eveleen Fogarty, Catherine
Loughnane, Anastasia
O'Halloran, Dolores
Cummins. Absent from
photo – Kathleen Stapleton,
Joanne Stapleton.

**School Year:-
1978-'79 Sixth Class**
Back row:- Elizabeth
McCormack, Caitríona
Cooney, Mary  Kirwan,
Liam Ó Donnchú
(Principal) Helen
Ryan, Catherine
Flanagan, Dolores
Croke. Front row: Mary
Dunne, Liam Costello,
Niall Brennan, Gerard
Coonan, Maurice
O'Halloran, Bridget
Cummins, Helen
Lahart. Absent from
photo:- Dolores Coman.

# Shine's Shop

WHEN I STARTED teaching in Pouldine School in the mid 1970s, the forlorn ruin of Shine's Shop was a significant landmark at the cross-roads, beside the school. There it stood silently, this relatively new building, lifeless and slowly deteriorating into a ruin. My curiosity was aroused and it wasn't long before I was enlightened about the 'myths and legends' relating to the place.

The people of the locality remembered it with great fondness and with the mention of Shine's, the mind immediately sped to memories of childhood, of schooldays at Pouldine, sweets and other goodies that were purchased there. Black Jack, Cleeve's Slab Toffee, Gob Stoppers, Lucky Bags, N.K.M. Toffees, Penny Bars, Cadbury's, Urney and Fry's Chocolate, Barley Sugar, Brown Cushions, Gallon Sweets etc. all got a mention, as did the scarcity of money during the Economic War and Emergency years. The attitude of the school-teachers wasn't forgotten either, as pupils were severely warned not to leave the school to visit Shine's during school breaks.

Others talked of the famous galvanised shed that was at the back of the shop. Many related that it was here that the Seán Treacy Pipe Band was formed in the thirties. Tales of the band, on a summer's evening, marching to the Jockey and back by Ballymoreen were related. The fun they had and the tricks that were played were recalled, but the camaraderie that was nurtured there lasted a lifetime. There was also mention made of the 'platform dances' that took place at Pouldine Cross, of musicians and 'all night dances', that often incurred the wrath of the clergy. John Shine was very interested in all musical instruments especially the violin.

Talk of the Emergency, during the Second World War, recalled stories of rationing and Ration Books. Commodities rationed during the war included tobacco, tea, sugar, flour and soap. These items were scarce as they needed to be imported. Households were issued with Ration Books and Shine's Shop became a hive of industry when supplies became available.

John J. Shine was a builder by trade and built his premises at Pouldine in the thirties. He was helped in this by a young man named Neddie Bourke. The design of the building was unusual for its time.

*John Shine, his nephew Paddy and brother Pat.*

John, who was a Limerickman from Athea, had taken part in the War of Independence in his younger days. This involvement resulted in his imprisonment in Limerick Prison in 1921 and facing the death sentence. Luckily for him, the Truce intervened and he was released in December of that year. While in prison he used his talent for composing poetry; one called Sweet Athea was published in the local paper.

Although he died on Christmas Day in 1970, fond memories of John J.Shine, his shop and of all its associated activities are still fondly recalled by his aging customers around Pouldine.

### Sweet Athea

"I'm sitting in my cell dark
and lonely
As the twilight through my
window strays
And I'm thinking of a little
hamlet only
So distant and so far away.
In a valley where the little
brooks are tinkling

From the hillsides down so
old and grey
And the sunbeams from old
Ireland's cares are sinking
Cast a halo o'er you sweet
Athea.
And the shades of night upon
your hills are creeping
While your homesteads all
in peace repose
And the silvery moon into
your vales is peeping
To sparkle on your watery
flows.
For peace is never found by
those who wander
Or happiness by those who
stray,
But absence makes the heart
grow ever fonder
And faithful to you sweet
Athea.

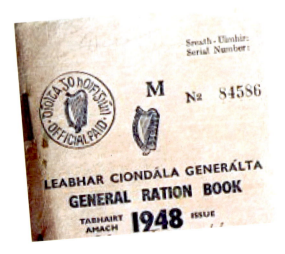

# 120 Years ago . . .
## . . . as Bassett saw us

IN 1889, The Book of County Tipperary was published by George Henry Bassett. He described his work as a manual and directory for manufacturers, merchants, traders, professional men, land-owners, farmers, tourists, anglers and sportsmen generally. One hundred and twenty years have since passed and it is both interesting and informative to read his entries for places in this locality, such as:- Horse and Jockey, Littleton and Two Mile Boris.

### HORSE AND JOCKEY, THURLES.

HORSE AND JOCKEY, a village of 6 houses, in the parish of Moycarkey, barony of Eliogarty, is a station on the Southern Railway, 5¾ miles, English, south-east of Thurles. The land of the district has a limestone basis, and is good for pasture and tillage. It is an excellent sheep country. There are extensive remains of the castle of Moycarkey, on the estate of Mr. John Max. It was at one time occupied as the residence of the Cantwell family, and has a large square tower, with high surrounding wall. A fissure in the tower was caused by lightning over a hundred years ago. There are remains also of Granna Castle, on the estate of Mr. James Myers. The village of Ballinure, 6 houses, 3½ miles, Irish, to the south, is part of the postal district of Horse and Jockey.

Catholic Church: Rev. John Bourke, P.P.

Grocers: John O'Keeffe, Horse and Jockey: Thomas Bulfin, J. Grady, T. Heffernan, Ballynure

Grocers and Spirits: Thomas O'Keeffe, E., Shanahan

Post M. : Lce. Barry

Railway : James Ryan, S.M.

School, Nl. : Denis Commons

FARMERS AND RESIDENTS.
Bulfin, Edmond, Noan
Butler, John, Ballyhudda
Davern, John, sen., Ballaghboy
Delaney, Martin, Curraheen
Dwyer, Wm., Ballinure
Fitzgerald, James, Graigue
Flanagan, Thady, Graigue
Grady, Edmond, Graigue
Gleeson, John, Curraheen
Hogan, Ptk., sen., Knocknanuss
Hogan, Patrick, Coolkip
Kavanagh, Francis, Shanbally
Lamphier, John, Laurel Lodge
Lamphier, Vernon, Laurel Lodge
Maher, Thomas, Knockroe

Max, John, Maxfort
Max, Mrs. M., Maxfort
Melbourne, William, Curraheen
Mollumby, Mrs. M. A., Rose villa
Mullins, Michael, Grallagh
O'Brien, John, Ballaghboy
O'Brien, William, Ballaghboy
O'Keeffe, Thomas, Curraheen
Power, Thomas, Noan
Shanahan, Mrs. Cth., Curragheen
Shanahan, Thos., Ballinure
Shanahan, Thos., Knockroe
Sullivan, Denis, Ballinure
Sullivan, Patrick, Grallagh
Tennant, John, Parkstown

*This photograph of the Horse and Jockey was taken in the early 1920s. It includes (l.-r.): John Joe O'Keeffe, Neddy St. John, Kitty O'Keeffe, Nell St. John and Nell Hassett. Johnny Harris is standing across the road outside Shanahan's premises.*

## LITTLETON, THURLES.
*Population 157 in 1881.— Trout-fishing*

LITTLETON, in the parish of Two Mile Borris, barony of Eliogarty, is 4 miles south-east of Thurles. The land of the district is used chiefly for tillage Barley, Oats, potatoes, and turnips are the principal crops. In the district there are ruins of Ballybeg castle, the old church of Ballymoreen, and the remains of a large Danish fort at Ballydavid.

Catholic Churches at Moycarkey and Two-Mile-Borris: Rev. Edw. O'Kane, c.c.; Rev. Nichl. Duggan, c.c., reside at Littleton
   Church of Id.: Ven. Archdeacon John O'Connor
   Dispensary: Dr. Ml. J. Barry
   Grocer: Thos. Stapleton
   Grocer and Spirits: Mrs. My. Boyleson, Ml. St. John
   Post M.: Jno. Alcock
   R. I. C.: Sergt. J. Boylan
   School, Nl.: Mrs. My. Commons
FARMERS AND RESIDENTS.
Brennan, James, Ballybeg
Burke, James, Rathcunikeen
Burke, Ptk., Rathcunikeen
Cantwell, Anthony, Ballyerke
Cantwell, Mrs. Ptk., Ballybeg
Carey, James, Coolcroo
Carrigan, James, Rahinch
Delaney, Daniel, Rahinch
Donnelly, Thos., Ballynamona
Doran, John, Galbooly
Going, O. L. M. (j.p.), Liskeveen
Murphy, Mrs., Ballymoreen
Phelan, Martin, Galbooly
Power, Rd. (j.p.), Ballydavid Ho
Ryan, John, Ballydavid
Ryan, Thomas, Galbooly
Wallace, George, Liskaveen

## TWO MILE BORRIS, THURLES.

TWO MILE BORRIS is a village of 20 houses, in the parish of same name, barony of Eliogarty, 3 miles, Irish, east by south from Thurles. The land of the district is good for pasture and tillage. There are remains of castles at Two Mile Borris and Coolcroo.

Catholic Ch., Priests, see Horse and Jockey and Littleton
   Church of Id., Littleton
   Grocers: Jas. Dwyer, Ellen St. John
   Post M.: Jas. Cooke
   School, Nl.: Jno. Manning
   Spirit retailers: Pat Bannon, Cath. Hayes, Edw. Maher
FARMERS & RESIDENTS.
Commins, Thomas, Blackcastle
Cushing, Miss Mt., Borris
Dalton, Jeremiah, Noard House
Duggan, Michael & Thos., Borris
Fanning, Martin, Borris
Guilfoyle, Michael, Ballyerke
Hayes, Daniel, Leigh
Hayes, Daniel M., Borris
Hayes, Mrs. A., Leigh
Hayes, Thomas, Leigh
Large, Christopher, Leigh
Maher, Edmd., Coolcroo
Morriss, Thomas, Borris
Ryan, John, Borris
Ryan, Thomas, Coalfields

# Tales Out of School

MY YOUNG LIFE was lived in the setting of home, Pouldine School, the Church and hurling in Fitzgerald's field in Forgestown. The roads were not tarred and the potholes were filled with broken stone, with gravel spread over them. The first tar road we saw was from Ballymoreen to the Yellow Lough. We spent nights speeding on this "wonder" – listening to the whiz of the tyres on the beautiful surface. We walked to school by road, enjoyed going barefoot in good weather, and sometimes came home across the fields.

Mrs. Danny Maher was my first teacher. She lived in Turtulla and cycled to school. One very frosty morning she fell and broke her wrist, but this did not prevent her from coming into school. She was a most pleasant and deeply religious woman. She was a

*Photograph taken on 14th December 1997 in Mullinahone on the occasion of unveiling of memorial plaque to Garda Henry Phelan. Garda Phelan was the first member of the newly formed Garda Siochana to die while on duty in Mullinahone on 14th November 1922. From left: Garda John Moloughney (Littleton), Fr. John McGrath and Garda Chief Superintendent Liam Harris (Grallagh).*

teacher 'before her time' because she had a "computer" on each infant desk. It consisted of 10 empty spools (from sewing thread) tied by string across the top of each desk – behind the inkwell. We learned to count by moving the spools sideways. She prepared me for my First Confession and First Holy Communion.

Pat Loughnane (whom we called "Lux") was teaching in the room at the road end. He lived in digs at Hayes's of Ballymoreen. He was a unique man. He arrived at school each day with a bottle of porter for his lunch. It rested on top of the press in a lying position. One hot day the cork flew and hit him on the head.

Mary Condon (Quinn) replaced Pat Loughnane on his retirement. She was young and beautiful, but her arrival was strange because we thought teachers were like oak trees that went on forever.

Timmy Maher was the Principal and taught in the room beside the Jockey road. The Master always dressed well and had a good influence on us both in school and through his involvement in hurling. He prepared us for Confirmation. We had an easy run for Confirmation that year. Archbishop Kinane was sick and we had no nerve-wracking examination in the Church to go through. Bishop Rodgers of Killaloe confirmed us. The Master also taught us how to serve Mass in Latin. The budding altar boys were gathered in a circle around him and he worked the miracle of teaching us the "tune" of the Latin responses – because we had no idea what we were saying in this strange language.

The school had three heating systems: a turf fire in each room. Turf was stored in a little shed at the top of the yard. When supplies were running low The Master picked a pupil and said "tell your father bring a load of turf to the school" – this meant a horse-cart of course. When it arrived, the bigger boys in his room were delegated to bring the turf from the road to the shed. Bringing in the turf was our first experience of Union Rules. Each boy carried a few sods at a time, to prolong the operation and avoid class!

Our lunches consisted of two slices of bread, homemade, with butter and sometimes jam as well, all wrapped in newspaper. In junior classes, a bottle of milk was common: often corked with a lump of paper. In autumn, an apple with your lunch was a real luxury and to get a bite from a friend's apple was a real treat. However, you had to be careful and keep your fingers firmly around the apple, because some boys had an "asses bite" and could split the apple in two halves.

The toilets were outside, very open plan, having no doors! A major operation was negotiated by sitting on the timber frame over the open pit below – no flushing water or toilet paper then! There was no water in the school at all.

When playtime came, there were two separate yards – the boys at the Jockey roadside and the girls at the other side of the high wall. In our time, the Dentist came to the school to extract our bad teeth. All my front teeth disappeared in one go!

Across from the school was Mrs Shine's shop. The sign over the door read: H.C. O'S. Shine, properly interpreted was Hanna Christina O'Sullivan-Shine: not quite the versions we used to come up with! She always kept the shop door locked and you had to knock and identify yourself before she would let you in. Mrs Shine is buried in Moyglass Graveyard. Behind the shop was the band hall for the Sean Treacy Pipe Band. Two of our neighbours were prominent members, Jimmy Heffernan on pipes and Mick Brien on the big drum. Eileen Costello from Littleton tried to teach us stepdancing in the hall. I must admit she had no success with the boys because there was no emerging Michael Flately among us!

Canon John McGrath was the Parish Priest. He was a big pleasant man and visited the school on a bicycle. He gave me a bar of chocolate at Christmas when I went to confession. He also told me he would give me his red hat when he died. I never got the hat, but I suppose it is hard to remember something when you are dead! On the afternoon that he died all work stopped. I remember my mother sending me down to Drumgower where my father was ploughing and he came home immediately.

As an alter server I remember serving Winnie Kirwan's marriage to Dan Maher of Forgestown. To get a half crown for serving a wedding or funeral was mega money. On Ash Wednesday, we walked from school to Moycarkey Church for confession – a big event. I suppose in today's terms you could call it our annual school outing! The death of Paud Maher, the Master's son, at a young age was a huge sadness in the parish. It was our first time seeing a white coffin. We formed a guard of honour at Shanbally cross and walked beside the hearse to the Church.

We never had summer time until I was in Secondary School. Fr. Breen, the new Parish Priest, tried to introduce it but there were objections. Eventually a compromise was reached: with a half hour change instead of the full hour: you could call it "halftime"...

Living across the road from the Church had certain advantages, especially if you went to first Mass. Then you could test-drive any new bicycle on offer during second Mass. There were only five or six families in the parish that came to Mass by motorcar. There were two "carparks" in the village, our yard and Ned Molloy's long shed.

I think my mother must have been a 'girl racer' in a horse and trap for the time she got a summons in Thurles one evening for cutting the corner, as she exited from Liberty Square into Friar Street.

I was an expert on gravedigging because I watched Ned (Randie) and Jack Molloy dig all the graves. Gravedigging then was different because you went down to the same depth as before. This meant you came on the bones of the person buried there many decades before. Ned said to me "don't they all look the same on the shovel". Ned Molloy sat at our fireside every night. I never heard Ned or Jack use a bad or ugly word in all the years I knew them.

The hall in the village was the social centre, hosting plays, dances and whist drives. The Pioneer social was special with Phil Mooney sitting on a table, playing the accordion. Tea and buttered barnbrack was served. I can still hear the announcement at Mass: "the Pioneer bus to Tramore will leave after first Mass next Sunday – the local wit would say, "Yes, for the annual wash".

Joe Cleere came from an Industrial School to the Cummins family, Killough. He was a lovely happy young fellow and he was like a brother to all of us. He later married and spent his life in Thurles. Our friendship was strong to the day Joe died.

Radio played a very important role in our lives. I remember hearing Michael O'Hehir broadcast matches at Ann and Pake Molloy's house on their radio that was powered by a windcharger.

Religion was also very central to our lives. Catherine and Mick Ryan-Smith lived at the butt of the railway bridge. On an October evening, we were having supper after picking potatoes and word came that Catherine had died suddenly. Mick never put on the radio for 12 months in respect.

I recall going up to "Mud" Shanahan, Maxfort, to collect eggs on a Good Friday and I sat with my legs dangling from the seat beside the open fire. After a while, I said "it's time for dinner" and up I got. "What" she said, "a young strapping lad like you eating dinner on the day Jesus died on the cross for you". I have never eaten a dinner on a Good Friday for my adult life.

Nan Costello, the Master's sister taught in Ballytarsna School. She travelled on her bicycle from Knockroe and came home by the Church to do the Stations of the Cross, three times, each evening. She, with other women spent three hours vigil on Good Friday leading up to the 3.00 p.m. ceremonies.

I lived my young life in the shadow of saints in the making. For this blessing, I am eternally grateful.

*Fr. John McGrath*

*Outside Moycarkey Church on Confirmation Day: Jim O'Hea, Diarmuid Ryan and John Shanahan.*

# If those Walls
# could speak

I FIRST ENTERED Pouldine School in 1950 on a sunny September morning and sat beside Harry Maher in Infants. The Teacher was Mrs. Danny Maher, who made a bit of a fuss, and I can still sense the smell of the old classroom and the chalk dust with the blackboard on its tripod at one side towards the front. Three classes occupied that room, lower infants, high infants and first class, while Mrs. Maher kept control of all three.

I remember it was always important to move up to another class each year and by the time we got to first class the room and its walls became your home from home. By the time I reached first class there were an unequal number of boys and girls so I shared a desk with Maureen Kelly, whose father was Paddy

*Fr. Phil Fitzgerald*

Kelly, employed by Ted Ryan at Maxfort. Maureen kindly brought me apples sometimes which she got from Ryan's orchard and very nice they were. Maureen later became Sr. Marie Goretti of the Presentation Sisters in Cashel, where she taught for years, and is now with a foundation founded by the Cashel nuns in California U.S.A.

After three years with Mrs. Maher, I moved onto Mr. P. Loughnane for second and third class. This move was always seen as a challenge as our new teacher was so different from Mrs. Maher and his use of that little stick was legend. He consumed a drink of Guinness with his sandwiches each lunchtime and was in the habit of throwing the last drop at any child passing the door, until Canon McGrath the P.P. was the receiver of the black drops and the drink changed to 'seven up' from that day on. I can still see the black piece of roofing felt stuck to the wall with the seasons of the year written in Irish

*Back: Jimmy Fitzgerald. Middle: Dick Fitzgerald, Jimmy McGrath, Paddy McGrath, James Fitzgerald.*
*Front: John Fitzgerald, John McGrath, Margaret Fitzgerald, Phil Fitzgerald.*

and the arrow was moved ceremoniously at the beginning of each season. Others in second class with me were my later brother, Dick, Tommy Britton, Seamus Grady, Noel Walsh, Michael Dwyer, Breda Skehan, Bridie Dwyer, Patrick Buckley, Paddy Joe O'Connell, Eddie Shannahan, Mary Shannahan and Bessie Twoomey to name a few.

It was in second class that we were often given the job of bringing the turf from the roadside when it was delivered by some generous donor. The smoke from that turf blinded us when it came back down the chimney because the wind was blowing in the wrong direction. Bringing in the turf was not the only dirty job we had to do. There was the sweeping of the floors after school. They were sprayed liberally with water to keep down the dust and the mixture of water and dust did not help the look of the floor afterwards. It was in second class we learned the damage we could do with a ruler and a piece of blotting paper dipped in ink. Missiles did not always hit the intended target. A girl's long hair dipped in the inkwell caused a real mess, when she was called by name.

The visit to the school dentist was an occasion to be dreaded. Teeth were extracted in the spare room, while the screeches and the moaning with pain was enough to put the fear in anybody's heart. After the butchery, blood was often spat into rat holes in the timber floors with perfect aim.

Another visitor to the school was the Catechism Inspector Fr. Lee, who performed his duties in a serious and reverend manner, which meant we all stood there dressed in our Sunday best with hair neatly fixed to our heads and a terror passing through us in case our teacher, our parents, ourselves and God knows who else gone before us were disgraced by any spot of ignorance in our part. Fr. Lee was later succeeded by Fr. Keown who came with a smile and gave us all a bit of praise, whether we deserved it or not.

The visit of the school nurse was not something taken lightly especially when you were about to be injected by a needle, which in the opinion of those who know, had already inoculated half the country before it was pressed mercilessly into your tender, precious skin by a practitioner who seemed to be oblivious to the fact that you felt the room going round in circles and all life was disappearing before you, as you fell in a faint on that hard timber floor.

When the inspector from the Education Department came, we had to take his visit very seriously. The tension ran through the school and everyone was a target for his questions. Teachers were watching every move a child made and it seemed that the whole future of the school depended on correct answers and good behaviour. What a sigh of relief was expelled, when he had left the premises.

Moving on to fourth class meant that you had to cope with two new subjects namely, History and Geography. Fourth, fifth and sixth classes were taught by the Master – Mr. Tim Maher. He sometimes tried to teach us the rudiments of singing and 'doh, ray, me, fah, soh' etc. became engraved in our brains like Japanese torture. If only the Sound of Music had been available then we might have got the message.

In fourth class, we shared with Boylsons, Hewitts, Stapletons, Hogans, Ryans, Tynans, Shaws, Heffernans, McGraths, Scotts, Gleesons, Twoomeys, Skehans, Shannahans, Fells, O'Regans and many others. I left after fourth class ands went to the C.B.S. in Thurles.

Any note about Pouldine School is not complete without a mention of Mrs. Shine and her greeting when we entered her shop across the road. For one penny, we had a fist of sweets and the penny bar was the favourite with everyone.

Pouldine School was replaced by a new building and the two buildings could tell a great story, if only those walls could speak.

*Fr. Phil Fitzgerald*

*School Year:- 1979-'80 Sixth Class*

*Back row: Richard O'Keeffe, Andrew Bourke, Philip McCormack, Siobhan O'Reilly, Bridget Cawley, Eoin Dunne, Patrick Cambell, Kathleen Doyle. Front row: Martina Scott, Josephine Shaw, Blanche Lanphier, Eileen Kelly, Elaine Higgins, Nora Doyle. Absent from photo – Mark Ryan.*

*School Year:- 1980-'81 Sixth Class*

*Back row: Thomas Cawley, Michael Bourke, Michael Loughnane, Ian Kavanagh, Thomas Dunne. Front row: Jimmy Cawley, Denis O'Sullivan, Donal O'Dwyer, John Abbott, Martina O'Regan, Caroline Dunne, Linda Shaw, Suzannah O'Reilly, Ella Cooney. Absent from photo: David Abbott.*

*School Year:- 1981-'82 Sixth Class*

*Back row: Henry Bourke, Kenneth Higgins, J. J. Fogarty, Liam Ó Donnchú (Principal) Robert Stapleton, Thomas Flanagan, Kevin Barry, Seamus Fahy. Front row: John Maher, Teresa Cummins, Deirdre Rayel, Catherine Cummins, Majella Dunne, Michelle Kelly, Noel Stapleton. Absent – Mary Doyle.*

# 170 Years Ago . . .
# . . . Samuel Lewis wrote

**M**OYCARKEY, a parish, in the barony of ELIOGARTY, county of TIPPERARY, and province of MUNSTER, 3 miles (S.) from Thurles, on the mail road from Dublin (by way of Cashel) to Cork; containing 1373 inhabitants. This parish, which is partly bounded by the river Suir, comprises 3554 statute acres, as applotted under the tithe act, of which about one-fifth is pasture, nearly the same proportion waste and bog, and the remainder arable land. Turtulla, the

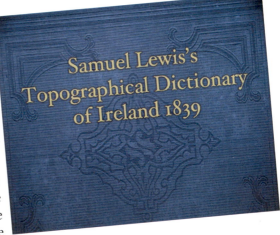

Samuel Lewis's Topographical Dictionary of Ireland 1839

property of Valentine Maher, Esq., and now the residence of John B. O'Brien, Esq., is pleasantly situated in a well-planted demesne on the river Suir: there is a flour-mill on the estate. The other seats are Maxfort, the residence of Wm. Max, Esq.; Cabrae Castle, of P. Fogarty, Esq.; and Moycarkey Castle, the property of Viscount Hawarden, now in the occupation of Mr. Wm. Foley. It is a rectory and vicarage, in the diocese of Cashel, forming part of the union of Clogher, and of the corps of the chancellorship of Cashel, in the patronage of the Archbishop: the tithes amount to £200. In the R. C. divisions it is the head of a union or district, comprising also the parish of Two Mile Borris forming part of the R. C. archbishop's mensal. In each parish is a chapel; that of Moycarkey is a modern structure, situated near the ruins of the old church, of which there are considerable remains. About 210 children are educated in two private schools. The ancient castle of Moycarkey, formerly the residence of the Cantwell family, consists of a large square tower, surrounded by a considerable area, which is enclosed by a strong high wall having small towers at the east and west angles; it was struck by lightning nearly half a century since, when a large breach was made in the great tower, and also in the eastern wall.

**LITTLETON**, a post-town, in the barony of ELIOGARTY, county of TIPPERARY, and province of MUNSTER, 4 miles (E.) from Thurles, and 79 (S.) from Dublin, on the road by Cashel to Cork; containing 44 houses and 283 inhabitants. This place is of modern date, having been chiefly erected by the late Rev. Thomas Grady, who expended considerable sums on its buildings, and in the ornamental improvements of the vicinity: it is now the property of Valentine Maher, Esq. Here are a station of the constabulary police, a public dispensary, and the parochial church, which is a handsome structure with a tower and spire.

**BALLYMOREEN**, a parish, in the barony of ELIOGARTY, county of TIPPERARY, and province of MUNSTER, 4 miles (S. S. E.) from Thurles, on the mail coach road from Dublin to Cork; containing 1237 inhabitants. It comprises 2870 statute acres, as applotted under the tithe act; there are about 500 acres of bog and of the remainder of the land, the greater portion is under tillage. Parkstown is the residence of J. P. Lanphier, Esq.; and at Liskevin are the residences of R. Beere, T. Millet, and J. Going, Esqrs. The living is a vicarage, in the diocese of Cashel, and in the patronage of the Archbishop; the rectory is impropriate in the Marquess of Ormonde. The tithes amount to £200, of which £60 is payable to the impropriator, and £140 to the vicar. There is no church, glebe-house, or glebe; the members of the Established Church attend divine service at Littleton, about 2½ miles distant. There are two pay schools, in which are about 100 boys and 60 girls.

*(From A Topographical Dictionary of Ireland by Samuel Lewis)*

*Old views of Littleton*

# Happy Memories of School 'Daze'!

*Sr. Maria
(Mary Maher).*

**W**HEN ASKED to write of my early school days I was at first a little 'lost' – where to start? Then the memories trickled back through colour, aroma and the sense of joy, fun and gratitude which I was privileged to experience in my childhood. The first colour 'memory' was of our trusted and faithful black Morris Minor in which Mammy drove Séamus and me to school each day. Every morning was an adventure as any pupil on foot along the way came on board. Sometimes, after school, the delicious aroma of dinner greeted us as we climbed into the car – another adventure as we munched with delight in the back seat on our way to a shopping spree!

In our later years, we cycled to school, often with a Garda /escort! Ned O'Hea cycled with David sidesaddle on the crossbar, as Jim peddled ahead. The rules of the road were applied as Ned, our Guardian Angel, insisted that we dismount and walk at the crossroads and around turns – not much to our liking as it slowed us down – but it was for our good. We loved to wait on the bridge while the train passed, watching with wonder the beauty all around us.

My memories of school from 1958 – 1966 are very happy. The building with its cream/yellow walls and green paint on timber, doors and windows formed a welcoming place where Mrs. Butler, Miss Treacy, Miss Ryan and, of course, the Master – Timmy Maher, all worked hard to provide us with an excellent education. The Master's sister, Nan Costello cycled passed our home each morning on her way to teach in Ballytarsna School. Mammy was a past-pupil of hers. I also recall Daddy talk about his own days in our school where his Aunt Ellen and her husband Gerry Coman were the only teachers.

Mrs. Butler, with her gentle and motherly care for each of us, gave us such a good introduction to school, setting an atmosphere conducive to learning from Infants onwards. The doll's house in the corner, the colourful 'counters' and the bright, spacious room all live vividly and happily in my memories. Mrs. Butler also initiated me into the mysteries of knitting, which so fired my imagination that I used to knit under the blankets after 'lights out'! Turning the heel of a sock was mastered and worn by a proud Dad. Mrs.

Butler allowed us to gather around the potbelly coal stove on winter days to warm our cold hands - a thoughtful treat.

Miss Treacy taught first and second-class. She set high standards and laid the foundations for a lifetime needlework 'career' – (well more-than-useful hobby!) She encouraged and challenged us and her ideas were endless. (In 5th and 6th class, when the red, pleated hand-stitched skirt was completed, she initiated the keener pupils into embroidery and drawing thread work) Both knitting and needlework skills, which I learned so well in Moycarkey, serve me well to this day. Miss Treacy was very inventive. She fashioned a 'radio' out of some cardboard, complete with 'knobs'. I loved to sit on her chair and speak into the back of this 'radio'. We used it to report on news from home, new life in the family or on the farm. It was a clever and a 'before its time' way of developing communication skills.

Sums were another story – and much less appealing to me. The numbers 'clock' on the flip chart, pointed to with a long cane, called us to order and some of us trembled as random questions were fired at us. Sometimes you got a second chance; otherwise it was the writing out of the 'table' chore! The blue and red lined blackboard helped us to join our letters – an important step on the ladder of learning.

On preparation for First Holy Communion, which occurred on Holy Trinity Sunday that year, was very thorough. Reverence and respect for the Blessed Sacrament was instilled and no detail left to chance. We practised holding our head back and closing our eyes to receive, and our prayer leaflet was explained and taught.

Moving into third and fourth class, where the lovely, regal figure of Miss Ryan towered over us, was like going into 'big' school. Many things flash through my mind for those two years. Light coloured wooden desks, with two-brass-covered inkwells, where the pen and nib adventure started. Bundles of copy books, with tight fitting band on the teachers desk or shelf, the tuning fork, Irish songs like 'Beidh Aonach Amárach' etc. printed on the flip chart and the d' r 'm' scales on the blackboard for the singing class.

The sewing copybook with needlework samples of various stitches, seams, buttonholes etc. each one stamped with the date when completed. Questions from the catechism were memorised for the Diocesan Examination. We wore our 'Sunday best' clothes on the day that the diocesan examiner came to question us, adding to the excitement and nerves!

The Master's Room, for fifth and sixth class, had an awesome feel to it, with its high windows and no view out. A small blackboard with the attendance numbers hung on the wall; a map of Ireland rolled up and pulled down for geography lessons. Oh! Every town, in every county, learned off in Irish! However, fifth and sixth classes had privileges. If the Infant's teacher was absent two of us were sent to 'Sub' for the day – it was glorious, no homework that night! We loved to play the role of 'teacher' – things are very different

Sr. Maria (Mary Maher) with her mother Winnie and brother Seamus at their home in Knockstorey.

today! It was during one of these days that Marie Lanphier and I were called to assemble in Miss Ryan's classroom for the class photo – a great event. Seamus or myself would bring milk, in a 'Baby Power's' bottle, for the teacher's lunch. In the summer months, there was no stove to boil the kettle on, so I would leave class before lunch break and go out to the Master's house next door to collect the teacher's teapot. They took their lunch in Miss Treacy's room, while the Master went home for his. His wife was so gracious and kind and her home sparkled with welcome and neatness.

Because of our date of birth about six of us had to return to Moycarkey, from secondary school, for Confirmation. You could not imagine how nervous we felt returning to our Alma Mater and standing before the Archbishop for examination!

School was not all work – the playtimes were wonderful. A new game each season! We did lots of 'skipping' in the school yard with a large rope where you had to queue up, then run in, skip to a rhyme ('Two little dickey birds sitting on a wall, one named Peter the other named Paul!') and run out again. If you were tripped up, you had to take your turn at turning the rope. Whenever I meet Ann O'Regan, she recalls our football days. Yes, she would drag her heel across the yard to mark the 'centre line'. We did not hold 'Sam' in our hands, but hold and treasure the memories still.

I am blessed that I have such good memories to treasure. I end with a small prayer from our First Communion leaflet:

"....Bless my Father and my Mother,
Bless each little Child of Thine,
Bless my teachers and my friends,
Bless our missionaries, bishops, priests and nuns
Bless all men with love divine"
Any may God bless all who read this too!

*(Sr. Maria – Mary Maher, Pupil at Pouldine School, 1958 – 1966)*

**School Year:- 1983-'84 Sixth Class**

*Back row: P.J.Butler, Cormac Cassidy, Timothy Scott, Michael Dee, Bill O'Sullivan, Declan O'Dwyer, Declan Hogan, Thomas McCormack, Richard Stapleton, Michael Cooney. Middle row:Vanessa O'Reilly, Sharon Croke, Eileen Flanagan, Helen Flanagan, Maria Maher, Geraldine Lahart, Michelle Delahunty, Elizabeth Cummins, Mary Fahy. Front row: Gregory Sweeney, Brendan Stapleton, Irwin Bannon, Micheál Kavanagh. Absent from photo: David Sheppard.*

**School Year:- 1982-'83 Sixth Class**

*Back row: Damien Loughnane, Patrick O'Connell, Martin Flanagan., Dennis Rayel. Liam Ó Donnchú (Principal), Seamus Lahart, Andreas Maher, John Mcormack, Pat O'Brien. Middle row: Martin Cambell, Adrian Delahunty, Cristin O'Reilly, Martina Croke, Siobhán Bourke, Siobhán Hogan, Esther Ryan, Esther Butler. Front row: Patrick Dunne, Thomas O'Halloran. Absent from photo: Trevor Abbott, John Kelly.*

**School Year:- 1984-'85 Sixth Class**
*Back row: Kenneth Concagh, Seamus Stapleton, Donal Hogan, Maura O'Connell, Mairéad Bourke, Emer Bannon, Laurence O'Sullivan, Liam Ó Donnchú (Principal). Middle row: Helena O'Keeffe, Ann-Marie Shanahan,*  *Josephine McCormack, Mary Callanan, Jennifer Shaw, Katie Bourke, Mairéad Cooney. Front row: Pat Costello, Joseph McCormack, Paul Skehan.*

– 96 –

# Milestones of History in Moycarkey

*John J. Hassett*

**A**S ONE OF several Moycarkey parish pupils, who attended Ballytarsna National School located across the parochial boundary in Boherlahan, I almost daily shared experiences of the kind of homework and of the demanding teachers we had with my peers of Pouldine National School. They too thought that school was a nuisance and a terrible waste of time, bad enough having to attend it, but most unfair to have school homework when you returned home at evening. It is the things that make us different that also make us more interesting to each other. Pupils from Moycarkey parish attending Ballytarsna National School received their First Holy Communion in Boherlahan Parish Church and later on the Sacrament of Confirmation. In Moycarkey Church for the Confirmation Ceremony, the Sean Treacy Pipe Band was present to welcome the Archbishop of the time with appropriate music. Boherlahan had no such musical welcome on Confirmation day, and we perhaps felt we should have the same as Moycarkey being from that parish. How children's minds display the competitive edge or perhaps the desire for equality, from an early age!

The old Pouldine National School gave me in childhood the impression of a fortress much more than of a school, as we passed it on our way to and from Thurles. Built beside a junction of four roads linking Thurles with Horse and Jockey and Holycross with Littleton, it is centrally located in a region steeped in ancient, medieval and modern Irish history. One of the founding fathers of the Irish State General Dick Mulcahy who in his childhood and teenage years resided in Littleton chose nearby Ballymoreen cemetery as his last resting place. Colonel Jerry Ryan, Captain Bill Donnelly and General Dick Mulcahy became active IRB members from early youth, probably through a former Town Clerk of Thurles, the late J. M. Kennedy, then head of the secret society in the region. The local Moycarkey Branch of Sinn Fein was formed in Lambe's House Maxfort; Moycarkey in 1918. It is now the residence of their nephew Paddy Fanning.

The well planned capture of Littleton Royal Irish Constabulary Barracks during the War of Independence reflected quality intelligence work and perfect planning that resulted in the rushing by a small select group of IRA men of the barrack and the over powering of the garrison while having their mid day meal, and without loss of life, has no parallel of which I am aware in the War of Independence. The capture of much needed guns and ammunition from the police in the raid gave a major boost to the local Moycarkey Company and the Mid Tipp Brigade IRA at the particular time. Some past pupils of Pouldine National School were involved in the capture of Littleton police barrack and served well in the fight for Irish Freedom ninety years ago.

At Knockroe within one mile of the school and beside the Thurles road on September 25th 1845, one of the largest public meetings of the Daniel O' Connell Repeal Movement for the restoration of an Irish Parliament was held. O' Connell believed it was the largest meeting of his Repeal campaign; others thought Tara had a bigger crowd. Figures from a quarter to half a million people as estimated have been given for the Tara and Knockroe gatherings, the population of Ireland was close to 9 million people at that period. No greater gatherings of people have ever been recorded since in Ireland for any public meeting or gathering.

The Horse and Jockey village is a place of habitation and enterprise over several centuries and is linked with the legendary Gobaun Saor of Irish folklore who resided according to tradition at Derrynaflan, where the famous medieval hoard, now in the National Museum, was found a quarter of a century ago. Irish folklore through the ages recalls the alleged internationally famed Irish Master Stone Mason and Architect and his achievements and roles in many places. Derrynaflan was in recent centuries if not always, known to the locals as the Gobaun Saor Island and not by its current name. One thing we can be relatively certain of is that it was a place of habitation and enterprise from before the birth of Christ.

The Horse and Jockey Hotel is now centre stage of a village that had the horse drawn mail coach of the 18th and first half of the 19th century passing through it daily, linking Dublin with Cork. Located in the centre of quality land, the Horse and Jockey village was and still is one of the great cross road junctions of mid Tipperary and East Munster and a meeting place for people. In the last decade of the 18th century Wolf Tone, the father of Irish Republicanism and leader of the United Irishmen, visited the Horse and Jockey Inn, now a part of the modern hotel, to meet local leaders of the United Irishmen. He was accompanied by Thomas Russell a native of Mallow an organiser and co-ordinator of the United Irishmen for the region and known in history as 'the man from God knows where'. It was a significant meeting of local leaders and as a result lived on in local folklore

*Thomas Russell*

*Huntsmen under the oak tree outside the old Horse & Jockey Inn and overhead the famous sign which gave the name to the crossroads.*

to present times. One of the few centres of conflict in County Tipperary in 1798 was the Battle of Tubberadora four miles distant, where a poorly armed group of United Irishmen in the process of assembly were surprised by a mounted Company of Militia and a brief encounter developed resulting in fatal casualties among the United Irishmen as well as some being taken prisoner and later executed. An account of the Tubberadora incident reached Wolf Tone, then in Paris, and he recorded it in his diary.

Moycarkey Parish and its schools are all hurling nurseries since the formation of the GAA 125 years ago. In 1898 the Horse and Jockey hurlers to celebrate the centenary of the 1798 Rebellion against foreign rule in Ireland, celebrated the village Inn link with 1798 by registering themselves for that year's Tipperary county championship as the Horse and Jockey Wolf Tones and went on to win the All Ireland senior hurling championship of 1899 for County Tipperary . In 1998 both Thomas Russell and Wolf Tone were commemorated in the Horse and Jockey Inn by the Irish Bardic Federation, when Derek Warfield leader of the famous Wolf Tones Band, and eminent historian delivered the lecture followed by an evening of music and song enjoyed by all present. The modern Moycarkey National School at Poudine, is and always will be a part of an Ireland that will uphold and enrich our National Culture protect our Sovereignty and abide by the Christian faith, to steel us in our resolve to create a better tomorrow for all, as we salute the major achievements of previous generations, who passed on the benefits of their demanding labours to us of this generation.

*By John J. Hassett*

*Outside O'Keeffe's Grocery in 1955: Mary O'Keeffe on her First Communion Day with her cousin Catherine Fitzgerald.*

*ABOVE: All aboard . . . next stop Laffan's Bridge as train prepares to leave the Horse & Jockey.*

*RIGHT: The signal box at Horse & Jockey Railway Station photographed in September 1963.*

# The Changing Face of . . .
## . . . Horse & Jockey

ONE hundred years ago, the Horse and Jockey was a picturesque little village, nestling at the foot of the famous hump-backbridge. An industrious little village, I might add, because it boasted of having a tailor Michael Caudy, a cobbler and shoe-maker, Jack Carthy, Tom Barry, the blacksmith, two threshing mills owned by Dick O'Keeffe, also the Post Office owned by Tim Barry. The railway line from Thurles to Clonmel served the station at Horse and Jockey – goods trains and passanger trains all made a stop there. Deliveries of goods to the pub – Richard O'Keeffe and grocery – John O'Keeffe (of which there was one of each) came by

*Joan O'Keeffe*

goods train. The people of the village and surrounding area travelled by train to nearby towns of Thurles, Templemore, Fethard or Clonmel and on excursion trains (as they were called then) to Dublin or in summer to the sea-side. Life was tranquil and unhurried then and it seemed that nothing would ever change. In the early sixties, road-widening commenced and most of the branch lines, including Horse and Jockey, were about to be closed.

The famous bridge was reckoned to be dangerous because large heavy-laden haulage trucks were now transporting goods and frequently got stuck on the bridge.

The photographs show the demolition of the bridge and clearing of existing out-offices. New houses sprang up. A filling station was erected to meet the needs of passing traffic and so the once sleepy village woke up to a complete transformation

People who have been away for years have said that they would not recognise the place from what it was when they left.

*(This article, written by Joan O'Keeffe R.I.P., is re-printed from the Horse and Jockey Centenary Booklet, published 1999)*

**School Year:-**
**1985-'86 Sixth Class**
Back row: Johnny Flanagan, Brian Delahunty, Jerry Fahy, Eugene Dunne, Denis Costello, Liam Ó Donnchú (Principal). Middle row: Yvonne Shaw, Caroline Lambe, Miriam Mooney, Martina Loughnane, Catherine Barrett, Joanne Maher.

Front row:- Mary Teresa Butler, Cora Delaney, Norma Stapleton, Bridget Kane, Treasa Murphy, Isobel Coman, Ann Barry. Absent: James Moriarty.

**School Year:- 1986**
**– Senior Infants**
**and First Class**
Back row:-Mrs Mary Minchin, George Webster, Frank Molloy, Michael Minchin, Tom Higgins, James Dunne, Patrick Shahanan, John Paul Shanahan. Middle row: Marie Cummins, Ann Harrington, Pamela Quigley Niamh Ryan, Claire Hogan, Colin Ryan, Patrick

McCormack, John Butler. Front Row (seated): Catriona Ryan, Susan Leahy, Muireann O'Donoghue, Claire Dee, Siobhán Nagle, Sinead O'Mahony, Caroline Roche, Katie O'Connell. Front (kneeling): Louise Shortall, Angela Cummins, Ann Barrett, Loraine Dunne, Lorainne Stapleton. Missing from photo: Rosemary Fanning, T.J. O'Brien, Jason Roche.

**School Year:- 1986-'87 Sixth Class**

Back row: Teachers Ms. Catherine McGrath, Ms. Lucy McGann, Oliver Hogan, Daniel Maher, Cyril Stapleton, Liam Ó Donnchú (Principal Teacher) Séamus Concagh, Gerard O'Dwyer, Mrs Mary Minchin, Ms. Bríd Ryan. Front row: Bridget Ryan, Elaine Mooney, Janette Butler, Tara Coman, Tracy Browne, Nollaig Ryan, Agnes Kane.

# Birthplace of vision, imagination and wisdom

*Pat Costello*

WITH THE advancing years and the challenges of memory it becomes more difficult to find a window through which one can return and explore early childhood and of course, schooldays. There is an old saying in the Hebrew that "a child's mind is not a vessel to be filled but, a lamp to be lit", but such wisdom would have eluded the curiosity of a five year old setting out on life's excursion in the early nineteen fifty's.

Still, the frenzied babble of schoolyard voices, the smell of new books, a line from a poem perhaps, and the great maps dangling from the classroom wall taunting us with strange names and strange places yet to be explored, all conspire to illuminate that corner of our minds where the memories of those days at school have taken refuge.

Much of our current understanding of school stems from our children's experiences and indeed from those of our grandchildren. Play school, play groups and early learning opportunities all help to smooth the transition of the young scholar from home to the world of education. My arrival at Pouldine School was a very different affair. Holding my mothers hand we stopped at the stone piers which marked the entrance to the boys yard, and an imposing entrance it was, looking like the portals of some ancient fortress with the sounds of what appeared to be a major battle coming from within. Mrs Maher, herself an equally imposing figure, took my outstretched hand and marched me past a sea of curious faces, who had paused in their endeavours to observe the new boy, around the "Masters" classroom and into her seat of learning where I was embraced into the fold of Low Infants. New faces, new voices, a special place to sit, a turbulent symphony of the senses, the squeak of chalk on the little blackboards and the songs of the older children projected in unison, reminding you that you had yet to fit in. Above all rose the voice of Mrs Maher, nursing a regime of rhyme and reason and of course routine, a routine that spilled out into the schoolyard for the sos beag and the lón, soon the once formidable school walls would become a platform to provide our young eyes with a new vantage point on the world.

Great civilisation throughout the centuries have always been judged, among other things of course, by the quality of their architecture. In our little community Pouldine School presented a most imposing edifice. Built at the confluence of four roads the school immediately exerted a powerful influence upon the landscape. One cannot even imagine the circumstances prevailing in the area when the school came into service during the middle of the nineteenth century, into an Ireland tormented by famine, despair and political unrest. Despite this a correspondent to the Ilustrated London News in 1847 reported on the vibrancy of the market day and the numbers of people present, in the town of Thurles, a fact to which I was oblivious as I flew past Pouldine for the first time on the carrier of my father's postbike.

First Holy Communion would be without doubt the most important early milestone in our days in Pouldine. Passage through the relatively calm waters of Low and High Infants was accomplished without incident and then, onwards and upwards to confront vexing theological concepts and questions, wrestle with the implications of sin and prepare for the demands of the First Confession. It must have been successful for we emerged contrite, pious and ready for the big day, "First Communion" in those days was a gentle, simple affair without any of the social complications which are commonplace nowadays. I remember visiting my neighbours, Biddy and Jack Carrie after coming from the Church in Moycarkey. Jack demanded a full account of the procedures and I was happy to oblige and in fact with my newly acquired religious knowledge I was able to point out a number of facts about the Sacrament with which he was not familiar. As a result of the consultation I received a shining two shilling piece which contributed greatly to the afternoons celebrations which included Dwans red lemonade and a couple of bars of chocolate.

I think it is fair to say that journeys, great and small, play a significant part in all our lives. As I got older and was able to set out alone, the journey to school took on a new life all of it's own. Just below our house at a bend in the road was a favourite camping place for two travelling families who stopped there at different times of the year. They were quiet gentle people who would pass the time of day and ask you what you learned in school. Fanning's gate was surrounded by a great brooding grove of trees which provided ample opportunity for would be sculptors to carve their names and leave a legacy for posterity. At Shanballa cross you were likely to catch your first glimpse of fellow scholars making their way from Graigue and Moycarkey and as the years passed it became an important meeting point where the previous day's conversations were taken up afresh, embellished I'm sure, and helped to soften the journey to school. There was a fine dramatic view of Pouldine as we came over the brow of the hill, sometimes we deceived ourselves into thinking we could even judge the mood of the day from that particular vantage point. One final distraction awaited, in the form of a little bridge and stream which crossed the road and provided years of exploration and curiosity. Bricín's, frogs and other obscure life forms occupied this little stream at certain times and the temptation was ever present to explore this mysterious waterway to it's source but, school beckoned.

THURLES ON MARKET-DAY.

The middle years in Pouldine, third and fourth class, seem to convey memories of a period of great stability and calm, a sort of golden age of learning as one might say. Poetry arrived, and the stories in the sweet smelling new books became longer and more complex. The threepenny and sixpenny copy, with a majestic warrior accompanied by a hound, set against the background of an elegant round tower on the cover, were used to contain our intellectual outpourings. The "composition" would become the natural extension of the gift of storytelling we received from our parents and the older people in our neighbourhood. Bhí an Gaeilge ann go flúirseach freisin. Mar is gnáth bhí Mamaí ag obair go dian sa chistin, agus Dadaí amuigh faoin spéir, ag tabhairt aire do na mbeithíoch. Bhí ceol an nadúr agus an talamh ag eirí ó gach leathanach. Sceal indiadh scheal, Cúchulainn, Ferdia agus a mhuintir in aice le Clann Lir ag casadh timpeall istigh in ár gchinn óga. Maths, disguised as "sums" accompanied by "Tables", chanted with all the fervour of an ancient mantra laid the foundations for decades of problem solving yet to come. Miss Condon would speak of higher things, like music and the beauty of the human voice. Beidh aonach amarach í gContae an Chláir and Oró mo Bháidín ag Snámh ar an Loch would resonate with almost prayerful intent around the walls of our little classroom. Schríbhneoireacht, writing, took pride of place in the order of demands on the young scholar. The tiny white vessel which lurked behind the sliding brass plate on the desk and contained that dark vile liquid known as ink suggested nothing short of witchery. Propelling the pointed piece of metal with the little wooden stem across the page, without leaving substantial deposits of ink, unintentionally of course, called for the most sublime skill.

During the Sos and the Lón we would exchange the confinement of the classroom for the broader reaches of the boys yard, the girls would conduct their affairs in another yard, behind an appropriately proportioned wall. The need for such segregation was not apparent to us at this stage. The world was a different place looking out over the school wall, and regularly drama unfolded before our very eyes on the road outside. Jimmy Purcell would arrive with a donkey and dray car with two churns en route to the creamery in Littleton. Some of the more villainous sixth class boys would shout dubious words of encouragement as they passed, however if Jimmy was unfortunate enough to meet Jack Dwyer with his noisy tvo powered tractor this was more than the poor donkey could take. It was a stirring sight to see Jimmy trying to restrain the bouncing churns and the donkey as they charged down the Ballymoreen road, reminiscent of the final stages of the great chariot race in Ben Hur. A great personal treat of course was if my Father passed on his bike, whistling as usual, on his way to deliver the post.

The only challenge to the architectural dominance of our School at Pouldine cross was Mrs Shines Shop. I remember Mrs Shine as a saintly women, if one was fortunate enough to have the resources to buy a pennie's worth of bulls eyes she would descend the stairs chanting, Jesus, Sweet Jesus and give you the sweets in a little cone of bright white paper. A very large sign on the wall outside had the picture of a sailor and extolled the virtues of Players Navy Cut. Behind the hedges was the band hall, the spiritual home of the Sean Tracy Pipe Band a place of magic and mystery. There is no sweeter memory than sitting on the wall outside our house in Shanballa in the quiet of a summer evening and hearing the sound of the pipes drifting across the fields from Pouldine as the band were practicing, ancient music caressing an ancient landscape.

The Master, Timmy Maher was an elegant man. He always appeared as an elegant man even if you met him walking the greyhounds or attending a match so, it was no accident that the pace of life quickened when we went to the Master's classroom. One served one's apprenticeship in fifth class, playing understudy to the Dons and Dames in sixth class but, our turn would come. And come it certainly did with a bewildering array of new challenges and experiences. Timmy would draw down the great maps of Ireland and Europe and through the medium of Stair and Tír Eolas would flit effortlessly between the West of Ireland and the Balkans with only the aid of a wicked looking pointed stick. The spectre of the Primary Cert loomed on the horizon and of course Confirmation. A number of unexplained mysteries remain from that final period in Pouldine. One particular mystery concerns the arrival of a tiny Nun who was introduced to us by the Master, she then proceeded to show us moving pictures of apparitions and other supernatural events using a very noisy machine, there was no sound in evidence to the best of my knowledge. The Masters room had to be darkned and I recall John D'Alton from Galboola sustained an injury while assisting the little Nun to black out the tall windows. A pressing engagement with the Diocesan Inspector meant that the Green Catechism was one's constant companion for months, there was no time for questions or philosophy, only answers – the correct answers. Preparation for confirmation was wonderful. We would assemble in the choir gallery in Moycarkey Church and with the aid of a wheezy harmonium fill the air with the beautiful latin hyms that were part of the Church's liturgy at that time. With the Inspector satisfied, we could look forward to the great day even if some mischief makers suggested that part of the ritual was a devastating right hook from the Bishop. It turned out to be only a rumour.

One of the great advantages of being in the Masters class was the daily football match during am lón. Timmy loved sport and each day when he retired for his lunch we were given the freedom of the little field at the back of his house to play football. Many heroic encounters took place during those short games. The talents and abilities of the participants were diverse, knowledge of the rules was scant and by and large the whole event was, in the absence of a referee, self regulating – a triumph for democracy.

The journey home from school was no less important, the games of marbles, kicking a soft sponge ball ahead of you until it disappeared into the ditch, swapping comics, a practice frowned upon at the time. There would be visits to Jim Reilly's garden to retrieve a juicy young turnip, which would be peeled with the aid of a five bar gate. Rumblings in the bolg would follow, but it would not deter us from trying it again.

I'm sure the journey home on the last day from Pouldine was no different but perhaps this time filled with a little more apprehension and uncertainty, and then I think maybe there is no last day, that we constantly return in spirit to that place where vision, imagination and wisdom is born and when confronted by an inquisitor with

"What did you learn in school today?" , we will have an answer !.

*Pat Costello*

*The old parochial house in Moycarkey.*

**School Year:- 1987-'88**

Back row: Francis Ryan, Paul Molloy, Ann Butler, RoseMary Lanphier, Caroline Stapleton, Risteárd Cassidy, Michael Moriarty. Front row: Valarie Lanphier, Tríona Murphy, Ellen McCormack, Louise Delaney, Fíóna O'Mahony, Olivia O'Brien, Phylis Abbott.

**School Year:- 1988-'89 Sixth Class**

Back row: Ann Marie Maguire, Thomas Delahunty, Nigel Callanan, Brian Shanahan, Liam Ó Donnchú (Principal) , Brian Croke, Vincent Stapleton, Derek Leahy, Julie Harrington. Front row: Kate O'Sullivan, Elllen McCormack, Onagh Nagle, Jenny Harrington, Chanelle Shanahan, Mary Ryan, Majella Fitzgerald.

**School year:- 1989-'90 Sixth Class**

Back Row: Donal Shanahan, Patrick Delahunty, James Kennedy, David Minchin, Michael O'Regan, Donncha Looby, Paul Hogan, Eoghan O'Donoghue, Robert Nagle, Noel Butler.
Middle Row: Barbara Dunne, Catherine Harrington, Imelda Britton, Catherine Stapleton, Eileen Looby, Ciara McCormack, Maria O'Brien, Clare Molloy, Dervla Fitzgerald. Front row: Caroline Abbott, Andrea Murphy, Alma Delaney, Breda Coman, Liam O'Donnchú (Principal), Paula Coman, Catherine Moriarty, Fionnuala Concagh, Debbie Quigley. Absent from photo: Niall Bannon.

# Next Stop
# – "The Jockey"

HAVING a railway line at Horse & Jockey eased the transport problems for locals in years gone by. Its existence also added to the status and potential of the village and was a vital entity in the daily lives of the members of the locality, who recall it nostalgically. Here are a few facts about this railway line:-

1. The Thurles-Clonmel railway line, which passed through The Jockey, was 25 _ miles long, with a 4 _ foot gauge and opened on July 1st, 1880.

2. It was a single-track line throughout its existence, although the original plans hoped for a double track, hence the many double arch bridges on the line.

3. In the remaining years of the nineteenth century, three passenger trains travelled daily in each direction. Usually a Vulcan 2-4-0 engine No. 36 – Lily worked the line.

4. In the first decade of the twentieth century G.S. W.R. provided an "84" class 0-4-4 tank engine to power the trains on this line.

*Mick Maxwell, who was the last Station Master of Horse & Jockey on the platform with his son P.J. Photograph taken in 1963.*

5. The Railway Company had a stone crushing plant at Laffan's Bridge (1901 – 1907). When they failed to get extra land near the quarry, they moved the entire concern to Lisduff, north of Thurles.

6. The line suffered extensive damage during the War of Independence and the Civil War. The track was ripped up in eight places, seven bridges were destroyed and signal cabins at Clonmel, Laffan's Bridge and Horse and Jockey were burned.

7. In the late 1940s, the railway suffered from acute coal shortage. Only one train ran daily in each direction taking 2 hours for the up journey and 97 minutes for the down. All services were suspended, due to fuel shortage for some months in early 1947.

8. In 1954, C.I.E. introduced the Railbus to this line. Road buses were converted at Inchicore Works to railway running by the fitting of steel train wheels, especially made to fit the railway gauge. This service was entirely inadequate as the vehicle had seating for a mere 34. It could not serve every platform as it had an entrance on only one side. A hurried alteration was needed to make it accessible from either side. After 1956, it was seen no more.

9. Horse and Jockey station had a layout almost completely opposite to that of Laffan's Bridge and Farranalleen, the platform being on the down side in this case and the siding on the other. The siding allowed trains to cross here as happened daily when the morning down goods took refuge in the siding to allow the up passanger train to proceed to Thurles.

10. There were several level crossings on the line, one being at Curraheen. Each crossing had a gatekeeper who resided nearby.

11. Passanger trains were discountinued on September 9th, 1963 but specials and freight trains ran until all traffic ceased on March 27th, 1967.

12. The last three stationmasters at the Horse & Jockey were Dan O'Keeffe, Michael Fleming and finally Mick Maxwell.

Map of the railway from Clonmel to Thurles and its associated lines.

# American conquerors feted in Pouldine in 1926 – Dancing until dawn

TIPPERARY, All-Ireland champions of 1925, undertook the second great American tour the following year and included John Joe Hayes, Bill Ryan, Martin Mockler, Phil Purcell and William O'Brien from the Moycarkey-Borris club. The tour was organised by Paddy Cahill, a native of Holycross and prominent in Chicago GAA circles. The object of the tour was to promote hurling in the United States. The party left Ireland in May, 1926, and returned in July, having won all their games, defeating the American champions Offaly; a Cork selection in Boston; a Chicago selection in Chicago; San Francisco in that city, a Buffalo selection in Buffalo and then back to the Polo Grounds, New York, for the grand finale.

The "Welcome Home" celebrations in 1926 were held in Pouldine Schoolhouse and the function aroused great interest throughout the whole county, and was, in every aspect, a magnificent success. The only drawback was that the accommodation provided by the building was inadequate. The banquet began at 7 p.m. and both from the point of view of excellent speeches delivered the great songs that were sung and last but not least, the choice of fare provided, was one of the most enjoyable social gatherings held in the parish of Moycarkey-Borris.

The Ladies' Committee, under the leadership of Mrs T.A. Byrne, Ballyroe House, Cashel, received lavish praise for the manner in which they carried out the catering. Members of this committee were: Miss Nell Hayes and Miss Mary Anne Hayes, Ballyerk, Miss Mollie O'Brien and Miss Peg O'Brien, Moycarkey, Miss Josie Tuohy, Moycarkey, Miss Bridie Hogan and Miss Nora Hogan, Coolkip, Miss Josie Ryan, Riverdale House, Horse and Jockey, Miss Kathleen Cahill and Miss Ellie Shanahan, Maxfort, Miss K. Shanahan and Miss M. Hunt, Kylenoe.

The general organising committee consisted of:- Messrs. D. Heaney and Thomas Purcell, Knockroe (Hon. Secretaries); William O'Callaghan, Parkstown House and P. Maher, Pouldine (Hon. Treasurers); M. Condon, Ballinure; M. Hayes, N.T. and R. O'Keeffe, Horse and Jockey; William Gleeson, Drumboe; Joe Fitzpatrick, Ballyerk; P. Mullins,

Grallagh; Paddy Hayes, Two-Mile-Borris; Captain Thomas O'Grady, Archerstown; Pat Shanahan, Pouldine; Andy Fogarty, MCC, Grange; Pat Molloy, Moycarkey; Jack Gleeson, Dromboe; Paddy Maher (Best), Phil Leahy, Laharden. Very Rev. D. Moloney, P.P., Moycarkey, presided, and on his right were Captain Thomas O' Grady, hero of the 1888 tour, and still hale and hearty, and Mr Frank McGrath, the team manager. On his left were Captain Johnny Leahy, and Mr M. Condon, chief of the reception committee. The clergy present were: Rev Timothy O'Dwyer, C.C., Moycarkey, Rev. J. Maher, C.C., Templemore and Rev. E. Byrne C.SS.P. The company included ex-Colonel Jerry Ryan, MCC, Thurles, and Mrs. Ryan, T.P. Stapleton, P.C., Thurles, Andy Mason, Secretary, Mid Tipperary Board GAA, Thurles, Joe Moloughney,U.C., Treasurer County Board GAA, P.J. Fennessy Editor, "Tipperary Star", and J.J. Halpin, journalist, Tipperary.

The hall was decorated with the blue and gold colours of Tipperary, the Tri-colour and the "Stars and Stripes" of America. Over the top of the main table was suspended a banner bearing the inscription: "Welcome to Moycarkey – the World Champion Hurlers, 1926." The hurlers on their arrival in the hall were greeted with prolonged applause.

## WELCOME HOME

The Rev. Chairman of the reception committee said it was his privilege as well as his great pleasure to welcome home the hurlers of Tipperary from the land of the 'Stars and Stripes' and to tell them how proud their fellow-countrymen were of the name which they had estalished for themselves and for our great Irish game from New York to the Golden Gates. 'We are proud of them, Tipperary is proud of them and Ireland is proud of them. They have brought back to Ireland a record of unbroken success. We congratulate them and we give them both our thanks and our welcome this evening. These young men come of a breed of hurlers. If you go back for one hundred years or more, you will find that the reputation of the Tipperary hurlers was almost as brilliant then as it is today.'

Concluding, the Rev. Chairman said: 'Whether you come from Moycarkey where the game was resuscitated, or whether you come from Tubberadora or Boherlahan, where it struck root, or Toomevara or other parts of North Tipperary where it flourished and flourishes still, I congratulate you, champion hurlers of the Premier County, on the great record you have made.'

Mr D. Heaney read the following address of welcome: "To the members of the Tipperary Hurling team – the World's Hurling Champions of 1926". We the undersigned on behalf of the Gaels of Moycarkey and Two-Mile-Borris, have great pleasure in extending to you a hearty Céad Míle Fáilte on your coming amongst us. We desire to assure you of our high appreciation of your noble deeds in the land of the Stars and Stripes – deeds that not alone have proved that Tipperary is still the Premier County, but have uncontrovertedly demonstrated that however poor and insignificant that Ireland may be in other respects, she can yet produce athletes who are able to advantageously compete with those of the greatest nation of the world. You have shown to all Irish men that if

*Tipperary Team (All-Ireland Champions 1925) in U.S.A. in 1926.*
*Front row: Martin Kennedy (Toomevara), Paddy Leahy (Boherlahan), Thos. Duffy (Lorrha). Centre Row: T.J. Kenny (Portroe), Frank McGrath (Manager), Johnny Power (Boherlahan), Michael Leahy (Boherlahan), Stephen Kenny (Cloughjordan), Johnny Leahy Capt. (Boherlahan), Phil Cahill (Holycross), William O'Brien (Moycarkey Borris), Patrick O'Dwyer (Boherlahan), J. J. Hayes (Moycarkey Borris). Back Row: Paddy Power (Boherlahan) Jim O'Meara (Toomevara), Phil Purcell (Moycarkey Borris), Arthur O'Donnell (Boherlahan), Martin Mockler (Moycarkey Borris), William Ryan (Moycarkey Borris), Wedger Meagher (Co. Board Sec.).*

they want to command the respect and admiration of the people of other lands, as you have done, they must go to those lands as the manly exponents of the national games and not as the foppish imitators of those of the stranger. Concluding, Mr Heaney said: "We welcome you to Moycarkey with the spirit of the Gael, we are happy to see you back again hale and hearty. It is our earnest prayer that you may long be spared to do honour to our grand old pastimes and to maintain at home and abroad the present position of unconquered Tipperary.

Signed:- Michael Condon (chairman) Tom O'Grady, Richard O'Keeffe, John Manning, James O'Keeffe, Paddy Hayes, William Gleeson, John Gleeson, William Callanan, Paddy Maher,Pat Shanahan, Patrick Molloy, Pat Maher, Thomas Purcell, Hon. Secretary.

Mr. Frank McGrath thanked the organisers of the banquet given in honour of the returned party, a function the members of the team would always remember with pride.

Rev. Father John Maher said that he was glad to see around so many of his old friends, not a few of whom he went to school with. He himself began hurling at an early age. He went to school with the Gleesons, Keeffes and Spillanes and others and he was a next-door neighbour of their guest- Captain Tom O'Grady.

Mr John Joe Hayes (Ballyerk), a member of the undefeated team, said they were all pleased to have with them that night one of the greatest Gaels that Tipperary had ever seen – Captain Tom O'Grady, one of the men who went out in the 'eighties' to put forward the interests of the GAA. They had found in the USA that the Gaels there were practically as good as those at home; the Americans had said that hurling was one of the greatest games they had ever seen and yet here in Ireland they had young Irishmen who won't play hurling because they think it is too "common." They prefer to play rubgy, hockey and other foreign games. When Americans are taking up hurling and declaring it to be the finest game in the world, it is a disgrace to see young Irishmen ashamed to play it and playing foreign games instead.

An enjoyable social evening followed with dancing starting at 10.30 p.m. and lasting with unabated enjoyment until daylight. A capital musical programme was contributed by an orchestra composed of talented Thurles and Cashel instrumentalists. Mr T.W. Gerathy, Thurles, presided at the piano.

"A great Moycarkey-Borris night in Poudine for the champion hurlers of the world."

*Group photographed at the unveiling of Paddy Maher (Best) memorial in 1979. Back row (l.-r.): John Phelan, Paddy Moloney, Harry Ryan, T. K. Dwyer, Jim Burke, Joe Ryan, Bill Moloney, Liam Hennessy, Eamon Barry, Jimmy Tobin, Sean Barry, Harry Melbourne, Billy Shanahan, Liam Ryan. Front row (l.-r.): Bill O'Keeffe, Johnny Ryan, John Mullins, John Joe Hayes, Tommy Gleeson, Paddy Ryan (S), Thomas O'Keeffe, Tommy Fogarty.*

# Schools Folklore Collection

URING THE school year 1937 – '38, schools all over the Republic of Ireland were asked to collect the folklore of their area. Almost 100,000 children aged eleven to fourteen, in 5,000 National Schools were involved in seeking out and setting down for posterity material dealing with a wide range of Irish folk tradition. This collection included folk tales and folk legends, riddles, proverbs, songs, customs and beliefs. Games and pastimes as well as descriptions of traditional work practices and crafts were to be included. The children collected the material mainly from their parents and grandparents and other older members of the local community. The result nationally extends to more than 500,000 manuscript pages. The collection is now preserved in the Department of Irish Folklore in University College Dublin.

Mr. Michael Myres was Principal Teacher in our school at the time of the collection and he, his staff and the pupils set about recording the information from this area. When their work was complete, they had a very impressive collection of 204 handwritten pages, some in the teacher's hand but most in the pupil's own handwriting. Most of the writing was done between January and July 1938. The process of collecting the information brought the pupils of the time in very close contact with their local culture and must have formed a special link between the generations, which might not otherwise have been secured. While examining the collection, one is very impressed, by the beautiful flowing penmanship of the pupils.

The main sections of the Moycarkey collection and their sources are:

- *Stories* – Larry Buckley (Knockroe) from Mrs. Buckley aged 80. William Ryan

*Michael Myers – School Principal at the time of the Schools Folklore Collection.*

(Knockroe) from Mrs. John Stokes (Knockroe) aged 70, Maura Myres (Dromgower) from Kate Dalton (Dromgower) aged 60, Maggie Buckley (Cloghmartin), Philomena Maher (Turtulla) from her grandfather Daniel Maher, Maggie Meehan (Knockroe) from William Carrie (Knockroe) aged 60, Joe Callanan (Parkstown) from Mrs. Lambe (Moycarkey) aged 75, Mary Shanahan (Turtulla) from her mother, Dan Fanning (Ballytarsna) from his father Joseph, Eileen Scott (Kylenoe) from Dan Purcell (born Knockroe, living in Kylenoe). James Tynan (Curraheen) was also named as a source for a story.

*Ink bottles*

- *Local Marriage Customs* - Maura Myres (Dromgower) from her father Michael Myres, Maggie Buckley (Cloghmartin), Christina Mackay (Curraheen)

- *Food and Recipes* – Collected by Maggie Meehan (Knockroe) and Teresa Costello (Graigue)

- *Placenames and Local History Stories* – Kitty O'Keeffe (Parkstown) from her father Richard, Joan O'Keeffe (Parkstown), Dominic Maher (Turtulla) from his father Daniel, Mary Gooney (Galboola), Dan Fanning (Ballytarsna) from his father Joseph, Joe Callanan (Parkstown), Mary Gooney (Shanaclune) from Richard Dwyer (Shanaclune) aged 87, Margaret Meehan (Knockroe) from her grandfather - John Bermingham (Knockroe), Philomena Maher (Turtulla), Josie Shanahan (Turtulla), Jerry O'Keeffe (Horse and Jockey), Pat Buckley (Pouldine) from Mrs.Buckley of same address, Mary Shanahan (Turtulla) from her mother.

- *Food in Olden Times* – Several Children

- *Fairs* – Joan O'Keeffe (Parkstown) from her father

- *Travelling Folk* – Dominic Maher (Turtulla), Maura Myres (Dromgower) from her parents.

*Ink wells.*

- *School in Olden Days* – Teresa Costello (Graigue), Jerry O'Keeffe (Parkstown)

- *The Games we Played at Home and School* - Joan O'Keeffe (Parkstown), Mary Shanahan (Turtulla), Maura Myres (Dromgower)

- *Proverbs* – Several Children

- *Lore on Certain Days* – Josie Shanahan (Turtulla) from her mother.

- *Customs on May Eve* – Maura Myres (Dromgower) from her father Michael, Josie Shanahan (Turtulla) from her mother.

- *St. Stephen's Day Customs* – Dominic Maher (Turtulla),

- *St. Martin's Day* – Joan O'Keeffe (Parkstown)

- *Halloween* – Philomena Maher (Turtulla), Eileen Scott (Kylenoe)

- *St. John's Day* – Joan O'Keeffe (Parkstown)

- *Palm Sunday* – Maura Myres (Dromgower) from her father Michael.

- *Religious Stories* – Maura Myres (Dromgower), Joan O'Keeffe (Parkstown), Eileen Scott (Kylenoe), William Ryan (Knockroe) from John Stokes (Knockroe) aged 78, Mary Shanahan (Turtulla) from her mother.

- *Forges* – Margaret Meehan (Knockroe), Joan O'Keeffe (Parkstown), Dominic Maher (Turtulla), Joe Callanan (Parkstown) from his father.

- *The Potato Crop* – Many Children

- *Terms used for Farm Animals* – Many Children

- *Churning* – Many Children

This was a time in Ireland, just before the outbreak of the Second World War, when the country was still in the grip of the Economic War with Britain. Money was very scarce, cattle prices were low and the emigrant ship was to be the fate of many. Yet for all that, we get no feeling of depression reading these pages, rather an acceptance of the reality of the time.

We owe a great debt of gratitude to all those involved with this folklore collection. They have left us an irreplaceable and priceless store of knowledge on their lives and of the Moycarkey of their time. A copy of the collection is available to the public at the Local Studies Section of the library in Thurles and we also have a copy in the school. Two sections of the collection are reproduced on the following pages.

*Confirmation Day in Moycarkey in 1967. Archbishop Morris and Fr. William Breen P.P. being welcomed by the Sean Treacy Pipe Band.*

# Millennium at Moycarkey N.S. Pouldine

*December 22nd 1999 was the last school day of the old millennium at Moycarkey N.S., Pouldine, Thurles. The following attended on that day:-*

*Front row (l.-r.):* Ivan Chadfield, William O'Dwyer, Marguerite McCormack, David Ryan, Aaron Flanagan, Tommy Noonan, Conor Hayes, Aidan Fitzpatrick, Niamh Butler, Nora Connolly, Melissa Morris, Antonia McGrath, Michaela Graham, Sean-Michael Cawley, Sarah Abbott, Michelle Sheppard, Michelle Rose Ryan, Tomas Ryan, Marese Noonan, Donna-Marie Cawley, Jamie Costello, Gavin O'Brien.

*Second row (l.-r.):* Marita Moloney, Karen Cobett, Shauna Flanagan, Michelle Carew, Brian Butler, Joey Coman, Andrew Fogarty, Timothy Ryan, Cathal Gleeson Fahey, Peadar Kinane, Jamie Maher, Richard O'Keeffe, Christopher Byrne, Marguerite Gooney, Ciara Maher, Corina Abbott, Kieran Stapleton, Lesley O'Sullivan, Edwina McGrath, Laurie O' Sullivan, Ryan Hayes, Ryan Noonan, Thomas Quigley, Neil Hewitt, Jamie Barry

*Third row (l.-r.):* Ms. Catherine O'Keeffe, Finbarr Hayes, Megan Ryan, Aisling O'Dwyer, Stephen Kirwan, Clare Singleton, Laura Kirwan, Adam Carew, Peter Kinane, Cillian O'Hara, Daniel O'Regan, Iain O'Brien, Lorcan O'Hara, Andrea O'Regan, Katie Quirke, Laura Maher, Anna Harnett, Aisling Hogan, Ailish O'Keeffe, Michael Roche, Colm Skehan.

*Fourth row (l.-r.):* Ms.Lucy McGann, Mrs. Maire Sheehy, Mr. Donie Shanahan, Noel Kinane, Niall Barry, Seamus Cummins, Eamonn Flanagan, Conor Skehan, Robbie Delaney, Martha Dempsey, Sheena O'Dwyer, Margaret-Mary McGrath, Conan O'Hara, Jack Harnett, Kilian O'Donoghue, Denis Roche, Cathriona Delahunty, William Foley, Karen Mullins, Karen Hogan, Ann Kirwan, Shanon Hayes,Sarah Kinane, Sinead O'Hara, Rory Ryan, Liam O'Donnchú (Principal), Mrs. Mary Minchin (Vice-Principal), Mrs. Aileen Colton, Ms. Ann-Marie Shanahan.

*Fifth Row (left to right)* Conor Fanning, Rachel Bourke, Méire O'Regan, Marie Kirwan, Anita Bannon, Sean Quirke, Shane Barry, Eoghan Nagle, Tomas Quinn, Eoin Ryan, Tony Flanagan, Patricia Coman, Rosaleen O'Keeffe, Christine Ryan, Felicity Dempsey, Hannah McGrath, Marie Carey, Laura Cleary.

# Home Cures

## Source – Moycarkey N.S.
## – Schools Folklore Collection 1937-'38

## WHOOPING COUGH

1. Drink the milk left by a ferret after his meal.
2. Mr Patrick W.Hogan (lately deceased) had a cure for whooping cough. It was some words – probably a prayer – written on a piece of paper, which was then folded and placed in a little bag or purse. This latter was to be hung round the sufferer's neck by a string.
3. A lock of hair from the head of a posthumous person sewed in a little bag and worn over the sufferer's chest.
4. Ask the rider of a grey horse whom you meet on the road for a cure, and do what he tells you.
5. The beaten-up white of an egg with ground sugar, candy and some brandy, a teaspoonful to be taken when the fits of coughing are troublesome.

## JAUNDICE

1. A quantity of barberry bark is steeped in a gallon of porter for 24 hours. It is then strained until it becomes quite clear. A half pint of whiskey is added. A wine glassful to be taken every morning fasting and before sunrise. No salt, meat, grease or milk should be used until the patient is well.
2. A few sprays of an herb called Cranesbill are brewed in a cupful of milk, and then strained. A half cupful is taken twice a day until the patient is cured.
3. Archangel weed found growing in tillage fields.

## HEADACHE

1. (a) Lift the Goban Saor's cap three times on to your head, or (b) lift the same cap on your head and walk around the Goban Saor's island three times.
   This cap is a round stone shaped like a cap, and is to be found at the Goban's grave on the Goban Soar's island in the townland of Lurgoe, parish of Killenaule, Barony – Eliogarty.
2. Moisten well a small sheet of brown paper with vinegar, and apply it to the forehead, and bandage tightly.

3. Collect a number of ribbons on St. Bridget's night and say five Our Fathers and five Hail Marys over them.  One of those ribbons rubbed to the patient's head will relieve the pain.

## ANTHONY'S FIRE OR 'WILD FIRE'

The blood of a person named Cahill whose father and mother were both Cahill cures Anthony's fire.  A piece of thread or string is tied lightly round finger, and the finger is then pricked with a needle.  The blood is rubbed to the affected part.

## SCIATICA

Turpentine to be taken in the folowing manner:- Begin with one drop the first day, two drops the second, three drops the third,   increasing the amount taken by one drop daily. Continue for 21 days.  Then reduce the amount taken daily by one drop each day till you come back to one drop.  The whole course runs over a period of 41 days.

## STYES

1. Make the sign of the cross with a gold wedding ring over the affected eye three times in succession, saying each time :- "In the name of the Father and of the Son, and of the Holy Ghost."
2. Point a gooseberry thorn three times at the stye saying: -"In the name of the Father, Son and Holy Ghost."
3. Bathe the eye with Cold tea.
4. Bathe the eye with the fasting spit every morning till the stye disappears.

## WARTS

1. Rub each wart with a pebble, using one pebble for each wart.  Place these pebbles in a little bag or purse, and drop the latter on the road.
   The first person who picks up and examines the contents will take your warts, and you will be rid of them.
2. Steal a piece of fat meat and bury it secretly in the dung heap.  As the meat rots the warts will disappear.
3. Rub a snail to the warts, and then stick the snail fast on a growing thorn.  As the snail, decays the warts will disappear.
4. Rub the fasting spit each morning to the wart, and it will gradually disappear.
5. If without intent, you happen to come on a flat stone containing some water in a hollow therein, and if you bathe your warts in this water, they will quickly disappear.
6. Make the sign of the cross over the wart with a knot of straw, and bury the knot in mud or in the manure heap.

## PAINS OR RHEUMATISM

1. With a bundle of nettles, sting well the affected part of your body.  Repeat this again

and again and you will before very long find your rheumatism improved, if not entirely cured.

2. Carry a small potato in your pocket, and as the potato withers the pains will leave.
3. Carry a nutmeg in your pocket, and say one Our Father, Hail Mary and Glory for the poor souls.

## FAINTING FITS OR 'WEAKNESSES'

Burn the patient's shirt behind the fire.

## SORE FOOT

Supply poultices of pounded up rib grass.

## BURNS AND SCALDS

1. Sweet oil and limewater applied to the burn.
2. Mix bread soda and sweet oil and apply to the affected part.
3. Boil the bark of elm in water, strain, and apply the water to the burn.

## BLEEDING

James O'Keeffe, Parkstown, Moycarkey can stop bleeding without seeing or touching

*The O'Keeffe family photographed in 1927. Back row: Thomas, Jack, Harry and Maureen. Middle row: Peg, Jim, Mary Ellen. Front row: Joan and Kitty.*

the patient. The cure is an unrevealed prayer which he recites on request. He has never been known to fail in stopping bleeding.

## BITES FROM DOGS

Place some of the dog's hair on the wound, and bandage.

## CUTS

A cobweb put on the wound, which is then bandaged.

## PAIN IN THE BACK

Turpentine sprinkled on red flannel and applied to the back.

## LUMBAGO

A mixture of salt and mustard on red flannel.

## SORE THROAT

Well heated salt placed in a woollen stocking which is tied round the throat on retiring to bed.

## A COLD

1. An onion is boiled in a pint of new milk and drunk as hot as possible. The patient must remain in bed for a day or two.
2. Bathe the feet in hot water and mustard.

## EAR-ACHE

1. A piece of cotton wool steeped in hot olive oil placed in the ear gives relief.
2. Hold the ear over the steam of jug of boiling water.
3. Squeeze a portion of a cut onion, and allow a few drops of the juice into the ear.
4. The centre of an onion heated at the fire and inserted in the ear.

## CHILBLAINS

1. Well boil crabs in water, strain, and bathe the affected parts in the liquid.
2. Rub goose grease to the chilblains, and allow it to soak in before the fire.
3. Bathe the affected parts in paraffin oil.

## CORNS

1. Steep an ivy leaf in vinegar and place on the corn.
2. Bathe the corn in alum water.
3. Apply ivy leaf steeped in paraffin oil.
4. Apply the skin of a boiled potato.

## RINGWORM

1. Sulphur and fresh lard.
2. Write your name in ink round the ringworm taking care that you leave no break in the ring.

## WHITLOW

1. Boiled onion and linseed meal poultice.
2. Dip the whitlow frequently in the water in which potatoes have been boiled.

## TOOTHACHE

1. A strong sniff of whiskey taken through the nose gives relief.
2. Insert a plug of tobacco into the hole in the tooth.

## HICCOUGHS

1. Take nine sips of water without drawing breath.
2. Sip water from the side of the container furthest from you.

## STOMACH PAINS

1. A linseed meal poultice.
2. Apply heated pot-lids rolled in flannel to the stomach.

# *Cures for Animals*

## FARCY IN HORSES

The symptons of this disease are:
1. A large swelling usually appearing on the underside of the animal's body or in a leg; and
2. If the finger were pressed on this swelling, a small dent or hollow will remain for some time after the pressure has been removed.
   Thomas Casey, Ballydavid, Littleton, Thurles cures this disease by prayer and holy water.

## "MENINGITIS" IN CATTLE

1. A bruised onion put in each ear of the beast and secured there.
2. Put the beast lying on her side. With a strong cord make five loops three times over the beasts head.

## SWELLING IN A BEAST

One man catches a dog by the hind legs, while another seizes him by the forelegs. They see-saw the dog across the beast's back.

**School Year:- Sixth class 1992-'93**

Back row: Anthony Shiels, Eoghan Butler, John Butler, Kevin O'Regan, Michael Minchin, Jacqueline Fahey, Ryan Fogarty. Middle row: Janette Bourke, Elaine Carey, Regina Fanning, Eveleen Roberts, Rodge Heffernan. Front row: Louise Shortall, John Paul Shanahan, Joanne Corcoran, Stephen O'Sullivan, Anne Barrett, Angela Cummins, David O'Dwyer,Muireann O'Donoghue, George Webster.

**School Year:- Sixth Class 1993-'94**

Back row: James Egan, Gary Ryan, P.J. Flanagan, Shane Quigley, Martin Shortall, Joseph O'Dwyer, Christopher Mooney, Kevin McGuire, James Fitzgerald R.I.P., Edward Moloney, Kevin Leahy, Adrian McCormack, Patrick McCormack. Front row: Aisling Concagh, Laura Cooney, Máire Skehan, Catherine Ryan, Maria Skehan, Maria Kiely, Lyana Maguire Vanessa Purcell, Lorraine Stapleton. Absent from photo: Maria Carey.

**School Year:- Sixth Class 1994-'95**

Back row: Matt Roche, Aidan Bourke, James Cleary, Noel Carey, Frank Roche, Thomas Lanphier. Middle row: John Harrington, Mark Shanahan, James Scott, Paul Egan, Diarmaid O'Dwyer, Bill Bourke, Paul Dempsey. Front row: Emma Sweeney, Elaine Nagle, Sarah Looby, Emma Delaney, Lesley Abbott, Tracy McCorthy, Louise Fahey.

# The Games we Play at Home and in School

Source – Moycarkey N.S.
– Schools Folklore Collection 1937-'38

## DAN, DAN THREAD THE NEEDLE

**"Dan, Dan Thread the Needle"** is played in the following manner. Two girls with joined hands stand facing each other, and think of two words such as a "watch", and "chain"while the other girls who are all in a line, pass under their joined hands, and say at the same time. "Dan, Dan thread the needle, Dan, Dan sew" and as the last girl passes under the joined hands she is asked by both girls which she prefers a watch or a chain. According to the answer she gives she takes her proper place, and so the game continues until all the players stand in two rows. The game is now finished by a tug of war between the two rows of girls.                                *(Source – Mary Shanahan, Turtulla)*

## OLD HAG

One girl is supposed to be the 'hag'. Several other girls line up after each other, The 'hag' does not go with those. The first girl of the row is called the "mother" and as they pass the 'hag' the "mother" asks "what time is it?" The "hag" tells them and as they pass her a second time, she pretends to be looking for something, and the mother says "what are you looking for?" "a needle" the 'hag' answers. "What do you want the needle for"? "To sew a bag". "What do you want a bag for"? "To bring in turf". "What do you want the turf for"? "To boil a pot of water". "What do you want the water for?" "To roast all your chickens" and at the same time she tries to catch one of the "chickens" but the mother defends her brood as best she can. The game is finished when the "hag" has all the "chickens" caught.                                *(Source – Joan O'Keeffe, Parkstown)*

## CONTRARY

Some children hold a cloth or a large sheet of paper and another is chosen as the "leader". When the "leader" says "hold tight" all the players let go and when the "leader" says "let go" all the players must hold tight. The player, who does what she is told instead of the opposite, must go out of the game. This is continued with the remaining players until there is but one player left, and it is she who wins the game and she also becomes "leader" in the next game of "Contrary". Any number can take part in this game, and it can be played indoors or outdoors. *(Source – Mary Shanahan, Turtulla)*

## HIDE AND SEEK

**"Hide and Seek"**. One girl has to seek, but first she has to be in a den while the others are hiding. When the other players say "cuch" she goes to look for them, and the last girl she catches has to seek in the next game, but if she catches no one she must seek again, until she catches someone. *(Source – Mary Shanahan, Turtulla)*

## HIGH GATES

Several girls catch hands, hold them up high, and form a ring, and one girl goes outside this ring and calls another girl out of the ring to follow her. If she is caught the other girl takes her place outside, but if she is not caught, she stays outside and calls another girl. She stays outside until she is caught by some of the girls whom she called out. (Source – Mary Shanahan, Turtulla)

## FOUR CORNERED FOOL

**Four Cornered Fool!** There are five players, four of them stand in the form of a square. The fifth stands in the centre. The four players then exchange places. It does not matter whom they exchange with as long as they still retain the form of a square. While this exchange is being made, the player in the centre tries to get to one of the vacated places. If she succeeds, the person who is left without a place has to stand in the middle, but if she fails, she has to return to her former position.

*(Source – Mary Shanahan, Turtulla)*

## CHARLEY OVER THE WATER

The players catch hands and stand in the form of a ring and one stands in the centre. The players walk or run round and round the one in the centre, repeating the following ryhme:-

*Charley over the water,*
*Charley over the sea,*
*Charley caught a blackbird,*
*But he could not catch me.*

The player in the centre, meanwhile, with shut eyes, strives to catch one of the others – guided of course by the sounds of their voices. When she catches one she has to guess whom she has caught. If she succeeds the player, whom she has caught takes her place, but if she guesses wrongly, she has to return to her former position, and the game begins over again.

*(Source – Maura Myers, Dromgower)*     *Maura Scully (née Myers)*

## DIVE, DIVE DUCKS IN THE WATER

The players stand in a line each player having a partner. The first pair hold up their hands and join them together, the others doing in like manner, in such a way as to form a bridge. The last two girls in the line with joined hands have to pass under the bridge saying while they are passing through: - "Dive, dive, ducks in the water". The next pair follows and so on until the whole line of girls have passed under the bridge. The game is continued until the players grow tired if it.

## RYE SALLY WATER

**Rye Sally Water.** All players except one-catch hands and form a ring. One goes into the middle and she calls in a partner. Those two go around the ring inside together while the ring of players swing around them saying:

*"Rye Sally Water, Rye Sally ban,*
*Try to follow your own young man,*
*Dukes to the east and dukes to the west,*
*And dukes to the girl that I love best.*
*Now those couple marry and joy.*
*A pretty young girl and a handsome boy.*
*Seven years after, seven years ago*
*Kiss that girl and leave her so."*

When this rhyme is finished the player who went into the ring first goes out and her partner seeks another player as partner and the game continues in like manner.

*(Source – Joan O'Keeffe, Parkstown)*

*Confirmation at Moycarkey Church 1951. Back row (l.-r.): Mary Fanning, Nora Grady, Mary Buckley, Christina Stapleton, Claire Reilly, Mary Molloy, Sheila Murphy. Front row (l.-r.): Peggy Twomey, Kitty Wilson, Kitty Philips, Carmel Scott, Sheila Fitzpatrick, Flora Wilson.*

### Preparing for Confirmation – 1984-'85

Back row: Yvonne Shaw, Margaret O'Halloran, Mary O'Halloran, Jennifer Shaw, Katie Bourke, Ann-Marie Shanahan, Helena O'Keeffe, Maura O'Connell, Mary Callanan, Josephine McCormack, Mairéad Bourke. Middle row: Gregory Sweeney, Emer Bannon, Mairéad Cooney, Elizabeth Cummins, Vanessa O'Reilly, Sharon Croke, Michelle Delahunty, Eileen Flanagan, Helen Flanagan, Maria Maher, Geraldine Lahart, Michael Cooney. Front row: Mícheál Kavanagh, Joseph McCormack, Pat Costello, Brendan Stapleton, Declan Hogan, Paul Skehan, Séamus Stapleton, Irwin Bannon, Donal Hogan, Laurence O'Sullivan, Kenneth Concagh, Declan O'Dwyer.

### Confirmation Class – 1986

Back row: Fr. Danny Ryan P.P., Cora Delaney, Breda Kane, Mary Teresa Butler, Miriam Mooney, Norma Stapleton, Martina Loughnane, Catherine Barrett, Joanne Maher, Caroline Lambe, Isabel Coman. Middle row: Eugene Dunne, Nollaig Ryan, Janette Butler, Tracy Browne, Bridget Ryan, Archbishop Thomas Morris, Elaine Mooney, Tara Coman, Gerard O'Dwyer, Liam Ó Donnchú (Principal Teacher). Front row: Cyril Stapleton, Oliver Hogan, Brian Delahunty, Johnny Flanagan, Denis Costello, Séamus Concagh, Agnes Kane, Daniel Maher.

# From Graigue to Pouldine

OCIAL LIFE in the fifties was limited. It consisted of interaction with neighbours and sometimes visits to and from uncles, aunts and cousins. Attending Mass was another outlet, but children were only allowed to go when they knew how to behave properly, which meant kneeling, sitting or standing at the appropriate time, and never looking around. Of course, when parents went up to the altar to receive Holy Communion the strict code of discipline was relaxed somewhat. Starting school promised a whole new adventure, a widening of horizons, and an increase in your little circle of friends. Generally, children started Primary School when they were five years old. Having an older brother Paddy to bring me to school gave the reassurance that I needed to cope with this daunting event in my life. Later on, I became a punctuality addict and I would not even wait for my siblings, in case I would be late for school.

As was customary we walked to school, sometimes taking a short cut across the fields, coming out on to the road just before Moloneys' farm. It was necessary to cross the

*Margaret, Paddy and Mary Flanagan, Graigue.*

railway line. Parental warnings to be careful were common. We familiarized ourselves with the train times but always treated the railway with the utmost caution. The trains had their own fascination for us. We loved to watch goods trains and passenger trains roll by thinking how wonderful it would be to travel by train to far away places.

On the way to school, we met up with other boys and girls all heading to the same destination, Pouldine School. If we were lucky, we might get a lift on a creamery cart. Our hearts would jump with delight if we saw Burkes' cart coming up from Ballyhudda or Paddy Moloney emerging from the farm. We were guaranteed a lift all the way to school since the creamery was located in Littleton.

Later we became the proud owners of bicycles. The bike was a treasured possession and opened the window to many opportunities. You could travel to places until then unexplored or visit school friends who lived at the other side of the parish. Owning a bicycle meant you learned how to mend a puncture just in case you were unlucky and had a flat tyre.

Children started school in June. There was a type of induction period until the summer holidays and then the first Monday in September, traditionally the day after then all Ireland Hurling Final, real school commenced.

In the fifties Pouldine had three teachers. Mrs. Maher took charge of the Infants and First Class. Mr. Loughnane had the middle classes and the Master, as we called the principal, looked after the senior classes. Timmy Maher, a typical country schoolteacher was the Master. He was a gentle character but when someone misbehaved or was sent to him for correction by one of the other teachers he took his role very seriously and gave the appropriate punishment for the particular misdemeanour. Although corporal punishment was used, the occasional slap did not seem to have any ill effects on us.

The master's room had high windows, specially constructed so that pupils were unable to see out and so would not be distracted by passing traffic or people on the road. High on the wall behind the master hung a large picture, which reflected in its glass any movements outside, and for us this compensated for the high windows. We were able to keep up to date with all passing traffic. I do not know if Mr. Maher knew the real value of that picture. At sos (morning break) and lunchtime the girls went to one yard and the boys to another. We played games like 'tig', hide and seek, hop scotch, skipping etc. A very popular pastime for girls was to play shop and at all our homes we had a shop set in some corner or unused outhouse. We stocked it with empties from the kitchen and used pebbles for money. We visited each other's houses to see the shops and we got hours of satisfaction taking on the role of either shopkeeper or customer. Lunch, which consisted of a bottle of milk and two slices of bread, was taken in the schoolyard or in the porch on a wet day.

In the early school days, turf for the school stove was provided by local families and later purchased by the school. When a load arrived, the big boys were delighted to be released from class to put in the turf. Pupils were assigned various chores in school, lighting the fire, sweeping the floor, going to the other classrooms with the Rolla. An occasional trip to the master's house on a message was a job for the specially selected student.

The curriculum was mainly based on education in Catechism, Irish, English and Sums. Great emphasis was placed on Religion. The parish priest Canon McGrath and his curate Fr. O'Dwyer would drop in and ask questions randomly around the class. The diocesan inspector Fr. Keogh and later Fr. Curtin came once a year to examine all students. This was a very important occasion. You learned your catechism thoroughly in preparation, wore your best clothes, and were so relieved when you had answered well. The anticipation of the half day that would follow compensated for the fear of not answering correctly. Receiving First Holy Communion and Confirmation were as important then as they are now but after the ceremony, families returned home and got on with the day's work. At the end of sixth

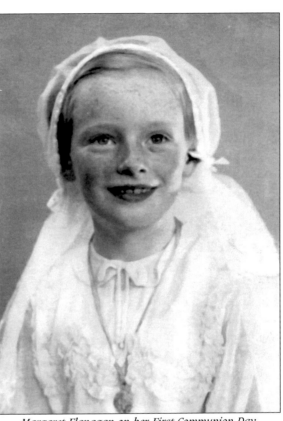

*Margaret Flanagan on her First Communion Day.*

class, we sat the Primary Certificate Examination. This was our first major examination. Principals exchanged places with principals from the other schools in the parish to supervise the examination.

Going home from school in the evening was always interesting. Firstly a trip to Mrs. Shine's sweet shop across the road, if the money situation allowed it. She stocked an amazing selectin of big glass jars of sweets. Lucky bags, chocolate money, liquorice, marshmallow mice etc. Generally, we purchased a penny worth of whatever we wished to buy.

It was quite common to see travellers living in canvas tents erected on the grass margin by the roadside. Often we saw them having their meals by the campfire.

Although we knew their names and the same families returned to the same places at regular intervals, we never engaged in conversation with them, but we admired their skills such as bucket, gallon, flower and picture making.

Before we reached Shanbally cross we might have a chat with the O'Reillys who lived in the now derelict house. At the cross, we parted company with our Moycarkey and Knockroe friends. Tommy Corcoran with his long white hair and matching beard, like a character from ancient Irish literature, seemed to be always sitting on the seat outside his house. We loved to have a reason to call to Fannings of Shanbally house. A warm welcome was always guaranteed by Maura and her brothers John and Paddy. If we were selling tickets, for the missions we never left empty-handed. Selling tickets or collecting members for the non-stop draw gave us a licence to visit houses. In the autumn visits to Moloneys' orchard full of apples and plums were regular. Mrs. Bourke's puck goats scared the lives out of us. We passed there as quickly as possible. Occasionally we wandered into Cormacks, the home of Kate, Paddy and Tom. If we were selling tickets visits were always fruitful. Their brother Ned, a colourful character, known as Ned the Yank came home to retire from America and gave us all a whole half-crown. We thought that we would never see a poor day again. Mrs. Griffin, her daughter May and son Jimmy lived in the next house, Mrs. Griffin came to our house on Mondays to do the washing. She used a big tub and a washboard since a washing machine was unheard of in rural Ireland. To the right of Graigue Bridge was John Buckley's house whose family Paddy, John and Mary were colleagues in Pouldine, Peg Wilson lived immediately after the bridge. Peg loved the local news and we were always glad to pass on the news. Her nephew Noel and niece Maura were attending school at this time.

At this stage of the journey home from school, the Dwyers and the Flanagans turned in Graigue boreen and back to the farms and the jobs that had to be done before the lessons. Cows had to be brought in, calves fed, help with turning the cows back to the fields after milking. Farms produced almost all of the food that was used. Consequently there were endless chores around the farm for children of all ages. We were never bored during holidays. We enjoyed particularly the hay making when we were allowed travel on the big hay float. The magic of the threshing machine arriving to complete the harvest was amazing. All the neighbours came to help.

Many years have passed since we travelled from Graigue to Pouldine and back again. The railway line, which was such an important feature in our childhood days, is no longer there. Many of the old houses are gone and several new houses reflect the prosperity of the twenty first century. The memories of those happy days in Pouldine are still alive and are shared with former classmates from time to time. My career is in education and I appreciate the foundations for learning which were put down and the values, which were set during my primary school years in Pouldine.

*Margaret Flanagan*
*(Pupil at Pouldine School, 1950 – 1958)*

# If St. Peter's Church
# could speak . . .

*Fr. George Bourke P.P.*

**O**LDER PEOPLE may remember that at one time a recurring theme for essays, or 'compositions' as they were called in those days, was rud nó duine éigean ag insint a scéal féin. If that were the theme for these few lines, St. Peter's Church, Moycarkey, would have a long and varied story to tell, a story of links with the present National School, the Old School and its predecessors.

Archbishop Patrick Everard, Co-adjutor Archbishop from 1814, had been urging Parish Priests of the time to replace the old thatched chapels with more modern and fitting places of worship. The old Chapel in Moycarkey was a very plain and dilapidated thatched building just outside the back wall of the Old Graveyard in the village. Fr. Robert Laffan was Parish Priest here until 1823, and he didn't get round to complying with his Bishop's pleas. Then in 1823 the same Dr. Robert Laffan became

Archbishop of Cashel and Emly, and at once the same letters were going out to his successor, Fr. David Dee, Administrator of the Parish of Moycarkey / Borris. Fr. Dee, with the support of his parishioners began the construction of the Church in the year of Catholic Emancipation, 1829, on a site given free by William Max of Maxfort. Fr. Dee was a noted Irish scholar and frequently preached in the native tongue.

Fr. David Dee was transferred to Loughmore parish in 1832 before the Church was fully completed, and it was left to his successor, Fr, Robert Grace, to add the ceiling and erect the galleries, with external stone stair-ways. Because of poor roof construction, Moycarkey Church had to be re-roofed after ten years, and again because of inferior nails another re-roofing was required before the end of the century. Fr. John Bourke was by then the long serving Parish Priest (1853-1891). It was he also who, with the backing of the parishioners, added the dressed limestone façade and put in new windows. He then intended to dedicate the Church to St. Peter in Chains, inspired by the great Roman Basilica of the same name. Other refurbishments have taken place over the years, the last

major one during the pastorate of Fr. William Breen, whose work included the addition of the external porches. Further adaptations were necessary after the Second Vatican Council, with on-going maintenance and decoration continuing to the present.

*Internal and external views of St. Peter's Church, Moycarkey, in the early 1900s.*

The Church of St. Peter in Chains or as it is often called nowadays the Church of St. Peter has served the people of this rural community for 180 years, through times of poverty and plenty. Older people have memories of a packed Church for Sunday Mass, people coming on foot, by pony and trap, on bicycles,  on the numerous Mass-paths or

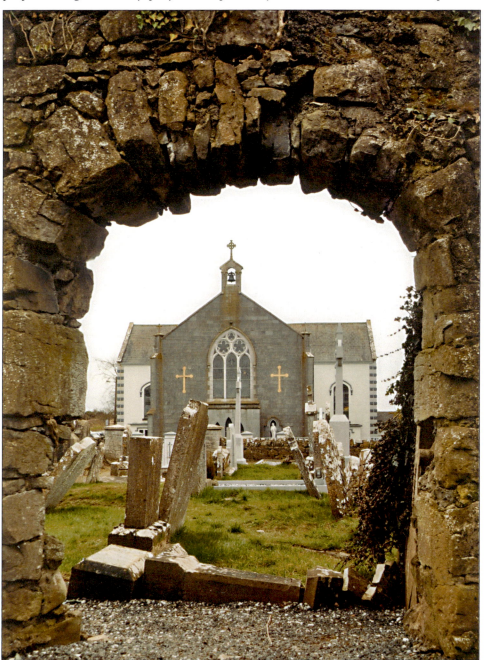

*St. Peter's Church, Moycarkey, photographed from the ruins of St. Andrew's Church and the graveyard.*

walking along by the old railway line. In the early days there were no seats in the Church; people stood on the mud floor.

If the Church could speak, it would tell of the poverty and deprivation of the Great Famine. The population of the parish dropped from 8,638 in the 1841 census to 5,335 by 1851. In those Famine times and long afterwards, the early part of the year was the most popular for marriages, e.g. in 1846 there were 45 Marriages in the parish, between January and February, with eight on the 23rd February and nine on 24th February (probably Shrove Tuesday that year). St. Peter's Church continued to be the place of Worship, Prayer and Devotions, through civil unrest, Fenianism, World Wars, Troubled Times. For example, what is the story behind Confirmation taking place on 6th October, 1921? Archbishop John M. Harty confirmed 233 children in St. Peter's Church at that unusual time of the year.

Still ag insint a scéal féin there were the Missions, the long sermons, the harshness and authoritarianism betimes, women sometimes made to feel inferior, all alongside an enduring faith, a spirit of neighbourliness. A large Mission Cross was erected in the Church in 1881 in memory the Mission preached by the Passionist Fathers, and as a reminder of promises made during the Mission week.

The Church and its parishioners seems to have had an ecumenical spirit long before it became the norm, with the initial granting of the free site by John Max, and later in 1838 Miss Emma Stanwix presented a beautiful painting of Our Lady with the Child Jesus to St. Peter's Church, were it hung in the sanctuary, over the Tabernacle for many years.

And of course for every generation since its construction St. Peter's Church has been the place for the celebration of the sacraments, for innumerable young children their place of Baptism – our Baptismal Parish Records go back to 1794 and our Marriage Records to 1793. The links with Moycarkey School have been abiding – the place of First Confession, First Holy Communion, and Confirmation, the invaluable work of the teachers, and all the changes surrounding these celebrations over the years. The Mass Servers, learning the Latin of yore, ringing the Bell, and then for the last forty years the vernacular; the girls joining the boys as Mass Servers in more recent years.

St. Peter's Church has seen so many changes - declining numbers at Mass, more empty pews. Baptisms, Weddings and Funerals, happy occasions, sad occasions, the Church is always open, welcoming and supportive, through the different liturgies. The Church Bell still calls us to prayer, worship with the community, the quiet visit to light a candle or say a silent prayer. 180 years in our present Church is part of the long history of faith handed down through family, School and parish. May the links be enduring; may the deep-rooted faith continue to be cherished. Críost linn, Críost rómhainn ………

*Fr. George Bourke P.P.*

# Far From Grallagh

**A**FTER AN hour's walk with my older brothers, Seán and Eamonn, from Grallagh Castle I arrived at Pouldine in early Sept. 1943 in fear and trepidation at the age of five years. Mr. Myers, soon to retire, greeted me and gave me the lordly sum of six pence, as did Mrs. Maher, who was in charge of the junior classes.Thus, started my education and for the past sixty six years, I have been involved in schools in three different countries mainly south of the Equator.

1943 was in the middle of the Second World War and rationing of food and clothing was the frequent topic of discussion. Coming from a small farm, my parents Jack and Ellen Barry, were perhaps a bit better off than some others, as we produced a good deal of our own food and managed, like other families, to supply, free of charge, a cart load of turf to the school each year.

At that time the three classrooms had no central heating in the old school and the rooms were high-ceilinged and very draughty. With three teachers and a school population of approximately 100, multiple classes were the order of the day. Tadhg Ó Meachair was the master and Mrs. Maher and Mr. Loughnane were the other teachers.

I think I was an average student, somewhat garrulous and keener on sport than study. The round trip of approximately 8 km each day on foot was taken

*Br. Charles Kevin Barry, Grallagh with Timmy Maher, Principal of Pouldine NS.*

*Left to right: Pat Barry, Br. Kevin, Michael Lambe – all from Grallagh.*

as normal and we often brought hurleys along to practise our skills and make the journey more enjoyable. A great disappointment for us was that we had no hurling field at the school and no organised sport.

When I was in fifth class, my father died and it had a significant effect on me, so people told me years later. Since I was very close to him, I grieved in my own childish way and felt I had been cheated to some degree. From all accounts, I became more independent, even aggressive and got into a fair share of strife both at school and at home.

I finished in seventh class in 1952 and went to the Patrician Brothers Training College in Tullow, Co. Carlow that same year. I completed my Leaving Certificate and was professed five years later. My studies at University College Galway ended in 1959 and I was sent to Botany Bay, Sydney, Australia that year.

Posted to a suburb called Fairfield in a secondary school of 1,200 pupils, I spent eight years there, three of them as Headmaster. I then volunteered to go to a very remote part of a very underdeveloped country called Papua New Guinea, where I spent 28 years mainly in jungle conditions. I was in charge of four different secondary schools at various times. These were the best years of my life, I had to learn new languages, had no access to electricity, phones, radios or roads for most of the time.

Schools there had basic clinics, catechist training and adult education centres and the pupils often walked up to two days to get to school, where we had to provide food and accommodation. The nearest town was about 250 km away, with only a small plane for transport, a couple of times yearly. Malaria, which I still suffer from, was only one of the many tropical diseases in those regions.

*(Kevin Barry, Grallagh, Pupil at Moycarkey N.S., Pouldine 1943 – 1952.)*

# A Child
# of the Sixties

IN 1969, a man landed on the moon. In the same year, I took the giant step from Pouldine N.S. as we called it.

This sense of security that I felt there was due in no small way to the care I received on my first day going to school.

My twin-sister Alice and I were very fortunate to be taken to school by our very good neighbour Eileen Heffernan.

*Helen Regan*

*Alice Regan*

We walked the mile to school in very safe hands. This was a generation before the days of the "helicopter parents".

On arriving in school, we were greeted by a very gentle person Mrs. Maura Butler. Mrs. Butler, as we knew her, became our second mother. She indeed took her responsibility "in loco parentis" very seriously. The highlight was having our own slate and making all shapes and sizes from "Márla". Our move from Junior Infants to Senior Infants also coincided with learning the "old Irish script". However, this ended very quickly. No doubt, a decision was made from on high that we were not to continue with the Book of Kells style script.

I thoroughly enjoyed the three R's especially the "sums". They made great sense and were a real joy. The biggest challenge was to fit the letters between the red and blue lines in the ruled copy. Needless to say, many loops were made trying to reach up to the top red line. This challenge was compounded when I graduated from pencil to pen and ink. The inkwells were inset in the desks. The blotting paper performed its mopping up function very well. The small blops of ink were likened to venial sins and the big ones were likened to mortal sins.

Miss Brid Ryan opened up the world to us with History and Geography, which she presented in a very interesting fashion. It is no surprise that Brid is a globetrotter to this day!

The day we entered the master's room we felt like veterans. Learning continued to be great fun and I especially enjoyed Algebra and Geometry.

Mr. Timmy Maher entertained us with stories of how Moycarkey got its name. "A woman was out feeding her hens one day and as she called them she said "Mo chearca" and the name stuck – Moycarkey".

This was pre-women's' liberation and so once a week the Fifth and Sixth class girls went out to Miss Pauline Treacy's classroom to learn knitting and sewing. The boys stayed behind in the master's room and to this day, I do not know what they learned. The girls were rewarded with Pauline Treacy's high standards. We learned how to embroider a tablecloth when it was a curriculum requirement to do only a tray cloth. Miss Treacy also taught us to knit an Aran sweater with all the intricate stitching, when in fact a plain jumper was the standard required.

The girls and boys were segregated at break-time and lunchtime. The girls played 'Marbles, 'Hide and Seek', Skipping, 'Tigh', 'Chain-following' in the gravelled yard, while the boys enjoyed football in the lush green field beside the master's house. We enjoyed a monthly feast of Pudsy Ryan in the "Far East"; little did we know that Pudsy was ahead of his time. Decades later, we are all using Pudsy's system in our texting!

On a cold winter's morning we were invited to stand around the stove to warm our hands, of course it was not lit without some effort from the pupils. Two 'big' boys were sent to collect the sticks and when the two were not back within a respectable time, two more were sent to rescue the offending pupils.

It was custom for a Sixth Class girl to fetch the tray with freshly brewed tea from the master's house for the teachers' lunch. It was my duty when in Sixth to go to the master's house and wait for the tray. I learned interesting bits of international news from Mrs. Maher and it was here that I learned that Bobby Kennedy was shot.

*(Helen Regan, Ballymoreen. Pupil at Pouldine School, 1961-69.*
*My sisters – Alice, Breda and Martina, and my brother Willie*
*also attended the school.)*

*Alice and Helen on their first day at school accompanied by Eileen Heffernan (centre).*

Confirmation 1988

Back row: Brian Shanahan, John Maguire, Francis Ryan, Michael Moriarty, Paul Molloy, Risteard Cassidy, Paul Britton, Brian Croke, Liam Ó Donnchú (Principal), Nigel Callanan, Oliver Moriarty, Tomás Delahunty, Fr. Ryan, Vincent Stapleton, Derrick Leahy, Noel Murphy. Front row: Ann Butler, Tríona Murphy, Valerie Lanphier, Rosemary Lanphier, Louise Delaney, Caroline Stapleton, Channelle Shanahan, Jenny Harrington, Most Rev. Dr. Thomas Morris, Mary Ryan, Oonagh Nagle, Julie Harrington, Majella Fitzgerald, Ann-Marie Maguire, Ellen McCormack, Olivia O'Brien, Fiona O'Mahony, Kate O'Sullivan.

Confirmation Class 1994

Back row: Liam Ó Donnchú (Principal) Martin Shortall, P.J. Flanagan, Christopher Mooney, Kevin Maguire, Edward Moloney, James Fitzgerald, Matt Roche, Shane Quigley, Gary Ryan, Kevin Leahy, Adrian McCormack, Patrick McCormack, Noel Carey, Paul Egan, Aidan Bourke, James Egan, Joseph O'Dwyer, Frank Roche, Fr. Richard Ryan P.P. Middle row: Aisling Concagh, Laura Cooney, Catherine Ryan, Vanessa Purcell, Lyana Maguire, Most Rev. Dr. Dermot Clifford, Máire Skehan, Lorraine Stapleton, Sarah Looby, Maria Kiely, Tracy McCarthy, Louise Fahey, Emma Sweeney, Elaine Nagle, Lesley Abbott. Front row: Bill Bourke, Thomas Lanphier, Paul Dempsey, Emma Delaney, John Harrington, James Scott, Mark Shanahan, Diarmaid O'Dwyer.

# School Managers
# 1847 – 1975

## FR. ROBERT GRACE

*Administrator at Moycarkey 1832, Parish Priest 1848-'52*

Fr. Robert Grace was a native of Ballingarry and entered Maynooth in 1816, being ordained in 1823. He served as curate in Boherlahan parish before coming to Moycarkey as Administrator, in 1832.

He lived at Coolkennedy, in a two storey thatched house, where he held 31 acres from George Fennell; he also held 10 acres in Butler's Farm, Moycarkey, from Miss Emma Stanwix.

In 1838, a time of great distress, Fr. Grace expended £700 on oatmeal for his poor parishioners. Fr. Grace built the church in Two-Mile-Borris; in Moycarkey he ceiled the church, put in a new altar, erected the galleries, built a wall around the chapel yard, and towards the end of his life, re-roofed Moycarkey Church.

Fr. Robert was ever conscious of the importance of education and was to the forefront in securing the first National School at Pouldine Cross, which opened in 1847.

Fr. Grace died suddenly at Mallow Spa while on holidays in October 1852, and was buried in Moycarkey church.

## FR. JOHN BOURKE

*Parish Priest of Moycarkey 1853-'91*

Fr. John Bourke was a native of Moycarkey parish, having been born at Rathcunikeen in 1809. He was an uncle to Archbishop Thomas Fennelly. Fr. John was ordained in Thurles in 1840, having previously studied at Maynooth. He served as curate in Kilcommon and Holycross before being appointed parish priest of Moycarkey in March 1853.

In Moycarkey, he built a residence for himself on a 20 acre plot at Parkstown. This was occupied by his successor as Parish Priest, his nephew, later Archbishop Thomas Fennelly, who lived there again after his retirement (1913-1927) having sold the land, except 6 acres, all of which he willed as a residence for future curates of Moycarkey. When the new church was built in Littleton (1977), a residence was also built for a curate on the site, and the Parkstown property was sold. Fr. Bourke re-roofed Moycarkey church, erected the dressed stone façade and put in new windows, helped by a legacy from Mrs. Fallon of Cabra Castle. He also re-roofed Two-Mile-Borris church, put in a new altar and erected galleries in the transepts. He built new schools in Borris, Pouldine and Littleton. Fr. Bourke died 2nd August 1891, aged 82, and was interred in Moycarkey Church.

## FR. THOMAS FENNELLY

*Administrator/Parish Priest of Moycarkey 1891-1901*
*Archbishop of Cashel and Emly 1902-'13*

Fr. Thomas Fennelly was born at Cooleeny, Moyne, and baptised in Moyne, 30/1/1845. He got his primary education in Moyne N.S. and did classics from 1857 with Ned Shanahan, an eccentric old teacher who lived on The Pike, Thurles, and with whom young Tom lodged. He entered Thurles College, 1860, but had to leave after about six months because of the College "Strike". After a year at home, he went to Castleknock College in 1861. He re-entered Thurles College in 1862 and Maynooth in 1865, where he was ordained in 1870.

He was curate to his uncle, Fr. Bourke, in Moycarkey, 1871-'79; CC Thurles 1879-89; in December 1889 he was appointed Adm. to his uncle in Moycarkey and became Parish Priest there after his uncle's death in 1891. Fr. Bourke left him his house and lands at Parkstown as well as all his means with instructions as to their disposition. With these funds Fr. Tom tiled, seated and decorated Two-Mile-Borris church, seated and decorated Moycarkey church; he made improvements to the schools of the parish and built teachers' residences at Borris, Pouldine and Littleton. Dr. Fennelly was appointed Coadjutor Bishop of Cashel and Emly and Titular Archbishop of Ostracene in April 1901. He was consecrated in Thurles Cathedral, in June 1901. In 1902, he succeeded as Archbishop of Cashel and Emly, on the death of Dr. Croke.

*Archbishop Thomas Fennelly*

Renowned for his common sense, rightly described as a man of the people, he was beloved by the priests and people of the diocese. A most charitable man, every cause, deserving and not so deserving, kept his purse empty. He had a wonderful memory for people and relationships and a penetrating sense of humour. His preaching was popular in the best sense.

He retired to his house at Parkstown and enlarged the house so that the curate could live with him; he died there on Dec. 24th 1927 and was interred in Thurles Cathedral beside the altar of the Blessed Virgin Mary. He left the house at Parkstown, with 6 acres as a residence for the curate of Moycarkey.

## FR. NICHOLAS DUGGAN

*Parish Priest of Moycarkey 1901-1926*

Fr. Nicholas Duggan, a native of Gortnahoe parish was born in 1849. He was ordained in Thurles by Archbishop Croke in July 1877.

Fr. Nicholas served as curate in Westminister, Ballina and Moycarkey before being appointed Parish Priest here in 1901.

He built a parochial house on a site of 6 acres at Butlers Farm, most of the cost coming from his own private means. The Parochial house was built between 1903 and 1906 at a total cost of £1700. He was created Cannon in 1919 and died in January 1926. He was buried in Moycarkey church grounds.

He negotiated changes in parish boundaries in 1903; Tubberadora and part of Gaile were transferred to Boherlahan parish, in exchange for Lower Ballytarsna.

## FR. DANIEL MOLONEY

*Parish priest of Moycarkey 1926-'35*

Fr. Daniel Moloney was born at Ardmayle, parish of Boherlahan Dualla, in 1856. Before going for the church, he was Principal Teacher of Cashel Boys' School in Agar's Lane. He made a private study of the classics and, at the age of 29, he entered the philosophy class, Thurles College.

He was ordained in Thurles Cathedral by Archbishop Croke in 1893.

His ministry included:- Temporary mission in Liverpool to 1905; chaplain to Workhouse, Thurles, 1905-'07; CC Bansha, 1907-'26; appointed Parish Priest of Moycarkey in Feb. 1926, and died there on Sept. 16th 1935.

He was buried in Moycarkey Church grounds.


## FR. JOHN MCGRATH

*Parish Priest of Moycarkey and Two-Mile-Borris 1935-'55*


Fr. John McGrath a native of Emly Parish was born in 1877. He was educated in Thurles College, 1895-'96, and Irish College, Paris, 1896-1902; ordained in the chapel of the College by Dr. Henry O'Neill, Bp. Dromore, 13/6/1902. Temporary mission in Darlington, diocese of Hexham & Newcastle 18/8/1902 – 17/02/1915; CC Golden, 28/02/1915 – 1922 CC Tipperary, 22/11/1922 to 20/10/1935, on which date he became Parish Priest of Moycarkey.

After the retreat in June 1953, he had a slight stroke and after some recuperation he resumed his pastoral work. On February 10th 1955 he suffered a grave brain haemorrhage and died that evening. He was buried in Moycarkey Church grounds. Tall, erect, zealous and energetic, his cheerful personality made him a favourite with priests and people.


## FR. WILLIAM BREEN

*Parish Priest of Moycarkey, Two-Mile-Borris 1955-'68*

Fr. William Breen was born at Ayle, Cappawhite in 1902. Folowing studies at Thurles and Maynooth, he was ordained in June 1928. He served as curate in Kilcommon, Castleiney, Fethard and Cashel. In 1955 he was promoted to the pastorate of Moycarkey. During his time here, he undertook the reconstruction and re-decoration of the churches in the parish - Moycarkey and Two-Mile-Borris, at a cost of over £40,000.

In the mid sixties he saw the need for a new school at Pouldine and initiated the purchase of a suitable site for that purpose. Fr. William was very involved in various community affairs including the promotion of a local drainage scheme, when severe flooding occurred around the village of Moycarkey.

In 1968 he was appointed parish priest of the parish of Cashel, also V.G. of the Archdiocese and Dean of the Chapter. He had been in hospital for a few days with abdominal pains and died of coronary thrombosis shortly after midnight on March 3rd 1974.

## FR. JAMES M. MOYNIHAN

*Parish Priest of Moycarkey-Borris 1968-'72*

Fr. James Moynihan was born at Cathedral Street, Thurles in 1909. He attended the local C.B.S., later attending Thurles College in 1926. He was ordained in Maynooth in 1934. His ministry included Killenaule, Knockavilla and Cappamore. He transferred to Moycarkey as Parish Priest in February 1968. While in Moycarkey he supervised the completion of the new school at Pouldine. His sudden death in October 1972 was most unexpected. Fr. James Moynihan is buried in the church grounds at Moycarkey.

*Moycarkey N.S. Pouldine School year:- 1995-'96
Back row: Siobhán Maguire, John McLoughlin, Catherine Bourke, Dara Maguire, AnnMarie O'Dwyer, Breeda Kirwan, Clare Kirwan, Rick Quigley, Shane Dunne, Aileen Ryan. Middle row: Seán O'Dwyer, Ann-Marie Dempsey, Conor Butler, Elaine Roche, Jacqui O'Halloran, Colette Fogarty,*

*Eoin O'Sullivan, John Minchin, Dolores Purcell, Liam Ó Donnchú (Principal). Front row: Susan Smyth, Neasa O'Donoghue, Ann-Marie Dixon, John Leahy, Paul O'Dwyer, Thomas O'Dwyer, Noel O'Dwyer, Dara Maguire.*

### School Year:- Sixth Class 1996-'97

*Back row: Nora Quinn, Catherine Moloney, Julie Kiely, AnnMarie O'Dwyer, Una Moloney. Middle row: Raymond Fanning, Gerard Dempsey, Colm Butler, Vincent Smyth, Liam Ó Donnchú (Principal). Front row: Patrick Cummins, Stephen Kiely, Mark O'Dwyer, Mary Hayes, Sinéad O'Regan, Michael Coote. Absent from photo: Rebecca Keogh.*

### School year:- Sixth Class 1997-'98

*Back row: Liam Ó Donnchu, (Principal) James Ryan, Joseph Dixon, Brian Hogan, Brian Mullins, Rory Coote, Fr. Richard Ryan P.P. Front row: Naomi Dempsey, Mary Jo Molloy, Patricia O'Mahony, Lisa Cleary, Ann Marie Molloy, Caroline Kiely.*

# Bandhall in Pouldine

THE ORIGINAL fife and drum band – The Borris and Moycarkey National Band, the earliest written reference to which is found in 'The Tipperary Advocate', dated Oct 8th 1881 – practiced at various locations, mostly around Littleton. It is also recalled that it held practices in Moycarkey Hall. In 1934 when the fife and drum band spontaneously metamorphosed into the Seán Treacy Pipe band. Initial practices continued to take place in the hall in Moycarkey.

*Sean Treacy Pipe Band – 1960*
*Back row: J. Heffernan, Michael Cooney, Donie Purcell, Thomas Dalton, J.J. Hayes, Michael Brien, Phil Mooney, Michael Dalton, P. Moore, Phil Cooney, Thomas McCormack, Pascal Ryan. Front row: Paddy Cooney, Larry Ryan (M), Jas Meaney, E. Donnelly.*

After some years the location changed to the back of Shine's shop at Pouldine Cross. J.J. Shine, a fiddle player, though never a member of the pipe band, was a strong supporter from the outset and accommodated the practices by making available a lean-to galvanised shed attached to the rear of his shop. Though relatively small, this room was the scene of many memorable practices, music classes and interesting meetings!

In the colder weather a stove was lit and John Joe Hayes from Littleton recalls bringing a bag of coal out from Thurles on his bike, on his way home from work. He would light the fire to have the place aired for practice later in the night. In the early nineteen fifties the Band committee hired a number of instructors to teach the pipers. One of these was a teenage prodigy from Waterford city who conducted classes several nights a week in this humble abode. Interestingly enough, the boy turned out to be a

*Sean Treacy Pipe Band – 1999*

*Back row: John Clarke, Andy Cooney, Seamus Sheppard, Phil Cooney ,Aoife Neville, Joe Cooney, Michael Treacy, Billy Foley, Paudie Skehan, Noel Cooney, Christopher Ryan. Front row: Mary Martin, Ml. Flanagan, Mary Ryan, Willie Sweeney, Deborah Bracken, Ger Neville, Martin Shortall, Eugene Ryan, Amanda Fennessy.*

widely recognised piper/instructor/adjudicator and returned to instruct the band from the mid eighties until recently.

The band was to remain at Pouldine till the late sixties, when it moved to the Muintir na Tíre Hall in Littleton. Alas, nothing remains of the Pouldine Cross bandhall today.

*Gerard Neville*

*Sean Treacy Pipe Band – 2009*

*Back row (l.-r.): Kathryn Cooney, Rodge Heffernan, Philip Doran, J.P. Cooney, Andy Cooney, Andy Bamberger, Michael. Flanagan, Gerard Neville. Front row: Andrea Cooney, Phil Cooney, Noel Cooney, Simone Strapp, Billy Noble, Sylvia-Anne Strapp, Jamie Corbett, Conor Cooney, Marguerite Corbett.*

# Tadhg Ó Meachair

TADHG Ó MEACHAIR affectionately remembered as Timmy Maher, a native of Beakstown, Holycross was born in 1911. He trained in St. Patrick's Training College, Drumcondra between 1929 and 1931 and came to Gaile N.S. as Principal on 1st October 1931. At this time he was classed a "Grade 2" teacher and received his Diploma in July 1934. His sister Nan taught in Ballinure N.S. and often stayed in Gaile teacher's residence with Timmy, from where she cycled to Ballinure.

Timmy was very active in school, parish and even county juvenile G.A.A. activities, being County Secretary of Tipperary Bord na nÓg for a number of years. He was also very involved in the G.A.A. affairs of his adopted parish Moycarkey-Borris and died holding honorary officership there. He was also instrumental in acquiring the playing field for Gaile School in 1936.

At the time of his marriage to Kathleen Mooney, she recalls that the Principal's salary was £14 per month. They travelled by motor cycle/side car. The Mahers had two sons, Paud and John and one daughter, Anne. In January 1945, Timmy moved with his family to Moycarkey N.S., Pouldine, having been appointed Principal and continued to teach there until his retirement in 1976. Timmy's great love of the game of hurling knew no bounds. As the playground in the school at Pouldine was too small for hurling, he allowed the boys use the plot attached to the teacher's residence for their games. He always took a great pride in the success of his past pupils, many of whom went on to represent the club and county with distinction.

Timmy was of a quiet disposition. He had a great way with the pupils in his care, enkindling in them a great thirst for knowledge and an ambition to reach their potential. The era of the 1960s brought great economic change to Ireland and as the decade progressed, the need for a new school in Pouldine became obvious. Timmy was to the forefront in achieving this end and had the satisfaction of seeing a dream become reality, when staff and

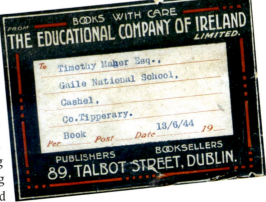

*From left: Timmy Maher Principal of Pouldine N. S.; Ann Maher (daughter) and Br. Charles Kevin Barry, Grallagh.*

pupils packed their bags and crossed the road to a brand new school, during the school year 1969 – '70. This was also the era of the New Curriculum and though in the twilight of his teaching career, he welcomed the changes with enthusiasm. Indeed the school in the early 1970s piloted some of subject areas of the New Curriculum.

A few years prior to his retirement Kathleen and Timmy Maher moved to Borroway, Thurles. He died suddenly, while playing golf at Thurles Golf Club on November 19th 1986 and is buried in the old graveyard in Moycarkey.

Solas na bhFlaitheas dá anam.

*RIGHT: Timmy on his last day as Principal in Pouldine – June 1976.*

# Moycarkey Castle

## *Notes on its History*

1. **The Castle** or Tower house was the baronial home of the Cantwells, Lords of Moycarkey. We find the first reference of a Cantwell in Moycarkey in 1303 A.D. They were an Anglo Norman family who in time became more Irish then the Irish themselves.

2. **The Castle**, which was built in the early 1400s, consists of a large tower, surrounded by a considerable area of ground. It is enclosed by a strong high wall having small towers at the East and West corners.

3. *Dimensions:* The castle is 10.5 m long from North to South and 7.5 m wide from East to West. Walls are 1.7 m thick and 15 m high. It was a four storey Tower house with an attic, the third rested on a stone arch, still remaining. Other floors were of wood. It had twenty windows.

4. *Bawn:* The Tower house is a remarkably strong one. It stands in the centre of a rectangular bawn (area between tower and outer wall) whose walls are 45.5 m North to South and 54.5 m East to West in length with round defense towers at two corners. The walls of the bawn are 9 m high and the towers are two storeys high. There is evidence of a wall-walk which provided access to cross-loops.

5. *Loophole:* At about 4 m from the ground there is a platform on the inside of the bawn wall. Soldiers could stand on this platform and fire at the enemy through six loopholes in the upper part of the small wall. There are also loopholes in the castle and in the

two towers.  The gun loops are square, round or cruciform.

6. *Cromwell:* In 1640 William Cantwell was the owner of Moycarkey Castle. During the Cromwellian Wars, (1649-'52) Cromwell and his forces spent over six months in Mid Tipperary.  His cannon shelled Moycarkey Castle doing considerable damage.

7. In the Civil Survey (1654 –'56) it was described as a "bawne and castle in  repaire."

8. After their lands were confiscated in the Cromwellian Plantation (1653) the Cantwells migrated to Cantwell's Court in County Kilkenny.  The head of the Cantwell family always included a capital "M" after their name to denote their connection with Moycarkey.   The last direct descendant of the Moycarkey Cantwells was John Cantwell who was one of Daniel O'Connell's solicitors in his famous state trials.

9. A Sheila-na-Gig, now lost, was formerly located in the south wall of the Tower house.

10. In 1740 the castle was the property of General Slaughter, who later changed his name to Stanwix.

11. About 1780 a large breach was made in the great tower and also in the eastern wall due to being hit by lightning.

12. 1837 – The Castle was the property of Viscount Hawardan of Dundrum and was occupied by William Foley.

13. In the late 1870's the Shanahan family, who lived in Pouldine up to recent times, were evicted from the castle.  They were not living in the Tower house but in one of the many buildings that were part of the defence walls.  The O'Dwyer family are the owners at present (2009).

14. Moycarkey  had authority to hold two fairs each year and two markets each week.

15. *"Like some old chief, robust and proud, Though years have made him aged and hoary, Stands still erect with head unbowed, And musing on departed glory."*

# Moycarkey and the Manor of Thurles

In 1303, an extent was made of the manorial barony of Thurles in County Tipperary, which belonged to Edmund Butler, a descendant of Theobald Walter, and father of the first earl of Ormond. Among the major free tenants, who owed rent, military service, and attendance at the lord's court, were members of many of the leading Tipperary families: Sir Hugh and Robert Purcell, Sir John Druhull, Sir William St. Leger, William and Roger Cantwell, Richard White of Arklow (another Butler manor), Sir James Keting, Richard son of Miles de Burgh, Grimbald de Samlisbury, and John Haket. At Thurles itself and at Ballihail there were burgess communities. Grimbald de Samlisbury held one knight's fee in Moycarkey of the manor of Thurles, owing for it, in addition to the normal services and in testimony to the insecurity of the area, the service of five armed men 'to keep the peace' whenever hue and cry was raised. The survival of an extent of Grimbald's own subordinate manorial organisation in Moycarkey, made in 1304, enables us to descend to a lower level in the hierarchy of dependence. Grimbald, whose ancestors had evidently not possessed the resources to build a castle, had a house, courtyard, garden and mill. He retained in his own hands 248 acres of arable, twelve acres of meadow and pasture, a wood of twenty acres, and a rabbit warren. He held a manor court, which his tenants were bound to attend. They ranged from major freeholders, such as William Cantwell and Lady Sibyl de Salle, who had a hundred acres or more, through small freeholders with less than ten acres, to cottagers with no land at all. Perhaps the most striking thing about the tenants is that of the sixty-two who are listed, no fewer than fifty-nine have names that suggest English or Welsh, rather than an Irish, origin. Certainly, some Irishmen may have taken English names; but the weight of evidence of this and other similar documents points to a sizeable immigration by, in the contemptuous words of the Caithréim, plebeian English.

**SOURCE:**
Extent of the Manor of Thorles (Thurles) 18th May 1303 Red Book of Ormond – The Red Book of Ormond is a 14th century manuscript, written in Latin, of legal records pertaining to the Ormond family in Ireland.

*Ruin of St. Andrew's Church in Moycarkey Village.*

*Múinteoirí
– 1983 –*

Back row:
Ms. Lucy McGann,
Liam Ó Donnchú,
Ms. Bríd Ryan.

Front row:
Ms. Pauline Treacy,
Mrs. Mary Minchin.

*Muinteoirí
1989:-*

Back row:
Ms. Lucy McGann,
Ms Bríd Ryan

Front row:
Mrs Mary Minchin,
Liam Ó Donnchú,
Ms. Catherine McGrath.

*Múinteoirí
1994 –*

Back row:
Ms. Lucy McGann,
Ms Yvonne Grogan.

Front row:
Ms. Bríd Ryan,
Liam Ó Donnchú,
Mrs Mary Minchin

# Through my rose-tinted Glasses!

*"No one can look back on his school days and say with truth that they were altogether unhappy"* – George Orwell 1903-1950

THE GROWN-UPS used to tell us that "Schooldays are the happiest days of your life". Of course we didn't believe them at the time, but looking back through my rose tinted glasses from this distance, I realise how true that was... The more I think about my time at the old school at Pouldine, the more memories come flooding back. What follows are a few of the ones that have stuck with me. I'm sure others could think of many many more.

*Billy Carrie.*

All I remember of my first day at Pouldine School in September 1959 is that my Mum brought me there and my next-door neighbour, Mary, brought me home. Miss Butler was my first teacher and was followed by Miss Treacy, Miss Ryan and Mr. Maher, the Principal, who was always referred to as 'The Master'.

The school building comprised four classrooms with two classes to each room. A memory which has never left me is the cold in mid-winter. The rooms were heated by pot-bellied stoves that only produced maximum heat as they 'reddened' on the outside when it was near time to go home. Each stove was surrounded by a wire cage to stop us getting burned. The stoves were fuelled by turf and coal and sticks and newspapers were used to start them. You were privileged to be selected to collect the firewood in the surrounding fields as it got you out of the classroom.

I remember at lunch break, the bravest of us would sneak back into the classroom and lean over the top of the cage to toast our bread by pressing it on the stove's red belly. Lunch was usually washed down by milk or cold tea from old Chef Sauce bottles. I can still hear the squeaks caused by the grinding of the sand and grit particles remaining in the bottle cap after Mum had rinsed out the last of the sauce before use – no Fairy liquid in those days!

Other clear physical memories are the stench off the dry toilets in warm weather and the smell of damp clothing as we crowded like cattle into the porches adjoining the classrooms on wet days – sheds were later built in the schoolyard for this purpose. We wore plastic sandals in the summer and wellies in the winter. I remember on hot days taking off the sandals to feel the melting tar on the road between my toes and in winter everybody had a black ring around their legs caused by friction from the tops of the wellies, as our socks kept falling down.

The popular games played in the schoolyard were 'tig', 'chain-follow (pronounced folly), marbles mainly by the boys and skipping by the girls. 'Conkers' was also popular in the autumn. There was a muddy field at the back of the Master's house, where we used to, in between staged boxing matches where nobody got hurt, play hurling and a little bit of football. Of course we were all playing for Tipp and wanted to be Jimmy or John Doyle.

The Master and his wife had a little brown and white terrier dog which they adored. His name was Figaro and he was a frequent visitor to the schoolyard especially at lunch time. One time he went missing and the Master nearly lost his mind. We searched everywhere for him. After a week or ten days had passed my sister and I one morning had to take a short cut through the fields as we were late for school. When hurrying through 'Brereton's Fort', which was a spooky place, my sister heard something yelping. We followed the sound and came upon poor Figaro tied to a tree in the middle of the fort feeling very sorry for himself. We untied him and carried him back to the Master, who was thrilled to see him. Figaro recovered from his ordeal but how he came to be tied in the fort remained an unsolved mystery.

Some time after this episode I was at Mass in Moycarkey with my friend Pat from Kylenoe. Like all young fellas we were easily distracted and spent our time chatting about matches, films or whatever. In the middle of the Mass, the Master separated us to stop the talking, which in those days was a 'hangin' offence. I never slept a wink that night thinking about what was going to happen to me, when I went to school the following morning. However, to my surprise, the Master never said one word to either of us. Looking back now, I think Figaro was looking after us – one good turn deserves another!

Of course First Communion and Confirmation were landmarks in everybody's time at Pouldine. I remember my Mum warning me weeks before not to get cuts or scars on my knees, as the photos would be ruined. In those days every fella had damaged knees from falls and scrapes in the schoolyard. On the eve of my Confirmation my knees were in pristine condition, not a blemish. As usual I collected the milk on my bike from Dowling's farm. On my dash home the milk gallon got caught between my knee and the handlebars of the bike and I took a right toss on to the road. I dusted myself down; my knees were still perfect, thank goodness. However, there was an ugly graze on my forehead where my head hit the road. How could I face Mum now? Well before I reached home I started roaring and crying as loudly as I could. Hearing the racket Mum came out on the road and seeing my distress took pity on me so I escaped a tongue lashing. Looking now at the Confirmation photo she must have worked hard to disguise the damage, as there is no evidence of it to be seen.

These are just a few memories of my time at Pouldine. I sometimes stumble upon the old black and white class photo and sit on the bed here in Dublin and challenge myself to name everyone in it. I remember Patsy, Seamus, Michael, Phonsey, Josie and Pat, Mary, Peggy, Angela and Breeda. Many of them I still meet regularly at funerals, matches etc., a handful have passed on and some I have no idea how they ended up. However, I do know that we are all united, wherever we are, by our common experiences and influences gained at the old school at Pouldine.

*"A teacher affects eternity; he can never tell where his influence stops"*
– Henry Brooks Adams

**Billy Carrie**
**(Pupil at Pouldine School, 1959-1967)**

ABOVE: *Michael O'Dwyer, Graigue and Christy Philips, Grallagh photographed in 1955.*

RIGHT: *First Communion Day 1956 (l.-r.): Margaret O'Hea, James O'Hea and Dolores Cahill (Moycarkey).*

Moycarkey N.S., Pouldine

A break from play – June 2008.

# Ministers for Education
# 1921 ⹍ 2009

| | | | | |
|---|---|---|---|---|
| 1. | John J. O'Kelly | 26 August 1921 | 9 January 1922 | Sinn Féin |
| 2. | Michael Hayes | 11 January 1922 | 9 September 1922 | Pro-Treaty Sinn Féin |
| 3. | Finian Lynch | 1 April 1922 | 30 August 1922 | Pro-Treaty Sinn Féin |
| 4. | Eoin MacNeill | 30 August 1922 | 24 November 1925 | Cumann na nGaedhael |
| 5. | John M. O'Sullivan | 28 January 1926 | 9 March 1932 | Cumann na nGaedhael |
| 6. | Tomás Ó Deirg *(1st time)* | 9 March 1932 | 8 September 1939 | Fianna Fáil |
| 7. | Seán T. O'Kelly | 8 September 1939 | 27 September 1939 | Fianna Fáil |
| 8. | Éamon de Valera *(acting)* | 27 September 1939 | 18 June 1940 | Fianna Fáil |
| | Tomás Ó Deirg *(2nd time)* | 18 June 1940 | 18 February 1948 | Fianna Fáil |
| 9. | Richard Mulcahy *(1st time)* | 18 February 1948 | 13 June 1951 | Fine Gael |
| 10. | Seán Moylan | 13 June 1951 | 2 June 1954 | Fianna Fáil |
| | Richard Mulcahy *(2nd time)* | 2 June 1954 | 20 March 1957 | Fine Gael |
| 11. | Jack Lynch *(1st time)* | 20 March 1957 | 23 June 1959 | Fianna Fáil |
| 12. | Patrick Hillery | 23 June 1959 | 21 April 1965 | Fianna Fáil |
| 13. | George Colley | 21 April 1965 | 13 July 1966 | Fianna Fáil |
| 14. | Donogh O'Malley | 13 July 1966 | 10 March 1968 | Fianna Fáil |
| | Jack Lynch *(acting)* | 10 March 1968 | 26 March 1968 | Fianna Fáil |
| 15. | Brian Lenihan, Snr | 26 March 1968 | 2 July 1969 | Fianna Fáil |
| 16. | Pádraig Faulkner | 2 July 1969 | 14 March 1973 | Fianna Fáil |
| 17. | Richard Burke | 14 March 1973 | 2 December 1976 | Fine Gael |
| 18. | Peter Barry | 2 Dec. 1976 | 5 July 1977 | Fine Gael |
| 19. | John Wilson | 5 July 1977 | 30 June 1981 | Fianna Fáil |
| 20. | John Boland | 30 June 1981 | 9 March 1982 | Fine Gael |
| 21. | Martin O'Donoghue | 9 March 1982 | 6 October 1982 | Fianna Fáil |
| 22. | Charles Haughey *(acting)* | 7 October 1982 | 27 October 1982 | Fianna Fáil |
| 23. | Gerard Brady | 27 October 1982 | 14 December 1982 | Fianna Fáil |
| 24. | Gemma Hussey | 14 December 1982 | 14 February 1986 | Fine Gael |
| 25. | Patrick Cooney | 14 February 1986 | 10 March 1987 | Fine Gael |
| 26. | Mary O'Rourke | 10 March 1987 | 14 November 1991 | Fianna Fáil |
| 27. | Noel Davern | 14 November 1991 | 11 February 1992 | Fianna Fáil |
| 28. | Séamus Brennan | 11 February 1992 | 12 January 1993 | Fianna Fáil |
| 29. | Niamh Bhreathnach *(1st time)* | 12 January 1993 | 17 November 1994 | Labour Party |
| 30. | Michael Smith | 18 November 1994 | 15 December 1994 | Fianna Fáil |
| | Niamh Bhreathnach *(2nd time)* | 15 December 1994 | 26 June 1997 | Labour Party |
| 31. | Micheál Martin | 26 June 1997 | 27 January 2000 | Fianna Fáil |
| 32. | Michael Woods | 27 January 2000 | 6 June 2002 | Fianna Fáil |
| 33. | Noel Dempsey | 6 June 2002 | 29 September 2004 | Fianna Fáil |
| 34. | Mary Hanafin | 29 September 2004 | 7 May 2008 | Fianna Fáil |
| 35. | Batt O'Keeffe | 7 May 2008 | Incumbent | Fianna Fáil |

# FORMER MINISTERS FOR EDUCATION
## – THE LOCAL CONNECTION

### *Richard Mulcahy*

Richard Mulcahy (1886-1971) served as Minister for Education for two periods, in the 1950s. Born in Waterford, he was educated in Mount Sion and Thurles C.B.S., the family having moved here when Richard's father became Postmaster in Littleton and later in Thurles. Elected to the first Dáil in 1918, Richard Mulcahy served as Chief-of Staff of the I.R.A. during the War of Independence. He was Fine Gael leader from 1944 until 1959. The Mulcahy family had many connections with this parish and Richard is buried in the family plot in Ballymoreen cemetery.

### *Mary Hanafin*

When the old Parochial House in Moycarkey was sold in the mid 1970s, it was bought by Mary Hanafin's parents - Des and Mona. It was to remain their family home for many years. Mary Hanafin was born in Thurles, in 1959, into a family that had a strong association with the Fianna Fáil political party. Mary was educated at the Presentation Convent in Thurles and St. Patrick's College in Maynooth. She was elected to the Dáil as a Fianna Fáil candidate at the 1997 General Election. She topped the poll in her constituency at the 2002 General Election. Following a cabinet reshuffle in September 2004 she joined the cabinet as Minster for Education and Science. In 2007 she was re-elected to the Dáil. In May 2008 Mary Hanafin was appointed Minister for Social and Family Affairs.

*Ariel view of Moycarkey N.S., Pouldine – early 1990s.*

# A Tale of
# Two Schools

C AN WE remember the first day of school? What were the first impressions? We hadn't really thought about them, until we were asked to write down the thoughts and some interesting things came rushing back to memory.

The first day in Pouldine NS, my cousin and I travelled to school together. I remember Mrs. Butler the teacher of the junior and senior infant's classes. There was a distinctive smell from the school and the teacher and the chalk and the crayons... I think there is a particular smell associated with all schools and institutions. I remember it with fondness and not with some of the more scary memories that some of my friends associated with their early school experiences. One of the longest lasting memories of Mrs. Butler was her knitting; she seemed always to have a basket full of knitting with her at break and lunch time and could knit without ever looking at the needles.

*Bridget Kirwan*

These were the days when desks were fixed to the floorboards and were made of solid timber attached to iron legs. There was the inkwell (empty for the early classes) and the seat was solid board with another board for the back. Each of us shared a desk with one other and the desks were laid out in rows all facing the teacher. I have seen these desks again recently in an African schoolroom. The floorboards were of the wide plank variety where there were hollow patches at the doors where many years of feet had worn an indentation into the floors. The walls had dado rails where the bottom was all panelled (I think the mice lived in there happily like in all old buildings) and the rooms all connected into one another. We could see into the next classrooms through the windowed doors.

The classroom was dark as it faced west and did not get much sun. We went to play in separate yards, the boys at one side and the girls at the other. The yard was surfaced in gravel and the games were revolved around a huge skipping rope, which had space for five or six children, but needed to be turned by fifth or sixth class and which most days spat out wet splatters at the children. We also played Red Rover and Sally Sally One Two

Three for variety but the most imposing feature of the 'yard' was the huge monkey puzzle which was planted in the 'Masters' house but which waved its long stems out over the school yard. The other imposing feature of the yard was the toilets. These were of what has become to be regarded as the 'sustainable variety.' There was no water and therefore no flush toilets, these toilets were freezing in the winter, carried interesting odours in the summer, and sometimes had other occupants along with you.

As we moved from Senior Infants, we prepared for entrance to Miss Treacy's class. The main feature of the classroom was the pot bellied stove, which sat at the top of the classroom beside her desk. In the winter, these stoves glowed with heat and it is probably a wonder they did not blow up at some stage. There was a protective fireguard around it to ensure that the passing child did not get burned to it and the boys were sent to collect the sticks to start the fire each morning.

Miss Treacy was formidable... she did not suffer fools gladly, operated on the principle that these were empty heads which she was going to fill, adopting a 'determined' approach to the task. Later when we were in Sixth Class, she was given the job of teaching the girls to knit (before the days of gender equality). On the journey to becoming a knitter, I was very grateful for my own mother's knowledge and skills, which saved me from many a tongue-lashing. Our biggest project at this stage was to knit a jumper for ourselves and mine was in a red wool and my cousins in purple and one day when we were supposed to have gotten to a particular stage in the project and things had not worked smoothly with the purple jumper she became so frustrated that the jumper needles and all were landed back in the lap of the hapless knitters with the infamous statement (as Gaeilge) 'What the idiot has made the idiot can unmake'.

The Holy Communion was a big event in the school year as it still is and we were trained and taught and got ready for the 'inspector' whose job it was to ensure that we had been properly indoctrinated into the ways of the church. These were still the days when all was learned off by heart and at seven we were expected to be able to put recite by heart all the various rules and regulations. I remember the day when the inspector was to come vividly. I had been sick the days before but because this was such an important event in the mind of a seven year old, I felt that I had to go to school. Off I went on the morning with a flask of tea and a packet of Marietta biscuits. The intention was that I would have a cup of tea and one or two biscuits to keep me going but Miss Treacy in her concern for me insisted that I eat more and the end result was that I remembered nothing of the 'inspector' (the kindly Fr. Curtain I think) and only that I was as sick as a dog for the rest of the day.

On the day of our First Communion we all arrived ready for the big event and at the same Apostles Creed Fr. Moynihan (who generally suffered from poor health) collapsed in the middle of Mass and had to be taken to hospital, (where he recovered later) I have a memory of a very long sit under Miss Treacys watchful eye, while the arrangements for another Priest to finish the ceremony were made.

*Patricia Hayes, 6th Class pupil at Moycarkey N.S., Pouldine, at the Image Art Display 2009.*

Fr. O'Meara was the curate in the parish at the same time and he used to arrive into school with boxing gloves to organise a boxing match or a football game between the boys and the girls. One day he asked me to recite the Apostles Creed at the school gate because he thought I had said it incorrectly at Mass the previous Sunday. It was a terrifying experience.

We moved into fourth class and into the new school at the same time. The 'new school' was a whole new experience, it was bright and airy, had a concrete yard and desks which could be moved and arranged and where we sat facing one another in groups of four. The shift in size of the chairs from junior infants to sixth class was a wonder and the colours! The walls were coloured and the desks were coloured, the desks that we first sat on are still being used by my children all of nearly forty years later. The other major change was that the girls and boys played together for the first time and one of the favourite games was the races up and down the yard, which came to an abrupt halt when one of the sixth class boys put his arm right through the window one day.

The other amazing thing about the new school was the subjects we learned and how we learned them, there was a change in the nature of the tasks, there was much more project work and art and 'participation' and 'discussion' became an important part of the school experience. We had Miss Ryan in third and forth class and the experience I remember as encouraging and supportive. Unfortunately she went through a period of poor health also during that time and we had Miss Ryan (who was a sister of the first Miss Ryan) Mrs Haverty and Mrs Fanning at different stages over that time. I remember also recycling X-Ray's (which were used for the very first acetates for the overhead projector I think) and early versions of printout paper which were used for a variety of purposes.

When we were in the 'Masters' (Timmy Maher's class), there were a number of eventful days. The school was broken into and flooded on what seemed to be a number of days one after another and there was great consternation about books and desks and disruption for a while. Around this time the 'Master' decided to move from the house into his own house in town and we had great fun in school while he held raffles for any unwanted items which were not making the journey to the new house. He had a big stick, which was there for disciplining any children that were out of line but to his credit I have few memories of it being used.

We were one of the last classes to travel to Boherlahan to get our Confirmation before the numbers in the schools in the parish were big enough to have our own and also before there were organised Primary Schools Games we have a memory of playing Littleton Girls in a field in Ballymoreen when Pouldine came off the worst for wear.

During the years that I was in primary school, we sometimes got a lift to school but mostly we walked home (along with most others) and in the summer, this was wonderful and we walked home barefoot and burst the tar bubbles with our toes as we wandered home. I am sure there were days when we got wet but they do no seem to have lasted in the memory as strongly.

Our class had an even number of boys and girls which I think was probably unusual (Lucy O'Keeffe, Brema Kirwan, Bridget Kirwan, Joanne Leahy, Josephine Graydon, Breda Costello, Ann Shaw, Kevin Croke, Seamus Ryan, Willie Regan, Paddy Fogarty, Terence Graydon, Pat Halloran, Pat Cormack).

*(Bridget Kirwan – School Years in Pouldine 1965-'73)*

*Millennium Memorial, Moycarkey Village (l.-r.):*
*Rev. Richard Ryan P.P.,*
*Stephen Hewitt*
*and John Lanphier.*

# The Jockey – for Characters and Craic

*P. J. Maxwell*

**A**S A VERY young small boy, I was always out wandering around the famous Jockey. My Father Mick Maxwell was Station Master at the local railway station. The Jockey was on a single line between Thurles and Clonmel. The Station was a hive of activity with people using the passenger service and local businesses delivering goods and parcels by rail. The house itself was a grand stone-built house and the windows were shaped in such a way that we could watch up and down the railway to see Daddy coming in for a sup of 'tae' or his dinner. I remember going for a spin one day to Clonmel with a fellow called Peter O'Shaughnessy and he brought me back that evening. It was like going on an adventure to the end of the world. We didn't have any electricity in the house. It was all Tilly lamps, and we had a nice green hanging lamp, which we had to be careful of when we were playing indoor football or hurling. There would be "Wigs on the Green" if any damage was done. My brother John was two years older than me and he was dropped off in Pouldine School to Mr. Maher every morning by my father on his black Raleigh bike with gears on it.

I was left at home to mind Mammy. When John was in school, I'd go off rambling out through the ditch next door to Stapleton's. Sylvie Stapleton, John Maxwell and Dick Keeffe were the big fellows then around the village. They would get up to all sorts of devilment and caused Mammy many sleepless nights. One time John ran away from home after getting a bit of a trimming in school and a second one when he came home for the same offence, as he let the family down by committing some terrible deed by "gawking out the window" while the Master was imparting very important knowledge. However, the whole village was out looking for him. Eventually he was found up on top of the "distant" signal, which must have been about two miles up in the sky. So when they found him, 'me' father says "Ah John, will you come down oura dat", "No" says our John, "You'll bate me", "be God then I won't "says me Father", but John's grip was frozen solid on to cast iron signal with fear, terror and dread, sure enough John came down and heat wasn't long coming into his hands and his legs and his backside.

When I'd be going into Stapleton's I'd be hoping Walsie was there, he was 'me' favourite and I thought he was God. The two of us would go off around the countryside selling calves in his blue scut truck. I used to climb up on the fireplace in 'me' Mother's room and whip a few fags out of the box with the sailor on it- John Player no tips. Some times all I'd get was a few butts, as Mammy was always lighting one and then topping it. I used to love smoking butts and holding them like "Boggan Healy"did, above in the Handball Alley, when he was telling us all about his deeds. I got a bad dose of ringworm and tetters from the calves and I had to go to the cure woman in Urlingford, Mrs. Britton I think. All I can remember is that feather she had and she putting that stuff on 'me' face and arms and worse than the burn of a fag when your finger would slide too far on the butt that stuck to your lip.

Rene Stapleton used to be minding Donie-Oliver and the Twins and I'd go in there till the Grandfather Bob got up. He was lovely, except the day that he went over to me father giving out about 'them two feckers' Sylvie and John, who whilst playing, pulled the head off the chicken that was under the barrel and could only be brought out through the lettuce wire. Another day the big boys were going off swimming in the swimming pool in Maher's of Parkston and they wouldn't let Concept O'Keeffe and myself go, as we were too small. We waited till the boys whipped off their clothes and ran in to the water and we had snuck up after them took their clothes home and they had to run home, through the Jockey, in their birthday suits.

Jimmy Stapleton was a fierce decent man, I heard 'me' father say several times. He always gave us the loan of a car, as we did not have one. Daddy needed to get to his new job in Goolds Cross. 'Twas funny the way the orange yoke would come out of each side to go left or right.

The best days of all were when Mary Joe would be going to town, ice cream and sweets for Connie and myself. One day we were in town and in the front of the car while Mary Joe was gone in to the Bank in the Square, we let go the handbrake and away goes the car off down the street. We were supposed to be heading for the river when Tom Flanagan jumped in and stopped the car. No goodies that day. Another day, when I was on 'me' rambles' I was passing by Jimmy Stapleton's reek of hay. 'Twas a windy day and I couldn't light me butt. I got a brainwave, I got a piece of cardboard marked Roscrea sausages and put it up against the reek on the sheltered side and lit the match to light the cardboard to light me fag. No joy, but as I walked away off she goes on fire. I ran straight in to Rene, to tell her that somebody had set fire to the hay. Well there were Guards and Firemen all over the place in a short space of time and the smell was awful. Nobody said anything to me but Mammy knew 'twas me and I'd say so did Walsie.

Connie and myself had a master plan one day for sweets. We went around the back of Keeffe's Pub and got a couple of empty "Kittys" and brought them in around the front to old Mrs. Keeffe and we codded her and got a few pennies. We then went over to John Joes for Black Jacks and Trigger Bars. Our John was accident prone. He pulled a kettle of boiling water down on top of himself and got roasted and I remember the roars out of him, when Mammy would be changing the dressing. Another day he was walking along the platform looking up at a plane and picking his nose, when he slipped and fell down on the railway tracks and busted his eye getting six stitches from Dr. Herlihy. A lovely man in a green American-style car brought them into town.

I can still smell the lovely dinners that Mrs. Dinny Keefe, Connie's mother, used to make. She would feed the whole lot of us. Mary O'Keefe used to mind us when Mammy was gone to town or gone to hospital to get a baby. All the auld lads would frighten us with stories of ghosts and quare fellows.

The bridge was dangerous and there would be a car or a truck every Monday morning in the garden after Sunday night. There were a lot of serious accidents. One man's head was rolling around the road and ended up at the road gate.

Jimmy Tobin and Nellie used to come down to Mammy of a Sunday. They were lovely. When Mrs. Wilson would come to the Station she always had a special car for her dogs and they were different than our Rose - a Jack Russell. Rodge and Ciss Callaghan used to take us to the Feis, where Anne and her sister would compete.

Looby's garage was a great spot and they would be talking about all the great men in the parish "Cusack, Mutt, Sweeper, Hayes of Ballyerk, Joe Bergin, Tommy Gleeson, Paddy "Best". There was a great lot of talk always about sport, whether it be hurling, greyhounds, coursing, flapper tracks, marbles, skittles, rounders, cross-country and

*Cigarette manufacturer Players with their promotional boat outside Horse & Jockey Service Station in the 1950s.*

above all handball. I remember no matter when we'd make our way up to the Alley, there would be a "Butler" there. They were great handballers. When the lads in Looby's were talking, you'd always hear about the Healy's of Coolcroo and Blake's of Coolquill.

I remember the "Travellers" used to camp up beside the Alley and there would

*Serious business at the 'Jockey . . . . Back row (l.-r.): Sean Barry, Johnny Ryan, Paddy Maher, Frank Gooney. Front row (l.-r.): Malachy Cullagh, Jerry Darmody, Dermot Shanahan and Harry Ryan.*

be murder with the locals. We didn't mind them as we used to go up and play with Maggie and Paddy McCarthy and they had a lovely dog Joey.

I remember when Jimmy Stapleton got a television, it was brilliant. We watched Rin Tin Tin, Daniel Boone, Lassie, Looney Tunes, Kit Carson, and the Marks Brothers, but our favourite was Mr. Ed - The Talking Horse. We knew a man who stopped at Keeffe's - Fred Winter and he had a horse that won a big race in England and had only one eye, but Mr. Ed was a bit better than him.

Sticks Shanahan used to show us tricks with matches, cards, and elastic bands. He could shoot like a bow and arrow with a band and one of Mammy's clothes pegs.

Fintan Stapleton and Peter Bulfin came home from America and we were amazed about the things they saw like on the telly. Dinny Keefe and 'me' father brought us in to Gussie Sheas in Thurles for a haircut but we preferred going to Teddy's as he had a singing bird. One year when the whole place was going to an All-Ireland final in Dublin, a rake of the men piled into the Guards Van at the back of the train and played cards. Dan Shaw, Roundy Mooney, Tom Devitt, The Joker, Sticks, and many more were there. Jimmy Scott won a Minor Medal with Tipperary and his father won a Senior Medal with Kilkenny when they beat Tipperary.

By the way, I was born on March 17th 1959 in St Anne's Nursing home in Thurles, where Dr. Paddy Moloney who like myself brought his name with him slapped my botty. Fr. O'Meara christened me in Moycarkey.

*P .J. Maxwell*

# Our School Crest

OUR school crest is composed of two main symbols – the Cross and the Torch.

The Cross symbolises the Catholic ethos of our school. This Cross, known as a Greek cross is based on a carving seen on a grave slab on the Island of Derrynaflan – one of the main monastic sites in this locality. The use of this cross is also indicative of the continuity of the Christian Faith in our parish, from the earliest Christian times. The circular feature of the cross states that God is eternal, without beginning or end – just like the circle. This cross can also be seen on the Millenium monuments in the villages of Moycarkey and Littleton.

The Torch symbolises the enlightment of the human being through education. It has historically been a symbol of hope, freedom and faith - the light of hope when all else is dark. In Christianity, the torch represents Christ as the Light of the World.

The torch also symbolises achievement in sport, as in the Olympic Torch and recognises the great sporting tradition of Moycarkey.

In the early years of this state, the road sign warning of the proximity of a school contained the symbol of the Torch and the word "Scoil".

The year 1970 is the year the new school was first occupied.

*School Staff 1999*

*Back row:*
*Mrs Mary Minchin,*
*Ms. Lucy McGann.*

*Front Row:*
*Ms. Ann-Marie*
*Shanahan,*
*Liam O'Donnchú,*
*Mrs. Máire Sheehy.*

*School Staff 2007*

*Back row:*
*Mrs Ann-Marie Carroll,*
*Ms. Lucy McGann,*
*Ms. Catherine O'Keeffe,*
*Liam Ó Donnchú.*

*Front row:*
*Ms. Fionnuala*
*Concagh,*
*Mrs Mary Minchin,*
*Mrs Aileen Colton,*
*Mr. Robert White.*

*School Staff 2008*

*Back row:*
*Mr. Robert White,*
*Mrs Catherine*
*Heffernan,*
*Mrs Ann-Marie Carroll.*

*Front row:*
*Mrs Mary Minchin,*
*Liam Ó Donnchú,*
*Mrs Fionnuala Hayes,*
*Mrs Aileen Colton.*

# Foireann na Scoile – School Staff

## MÚINTEOIRÍ - TEACHERS

New School Opened 1969-'70

**SCHOOL STAFF:**
*Principal Teacher* – Tadhg Ó Meachair
*Vice-Principal* – Ms. Pauline Treacy
*Assistant Teachers* – Mrs. Maura Butler, Ms. Brede Ryan

**PRINCIPAL TEACHERS IN THE SCHOOL:**
Tadhg Ó Meachair – Appointed July 1st 1944 - Retired June 30th 1976
Liam Ó Donnchú – Appointed July 1st 1976 – Retired September 1st 2009
Mr. Robert White – Appointed September 2nd 2009.

**VICE-PRINCIPALS:**
Ms. Pauline Treacy
Ms. Bríd Ryan
Mrs. Mary Minchin

**CLASS TEACHERS:**

Ms. Pauline Treacy – Retired Aug. 31st 1984, following 36 years teaching, mostly in Pouldine. (Died Aug. '98).

Mrs. Maura Butler – Resigned Sept. 30th 1976.

Ms. Brede Ryan – Appointed July 1st 1957, Retired August 31st 1998.

Mrs. Mary Minchin – Appointed October 1st 1976, replacing Mrs. Maura Butler.

Ms. Lucy McGann – Appointed January 1st 1978 (Due to an increase in pupil numbers), Resource Teacher 2002 -

Ms. Catherine McGrath – Appointed Sept. 1st 1984 (replaced Ms. Pauline Treacy), resigned 1992.

Ms. Anne Harrington replaced Ms. Brede Ryan during her career break 1989 – '90.

Ms. Gina Kenny replaced Mrs. Catherine Tierney (nee McGrath) during her career break 1991 – '92.

Ms. Yvonne Grogan – Appointed Sept. 1st 1992 (replaced Mrs. Catherine Tierney).

Ms. Ann Marie Shanahan – Appointed Sept 1st 1995 (replaced Ms. Yvonne Grogan).

Mrs. Máire Sheehy – Sept.1st 1998 (Replaced Ms. Brede Ryan), Resigned Aug 2000.

Ms. Claire O'Carroll appointed Sept. 1st 2000, replacing Mrs. Máire Sheehy. Resigned March 2001.

Ms Fionnuala Concagh appointed Sept. 1st '02. (New Teaching Post due to increased numbers).

Mr. Gearóid Ryan appointed 2002 (Replaced Ms Lucy McGann, who became Resource Teacher). Resigned March 2003. Gearóid died on June 1st 2005. R.I.P.

Mr. Robert White appointed Sept. 1st 2003, replacing Mr. Gearóid Ryan.

Ms. Fiona McCullagh appointed Sept. 1st 2008. (New Teaching Post due to increased numbers).

*Ms. Gina Kenny.*

## SUPPORT TEACHING (Remedial, Resource, Resource Teacher for Travellers)

1986 – Ms. Bríd McHugh

1999 – Mrs. Aileen Colton (Sept. 1st), shared post with Gaile, Dualla and Ballytarsna), Retired Sept. 1st 2008.

Ms. Lucy McGann, 2002

Ms. Mally Noonan 2002

Mrs. Ailish Clancy 2006 – '07

Ms. Siobhán O'Reilly 2007 – Æ08

Ms. Sara Horgan, Sept. 1st 2008

Ms. Elaine Brady appointed Sept 2nd 2008

*Ms. Anne Harrington*

## PART-TIME SUPPORT TEACHERS

Ms. Margaret McGarry

Mrs. Joan Nagle

Mrs. Bridget O'Gorman

## SPECIAL NEEDS ASSISTANTS

1999 – 2008 Ms. Catherine O'Keeffe (Sept.1st)

2002 – '03 Mrs. Frances Molloy

2006 – 2008 Mrs. Catherine Heffernan

## FÁS SCHEME – SCHOOL CARETAKER

John Lanphier, Curraheen. 1987

Danny Pyne, Coolkennedy. 1989

Donie Shanahan, Pouldine. 1990

*Mr. Gearóid Ryan.*

Tom Bourke, Graigue. 1991
Donie Shanahan, Pouldine. 1992
Willie O'Regan, Ballymoreen. 1993
Vivian Britton, Moycarkey. 1994
Donie Shanahan, Pouldine. 1995

## FÁS SCHEME – SCHOOL SECRETARY
Josephine Shaw, Ashill
Deirdre Donnelly, Holycross
Frances Molloy, Knockroe.
Catherine O'Keeffe, Holycross. 1998

## SCHOOL SECRETARY
Mrs. Catherine Walsh – Oct. 20th 2008

*Mrs. Catherine Walsh*

## CLEANING
Mrs. Mary Heffernan, Kylenoe. 1970 – 1986
Mrs. Catherine Loughnane, Pouldine. 1986 – 1994
Mrs. Margaret Cassidy, Coolkennedy. 1994 -

**McDonalds Soccer Winners 1999**
*Back row (l.-r.): Stephen Singleton, Elaine Roche, Majella Delaney, Claire Carey, Liam Ó Donnchú.*
*Front row (l.-r.): Karen Hogan, Sinéad O'Hara, Karen Mullins, Mairéad Dixon.*

*School Year:- Sixth class 1998-'99*

*Back row: Blain O'Halloran, David Kinane, Megan Quigley, Thomas Roche, Gerry Maguire. Middle row: Sarah Cummins, Mary Shortall, Shane Hewitt, Kieran McCormack, Paul Singleton, Siobhán Roche, Mairéad Dixon. Front row: Majella Delaney, Carol Sweeney, Damien Shanahan, Patrick Heffernan, Liam O'Donnchú (Principal), Clare Carey, David Maher, Mícheál Heffernan.*

School Year:- Sixth Class 1999-2000
Back row: Sean Quirke, Shane Barry, Felicity Demnpsey, Rachel Bourke, Laura Cleary, Máire O'Regan. Middle row: Tom Quinn, Dick O'Sullivan, (R.I.P.), Kevin Mullanney, Conor Fanning, Hannah McGrath, Marie Kirwan, Anita Bannon. Front row: Eoin Ryan, Eoghan

Nagle, Tony Flanagan, Liam Ó Donnchú (Principal) Patricia Coman, Christine Ryan, Rosemary O'Keeffe, Marie Carey.

*School Year:- Sixth Class 2000-'01*

*Back row: Brendan McCormack, Kilian O'Donoghue, David Ryan, Denis Roche, Noel Kinane, Conan O'Hara, William Foley, Liam Ó Donnchú (Principal). Front row: Catherine Delahunty, Shannon Hayes, Karen Mullins, Ann Kirwan, Sinéad O'Hara, Karen Hogan, Jack Harnett.*

# Developments through the Years

1969 – New School built, Scoil Naomh Peadar

1970 – Spring, New School occupied

1971 – Tuairisc Scoile, School Report. Cigire: Éamonn Mac Aonghusa

1972 - Very Rev. Daniel M. Ryan appointed Parish Priest and School Manager.

1973 – Tuairisc Scoile, School Report. Cigire: Éamonn Mac Aonghusa

1975 – Board of Management appointed for the first time

1975 – Tuairisc Scoile, School Report. Cigire: Éamonn Mac Aonghusa

1982 – Trees Planted on School Grounds

1982 – Basketball Posts and Nets installed

1983 – Joined Group Water Scheme

1983 – Mór Thuairisc, School Report. Cigire: Tadhg Ó Gláimhín

1984 – New Front Wall Erected

1986 – November, Tadhg Ó Meachair died, R.I.P.

1986 – Mór Thuairisc School Report. Cigire: Liam Ó hÉigearta

1989 – Front Hedge Planted

1989 – School Hall completed and opened

1990 – Whist started on Tuesday nights in School Hall

1992 – Mór Thuairisc School Report. Cigire: Seán Terry

1994 – School Re-Roofed, Double Glaze Windows Installed, Covered Walk-Way, New Carpets and Blinds, Lighting Upgraded (Cost Approx. £90,000)

1994 – Heating System installed in School Hall

1994 - School Uniform Introduced -   September 1st

1994 – Blessing of the School Oct. 7th

1995 - Book Rental Scheme started

1995 – June 17th, Pupils take part in the National Children's Choir, Cór na nÓg, concert at the National Concert Hall, Dublin.

1996 - Pupils receiving Confirmation wear their School Uniform

1998 – New Wall and Fence erected beside main road

1999 – Mór Thuairisc School Report. Cigire: Seán Terry

2000 – First Book Fair

2000-'01 – Asbestos Tiles etc.removed, new blinds installed, classrooms painted, Hot Water for Classrooms

2001 – New Drainage System for schoolyard installed

2001 – Alarm System installed

2001 – First time we participated in St. Patrick's Day parade in Littleton

2001 – Mural painted in school hall. Artist – Mark Shanahan

2001 – Plaque with School Crest erected. Sculptor – James Slattery

2001-'02 – One less class-teacher due to falling enrolment

2001 – First edition of Nuacht Scoile, our school newsletter, published

2002 – Front grounds ploughed, levelled and reseeded – Páirc an Bhóthair

2002 – New class teaching post, due to increased pupil numbers.

2002 – Artist in Residence – Desmond Scott

2003 – Two acres purchased from McGraths for new playing area – Páirc na Scoile

2003 – Tír na nÓg, (New Prefab) erected

2003 – Computer Room completed

2003 – New Tarmac Yard

2003 - In June athletes from the school took part in the Special Olympics Torch Run

2004 – June 9th School Hall named Halla Uí Riain

2005 – December. Grant of €5,000 received from Comhairle na Mumhan – Munster G.A.A. Council, towards the development of playing pitches.

2006 – Roof insulation, Halla Uí Riain

2006 – New Footpath, Kerbing and Tarmac outside school

2007 – March 15th, Curriculum Implementation Evaluation: Science and Mathematics. Reported: Nov. 8th '08. Cigirí – Pádraig Ó Néill, Carmel O'Doherty

2007 – Hotwater system installed in Halla Uí Riain

2007 – New Car Park for school staff. New storage shed.

2007 – November, Concert with Peter Kearney

2008 – Speed limit on main road reduced from 100 to 60 Km. per hour, at school opening and closing times.

2008 – Homework Club started

2008 – Applied for Green Flag Status to An Taisce

2008 – Food Dudes Healthy Eating Programme introduced

2008 – June, Tesco Great School Run

2008 – New class teaching post, due to increased pupil numbers.

2008 – An Bradán Feasa, (New Prefab). Principal's Office, School Secretary appointed (Part-Time).

2009 - Received our first Green Flag from An Taisce

Art Exhibition – Pupils' art was framed and exhibited

New Interactive White Board installed.

New Covered Walk-Way constructed.

Anseo – As Láthair, Present – Absent
An Leabhar Rollaí – An Leabhar Tinrimh

# Numbers On Roll
# 1890 – 2008

## An Sean-Scoil

| | | | | |
|---|---|---|---|---|
| 1890 – 128 | 1907 – 176 | 1923 – 155 | 1940 – 103 | 1957 – 157 |
| 1891 – 134 | 1908 – 179 | 1924 – 155 | 1941 – 100 | 1958 – 139 |
| 1892 – 131 | 1909 – 189 | 1925 – 152 | 1942 – 94 | 1959 – 163 |
| 1893 – 159 | | 1926 – 150 | 1943 – 99 | |
| 1894 – 168 | 1910 – 179 | 1927 – 149 | 1944 – 92 | 1960 – 166 |
| 1895 – 167 | 1911 – 180 | 1928 – 139 | 1945 – 104 | 1961 – 155 |
| 1896 – 169 | 1912 – 182 | 1929 – 134 | 1946 – 107 | 1962 – 138 |
| 1897 – 172 | 1913 – 181 | 1930 – 123 | 1947 – 110 | 1963 – 137 |
| 1898 – 159 | 1914 – 174 | 1931 – 130 | 1948 – 110 | 1964 – 139 |
| 1899 – 161 | 1915 – 166 | 1932 – 120 | 1949 – 106 | 1965 – 129 |
| | 1916 – 174 | 1933 – 121 | | 1966 – 128 |
| 1900 – 161 | 1917 – 174 | 1934 – 108 | 1950 – 103 | 1967 – 119 |
| 1901 – 168 | 1918 – 175 | 1935 – 109 | 1951 – 110 | 1968 – 111 |
| 1902 – 162 | 1919 – 164 | 1936 – 110 | 1952 – 116 | 1969 – 120 |
| 1903 – 167 | | 1937 – 113 | 1953 – 115 | |
| 1904 – 170 | 1920 – 153 | 1938 – 109 | 1954 – 124 | |
| 1905 – 169 | 1921 – 172 | 1939 – 100 | 1955 – 143 | |
| 1906 – 174 | 1922 – 153 | | 1956 – 146 | |

## An Scoil Nua

| | | | | |
|---|---|---|---|---|
| 1970 – 114 | 1979 – 152 | 1987 – 164 | 1995 – 145 | 2003 – 130 |
| 1971 – 120 | | 1988 – 166 | 1996 – 133 | |
| 1972 – 110 | 1980 – 145 | 1989 – 174 | 1997 – 129 | 2004 – 128 |
| 1973 – 116 | 1981 – 148 | | 1998 – 125 | |
| 1974 – 112 | 1982 – 147 | 1990 – 163 | 1999 – 120 | 2005 – 132 |
| 1975 – 127 | 1983 – 154 | 1991 – 162 | | |
| 1976 – 150 | 1984 – 147 | 1992 – 157 | 2000 – 113 | 2006 – 136 |
| 1977 – 161 | 1985 – 147 | 1993 – 149 | 2001 – 123 | 2007 – 151 |
| 1978 – 148 | 1986 – 142 | 1994 – 142 | 2002 – 131 | 2008 – 158 |

*June 2008 – Presentation to Mrs Aileen Colton on the occasion of her retirement from teaching.*

*Left to right: Rev. George Bourke makes the presentation to Aileen, on behalf of the Board of Management on right is School Principal – Liam Ó Donnchú.*

*Back row (l.-r.): Liam Ó Donnchú, Mary Ryan, Joe Byrne, Margaret Cassidy, Lucy McGann, Ann-Marie Carroll, Fionnuala Hayes, Robert White, Michelle Donnelly, Patricia Connolly, Annette Scott, Siobhán O'Reilly. Seated (l.-r.): Catherine O'Brien, Mary Minchin, Aileen Colton, Fr. Geroge Bourke.*

**December 2007 – Marking Christy Mooney's retirement after many year of service as Board of Management Treasurer.**
*Left to right: Rev. George Bourke P.P., Mr. Christy Mooney, Mrs Kathleen Mooney, Mrs Ann-Marie Carroll and Liam Ó Donnchú.*

# Moycarkey National School, Pouldine
# Board of Management

## FIRST MEETING

The first meeting of the Board of Management took place on October 22nd 1975. The members of this board were:

*Chairman* – Very Rev. D. M. Ryan P.P., Moycarkey.
*Secretary* – Tadhg Ó Meachair N.T., Thurles.
*Treasurer* – Patrick Maher, Ballymoreen.
Rev. Patrick Cooney C.C., Littleton; Joan O'Keeffe, Horse and Jockey; Anne O'Sullivan Kilmealen; Stephen Kirwan, Moycarkey.

## OFFICERS OF THE BOARD OF MANAGEMENT

*Chairman*
Very Rev. D. M. Ryan, Moycarkey. 1975 – 1986
Rev. Richard Ryan, Moycarkey. 1987 – 2002
Rev. George Bourke, Moycarkey. 2002 –

*Secretary*
Tadhg Ó Meachair, Thurles. 1975 – 1976
Liam Ó Donnchú, Ballymoreen. 1976 – 1979
Rita Barry, Curraheen.  1979 – 1982
Liam Ó Donnchú, Ballymoreen. 1982 - 2009

*Treasurer*
Paddy Maher, Ballymoreen. 1975 – 1979
Patrick Bourke, Maxfort. 1979 – 1982
Christy Mooney, Ashfield. 1982 – 2007
Joe Byrne, Moycarkey.  2008 – 2009

## BOARD MEMBERS DOWN THE YEARS SINCE 1975

Rev. Patrick Cooney C.C., Littleton; Joan O'Keeffe, Horse and Jockey; Anne O'Sullivan, Kilmealen; Stephen Kirwan, Moycarkey; Denis Bourke, Coolkennedy; Rita Barry, Curraheen; Daniel Butler, Parkstown; Patrick Bourke, Maxfort; Mary Kavanagh, Maxfort;

Michael O'Connell, Ashill; Mary Ryan, Newtown; Mary Butler, Parkstown; Frank Roche, Newtown; Margaret Hogan, Coolkip; Eileen Concagh, Shanballa; Mary M. O'Regan, Knockroe; Kathleen Kirwan, Moycarkey; Michael Dempsey, Shanballa; Margaret Carey, Forgestown; Geraldine O'Hara, Drumgower; Mary Minchin, Drumgower; Margaret O'Dwyer, Ashfield, Galboola; Tom Quinn, Graigue; J. J. Fogarty, Parkstown; Ann Marie Carroll, Curraheen; Joe Byrne, Moycarkey; Mary Ryan, Aughnagomaun; Breda Kinane, Kevinsfort; Annette Scott, Kylenoe; Robert White, Cashel.

# School Management

FOR OVER 140 years, primary schools were managed by the local clergy, mainly the parish priest. In 1969, following Vatican 11, the Catholic Bishops proposed that lay people should become involved in the management of the schools. Since 1975, management is shared by a Board of Management. The size of the Board is determined by the size of the school.

At present, our board comprises of eight members:-

- Two Direct nominees of the patron (Archbishop).
- Two parents of children enrolled in the school. (elected by parents)
- The Principal Teacher.
- One other Teacher (elected by the teaching staff)
- Two extra members proposed by the six nominees above.

These were the first Boards of Management appointed in this parish:-

## MOYCARKEY N.S. POULDINE

Rev. Daniel M. Ryan P.P., Chairman.
Tadgh Ó Meachair, N.T., Secretary
Patrick Maher, Ballymoreen, Treasurer.
Rev. Patrick Cooney, C.C.; Mrs. Larry O'Sullivan, Kilmealan; Mrs. J. J. O'Keeffe, Horse & Jockey and Stephen Kirwan, Moycarkey.

## GAILE N.S.

Rev. Daniel M. Ryan, P.P., Chairman.
Philip O'Dwyer, N.T., Secretary.
Mrs. Philip Fahey, Gaile Treasurer.
Rev. Maurice Morrissey, P.P., Boherlahan; William Flanagan, Galbertstown; Mrs. Martin Maher, Gaile, and Rodge Fanning, Gaile.

## LITTLETON N.S.

Rev. Patrick Cooney C.C., Chairman.
Denis Commins, N.T., Secretary.
William Ryan, McDonagh Terrace, Treasurer.
Rev. Daniel M. Ryan, P.P.; Mrs. Kitty O'Dwyer, Ballybeg; Mrs. Eileen Kelly, St. Brigid's Terrace and Mal Maher, Littleton.

## TWO-MILE-BORRIS N.S.

Rev. Robert Harkin, C.C., Chairman.
Tim Carroll, N.T., Secretary.
Gus Ryan, Grawn, Treasurer.
Rev. Daniel M. Ryan, P.P.; Mrs. Thomas Ryan, Two-Mile-Borris; Mrs. Sean Corcoran, Two-Mile-Borris, and John Connolly, Noard.

# BOARD OF MANAGEMENT CHAIRPERSONS
# 1975 - 2009

## FR. DANIEL M. RYAN

*Parish Priest of Moycarkey and Borris 1972-'87*

*Fr. Daniel M. Ryan*

Fr. Daniel M. Ryan was born at Ballykiveen, Cappawhite in November 1915.

He entered St. Patricks College, Maynooth in Sept., 1934 and was ordained there by Archbishop John Charles McQuaid, in June 1941. Following post-graduate studies at Maynooth, he was on the staff of Carlow College from 1942 until 1947. He was appointed to the teaching staff of St. Patrick's College, Thurles, in July 1947. He also served, from 1948 until '56, as Dean of Discipline at the College. Fr. Daniel was Bursar there from 1956 until 1960, when he was appointed vice President of the College. During his ten-year ministry (1962-'72) as President of the College, he supervised the construction of the new east wing.

In 1972, he was appointed Parish Priest of Moycarkey Borris. During those years, the expanding village of Littleton, with its growing population warrented the erection of the new church and priest's house there in 1977 and Fr. Daniel suprvised its construction. In the early seventies, a new house was built for the curate in Two-Mile-Borris and later Fr. Ryan undertook the building of a new parochial house beside the church in Moycarkey.

The mid seventies saw great changes in the management of schools, with the formation of new Boards of Management in 1975. Fr. Daniel guided the smooth change over from the old managerial system to the new boards in all four schools in the parish.

In early January 1987, Fr. Daniel became Associate Pastor at Lisvernane but before the end of that month, he was hospitalised with an aneurism. He never recovered and died, aged 71, on Feb. 1st (Lá le Bríde) 1987 and was buried in Moycarkey churchyard.

Fr. Daniel M. Ryan was much loved among his parishioners and is remembered as a very practical man and for his sincere dedication to the priestly service.

## FR. RICHARD RYAN

*Parish Priest of Moycarkey, Two-Mile Borris and Littleton 1987-2002*

Fr. Richard Ryan, born Aug. 1929, was a native of Bawnbee, Caherconlish, Co. Limerick, but spent most of his priestly ministry in Tipperary parishes. His first year of college was in St Patrick's, Thurles followed by seven in Maynooth, where he was ordained by Archbishop John Charles McQuaid on June 19th 1955. It was to Dublin he was first posted as curate in Raheny Parish (1955 – '60). While there, he was very involved with the youth and was always conscious of the need for

*Fr. Richard Ryan*

sporting facilities. He played an active role in the founding of Raheny G.A.A. Club in 1958. This club went from strength to strength and to-day Fr. Dick's contribution to the club is remembered on a plaque in their clubhouse and the naming of a playing pitch in his memory.

Following a few years as chaplain to the Mercy Sisters in Doon (1960 – '62) and a brief period of service in Ballylanders Co. Limerick (1962 – '64), he was assigned to the Cathedral parish of Thurles (1964 – '80). These were the mid sixties and the years folowing Vatican 11. Fr. Dick is fondly remembered in Thurles not alone for his priestly ministry but also for his involvement in organising many talents - contests in the new Premier Hall.

In 1980, he transferred as curate to Mullinahone Parish and following his ministry there, he was appointed Parish Priest of Moycarkey Borris and Littleton in January 1987.

A man of fine stature and impressive presence, Fr. Dick's kind and gentle disposition endeared him to everyone. Always available and welcoming, his wise counsel was greatly appreciated. The building of Moycarkey School Hall in Pouldine was one of his proud achievements and in the latter years, the various millennium monuments and celebrations.

A well-read man, his affability and warmth endeared him to the school children who always appreciated his classroom visits. Fr. Dick's communication skills, his education and understanding made him a fine preacher, conveying his uplifting message briefly and effectively.

In the later years Fr. Dick was restricted by increasing bouts of ill-health, which he bore with resignation and cheerfulness. Fr. Dick Ryan departed this life on 10th January, 2002. He is buried in Moycarkey Chruch grounds.

In 2003, the Board of Management of Moycarkey N.S., Pouldine unanimously agreed to name the school hall – Halla Uí Riain in his memory.

## FR. GEORGE BOURKE

*Parish Priest of Moycarkey,*
*Two-Mile-Borris and Littleton 2002 –*

*Fr. George Bourke*

Fr. George Bourke is a native of the parish of Ballinahinch-Killoscully. He was ordained in 1968 and began his ministry as a curate in Walkinstown, Dublin (1968-1971); and later served in Kilbehenny (1971-1982), Knocklong (1982-1990) and Borrisoleigh (1990-1993). In 1993, he was appointed parish priest of Cappawhite.

While in Cappawhite, as well as attending to his pastoral duties, he was much associated with the provision of facilities for the community. Fr. George was involved in the formation of the Cappawhite Community Council. Projects carried out by that body include the Community Resource Centre, which greatly enhanced the lives of so many, of all ages, including the 'senior citizens', in their now fully equipped Day Care Centre. Four new classrooms were added to the local National School together with major refurbishment of the existing school.

In June 2002 he was transferred as Parish Priest to Moycarkey / Littleton / Borris. Fr. George has always been very interested in promoting the welfare and well-being of the school community. He supervised the provision of extra accommodation at Moycarkey National School, Pouldine, and was actively instrumental in the purchase, in 2003, of additional land (Two Acres) for the school.

Fr. George's interest in local history is reflected in the publication of Parish Magazines or Journals in some of the parishes where he worked. Cycling and hill walking are among his pastimes, while his love for and willingness to use our native language is obvious to those who know him, and from his regular use of the "cúpla focal" in the weekly parish newsletter.

*Presentation to Tadhg Ó Meachair to mark his retirement from Moycarkey N.S.*
Left to right: Paddy Maher, Joan O'Keeffe, Liam Ó Donnchú, Pauline Treacy, Kathleen Maher, Rev. Fr. Cooney C.C., Tadhg Ó Meachair, Rev. Fr. R. Harkins C.C., Ver Rev. D. M. Ryan P.P., Stephen Kirwan, Bríd Ryan, Ann O'Sullivan, Maura Butler.

*Autumn 1984 – Ms. Pauline Treacy celebrates her retirement with the school staff.*
Left to right: Catherine McGrath, Liam Ó Donnchú, Bríd Ryan, Pauline Treacy, Mary Minchin, Lucy McGann, Very Rev. D. M. Ryan P.P.

*Members of the Board of Management celebrate with Ms. Pauline Treacy on the occasion of her retirement*

*Left to right: Ms. Pauline Treacy, Liam Ó Donnchú, Christy Mooney, Mary Ryan, Mary Butler, Margaret O'Connell, Very Rev. D.M. Ryan P.P.*

*Mrs Mary Heffernan, Kylenoe, gave sterling service to the school over many years.*
*This was marked by a special night of celebration to mark her retirement in 1986.*
Back row: Ms. Mamie Heffernan, Mrs Eileen Concagh, Mrs Madge Dunne, Mr. Christy Mooney,
Ms. Pauline Treacy, Mr Frank Roche, Ms. Bríd Ryan, Mrs. Margaret Hogan, Tadhg Ó Meachair,
Liam Ó Donnchú.

*Workers and Board of Management pictured at the opening of the New School Hall at Pouldine.*
Front row (l.-r.): Jimmy Ryan, Harry Ryan, Chairman, North Tipperary County Council; Very Rev Richard
Ryan P.P., Moycarkey; Liam Ó Donnchú, Mary O'Regan, Michael Purcell, Board of Works; Danny Butler,
Contractor. Back row: Pat, Joe and Seamus Ryan, electricians; Frank Roche, Paddy Ryan, Christy
Mooney, Tom Bourke. Missing from picture: Margaret Hogan, John Lanphier, Dick Cassidy, Danny Pyne.

*Moycarkey N.S. Board of*
*Management 2009*

*Back row (l.-r.):*
*Mrs. Mary Ryan,*
*Mrs. Annette Scott,*
*Mr. Tom Quinn,*
*Mrs. Breda Kinane.*
*Front row (l.-r.):*
*Mr. Joe Byrne (Treasurer),*
*Liam Ó Donnchú (Sec.),*
*Fr. George Bourke P.P.*
*(Chairman).*

*School Year:- Sixth Class 2001-'02*
*Back row: Séamus Cummins, Eamonn Flanagan, Liam Ó Donnchú (Principal), Niall Barry, Conor Skehan. Front row: Sarah Kinane, Margaret Mary McGrath, Laura Heffernan, Sheena O'Dwyer, Martha Dempsey. Absent – Ciarán O'Shea.*

*School Year:- 2002-'03 – Sixth Class*

*Back row: Lorcan O'Hara, Colm Skehan, Pat Molloy, Michael Roche, Daniel O'Regan. Middle row: Liam Ó Donnchú (Principal) Katie Quirke, Kilian O'Hara, Rory Ryan, Iain O'Brien, Jamie Barry. Front row: Laura Maher, Claire Singleton, Ailish O'Keeffe, Anna Harnett, Aisling Hogan, Laura Kirwan. Absent from photo: Jennifer Coote, Vanessa Cawley.*

*School Year:- 2003-'04 – Sixth Class*

*Back row: Niall Hewitt, Brian Butler, Aisling O'Dwyer, Laurie O'Sullivan, Leslie O'Sullivan. Middle row: Loughlin Walsh, Stephen Lirwan, Orlagh McCormack, Megan Ryan, Adam Carew, Helena Ryan, Liam Ó Donnchú (Principal). Front row: Ryan Noonan, Thomas Quigley, Peter Kinane, Finbarr Hayes, Andrea O'Regan, Edwina McGrath.*

# Poems

## *The Jockey*

On the Jockey road they travel fast,
With cars and lorries flying past.
Why don't they stop and rest awhile
And blend with our relaxing style.

They'll meet the men who hurled the ball
And those who alley-cracked the wall
The athletes bold who beat the best
And laid a challenge to the rest.

The Inn it stands with welcome door,
As it had stood in days of yore,
When Bianconi – the stage being done,
Food and drink for everyone.

They'll hear of how in eighty four
We won the 'county' yet once more,
With Bergin leading from centre-back
And Tobin throwing away his cap.

The station house in silence stands,
Recalling trains and travel grand,
While gazing down upon the scene,
Old Killough and its woods serene.

Down there at the cross, stands the school
    of Pouldine,
It prepared us for life and for those days
    I pine-
The best of our lives, no troubles or cares,
Before heading for Thurles and the big iron
    stairs.

If playing at cards appeals to you,
We play the Whist and Twenty-five too,
We love to chat, the yarn and song
And often stay up until forty one.

The farms about are a joy to view,
With corn, beet and barley too,
And cattle grazing in pastures green,
The best in Ireland can be seen.

The Gobaun Saor – he walked this land,
A mason skilled with chisel in hand,
On the 'chalice' Island of Derrynaflan,
He sleeps amid abbots and saintly men.

We'll dance a set before we go'
And drink you health a time or two,
New lifelong friendships found will be
In Tipperary's lovely Horse and Jockey.

*Liam Ó Donnchú*

# *Killough Hill*

At times we read of climbers bold who topped the towering peaks,
In foreign lands through ice and snow, enough to bring the creeps.
No avalanche assailed me and biting blasts were nil,
But linnets sang in hazels as I climbed up Killough Hill.

But sure those hardy climbers will never once describe,
The sights they saw while gazing o'er valleys far and wide
The reason is apparent; the views brought them no thrill,
I wished they scanned Tipperary's plains from the top of Killough Hill.

For from its summit I thought the view a treat,
Moycarkey's bounteous harvest lay spread beneath my feet.
And as a breeze came playing, the picture for to fill,
It waved in all its golden prime for miles around Killough Hill.

I thought of famous hurlers that district always knew,
O'Keeffes and Wall and Condon, Purcell and Sweeper too,
And there's the tendency to play the old game still
While ash will grow and flourish on the slopes of Killough Hill.

And looking to the westward, all foreign scenes might fail,
But that view so charming along the Golden Vale,
Where fertile fields, rich pastures yield, with many a sparkling rill,
And raths and forts, old towers and moats in view of Killough Hill.

Ah! What was 'neath the hazy blue I could not see so well?
But sure I knew that always true, down there was rare Clonmel,
Whose very name recalls some fame, that's sure to live until,
The morning's gleams and shadows fail to chase from Killough Hill.

And memories came crowding of that historic town,
Where Cromwell's mighty Ironsides lost all of their renown
And where its brave defenders the tyrant power did kill,
I felt like shouting 'Up Clonmel' from the top of Killough Hill.

Before I leave my pen away, I'd say to each and all,
If you take to climbing or if you get enthralled,
Don't sigh for great Mount Everest; don't mind the Alps at all,
But if you stray some glorious day, you're safe in life and limb,
The view is great, 'twill compensate for a climb up Killough Hill.

*Pat Bourke, Monamoe, Holycross*

# *Moycarkey Borris*

We salute Moycarkey, Newhill, Leigh,
Rich grasslands, bog and fallow,
Galboola, Ballybeg, Pouldine,
Cloughmartin, Coldfields, Grallagh.

Near Borris, Ballyerk and Noard,
The Black and Clover flowing;
Through Jockey, Littleton and The Pike,
The traffic kept on going.

The Plain of Corc in grandeur lies
In splendid continuity;
From Turtulla to Blackcastle's tower,
I viewed this 'Vale of Beauty'.

Moycarkey's graveyards guard the bones
Of hurlers famed in story,
And Borris boasts of Gaelic hosts
Who won honour, fame and glory.

Here is the grave of John Joe Hayes;
There Maher 'Best' lies sleeping;
In Ballymoreen, the ivy green,
O'er patriots graves is weeping.

The Moycarkey Ryans rush forth like lions
Saying 'Hurrah, my boys, what care we?
Moycarkey's name is held in fame
With the 'Blue and Gold' of Tipperary.

We salute Coolcroo, we've heard of you
And each brave athletic fellow;
To the Seán Treacy Band, and the hurlers grand
Who don the 'Red and Yellow'.

*Joseph Perkins*

# The Grallagh Back Road

THIS SONG used to be my late Uncle Jack Lambe's favourite party song. The song was written by the late James Mullins who was married to the late Josie McCarthy, who was a niece of Jack Lambe. James Mullins died on the 03 February 1946 at the age of 35 years so the song must have been written in the early 40's. They had one son, Davy Mullins and they lived in Ard Mhuire in Thurles. Josie Mullins was well known mid-wife and in later years worked as a nurse during the sugar factory campaigns.

*Paddy Lambe*

It was early one evening on the Grallagh back road
A band of ould tinkers took up their abode,
They remained there just for the night
And early next morning they had a big fight.

*Chorus:*
Singing fol de diddle arum tye arum tye

There were Hanrahan's, O'Reilly's and McCarthy's as well
Some of the names I won't mention to tell.
Said Hanrahan to Reilly, now what brought you here
Said Reilly to Hanrahan, I'm here since last year.

*Chorus*

Then Reilly got up and he looked for a stick
It was then that Hanrahan began to kick,
The kickin' and the beltin' and the noises they made
Sure the curses and swears they would waken the dead.

*Chorus*

I was there myself, all the fight I did see
I saw it all from a big tree,
And if I went out for to make the peace
You can be sure I'd get a fine rap in the face.

*Chorus*

Then just as the fighting was all o'er
Two civic guards came down the road,

And the handcuffs on them they did secure
And they brought them to the barracks in Ballinure.

*Chorus*

Now come all you young tinkers wherever you be
Wherever you go and whoever you see,
And if ever you pass by the Grallagh back road
Be sure and don't take up your abode.

*Chorus*

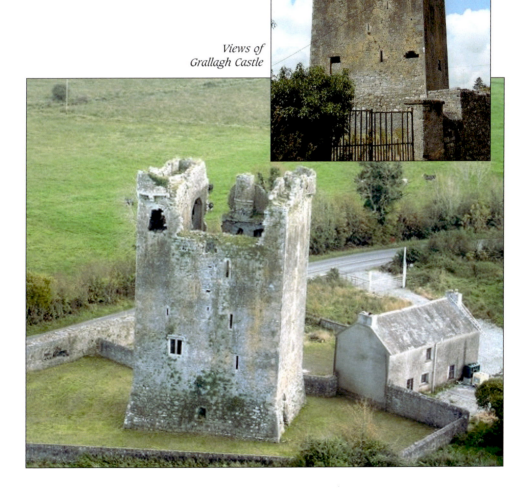

*Views of
Grallagh Castle*

*Shauna Fitzpatrick,
Sixth Class pupil 2008-'09
admiring her artwork
at the Image Art Exhibition
– Spring 2009.*

*St. Patrick's Day Parade, Littleton 2009.
On right is Conor Hartnett,
ready to lead our entry in the parade.*

*Locomotive No. 158 entering
Horse & Jockey Railway
Station in the early 1950s.*

*Ariel views of Moycarkey N.S., Pouldine – June 2009.*

*Confirmation Class 1990*

*Back row:- T.J. O'Brien, Neil Bannon, Noel Maher, David Minchin, Donncha Looby, Patrick Delahunty, Noel Butler, Paul Hogan, Seán Carey, Enda O'Callaghan, Nicky Hogan. Fourth row: Breda and Paula Coman, Dervla Fitzgerald, Shane Murphy, Donal Shanahan, Patrick Lambe, Robert Nagle, Eoghan O'Donoghue, Catherine Stapleton, Fr. Richard Ryan. P.P. Third row: Liam Ó Donnchú, Mrs Mary Minchin, Eileen Looby,, Mairead Looby, Maria McLoughlin, Sandra McCormack, Marguerite Minchin, Linda Dee, Bríd Ryan, Marie Webster, Maria Delaney, Alma Delaney. Second row: Jason Roche, Helena Power, Alma Mullins, Nicola Kavanagh, Fionnuala Concagh, Andrea Murphy. Front row: Linda Power, Catherine Moriarty, Claire O'Mahony, Tara Quigley, Debbie Quigley, ArchBishop Dermot Clifford, Barbara Dunne, Catherine Harrington, Imelda Britton, Maria O'Brien, Claire Molloy, Ciara McCormack. Absent from photo: Mark Leahy, Bríd Lamphier, Claire Skehan.*

*Confirmation Class 2009*

*Back row: Liam Ó Donnchú (Principal), Kathryn Connolly, Lorna O'Regan, Aoife Maher, Michael Flanagan, Maria O'Keeffe, Seán Darmody, Ann Connolly, Fr. George Bourke P.P. Middle row: Patricia Hayes, Eimear Martin, Aaron Hayes, Darragh Ryan, Pádraig Kirwan, Conor Ryan, Jack Kiely, Martha Kirwan, Fr. Joe Tynan C.C. Front row: Maria Kinane, Nora Donoghue, Shauna Fitzpatrick, Most Rev. Dr. Dermot Clifford, Nicole O'Brien, Thomas Mernagh, Rachel Byrne.*

# To Dublin
# via Pouldine

*By: Bríd Ryan*

*Bríd Ryan*

**D**URING MY final exams in Mary Immaculate Training College in Limerick, I was approached by the History Professor, Sr. Celestine and asked if I would be interested in a teaching post near Thurles. The Parish Priest of Moycarkey, Fr. Willie Breen, had asked for someone who could play the harmonium in church. My sights were on Dublin at that time but as this position had to be filled on July lst, I would be paid for the summer holidays. That was a big attraction, so I accepted.

There were no Boards of Management at that time and no formal interviews for teaching jobs in primary schools. Early in June 1957, I called on Fr. Breen and after a chat, he offered me the job. I saw Pouldine for the first time and wondered about the "Deep Hole".

*Pupils from Moycarkey N.S. who met the American Ambassador Jean Kennedy Smith at her residence in the Phoenix Park following success in an art competition. Photograph also includes their teacher Bríd Ryan and Ailish Mullins (parent).*

During the next two weeks I found accommodation in Thurles. My Dad brought me to the school the first morning with my bicycle on the back of the car. I met the Principal Tadhg Maher and the other teacher – Pauline Treacy for the first time. Pauline, very kindly, told me to send the bicycle home and that she would bring me to and from school in her car.

Pouldine School at that time was in what is now Walsh's house across the road from the present school. I had 2nd and 3rd classes in the classroom nearest the road. Pauline Treacy had Infants and 1st class and Tadhg Maher had 4th, 5th and 6th. In my room there was a round iron stove for heating in winter. The turf was supplied by the parents and I had to light the fire every morning. The chimney in my room was very bad and for the first hour or so each morning the room filled with smoke. There was electric light but no other electrical appliance or socket. The kettle for lunch was boiled on the stove. During summer months Kathleen Maher (Tadhg's wife) who lived beside the school provided us with boiling water. The toilet and fuel sheds were at the bottom of the yard.

Later in the sixties Maura Butler joined the staff. Increasing numbers and improved pupil/teacher ratio meant Pouldine was allocated a 4th teacher. Maura had previously taught in Moyne but because of the marriage ban, which applied to all women in the public service, she had to resign her job when she got married. The removal of the ban allowed those women who had resigned to re-enter the work force. Maura took the Infant classes in Pouldine.

It was probably due to the increase in numbers and the need for a new classroom that Fr. Breen began to consider building a new school. The site was across the road in Quinlan's field.

I was absent from school due to illness in 1969-'70 when the move to the 'new school' took place. On my return, I could not believe my eyes – A kitchen, teachers' room, indoor toilets, running water, projectors, tape recorders etc. There was also central heating – no more smoke!

In addition to all the changes in our working conditions, we had a New Curriculum for primary schools. The programme had become 'child centered', which for me was absolutely wonderful. History, Geography, Maths etc. were now centered on the environment of the pupils. Artifacts from childrens' grandparent's time began to appear in school; old oil lamps, box irons, sugán twisters and horses' harness. There were stories about parents and grandparents who had travelled by train from the station at the Horse & Jockey. They were great times.

Music, Art, Drama and Physical Education were also now a very important part of school life. There was even a new Irish programme, "Buntús" with filmstrips and audio tapes. Things were really looking up and we all began to enjoy ourselves. We went on walking trips along the old railway line to the station at Horse & Jockey. We followed the

*Moycarkey N.S. Parents Council make a presentation to Ms. Bríd Ryan to mark her retirement (l.-r.): Ella Coman, Michael Dempsey, Catherine O'Brien, Kathleen Kirwan, Mary Skehan, Bríd Ryan, Breda Kinane, Joan Singleton, Margaret O'Dwyer.*

Cloughrane River under the stone bridge on the Galboola Road. We climbed Killough and even went as far as the Devil's Bit and the Graves of the Leinster Men beside Lough Derg. The school inspector suggested I should get an ordinance survey map of the area. I still remember the day I walked across the Phoenix Park in stiletto heels to buy that map in the Ordinance Survey office. I had not realised the office was so far in from the main gate. We made great use of that map and it was on the wall until I retired with very little changes. I wonder what the present one looks like with motorways, roundabouts etc.?

Tadhg Maher retired in 1976 and Liam Ó Donnchú came as Principal. Maura Butler left to teach in the Presentation Convent Primary School in Thurles and Mary Minchin replaced her. Pupil numbers were still increasing and in 1978 Lucy McGann joined the staff. There were quite a few changes after that and now two of my past pupils, Ann-Marie Carroll and Fionnuala Hayes are teaching in the school.

A new hall was built in the school grounds in 1989. Now we could do Drama, Plays and P.E. in comfort with the assistance of Donie Shanahan who moved and arranged the furniture and equipment so competently. Thank you Donie for your patience and good humour. Thanks also to Mrs. Heffernan, Mrs. Loughnane and Mrs. Cassidy who kept the school in such good condition during my years on the staff.

Now that I have retired, I spend a lot of time in Dublin, where I had first intended going all those years ago. However, I am so glad I made the decision to go to Pouldine. They were very happy years due mainly to the wonderfully loving children that it was my privilege to teach. I still meet them everywhere. Sometimes they have to remind me of their names. They forget that they no longer look like ten year olds! It is always a great pleasure to meet them and I feel so proud of them all.

***(Bríd Ryan was a teacher in Pouldine School from 1957 until 1998)***

**School year:- 2004-'05 Sixth Class**

Back row:- Richard O'Keeffe, Christopher Byrne, Cathal Gleeson Fahey, Merriman Mogridge, Kieran Stapleton. Middle row: Andrew Fogarty, Joey Coman, Peadar Kinane, Fern Freeman, Michelle Carew, Timmy Ryan, Jamie Maher, Liam Ó Donnchú (Principal). Front row: Eleanor Kiely, Marita Moloney, Karen Corbett, Klara Martin, Ciara Maher, Corina Abbott, Shauna Flanagan, Roisin Mogridge.

**School Year:- 2005-'06 Sixth class**

Back row: Antonia McGrath, Maryese Noonan, Michelle Rose Ryan, Niamh Butler, donna Marie Cawley, Melissa Morris, Nora Connolly. Front row: Tommy Noonan, Conor Hayes, Aidan Fitzpatrick, Liam Ó Donnchú (Principal) William O'Dwyer, Jamie Costello, Kieran Lyons.

School Year:- 2006-'07 Sixth Class
Back row: Liam Ó Donnchú (Principal), Kathelln Donoghue, Michelle Sheppard, Michaela Graham, Ciara Darmody, Marguerite McCormack.
Front row: Tomás Ryan, Oisín Copeland, Cody Jackson, Aaron Flanagan, Paddy Donoghue, Gavin O'Brien.

# Donie . . . A Man
# for All Seasons

'Where's Donie?', is a call regularly heard around Pouldine School. When anything breaks down it is to the caretaker, Donie Shanahan that we look for help. This has been the case since 1990, when Donie first became involved with the school. Prior to that Donie had been employed as an assistant supervisor at Thurles Sugar Factory, until it ceased production in 1989. But Donie has 'more strings to his bow', as you will soon see.

Donie's childhood was spent in the Quarry, Mitchel Street, Thurles, growing up on Clobanna Terrace. Music has permeated his life ever since his mother bought him his first guitar at Hanafins in 1962. This was a Martini Electric Guitar and cost 150 guineas. Following a few pertinent pointers from neighbour and friend Ber Diggins, Donie was now ready for the stage and to face the world. The group *The Dy-Undead* was formed and they played at the 'Hops' in John Joe Bourke's carpentry shop on Friday nights and also in the Glenmorgan House and the Muintir na Tíre Hall in Thurles. Donie was a 'natural' guitarist, with a great ear for music and always found it easy to pick up tunes. Along with him in the group were the Murphys-Jimmy and John, Eamonn Lyons and Dick Keogh. The new Premier Hall opened in 1964 and the group entered a major talent competition at this venue. Packed houses and excitement gripped the town as the finals approached and especially when the *Dy-Undead* were proclaimed winners.

This beat-group now progressed to showband status. Their fame had spread outside

*School caretaker Donie Shanahan with school Principal Liam Ó Donnchú.*

*The Cossacks Showband (l.-r.): Donie Shanahan, Kevin Nevin, Dick Keogh, Pat Diggins, Martin Lanigan, Ber Diggins, Jimmy Byrne (lead singer).*

Thurles and the group, now known as The Gentiles (Hit Single-Marlene) and later Simon King and the Visions began to tour to venues not alone in Ireland but to the Irish Clubs in the major cities of England, Wales and Scotland. Managed by Honey Promotions, they also had the regular date at the Eamonn Andrews 'New Spotlight Night Out' in Cork and in Harcourt Street, Dublin. While here, they were voted the Best Young Band in 1970 in a competition compered by Larry Gogan.

Donie has great memories of playing at the American Airforce Base in High Wickham and on the revolving stage in the Gresham on Holloway Road. While touring, he also shared the stage with some of the 'greats':- Joe Loss, The Tremolos, The Trogs, Ronnie Wood and The Move, Steve Ellis and Love Affair, Dave Clark Five and many others including the legendary Jimmy Hendrix.

Donie, playing Rhythm or Lead Guitar, has from time to time been with other bands such as The Cossacks, Jack Hanly and in the 1980s with Mick Delahunty, until they disbanded. In more recent years he has been the main cog in the popular Cottonfields Band with Sean Boyle, Eddie Ryan and Tony Power, as they tour the pub circuit. The next generation is also there as Donie's eldest son Brian is now in that group.

Donie doesn't have much time for many of today's performers with their miming, manufactured music and backing tracks. 'None of that in our time', he says. He rates The Freshmen, a band from Belfast, as among the best he has seen. As guitarists he admires Jimmy Page of Led Zeppelin and Merle Haggard.

But back to Pouldine after all that travelling. As caretaker Donie takes great pride in the school and maintains the grounds impeccably, giving them the same attention as he

*The Visions Showband (l.-r.): Johnny Rush, Donie Shanahan, Eamon Lyons (lead singer), Kevin Nevin, John Murphy, Jimmy Murphy, Jimmy Cotter.*

would to his own lawn at home. For a rural national school the grounds are extensive and maintaining them is demanding. Donie on his ride-on mower is a familiar sight at any time of the day. He is an expert when dealing with mechanical and electrical problems in the school and is not fazed by modern technology. Be it a computer, printer, lawnmower or the like that breaks down, he is on hand with the necessary tools and the knowledge to repair the fault. Problem solving gives him great satisfaction, but he laughs it off and with a toss of his head makes light of his success.

During the summer holidays he can be seen, on his knees, painting the many markings in the school yard. The Hopscotch Squares, the Snake, the Circles etc. have to be upgraded after the wear and tear of the previous year and the pupils really appreciate the top-class play-areas that they enjoy. This is seen and heard at every school gathering when the biggest cheer from pupils, parents and staff is reserved for such a dedicated caretaker.

Donie is also involved with the many activities that take place outside school time. The school hall is popular for parish social activities e.g. Whist, Set-dancing, Medal Presentations etc. and Donie is again 'on call' to make sure that everything is in order. He is first to be called out when the school alarm sounds. This can be at any hour but whatever hour it is, he is there. A Hard Day's Night indeed!

Not all the tasks of a school caretaker are pleasant. Toilets get blocked, children puke, septic tank can act up, but Donie doesn't complain. His determination to solve the problem and to ensure that the situation returns to normal as soon as possible is paramount. He admits that he gets great satisfaction from the challenge offered by the variety of tasks he is asked to perform. The fact that the school is so near his home is an added attraction to his work.

Though born in the town, his roots are deeply embedded in the hills of Kilcommon and he likes nothing better than taking a spin there and meeting the cousins. Donie's wife Ann (Ryan) and the entire family have, over the years helped the school. They can all be happy in the knowledge that Donie's dedicated work is really appreciated by all the school community.

*Treasured memories of Santa's visits.*

(Organised by Parents Council)

# Moycarkey National School – Parents' Council

THE Parents' Council was established in October 1995. The first Chairperson was Geraldine O'Hara, who instigated the founding of the Council. It was decided from the start that the council would not simply be a fund-raising committee but would assist the Principal and staff in whatever way we could. We got involved with the School Sports Evening which had proved to be a tremendous success. Another big hit was the Graduation Disco held each June and attended by fifth and sixth class pupils. A certificate is presented to each sixth class member to commemorate their time in the school.

The Council also assists with the financing of the Swimming, which takes place each year. It also finances the Set Dancing in which first Paddy Cooney and now his son Michael teaches the pupils (no one with two left feet in the school now). Financial support has also been given for the provision of Computers, Sports Equipment, Music Lessons and Letterland etc.

The Book Scheme is a very beneficial scheme in the school. It facilitates the recycling of schoolbooks. That means no more boxes of old books stored in the home.

Fashion shows, Table Quizzes, Sponsored Walks, Card Nights and Race Nights are all functions used to raise funds to help us meet our financial commitments and a great deal of thanks is due to the parents and parishioners, who support us on every occasion.

The following are the founding Parents' Council officers:-

*Chairperson:* Geraldine O'Hara, Dromgower
(1995 – 1998)
*Secretary:* Breda Kinane, Kevinsfort (1995 – 1998)
Treasurer: Joan Singleton, Graigue (1995 – 1998)
*P.R.O.:* Mary Skehan, Knockroe (1995 – 1998)

*Geraldine O'Hara*

*Moycarkey N.S. Parents' Council 2008-'09*

*Front row (l.-r.): Robert Hayes, Mary Ryan, Catherine O'Brien, Joe Byrne, Paschalina Ely, Michelle Donnelly, Breda Ryan, Ann-Marie Looby. Back row (l.-r.): Sylvana Murphy, Caroline Stapleton, Hannie Maher, Pauline Whelan, Teresa Tobin, Norma O'Regan, Annette Scott, Esther O'Meara, Olivia Maxwell, Natalie O'Callaghan, Norma Ryan/Fahy, Patricia Connolly, Kathleen Brown, Helen Dowling, Demelza Butler, Una O'Sullivan, James White. Missing from photo: Ann Fogarty, Julia Kennedy, Marie Gilleece, Majella Tobin.*

*Peter Kinane struts his stuff.*

*Parents' Council Fashion Show – April 2000. On the Catwalk – David Kinane.*

*Rita Flanagan, Catherine O'Brien and Lucy McGann in fine style.*

*Fashion Show in Halla Uí Riain*
*From left to right: Lucy McGann, Ann-Marie Carroll, Joe Byrne and Mary Mullins.*

*Mr Joe Byrne*
*– Parents' Council*
*Chairman makes a*
*presentation to*
*Mrs. Aileen Colton*
*to mark her retirement.*

*Flowers for Aileen*
*– Mrs. Mary Minchin,*
*Mrs. Aileen Colton*
*and Mr. Joe Byrne at*
*Aileen's retirement*
*celebration.*

*Parents' Council members at the St. Patrick's Day Parade, Littleton (l.-r.): Kathleen Kirwan, Breda Kinane and Margaret O'Dwyer.*

Then followed by:-

*Chairperson:* Breda Kinane, Kevinsfort 1998 - 2004
Joe Byrne, Moycarkey 2004 - 2009

*Secretary:* Margaret O'Dwyer, Galboola 1998 - 2007
Michelle Donnelly, Aughnagomaun 2007 -

*Treasurer:* Michael Dempsey, Shanballa & Ella Coman, Galboola 1998 - 1999
Louise Meaney 1999 - 2000
Hannie Maher, Coolkennedy 2000 -

*P.R.O.:* Michael Dempsey, Shanballa 1998 - 1999
Joan Singleton, Graigue 1999 - 2001
Sylvana Murphy, Thurles 2001 -

*Book Scheme Co-ordinators:* Catherine O'Brien, Beakstown
Jacqueline Corbett, Shanballa
Nathalie O'Callaghan, Turtulla.

Moycarkey National School Parents Council

## Fashion Show

Wednesday 12th April
8:00 pm
School Hall

Participating stores:
CASUALS, DUNNES STORES
EN PARIS, HEATONS
LIFESTYLE SPORTS, STYLE MAN

Members of the Tipp All Ireland
camogie team will be taking part

Admission £5

# National Schools
# – Important Dates

| | |
|---|---|
| 1828 | Report from the Select Committee on Education in Ireland |
| 1829 | Catholic Emancipation |
| 1831 | Establishment of the National School System (Stanley Letter) |
| 1850 | Synod of Thurles. Establishment of Catholic University of Ireland |
| 1868 | Irish National Teachers Organisation founded, with Vere Foster as its first President. |
| 1872 | Payment of teachers by results made nationwide. |
| 1873 | Teacher contract of employment introduced |
| 1900 | Revised programme for National Schools |
| 1904 | Bi-lingual programme |
| 1918 | Salary paid monthly, directly to teachers |
| 1922 | New programme for National Schools |
| 1924 | Department of Education set up (in the Irish Free State). An Roinn Oideachais |
| 1926 | Compulsory attendance legislation passed. Founding of Preparatory Colleges for student teachers. |
| 1929 | Primary Certificate (optional). |
| 1934 | Marriage ban on female teachers introduced. Revised programme for National Schools. |
| 1943 | Primary Certificate made compulsory. |
| 1944 | Local Authority Scholarship Act introduced. |
| 1948 | Staffing of schools based on enrolment rather than attendance. |
| 1958 | End of marriage ban on female National Teachers, after 25 years. |
| 1961 | Preparatory Colleges closed |
| 1962 | First State Grant for National School maintenance. |

| | |
|---|---|
| 1963 | Reference Library scheme for National Schools introduced. |
| 1965 | Psychological service set up in Department of Education. |
| | Policy of closure of small National Schools announced and widely debated. |
| 1966 | Maynooth College opened to lay students. |
| 1967 | Free Second Level Education Scheme. |
| | School Transport Scheme introduced. |
| 1968 | Abolition of Primary Certificate. |
| | Third Level student grants introduced. |
| 1969 | First Regional and Technical Colleges established. |
| | Common salary scale for teachers. |
| 1971 | New Curriculum for National Schools introduced. |
| | New Equipment grants for National Schools. |
| | Opening of first Teacher Centre. |
| 1972 | Report on Education of the Deaf. |
| | School-leaving age raised to fifteen. |
| 1974 | Length of Training for National Teachers extended from two to three years. |
| 1974 | Bachelor of Education degree course instituted for National Teachers. |
| | Colleges of Education recognised by N.U.I. |
| 1975 | Boards of Management for National Schools established. |
| 1977 | Equal pay for all teachers introduced. |
| 1978 | Department grants for caretakers in large schools. |
| 1982 | Corporal punishment abolished in National Schools. |
| 1985 | National Parents' Council established. |
| | Career Break scheme introduced. |
| 1986 | Carysfort Teacher Training College closed. |
| 1990 | Psychological Service (pilot project) initiated. |
| 1993 | Stay Safe programme introduced. |
| 1996 | Breaking the Cycle scheme set up. |
| 1997 | RSE programme introduced. |
| | Board of Management reformed to include members of the wider community. |
| 1998 | Information Technology in Primary Schools.  Each school receives a computer and free access to the internet. |
| 2000 | Education Act passed. |
| 1999 | Revised Curriculum launched. |
| 2000 | Education Welfare Act passed. |
| | Irish Primary Principals' Network established. |
| 2001 | Teaching Council Act passed into law. |
| 2002 | Report from Benchmarking Body on Public Service pay. |
| 2003 | Education Welfare Board Established. |
| 2006 | Teaching Council Established. |
| 2008-'09 | Major cutbacks in Education Funding.  Moritorium on promotions and recruitment in the Public Service. |

# Liam Ó Donnchú
## School Principal 1976-2009

L IAM Ó DONNCHÚ was born in Hollyford, Tipperary, and attended the local national school, where his father was principal teacher. On his father's retirement, the family moved to Thurles and Liam was a student at Thurles C.B.S. secondary school. Following his Leaving Certificate examination in 1967, he accepted a 'Call to Training' at St. Patrick's College of Education in Drumcondra, Dublin. Having qualified as a National Teacher in 1969, his first post was at Holy Spirit B.N.S. in Ballymun on the northern outskirts of Dublin city. While in Dublin, he continued his studies gaining a B.A. from U.C.D. and the Higher Diploma in Education at Trinity College. In 1976, Tadhg Ó Meachair retired as Principal at Moycarkey N.S., Pouldine and Liam applied successfully for the position.

A great lover of all sports particularly hurling, Liam played for many years with Thurles Sarsfields G.A.A. Club and was, in later years, secretary and chairman of that club. Producing G.A.A. publications has occupied much of his spare time, over the years, as Editor of match programmes at Semple Stadium and as Secretary of Tipperary G.A.A.

*Newly appointed
School Principal
– Mr Robert White
makes presentations,
on behalf of the school staff,
to Liam Ó Donnchú
and his wife Catherine
to mark his retirement.
(June 26th 2009)*

***Múinteoirí 2008-'09***

*Back row (l.-r.):
Ms. Sara Horgan,
Liam  Ó Donnchú,
(Principal),
Mrs. Mary Minchin,
Ms. Lucy McGann.
Front row (l.-r.):
Mrs. Fionnuala Hayes,
Mrs. Ann Marie Carroll,
Mr. Robert White,
Ms. Fiona McCullagh,
Ms. Elaine Brady.*

Yearbook. A founder member of Lár na Páirce Interpretive Centre in Thurles, Liam has been for many years P.R.O. of Semple Stadium, where he mans the P.A. on match days. He has played an important role in the development of the Stadium, highlights being the Centenary All Ireland there in 1984, Féile music festival in the nineties, right through to the recent refurbishment and floodlighting of the venue. He also found time to continue his studies and was conferred with an M.A. at U.C.C. in the late nineties.

As Principal, Liam's early years were occupied with the introduction of the New Curriculum and the provision of resources to successfully introduce the changing emphasis of the curriculum. These years also saw major changes in the management structures of primary schools with the coming of Boards of Management. Even though the school building was new, it soon was proving too small to accommodate the pupil population and the lack of a proper school hall was being sorely felt. Liam and the Board of Management addressed these challenges not merely through the support of the Department of Education but on many occasions by using local initiative – Halla Uí Riain is testament to that. Over the years Liam has initiated many projects, refurbishments and developments at Pouldine.

As a teacher, Liam was always a great believer in the importance of pupils getting a solid grounding in the basics of literacy and numeracy, while in primary school. Their future education would have a sound foundation on which to progress. He also imbued in his pupils a thirst for knowledge, as he challenged their young minds – Give them Roots to Grow and Wings to Fly. He was also very conscious of the importance of support teaching being provided to pupils that needed it. Liam was always to the fore in the promotion of our native language and saw the local school the correct vehicle for the promotion of local customs and pastimes such as hurling, set-dancing, athletics etc.

Liam, who retired in Sept. 2009, is married to Catherine and lives in Ballymoreen. Their children: Eoghan, Muireann, Neasa and Kilian are all past-pupils of Pouldine. He can be happy in the knowledge that during his stewardship, the school went from strength to strength.

*Is saibhre ár n-iothlainn i do dhiaidh.*

*Sixth class pupils 2008/09. Also included are Pádraig Fahey, Donie Shanahan and Liam Ó Donnchú.*

*Whist nights in Pouldine*

# Will You Whist!

**W**HEN OUR school hall was built in 1989, it proved an invaluable resource for the pupils and staff of the school, but it was always envisaged that the facility would be made available to the local community for various activities. Many groups have used the hall over the years but none can match the whist players for their regular weekly gathering there.

Of course Moycarkey and its locality is famous for card players and their love of cards and the hall wasn't long in being before it was being "eyed up" as an ideal venue for whist. Indeed whist had been played in the old hall in the village of Moycarkey in the sixties and early seventies but this had lapsed in the following years.

*Whist Players at Pouldine – Summer 2009*
*Back row (l.-r.): Michael Gleeson, John Purcell, Christy Mooney, Michael O'Connell, Barry McNamee, Tess Hogan, Kay Hennessy, Margaret Butler, Nancy Ryan (Coldfields), Breda Moloughney, Annie Stakelum, Breda O'Regan, Alice O'Connell, Anne Bourke, Ellen Hennessy, Tom Allen, Joe Mockler, John McGinley, Pat Fanning. Front row (l.-r.): Liam Ó Donnchú, Kathleen Kelly, Annie Phelan, Peggy Bannon, Nonie Ryan, Statia Ryan, Roseanne Corcoran, Kitty Dwyer, Marie Scott, Nancy Eviston, Nancy Ryan (Maxfort), Joan Moloughney.*

Fr Dick Ryan P.P. was keen to see the hall in the school used by the locals and encouraged Christy Mooney, Ashfield, Ted and Nancy Ryan, Maxfort to give the whist a go, in the new hall. This was 1992 and what was started then, went from strength to strength, into regular Tuesday night whist, all year round.

Money generated by the whist had gone to support the school and many of the resources that the pupils now enjoy resulted from the whist. Not only did the school benefit but also many local organisations such as the I.C.A., Moycarkey Coolcroo A.C., Horse and Jockey Handball Club etc. who ran Whist Drives and Poker Classics in the hall.

The whist also supported the foreign missions with great card nights in the hall to benefit Fr. Jim Foley's mission in South America and Fr. Paudie Moloughney's (Laharden) work in Brazil and further afield.

*Nancy and Ted Ryan, Maxfort.*

It is impossible to quantify the great contribution made by Christy Mooney to the ongoing success of the Whist. He gets great assistance from Kathleen Kirwan – Laurel Lodge, Breda Kinane – Kevinsfort and Mary Bourke – Ballyhudda, Margaret Butler – Drom Inch and many of the regulars attending lend a hand as required, particularly Kathleen Kelly.

On the ordinary Tuesday night along with the locals from Moycarkey, you are likely to meet men and women from Littleton, Two-Mile-Borris, Holycross, Thurles, Loughmore, The Ragg, Templemore, Gortnahoe, Kilcooly, Johnstown, Dundrum and Cashel. For the bigger Whist Drives and the famous Christmas Monster Whist with thirty tables filled, the card lovers travel from as far a field as Kilmanagh, Piltown, Tullaroan, St. Mary's, Johnstown, Tipperary Town etc. Of course, the prizes are very attractive on these nights, and the excellent catering is a vital part of the night. No one will leave the hall hungry, whatever about winning a prize!

The night is billed to start at 8.30 p.m. but most will admit that it's nearer to 9.00 p.m. before the ball is thrown in and the action begins. They play twenty games with a break after ten. The break gives an opportunity for that important chat and maybe that longed for trip outside for a smoke. In the days before smoking bans, no such trip was necessary, the hall was famous for smoke and it was often difficult to see the end of the hall – so thick was the plume. The Whist finishes around 10.30 p.m. but the cards don't finish then as the games of "25" can go on long into the night.

The card – players are a happy-go-lucky bunch. They love the comradeship and the social aspect of card playing. For some however the skill of card playing is serious business and an unfortunate beginner or a slow player could regret not seeing the "obvious". Overall, it's a great night and the highlight of the week for many and long may it last.

As the poet wrote:-

*If playing at cards appeals to you,*
*We play the whist and twenty-five too,*
*We love to chat the yarn and song*
*And often stay up till "forty one".*

# Some Interesting Finds from Littleton Bog

*Ariel view of the monastic site of Derrynaflan, known locally as The Island.* (Photo: Kenny Fethard)

O
VER THE years, many objects have been found in Littleton bog. These have been accidental finds made by local turf cutters and in more recent years by Bord na Móna employees. The extensive machinery used by the Bord occasionally unearths secrets of the past. The list of finds demonstrates the great ability of bog-lands to preserve and the list of finds includes items of clothing such as coats and cloaks, leather bags and shoes, weapons of bronze and iron, shields, personal ornaments, well preserved wooden objects such as dishes and troughs, trackways, tubs of 'bog butter' etc. The fertile 'island' of Derrynaflan in Littleton bog, has yielded a treasure trove of ecclesiastical objects. The National Museum of Ireland now holds all these items. Hereunder is a brief account of some of these finds.

## CLONOURA OR LITTLETON SHIELD

In the 1960s, a small plain Iron Age shield was found in Littleton Bog in the townland of Clonoura. The shield board is made of thin sheets of alderwood, covered on the face and back in sheets of calf hide. These are fastened together with strips of leather stitching around the edges. The hand-grip is of oakwood, covered in leather. It is 57 x 35 cm. The front of the shield is scarred by ancient cuts and incisions which come no doubt from the field of battle. Some are slash marks while others resulted by stabbing.

## THE LITTLETON SWORD

In 1989 a local man found a Late Bronze Age leaf-shaped sword under a togher (trackway across the bog) in Littleton Bog, near Longfordpass North.

## THE HURLING BALL

In May 1960 a hurling ball was uncovered in Littleton bog. It was found in the townland of Bawnreagh by Mr. Todd Fanning of Ballydavid, Littleton, and came to light in the spoil from one of Bord na Móna's railway drains, which had been excavated to a depth of two metres. Archaeologist Etienne Rynne dated this find at about two hundred years. The core of the ball was hard and solid and made of the felted body hairs of either horse or ox. Around the core, twoply cord, made 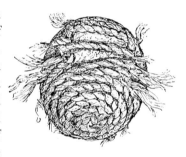 from the tail hairs of a horse was wound spirally. Another archaeologist, A.T. Lucas, concluded that the depth at which the ball was discovered was appreciably greater before the bog was drained. This would age the ball to at least six hundred years.

## TOGHER AT LONGFORD PASS NORTH

A togher is a wooden trackway traversing boggy or wetland areas. Following the discovery by a Bord na Móna worker of a Late Bronze Age leaf-shaped sword between the timbers of an exposed togher at Littleton Bog, Co. Tipperary, a team from the National Museum of Ireland investigated the site.

At least three toghers run through this section of Littleton Bog. That investigated is the most northerly. It runs in a south-west-north-east direction and can be traced on the ground for a length of 400m. It is cut through in several places by Bord na Móna drainage ditches. The surface of the trackway has been damaged by the passage of machinery and by having been exposed to the elements for a long period of time.

At the find spot of the sword, an area 6m x 8m was investigated. Here the trackway was approx. 4.5m wide. It was delimited on the south by a large oak beam 4.9m long. The rest of the trackway consisted of birch logs and some smaller redeposited planks - some with square perforations for pegs. On the north side of the trackway the planks were less rigidly structured and were lying at different angles to the main body of the togher. These were overlain by a series of birch logs parallel to the oak beam. The road at this point appeared to show two periods of construction. The oak planks were displaced and covered by the birch logs. The bronze sword was found amongst the redeposited oak planks. The deposition of the sword appeared to have taken place during the secondary rebuilding of the trackway.

## TOGHER AT 'DERRYNAFLAN', LURGOE

Peat-milling operations in the bog around Derrynaflan revealed traces of a number of wooden trackways. At least four could be traced between the bog islands of Derrynaflan and Derrynabrone to the east. Part of one of these was excavated. It consisted of straight, trimmed ash or hazel branches, up to 4m in length and 40-160mm in diameter, laid in a single layer along the line of the road. Small birch rods 15-30mm in diameter, with pointed ends, were scattered between the larger timbers. The trackway measured 1m in width and the timbers were held in place by vertical posts set 0.5m apart on either side. The trackway lay at a depth of 1.1 m and preliminary pollen analysis suggests that it is prehistoric – probably Bronze Age – in date.

## THE DERRYNAFLAN HOARD

Derrynaflan, also referred to as the Gobaun Saor, is a small 'island', thirty hectares in area, of dry fertile land situated in Littleton Bog in the townland of Lurgoe. The monastery there was an important foundation in the period preceding the Viking raids; the present modest ruins of a small Cistercian nave-and-chancel abbey church there, however, date from a later period. Situated on the territorial border of Éile and Éogonacht, Derrynaflan appears to have flourished between the early eighth century and the early-to-mid ninth century when it was one of the most important centres of the céli Dé reform movement. After the death in 847 of its patron Feidlimid mac Crimthainn, King-Bishop of Cashel, the monastery appears to have declined although there are ruins of ecclesiastical buildings of possibly thirteenth-century date.

The Derrynaflan Hoard was discovered on February 17th 1980 by Michael Webb from Clonmel and his son, also Michael, while they were exploring the ancient monastic site of Derrynaflan with a metal detector. It was concealed near the pre-Romanesque church within the monastic enclosure. The hoard was probably secreted during the turbulent 10th to 12th centuries, when Viking raids and dynastic turmoil created many occasions when valuables were hidden. The early and later 10th century is marked by a particular concentration of hoarding in Ireland.

## THE CHALICE

Similar in construction to the Ardagh Chalice, with a gold filigree band of panels below the rim, emblazoned with amber studs, the Derrynaflan Chalice is made from more valuable metals but with less decoration, although it does display more gold filigree ornamentation. In addition, its three main components (cup, stem

and foot) are connected more securely, by means of a hollow stem rather than a copper bolt. This advance in metallurgical connecting technique (along with the silver filigree decoration of the paten) suggests it was made after the Ardagh Chalice - probably in the ninth century.

## THE DERRYNAFLAN PATEN

The Derrynaflan Paten – type of shallow metal plate for holding the bread during the Eucharist – was assembled by Celtic metalworkers from over 300 separate components. The dish is made from beaten silver, trimmed with silver wire mesh bordered by a ring of gold filigree panels.

The fine gold wire is roped then woven into a zoomorphic pattern surrounded with a field of knotwork. The intricate metallurgical design-work on the twenty four panels includes images of kneeling men back to back, sharp fanged animals, one eagle and two serpents all part of a triskele pattern with spirals and interlace. The spirals and knotting are pressed out into gold and silver foil side panels bordered by knitted silver and copper wire. The rim of the paten is decorated with 24 gold and polychrome glass and niello (metallic sulfide) studs. The silver filigree workmanship indicates the influence of Viking craftsmen, while its design-work derives from traditional Celtic art.

## THE STRAINER

A decorated strainer-ladle made around the same time as the paten was also part of the Derrynaflan Hoard and was probably used for symbolic purification of the Eucharistic wine.

## THE LITTLETONIAN PERIOD

Knowledge of the human past is greatly enhanced by the study of the natural world connected with or modified by human activity. This environmental evidence derived from the study of pollen, spores and other microscopic particles (palynology) from the bogs in Tipperary has been such a rich source, that a phase of the current Irish postglacial period is known as the 'Littletonian' after Littleton Bog.

## SOURCES
North Munster Studies, Edited by Etienne Rynne
Department of the Environment, Heritage and Local Government. Website www.excavations.ie
Local History Notes, Liam Ó Donnchú
Scéal na hIomána, Liam P. Ó Caithnia
A Heritage Gazetteer of North Tipperary – Siobhán Geraghty
The Prehistoric Archaeology of Ireland – John Waddell
The Bogs of Ireland – John Feehan, Grace O'Donovan.

# The School
# at the Cross

**M**OYCARKEY National School played an important part in the local community of Moycarkey. Its influences stretched from the Horse & Jockey to Turtulla Cross, and from Graigue to Ballymoreen. And through it passed countless young Tipperary students who learned about numbers, letters and life – and I as a past pupil am proud to count myself as one of them.

*Robert Nagle.*

I was a young four year old starting school in 1982. Garret Fitzgerald was Taoiseach and Kilkenny with Brian Cody in the team were the reigning All-Ireland Hurling champions. My early memories are vague but I recall Ms. McGann as our teacher in Baby Infants. Through the exploits of Ann and Barry, we learned to read and write and back then through a child's eyes the school seemed huge. To run around the building during lunch was akin to a marathon!

Mrs. Minchin was next to shepherd us through High Infants and First Class. The big occasions of First Confession and Holy Communion loom large in my memory of this time- we might have been bold but we were also God-fearing. In the months before hand, we would be brought to Moycarkey Church for practise and we recited our prayers everyday. And when the big day came, we ran around the churchyard lawns in the May sunshine and collected cards with crisp pound notes in them.

In Second Class we were reunited with Ms. McGann again. I recall our collective shock one day when the boys were kept in for knitting and sewing, while the girls went out for football- such injustice! This is perhaps an example of the other important skills and crafts we learned outside of the academic lessons- including music, singing, dancing, painting and drama. Ms. McGann would even have us doing aerobics to warm us up on the cold winter mornings!

The highlight of the day would be the games we would play during sos and lunchtime, the football matches of course, but also 'tig', bulldog, stick in the mud and many more whose names are long forgotten. At the end of lunch we would all line up in our respective classes in the school yard before filing into the cloakroom to change into our indoors (slippers). We would also get great excitement out of the fortnightly visit to Thurles Swimming Pool and once a week the Master would bring us out to practise the skills of hurling and football from which many a fine Moycarkey player evolved.

Ms Ryan taught us for Third and Fourth Class. I can remember learning to play the theme tune to Glenroe on the tin whistle and wondering what the big fuss about *long division* was all about. Academics were coming more into focus at this stage and schemes such as the Chip Books helped foster a good learning environment. We were also discovering about our culture and the school tours down through the years were scenes of mayhem and merriment. The poor teachers trying to control a bus full of children giddy from Fanta and Mars bars while visiting the sites and scenery of the country. There was one memorable trip through the Vee where we ran around the hills like wild things!

The final years of Fifth and Sixth Class were taught by the Master, Mr Ó Donnchú. Along with the lessons and homework he would entertain us with quizzes and riddles and should you know the correct answer you could become the proud owner of a new pencil sharpener or ruler as a reward! As the senior kids in the school we were entrusted with responsibilities such as ringing the school bell, taking the roll (*an rolla* to some), collecting the school milk, and for the boys a morning off once a week to serve as altar boys. Those final years marked the building of the current school hall, which was a most welcome addition as it allowed us to play indoor soccer or enjoy set-dancing, when it was raining.

After leaving for secondary school and even beyond, the school still played a pivotal role in our lives as a centre of the community. We caught the secondary school bus into Thurles from Pouldine cross every morning and got dropped off there again coming home in the evenings. There we would hang around the bike shed for hours chatting and joking. There was also many a happy evening spent playing football in the yard or on the pitches. Into later life now, I still return to my old classrooms to vote in the elections and referendums which shape our broader society.

Looking back now I have many fond memories of Moycarkey NS. It was where childhoods were moulded and nurtured and it is a testament to the teachers and staff that many of the past pupils have gone on to live successful lives. It was where we gained valuable learning experiences and built friendships and it just goes to show that the friends I made at the school at the cross are still my best friends today.

*(Rob Nagle, Schooldays in Moycarkey N.S., Pouldine, 1982-1990)*

# Sport for All

*By: Robert White*

THERE IS more to life in school than 'The Three Rs'. Many people's fondest memories of their schooldays are associated with the games and sports they either played at break and lunch-time or during Physical Education classes. Indeed some of Ireland's greatest sports stars first developed their 'grá' of sport in Primary School. Pouldine is no different to the hundreds of other schools throughout Ireland in that respect. The locality carries with it a fine tradition of excellence in sport. The local GAA club, Moycarkey-Borris has no less than 14 County Senior Hurling titles to their name and the parish has a proud tradition of success in Handball and Athletics. Many of the players on those teams have attended Primary School in Pouldine.

Just as the school academic year runs from September to June, so too does its sporting calendar. The school enters numerous competitions each year in many varying sports as well as having 'in-school' competitions to hone and nourish the skills needed for competition. Here is a glimpse into the typical sporting year in Moycarkey N.S., Pouldine

## SEPTEMBER/OCTOBER

- Cumann na mBunscol Boys Football
- Cross Country County Championships
- School Gaelic Football League

*Past pupils of Pouldine who were members of the Dr. Harty Cup and All-Ireland Colleges' winning team with Thurles CBS 2009 on their visit to the school (l.-r.): Liam Ó Donnchú, Michael Roche, Pat Molloy, Jamie Barry and Mr. Robert White.*

**Moycarkey N.S. Pouldine – Hurling Team 1984**

*Back row (l.-r.): Donal Hogan, Paul Skehan, Michael Cooney, Bill O'Sullivan, Kenneth Concagh, Richard Stapleton, Cormack Cassidy, Gregory Sweeney, Irwin Bannon, Timothy Scott, Joseph McCormack. Front row: Micheál Kavanagh, Thomas McCormack, Johnny Flanagan, P.J. Butler, Brendan Stapleton, Declan O'Dwyer, Denis Costello, Declan Hogan, Seamus Stapleton, Laurence O'Sullivan.*

**Cross Country Running – Medal Winners 1986**

*Back row: Cyril Stapleton, James Moriarty, Tracy Browne, Nollaig Ryan, Bridget Ryan, Mary Theresa Butler, Cora Delaney, Janet Butler Denis Costello. Second row: Seamus Concagh, Christopher Browne, Nigel Callanan, Ristéard Cassidy, Francis Ryan, Brian Shanahan, Paul Molloy. Front row: Anne Butler, Úna Nagle, Mary Ryan, Ellen McCormack.*

*Moycarkey N.S. Pouldine School Football Team School Year 1986-'87 Back row: Daniel Maher, Gerard O'Dwyer, Seamus Concagh, Oliver Hogan, Paul Molloy, Cyril Stapleton, John McGuire, Ristéard Cassidy, Francis Ryan. Front row: Tracy Browne, RoseMary Lanphier, Anne Butler Bridget Ryan, Janet Butler, Nollaig Ryan, Tara Coman. In Front: Elaine Mooney.*

## OCTOBER/NOVEMBER

- Cumann na mBunscol Girls Football
- School Olympic Handball League
- School Uni-Hoc League
- Rás na Samhna

## DECEMBER

- Boys and Girls County Indoor Soccer Tournament
- Jingle Bells Race

## JANUARY

- Munster Indoor Soccer Tournament
- 5-aside Indoor Hurling Tournament

## FEBRUARY

- Irish Dancing Classes for 8 sessions culminating in a school Céilí
- School Hurling League

## MARCH-MAY

- Swimming in a local pool for 6-8 sesssions

## APRIL/MAY

- Boys and Girls 5-aside County Soccer Tournaments
- School Soccer League
- Rás na Cásca ( Easter Egg Race)

## MAY

- Cumann na mBunscol Hurling
- The Great School Run

## JUNE

- Sport for All – Day
- Sports/ Fun Evening
- School Basketball League.

*Maria Kinnane, Pouldine, was on the Tipperary Primary Schools' Girls Football Team in 2009.*

*John Corbett of Corbett Motorvillage sponsors a set of jerseys for the school (l.-r.): Rory O'Regan, Ms. Cáit Power, John Corbett, Liam Ó Donnchú, Mr. Ed Donnelly, Mr. John Corbett, Mr. Robert White, Patrick Maher, David O'Dwyer, Andrew Dunne.*

*School Year: 1995 Class 5th & 6th*
*Back row: Dick Quigley (Manager) John Minchin, John Harrington, Paul Dempsey (Captain) James Cleary, Noel O'Dwyer, Billy O'Dwyer (Manager). Front row: Paul O'Dwyer, Rick Quigley, Sheena O'Dwyer (Mascot), Paul Egan, James Scott, Matthew Roche, Mark O'Dwyer. Missing from Photo: Jessie Cleary.*

**Pouldine National School – Winners of the Moycarkey-Borris Under-9 Parish League 1998**

*Back row (l.-r.): Shannon Hayes, Eamonn Flanagan, Conan O'Hara, Rory Ryan, Noel Kinane, Sinéad O'Hara. Front row: Colm Skehan, Lorcan O'Hara, Finbarr Hayes, Pat Molloy, Michael Roche.*

*School Year: June 2001 – School Hurling Team*
Back row: Pat Molloy, Karen Mullins, Jack Harnett, Conan O'Hara, Ann Kirwan, Kilian O'Donoghue, Karen Hogan, Niall Barry, Eamonn Flanagan. Front row: Michael Roche, William Foley, Noel Kinane, Seamus Cummins, Sinéad O'Hara, Ciarán O'Shea, Rory Ryan.

*Snickers – Soccer skills 1995 Winners*

*Paul Dempsey, David Maher with school Principal Liam Ó Donnchú.*

*School Hurling League – O'Brien Cup Winners 1983*

*Pat Costello, Bill O'Sullivan, John McCormack, Patrick O'Connell, P.J. Butler, Irwin Bannon, Denis Rayel.*

*Class 5 – School Hurling League Winners 1983*

*Back row (l.-r.): Patrick O'Connell, P.J. Butler, Bill O'Sullivan, Denis Reale. Front row (l.-r.): Paul Skehan, John McCormack, Pat Costelloe, Irwin Bannon.*

**School Hurling League Finalists 1983**

*Back row (l-r.):*
*Laurence O'Sullivan,*
*Andy Maher,*
*Brendan Stapleton,*
*Donal Hogan.*
*Front row (l.-r.):*
*Declan O'Dwyer,*
*Martin Flanagan,*
*Michael Kavanagh.*

**Tipperary Futsal Indoor Soccer Champions 2008-'09**

*Back row: Maria Kinane,*
*Kathryn Connolly,*
*Eimear Martin Capt.,*
*Ann Connolly, Patricia*
*Hayes, Maria O'Keeffe.*
*Front Row: Rachel Byrne,*
*Shauna Fitzpatrick,*
*Gillian Fogarty,*
*Martha Kirwan.*

**South Tipperary School Boys League 1994**

*Matt Roche,*
*John Minchin*
*(Player of the*
*Tournament)*
*John Harrington,*
*Rick Quigley.*

Back: Martha Dempsey, Margaret Mary McGrath, Sarah Kinane.
Front: Laura Heffernan, Sheena O'Dwyer.
Performing in Star Stream (T.V. Show 2002).

*Moycarkey N.S. Pouldine 5-a-side Soccer County Champions 2008*

*Back row: Kieren Hennessy, David O'Dwyer, Rory O'Regan, Micheál Foley. Front row: Brian Maher, Patrick Maher, Darragh Ryan.*

**School Hurling Team 1983**

Back row: John McCormack, Timothy Scott, Thomas McCormack, Seamus Lahart, Brendan Stapleton, Irwin Bannon, Pat O'Brien, Declan O'Dwyer, P.J. Butler. Front row: Patrick Dunne, Patrick O'Connell, Andrew Maher, Adrian Delahunty, Bill O'Sullivan, Cormac Cassidy, John Cooney, Thomas Dunne, Martin Flanagan, Declan Hogan.

**Final of the School's Basketball League 2005**
Yellow Team: Seán Dalton, and Cody Jackson.
Blue Team: Micheala Graham, Kieran O'Grady, Michelle Sheppard, Gavin O'Brien.

*Moycarkey N.S. County Football Champions 2008 – 2009*
*Back row: Aaron Hayes, Michael Flanagan, Dean O'Connor, Brian Maher, Pádraig Kirwan, Kieran Hennessy, Conor Ryan, Thomas Mernagh, Micheál Foley, Jack Kiely. Front row: Keith Melbourne, Aaron Ryan, Conor Harnett, Eoghan Hayes, Maria Kinane, John Corbett, Darren Ryan, Kevin O'Regan, Tomás Darmody. On step: Darragh Ryan (Captain).*

*Rás na Cásca*
*Winners 2009*

*Back row: Darragh Ryan, Kathryn Connolly, Maria Kinane, Micheál Foley. Front row: Megan Lahart, Eoghan Hayes, Claire Ryan, Aaron Cawley.*

*Moycarkey N.S.*
*Hurling League*
*Winners 2005*

*Back Row: Micheala Graham, Seán Dalton, Corina Abbott,*

*Front Row: Richard O'Keeffe, Kieran Stapleton, Cody Jackson.*

*Moycarkey N.S. Soccer League Champions 2005*

Back row: Shauna Flanagan, Nora Connolly, Richard O'Keeffe, Michelle Carew. Front row: Cody Jackson, Jamie Maher, Klara Martin, Joey Coman.

*Moycarkey N.S. – Football League Winners 2004 – 2005*
From left: Karen Corbett, William O'Dwyer, Timmy Ryan, Cody Jackson, Ciara Maher, Joey Coman.

*Presentation of New School Jerseys by Cashel Communications in 2001.*
Steven Singleton, Joan Singleton, Breda Kinane, Liam Ó Donnchú, Breda Doherty, Margaret O'Dwyer.

*Schools County
Cross Country
Medalists 2000*

*Karen Mullins
– Gold Medal,
Rory Ryan
– Bronze medal.*

**2001 All-Ireland
Camogie Champions,
Tipperary visit the
school with the
O'Duffy Cup**

*Left to right:
Margaret Mary McGrath,
Edwina McGrath,
Sarah Kinane,
Sheena O'Dwyer.*

*McCarthy Cup
All-Ireland Hurling
Trophy visit 2001*

*Ann-Marie Carroll
and Lucy McGann
(Teachers).*

*Heineken Cup Visit – January '07*

Peter Kinane, Denis Leamy, Peadar Kinane, Denis Fogarty.

*Boys 5-a-side County Soccer Champions – May 2005*

Back row: Jamie Costello, Peadar Kinane, Christopher Byrne, Timmy Ryan, Richard O'Keeffe. Front row: Seán Dalton, Andrew Fogarty, Jamie Maher, Conor Ryan.

*Moycarkey 5-a-side Soccer County Champions 1999*

Back row: Paul Singleton, David Kinane, Shane Barry, Thomas Quinn. Front row: David Maher, Eoin Nagle, Damien Shanahan, Gerry Maguire.

**Girls Co. Football Champions 2008**

*Back row: Mr Liam Ó Donnchú, Ms. Elaine Brady, Kathryn Connolly, Patricia, Hayes, Ann Connolly, Leah Murphy, Rachel Byrne, Maria O'Keeffe, Gillian Fogarty, Mr Robert White. Front row: Martha Kirwan, Eimear Martin, Maria Kinane, Nicole O'Brien, Emer Whelan, Ann-Marie Carew.*

**Chess Time in 6th Class in 2003**

*Players:- Front: Anna Harnett, Aisling Hogan. Back: Daniel O'Regan, Ailish O'Keeffe.*

**Rás na Nollag Winners 2007**

*Back row:
Mr Liam Ó Donnchú,
Seán Darmody,
Kathryn Connolly,
Ann Connolly,
Gillian Fogarty,
Mr Robert White.
Front row:
Darragh Ryan,
Darren Ryan,
Tomás Darmody,
Emer Whelan.*

*Liam McCarthy Cup*
*visits the school*
*in 2001*

*Back row:*
*Adam Carew,*
*Tommy Noonan,*
*Tony Flanagan,*
*Colm Skehan.*
*In front:*
*Ciarán O'Shea,*
*Michael Flanagan.*

*Tipperary Minor Hurlers*
*visit the school with*
*the All-Ireland Trophy*
*in October 1996*

*Liam Ó Donnchú*
*(School Principal)*
*with Colm Butler*
*and Kilian O'Donoghue.*

*Inter-schools Basketball*
*Winners 1992*
*Back row:- Claire Hogan,*
*Caroline Roche, Rosemary*
*Fanning, Claire Dee.*
*Front row:- Jacqueline Fahey,*
*Marie Cummins, Angela*
*Cummins, Elaine Carey,*
*Elaine Carey, Ann Harrington,*
*Muireann O'Donoghue,*
*Siobhán Nagle, Sinéad*
*O'Mahoney, Katie O'Connell,*
*Lorraine Dunne.*

*Moycarkey N.S. Pouldine
– Semple Stadium 1988*

Back row: Kate O'Sullivan, Vincent Stapleton, Ristéard Cassidy, Nigel Callanan, Brian Croke, Paul Britton, Paul Molloy. Front row: Tomas Delahunty, James Kennedy, Brian shanahan, Francis Ryan, Derrick Leahy. In front: Noel Butler, Noel Maher.

*In 2001 Sinéad O'Hara was on the Tipperary Primary Game Football Team.*

*Moycarkey N.S. Pouldine – School Hurling Team 1994*

Back row: Paul Dempsey, Rick Quigley, Shane Quigley, James Scott, Shane Dunne, Martin Shortall, John Leahy, John Harrington, Joe O'Dwyer. Front row: Adrian McCormack, Aidan Bourke, Patrick McCormack, Conor Butler, Edward Moloney, Kevin Leahy, Kevin McGuire, P.J. Flanagan.

*Féile na nGael – School Visitation 1990*

*Harry Ryan, Johnny Ryan, Denis Ryan, Liam Hennessy, John Dowling (G.A.A. President), Rev. Richard Ryan, Mrs. Mary Minchin, Ms. Catherine McGrath, Ms. Lucy McGann, Ms. Anne Harrington, Liam Ó Donnchú.*

*Dan Breen Cup comes to Pouldine N.S. Moycarkey Borris – County Senior Hurling Champions 1982. Team Captain Jack Bergin with pupils celebrate the victory.*

*Young Sportsmen – June 1980*

*Back row: Pádraig Campbell, Eoin Dunne, Richard O'Keeffe. Front row: Philip McCormack, Mark Ryan, Andrew Bourke.*

**School Year:- 2007-'08 – Sixth class**
Back row:- Jack O'Dwyer, David O'Dwyer, Iain O'Dwyer, Michaela O'Meara, Sarah Abbott, Andrew Dunne. Middle row: Liam Ó Donnchú (Principal), Niall Barry, Stephen Lyons, David O'Shea, Andrew Moloney, Áine Hayes, Patrick Maher. Front row: Seán Cawley, Rory O'Regan, Siobhán Hennessy, James Whelan, Patrick Whelan, Claire Hassett, Shauna Noonan. Absent from photo: Kieran O'Grady.

**School Year:- 1995-'96 – Second Class**
Back row: Ellen Butler, Mary Shortall, Shane Barry, Dick O'Sullivan, Conor Fanning, Felicity Dempsey, Michéal Heffernan, Maria Carey, Máire O'Regan, Gerard McGuire. Middle row: Mrs Mary Minchin, Majella Delaney, Anita Bannon, Hannah McGrath, Eoghan Nagle, Thomas Quinn, Tony Flanagan, Sean Quirke, Marie Kirwan, Siobhán Roche. Front row: Laura Cleary, Rosaleen O'Keeffe, Patricia Coman, Fiona Purcell, Christine Ryan, Andrew Cope., Rachel Burke, Eoin Ryan, Shane McCormack.

**School Year:- 2007-'08 – Junior Infants**
Back row: Amy Cloonan, Adam O'Dwyer, Conor Dunne, Róisín Donnelly, Kelly Ann Gileece, Adam Costello, David Doyle. Middle row: Emmet Condon, Conor O'Grady, Aisling Meagher, Lauren O'Sullivan, James Shanahan, Thomas Whelan, Maria Kennedy. Front row:- Kaylee Stonestreet, Chloe O'Connell, Jack Corcoran, Rian Martin, Evan Tobin, Conor Clohessy, Queva O'Meara.

# 1995 – All Ireland Glory
# for Pouldine Boys

*Moycarkey N.S. – Pouldine All Ireland Champions 1995*
*Back row: Rev. Richard Ryan, Matt Roche, James Cleary, John Harrington, John Minchin, Liam
Ó Donnchú (Principal). Front row: Paul Egan, Paul Dempsey, James Scott, Rick Quigley.*

ON TUESDAY 20th June Moycarkey NS (Pouldine) became the first All-Ireland Primary School Soccer Champions from Tipperary, at St. Patrick's Training College, Dublin. Considering it was the first time entering the FAI's "Snickers" national competition for primary schools, this achievement is all the more remarkable.

Because of the thousands of Primary Schools throughout the country that enter this competition, the FAI (schools) divided the competition into three sections. Section A catered for schools with twenty-five or less pupils; section B for schools with twenty five to eighty pupils and section C for schools with more than eighty pupils. They also developed a 6-a-side game for schoolchildren that differs slightly from the 11-a-side one. A panel of eight players are used at specified times during the twenty-four minute match.

## THE FINAL (SECTION B)

Moycarkey, the Munster champions faced Burrenpoint, Donegal (Ulster), Dundalk N.S. (Leinster), St Edwards N.S., Sligo (Connacht) in three matches played between 1.30 and 4 p.m. Working to a plan that helped them win the Tipperary and Munster titles, Moycarkey came up against St. Mura's, Burrenpoint in the opening game. Due to the intense humidity on the day, they were happy to contain the Donegal side and with six minutes to go struck twice through Paul Dempsey and James Scott to take three points.

In their next match against Dundalk N.S, they had to rely on the reflex saves of goalkeeper John Harrington and the individual skills of James Scott to overcome this hurdle. Paul Egan put Moycarkey one up at half time. Dundalk equalised early in the second half but straight from the kick off James Scott waltzed through the Dundalk defence to score a brilliant individual goal and he was again on the mark two minutes from time to give the school a 3-1 victory.

To the delight of the Moycarkey "three wise men" Billy O'Dwyer, Dick Quigley and Jessie Cleary, word came down the line that those two wins were enough to give Moycarkey the All Ireland title, as the other two sides in the group had failed to secure maximum points.

In their last game against St. Edwards, Sligo, the exhausted but jubilant heroes of Moycarkey completed a memorable day winning 2-1 with a goal in each half from Rick Quigley.

*1994 – First Female Altar Servers in the Parish and past pupils of Pouldine N.S. Back row (l.-r.): Ann Marie Dempsey, Shanbally; Jackie O'Halloran, Graigue; Rita Barry, Curraheen (Sacristan, Moycarkey Church); Elaine Roche, Horse & Jockey. Front row (l.-r.): Ann Marie Dixon, Pouldine; Fr. Richard Ryan P.P.; Claire Kirwan, Moycarkey.*

# Liath Mór/Liathmore/ Leighmore

THE RUINS of the ancient monastic site of Liathmore stand just north of the Turnpike, Two Mile Borris, on the right of the old N8 – Dublin/Cork road.

## TWO CHURCHES

This site comprises the ruins of an early medieval monastery surrounded by a deserted late medieval village. The surviving standing monuments include an early church, a later church, and a roughly circular stone structure described as the base of a round tower. There are extensive views over the surrounding bogland from the flat roof of the larger church.

The smaller church is a single-celled oratory with thick, well built limestone walls. There are projecting antae at both gable ends. These are characteristic of the earliest phase of Irish stone churches. An 8th century date is suggested for this church. The abbot at this period was Cuangus (died 746).

*The smaller church at Liathmore.*

*The larger church at Liathmore.*

The larger church was built and added to over an extended period of time. The present structure consists of a nave and chancel. It is suggested that the chancel is the nave of the original church, with the remains of the first chancel lying in ruins to the east. The presence of antae on the eastern gable wall attests to the building's age; the early chancel was itself an addition to this building. The chancel was probably abandoned in the 15th century, at which time a new nave was added. This was considerably larger than most contemporary churches, and may never have been completed (it would have been difficult to roof so wide a span). Some of the stone used in this building phase may have been 12th century masonry originally from Holy Cross Abbey some 15 kilometers away, which became available when the Abbey's eastern arm was rebuilt in the 15th century. The present nave, of late 15th or early 16th century construction, is smaller and less elaborate than the earlier attempt. The monastery was founded by Saint Mochaomhóg around the year 590. He was nephew of Saint Ita and friend of Saint Fursey (600-650). Little is known about its later history, but the death of its Abbot is recorded in 1015; at the end of the 12th century it had manorial status, and by the 14th century belonged to the treasurer of the Diocese of Cashel.

## NAOMH MOCHAOMHÓG

Regarding Mochaomhóg, we are told that at his Baptism, he was given the name Caomh, which means 'the gentle one'. But, as his mother always addressed him as Mo Chaomh – my gentle one, in a short time he was known by no other name but Mochaomhóg. He was son of Bevan, a Connacht man and a skilled worker in wood and stone, while his mother's name was Nessa. Following the death of his father, Mochaomhóg was given in charge to his aunt St. Ita, who lived at Killeedy, Co. Limerick. He was educated under St Comgall at the monastery in Bangor, Co Down. In time he was ordained priest. Comgall then sent him to establish an abbey at Arderin. In 590, he founded the great monastery of Liathmore. The chieftain of Éile gave him the land for his monastery. Mochaomhóg was also associated with the foundation of other monasteries, particularly in the midlands but also in Scotland. The Latin version of his name is Pulcherius and this is the name referred to in many ancient texts. He died on March 13th 655 and was buried before the altar of his church. For five hundred years the monastery at Liathmore was famed for sanctity and learning. A long line of abbots succeeded Mochaomhóg, many of whom are buried at this monastic site.

## MOCHAOMHÓG AND THE CHILDREN OF LIR

The legend, The Children of Lir, has a very interesting association with St. Mochaomhóg. It is one of Ireland's best known and saddest stories and part of our mythological cycle. The story in brief: - Lir had three sons Aodh, Fiachra, Conn and one daughter Fionnuala. When

their mother died, Lir married Aoife. Aoife grew jealous of the children's love for each other and their father, so she plotted to get rid of the children. She used her magic to turn the children into swans. As swans, the children had to spend 300 years on Lough Derravaragh, 300 years in the Sea of Moyle and 300 years on the Isle of Glora (Inis Glóire), off Erris Head, Co. Mayo. To end the spell, they would have to hear the sound of a Christian bell and be blessed by a monk. It was at this time that St. Mochaomnóg was at Inis Glóire. The swans heard his bell ring and knew that the spell on them was broken. Before their eyes the feathers fell away and four very old, wrinkled humans were left. It was then Fionnuala said to Mochaomhóg: "Come and baptise us now, for it is short till our death comes; And make our grave afterwards," she said, "and lay Conn at my right side and Fiachra on my left side, and Aodh before my face. '' Mochaomhóg did as he was requested.

*Base of the Round Tower at Liathmore.*

While the tragic legend of The Children of Lir ends there, its link with Liathmore and St. Mochaomhóg continues to the present. Local people tell of the annual visit of swans to the fields around the old monastic site. This happens from September through winter each year and the swans can number up to one hundred at any one time. This is most remarkable, particularly as there is no water nearby.

## SOURCES

Department of the Environment, Heritage and Local Government. Website www.excavations.ie
Local History Notes, Liam Ó Donnchú
A Heritage Gazetteer of North Tipperary – Siobhán Geraghty
Moycarkey Borris – Parish Newsletters.

# Then and Now
# – from Poacher to
# Gamekeeper ...

POULDINE N.S. has played a huge part in my life so far, having spent eight years of a very happy childhood there and now I'm back in a teaching capacity (who'd have thought!). It's amazing to see exactly how much has changed since I left in sixth class and how much is still the same. To this day, I have very fond memories of my experiences in primary school.

*Fionnuala Hayes*

Starting primary school can be, of course, a very turbulent time in any child's (and parent's!) life, and although I don't remember all of the details too clearly, I'm told I took to it like a duck to water! Getting to school was no mean feat back then, as I graced the school gates on my first day on the back of my mother's bike! There were no Land Rovers or people-carriers in those days!

Having two older brothers in the school already probably made the transition much easier for me. I remember being in Infants playing with Márla, reading about Ann and Barry in our Infant reading book, lunchtime – chatting and eating together, and playing with friends. The games were similar to today – skipping, chasing, Red Rover, football etc. and we did not have to wear a school uniform back then. In later years, my brothers and I would walk to school and back, as the roads were a lot quieter then, and we sometimes took a shortcut through the fields. When my sister started school we were lucky enough to sometimes get a lift with neighbours.

The subjects were very similar to the subjects today. I particularly liked Nature Studies, English, Poetry and Irish and still remember going on local nature walks with our teacher Ms. Ryan, some poems from our book "Digging for China" and I carried on studying Irish in college. Learning tables and spellings "off by heart" was the norm, and more or less disliked by all, but had to be done! We were also taught how to knit and sew in Pouldine, which was quite enjoyable, only marred by the fact that the boys were outside playing football/G.A.A at the same time, tormenting us, knowing we would only have loved to be out there taking them on! Life was very cruel!

I can also remember my First Holy Communion and Confirmation days very clearly. The hustle and bustle of family and relatives, getting ready, the ceremonies themselves, photographs being taken. There was also a lot of preparation done in school, and I especially remember having to learn the "Catechism" off by heart, which was inspected in school by an examiner. (Nerve-wracking moments for both pupils and teachers alike!)

We were also lucky enough to go swimming in the old swimming pool in Thurles every Wednesday for a month or two and I can still remember that it cost 40p. Noel Gaynor was the lifeguard at the time and he taught us how to swim. Great fun was had by all on these days and everyone tried their hardest to earn their swimming badges. These badges were then sewn onto our swimming togs and displayed with pride. We would always return to the school very hungry but happy!

School tours came only once a year but were always looked forward to with much anticipation. It was the same routine each year, hardly any sleep the night before, checking and re-checking bags to make sure everything was packed and arriving in school as early as possible to make sure we got on the bus on time, so we didn't get left behind. This can probably be said of most school tours today, children up at the crack of dawn, dying to get to school! (If only it was as easy every other day!)

The main school building itself has not changed much since my time as a pupil, the chairs and tables are the same style and the fixtures and fittings are the same. Saying that, there have been a few modifications such as the addition of Halla Uí Riain (which was erected the year I was leaving Pouldine – Typical!) and our two new prefabs – "Tír na n-Óg" and "An Bradán Feasa". The school has also purchased a new hurling field, which gives plenty of space for each class to have their own designated play area. The teaching staff was very similar to the staff at the moment, with a few changes through the years. The Principal was Liam Ó Donnchú, Bríd Ryan (4th and 5th), Lucy McGann (2nd and 3rd) Catherine McGrath (1st and 2nd) and Mary Minchin (Infants). Mrs. Mary Heffernan was the cleaning lady back then and I can still remember the tables being brought out into the yard at the end of each term and given a thorough scrubbing.

Leaving Pouldine at the end of sixth class was both an exciting and unnerving time. We looked forward to the years to come, but at the same time we knew that we were leaving a place of safety and security. Luckily for us, we were given a great start in life, as Pouldine had laid very strong building blocks for our futures. And now, here I am, back again teaching children who are sitting in the same seats we sat in, playing together and sharing their childhoods together as we did. And I can't help wondering what lies in store for each of them. I hope that they gather as many great memories and friendships as I did and look back with the same fondness that I have for Pouldine National School.

*(Fionnuala Hayes (née Concagh) was a pupil in Pouldine from 1982 until 1990 and became a member of the teaching staff in 2002)*

# A New Motorway
# — M8

THE NEW motorway, M8 - Cullahill to Cashel Road, which divides the parish of Moycarkey-Borris, was officially opened by Mr. Noel Dempsey T.D., Minister for Transport, on Monday 8th December 2008.

## PROTECTION OF THE LOCAL ENVIRONMENT

Protecting the environment and providing mitigation to minimise the effects of the motorway on the surrounding countryside were important considerations in the development of the scheme. Extensive landscaping has been carried out to screen properties from the route and to help blend the scheme into the surrounding landscape. To minimise the impact of road traffic noise, low-noise surfacing has been provided throughout and barriers have been erected at certain locations along the route.

To protect wildlife, badger and otter passes were constructed under the motorway and substantial lengths of badger and otter proof fencing were erected to guide the animals to the underpasses and prevent them getting onto the motorway.

## ARCHAEOLOGY – "PRESERVING THE PAST"

Great care was taken in planning the new motorway to minimise the impact on archaeological sites and monuments. To ensure that any previously unknown archaeological remains were identified and investigated before construction, extensive test excavations were undertaken.

The excavated sites were diverse. They included settlements, burial sites and industrial remains, which ranged in date from the Bronze Age, four-thousand years ago, to the 19th century. Many archaeological artefacts were recovered including shards of pottery vessels, iron knives, medieval coins and personal belongings such as brooches, dress pins and buckles.

## *Archaeological Discoveries in Moycarkey Borris*

### EARLY PREHISTORIC

No evidence of our hunter-gatherer ancestors or the first Neolithic farmers was uncovered on this road scheme.

Evidence from pollen cores taken from the Littleton Raised Bog Complex suggests that the bogs were expanding from the middle of the Neolithic period and that at this time the landscape was dominated by hazel woodland. This suggests that, until the Bronze Age, the area was only very sparsely settled. Perhaps it was not attractive or suitable for settlement but it could have been used for hunting. A leaf-shaped Early Neolithic arrowhead found in topsoil on one of the excavated sites may have been lost during one such hunting expedition.

### BRONZE AGE

The presence of 27 fulachta fiadh (burnt mounds) found on this scheme reflect the lowland nature of the route.

A roundhouse excavated in Borris was defined by a curvilinear wall

*This castle-shaped object, along with a horde of 53 pennies, found at Two-Mile-Borris.*

slot (6.5 m in diameter); it had an east-facing entrance with an annex or porch feature. The location of internal roof supports was indicated by post-holes. Several pits were identified in the vicinity of the house, including one example that contained a flint scraper.

In Ballydavid, to the west of Littleton, a large oval ditched enclosure (internal diameter 125 m) was discovered. The site was located on a knoll that sloped steeply towards the east. A considerable amount of animal bone and antler was retrieved from the fills of the ditch. One bone had been worked to make a spindle whorl while a piece of antler showed evidence of cut marks. The remains of an undecorated vessel dating to the Middle Bronze Age was recovered from the base of the ditch.

Another large ditched enclosure was identified on low-lying ground in Borris, adjacent to Two Mile Borris. It measured approximately 100 m in diameter. Access to the interior of the enclosure was by way of a narrow east-facing entrance flanked by a pair of post-holes. A fragment of human skull was found in the base of the ditch to the north of the entrance. A cluster of six pits and 12 post-holes was revealed in the centre of the enclosure. Two cremation burials, a pit containing stake-holes and a deposit of cattle bones were also found within the enclosure.

Two Bronze Age pit cremation cemeteries were found on two adjacent ridges in Borris close to Two Mile Borris, the easterly one comprised 18 pits containing deposits of cremated bone while the other one comprised nine pits containing cremated bone and 12 pits which had no cremated bone. Downslope from the latter site (and close to the roundhouse described above) two circular ring-ditches were excavated, they were both just under 5 m in diameter. The fill of their shallow ditches contained small quantities of cremated bone and charcoal. A third sub-rectangular ring-ditch was found nearby. It enclosed a central cremation pit.

## EARLY MEDIEVAL

An early medieval settlement complex was uncovered at Two Mile Borris, - at least three phases of enclosure are represented on this site.

The earliest enclosure was oval in plan and had an east-facing entrance defined by a number of large post-holes. The ditch fills contained residues of iron working.

This early enclosure was replaced by a ringfort that was defined by a circular ditch (32m in diameter) with a north-east-facing entrance. Numerous features were present in the interior of the ringfort including four roundhouses defined by post-holes, curvilinear wall slots and drainage gullies. A bowl furnace and a number of shallow pits, one of which contained an iron knife and a pair of whetstones, were also found. The ditch fills contained animal bone, several iron knives, a glass bead, a bone comb fragment, a rotary quern-stone fragment, several bone pins, a stone gaming board and metallurigical waste.

In turn, the ringfort was cut by the construction of a large sub-rectangular ditched enclosure (65m wide and 50m long). This enclosure entirely enclosed both earlier enclosures and geophysical survey suggests that its construction was part of an extensive re-organisation of the agricultural landscape in this area.

Also identified within the various enclosures was a cemetery containing 19 graves, one of the individuals was buried with a copper-alloy ring-pin. Other features included three roundhouses, two cereal-drying kilns and an iron-smithing hearth.

## LATE MEDIEVAL

The modern village of Two Mile Borris is built on the site of an Anglo-Norman borough.

Excavations to the south of the village uncovered extensive prehistoric and early medieval remains. Activity contemporary with the late medieval borough was also found. These comprise a series of parallel ditches, which probably defined individual property boundaries, a large stone-lined keyhole-shaped grain-drying kiln and a complex of iron-working furnaces and hearths. A pit containing 61 silver coins of probable 14th century date was also discovered. The remains of a medieval vertical water-mill were found on the east bank of the Black River. On the opposite bank the foundations of a small rectangular (7 m by 6 m) earthen-walled building were uncovered. The building had a number of phases of use, the latest of which was as a smithy.

A post-medieval lime kiln was also excavated at Borris. These structures are found dotted throughout the landscape and were used for calcinating broken limestone to make powdered lime for use in industry, construction and agriculture and generally date from the 18th and 19th centuries.

## SOME MOTORWAY CONSTRUCTION FACTS

| | |
|---|---|
| Length of main carriageway: | 40km |
| Length of ancillary roads: | 11 km |
| Interchanges (4 no.): | Cashel |
| | Horse & Jockey |
| | Two-Mile-Borris |
| | Urlingford |
| Structures: (78 no.) | 21 road overbridges |
| | 4 road underbridges |
| | 1 Bord na Móna rail bridge |
| | 7 river bridges |
| | 3 accommodation overbridges |
| | 9 accommodation underpasses |
| | 33 significant stream/river culverts |

*arthworks:*

| | |
|---|---|
| Bulk Cut | 4.3 million cubic metres |
| Bulk Fill | 3.00 million cubic metres |
| | |
| CBM Sub-base and Base laid | 670,000 tonnes |
| Bituminous Surfacing laid | 470,000 tonnes |
| Structural concrete | 20,500 cubic metres |
| Trees and shrubs planted | 1 million |

*(Source – National Roads Authority, Archaeology Section – Public Information Leaflet)*

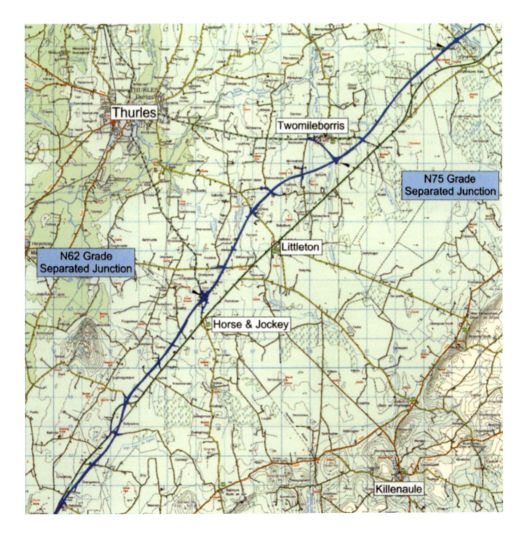

### School Year:- 1995-'96 – Second and Third Class

Back row: David Kinane, Thomas Quinn, Damien Shanahan, Thomas Roche, Teacher: Lucy McGann, Siobhán Ropche, Mairéad Dixon, Blaine O'Halloran, Anita Bannon. Middle row: Mary Shortall, Maria Carey, Marie Kirwan, Claire Carey, Megan Quigley, Kieran McCormack, Micheál Heffernan, Shane Barry, Dick O'Sullivan R.I.P., Rachel Bourke. Front row: Shane Hewitt, Carol Sweeney, Eoin Ryan, Eoghan Nagle, David Maher, Jerry McGuire, Sarah Cummins, Majella Delaney, Patrick Heffernan, Conor Fanning, Rowan Mills.

### School Year:- 1999-'00 – Junior & Senior Infants.

Back row: Michelle Sheppard, Maryese Noonan, Michaela Graham, Ivan Chadfield, Niamh Butler, William O'Dwyer, Michelle–Rose Ryan. Middle row: Aidan Fitzpatrick, Tommy Noonan, Jamie Costello, Nora Connolly, Melissa Morris, Antonia McGrath, Gavin O'Brien. Front row: Marguerite McCormack, Sarah Abbott, Tomás Ryan, Ann-Marie Carroll (class Teacher), David Ryan, Conor Hayes, Aaron Flanagan. Absent from photo: Donna-Marie Cawley, Seán Cawley.

### School Year:- 2008/2009 – Junior Infants

Back row: Kristian Ryan, Rachel Freeman Nash, Catherine Fogarty, Dean O'Donoghue, Michelle Flanagan, Sophie Ely, Joe Maher, Ben Ely, Gráinne Stapleton. Middle row: Emma O'Sullivan, Ciara Coffey, Eve Dardis, Joey Ryan, Tristan McCormack Ryan, Rebecca Hogan, Chloe Cummins, Adam Ryan, Luke Fell, Jack Fahey. Front row: Seán Flanagan, Joan O'Keeffe, Caleb Butler, Thomas O'Donoghue, James Webster, Ivan Cawley, Chelsie Hartigan, Lizzy Freeman, Neil Maxwell.

# Moira's Memories

1986, a year when an explosion in Chernobyl devastated northern Ukraine, Cork defeated Galway in the All-Ireland Hurling Final while Kerry beat Tyrone in Football, earning them a 3-in-a-row. It was also the year when I commenced my education in Pouldine N.S. I walked nervously, hand in hand across the school yard with my mother, in my other hand was a red vinyl case which contained some pencils and my lunch.

*Moira Skehan*

Ms. McGrath greeted us at the step. She would be my teacher for the next year – learning ABCs, finger painting, playing with márla and drinking warm school milk from small cartons. Ms. McGrath also had the unfortunate task of taking me home on one occasion to be changed after a 'little accident' on the classroom floor. The embarrassment of that scenario still disturbs me, especially having to get my sister from an older class to accompany me and I had to stand in the back of the car for the duration of the journey.

In Senior Infants, First and Second class, I was in Mrs. Minchin's classroom. It seemed to be a busier time. Our lessons were challenging, Ann and Barry were having more adventures in our reading books, as was Diarmuid an Dragúin 'as Gaeilge'. We got homework and we were champions at playing Red-Rover in the schoolyard at lunchtime. Preparations were soon under way for receiving our First Holy Communion. We learned our hymns, revised our prayers and equipped ourselves with plenty of sins for our First Confession, though not divulging too much information. Fr. Ryan might have been shocked.

Two strong memories of my years in that classroom were knitting class and Friday afternoon treats. My knitting capabilities were substandard to say the least. I am sure some of the boys created far superior hairbands and scarves than I did. My time was better served reading library books. Mrs. Minchin rewarded us with penny sweets on Fridays if we were well behaved. However, the most prestigious award was the 'Student of the Week' trophy presented every week. We grovelled for praise in the hope of that victory.

When I progressed to Ms. McGann's third class, I remember a very impressive nature table welcomed me inside the door. I spent the following 12 months often appearing with bunches of marigolds, wallflowers, daffodils or whatever else was in bloom in my father's garden to add to it. Irish classes were now through picture stories projected onto a screen on the blackboard. We all took turns rotating the reel on the telegóir, which was propped up on large books.

*Moira with her Pouldine classmates admiring their artwork.*

I think it was also around this time that we got our new school hall. The building work seemed to go on forever but the end product was worth it. We now had somewhere to have indoor P.E. classes with proper equipment. Circuit obstacle courses and indoor soccer leagues were common, girls and boys competing against each other.

Ms. Ryan had just returned from travelling the following year when I entered fourth class. I was now nine or 10 years old, my biggest worry was a 'Micra-T' reading test. The mobile library came to the school regularly and we got to choose a selection of books to keep us entertained and educated. Ms. Ryan always strove to extract our theatrical and creative selves. I reckon she was sometimes less than impressed at our attempts to be budding thespians. I did manage to become skilled at a few drama pieces however and shyly performed them at family gatherings.

My final two years in Pouldine National School were with Mr. Ó Donnchú. We were now considered the adults of the school, getting important jobs like taking the roll books to each class daily for completion, setting up the halla for occasions and ringing the lunch bell. This year also saw the introduction of a new school drink. Strawberry flavoured Benny Bunny replaced milk. A new school uniform was also brought in although I never got to wear it, as I was leaving.

The sacrament of Confirmation beckoned and we were yet again learning hymns and prayers. Fr. Ryan inspected our knowledge of the Ten Commandments. He asked a boy in my class, who shall remain nameless, what committing adultery means? Imagine his face when the boy confidently replied, "Not to be runnning off with married women, Father". We all erupted with laughter.

In hindsight, my eight years in Pouldine N.S. were very enjoyable. Other memories come to mind, such as school tours, part-time teachers, taking part in the Slógadh choir, camogie training on the pitch, jumping elastic bands and singing on Mary Morris's school bus every evening. I finished in June 1994 to commence Secondary School that September, leaving the building but keeping some great memories and great friends.

*Moira Skehan* – *(Moira Skehan was a Pupil in Pouldine from 1986 until 1994)*

# Archaeological Inventory, Parish of Moycarkey Borris

## RING-BARROW

A ring barrow consists of a low circular mound enclosed by an inner fosse and an outer bank. Barrows are associated with burial.

Ballyerk.

## STEPPED BARROW

This is an earthen mound with a ledge around its base.

Cloncleigh.

## MOUND

This is an earthwork whose function and date is difficult to ascertain.

Leigh.

## CRANNÓG AND WETLAND PLATFORM

A crannóg or lake dwelling is a defensive habitation site constructed on an artificial or natural island in a lake, river or marshy area.

Fertiana.

## RINGFORTS

A ringfort, also known as rath or lios, usually consists of a roughly circular or oval area surrounded by an earthen bank with an external fosse (moat). The typical ring fort was used as a dwelling-place, and would have contained one or more simple house made of upright wooden posts interlaced with a wattle-and-daub lattice construction. At night the domestic animals would have been herded into the enclosure through a gap in the bank, which would have been closed by means of a simple gate or other barrier.

Archerstown, Ballybeg (2), Ballydavid (2), Ballymureen (2), Blackcastle, Borris, Cloghmartin, Coldfields, Coolkip, Curraheen, Fertiana (4), Galbertstown (4), Galboola (2), Garraun, Graigue (4), Knockroe (3), Lahardan Lower (2), Moycarkey, Parkstown, Rathinch (4), Rathmanna, Shanacloon, Turtulla, Whitefort.

## SOUTERRAINS

A souterrain is an underground structure consisting of one or more chambers connected by narrow passages. The precise purpose of souterrains is unclear; some were probably for the storage of perishable commodities – cheese or grain – a kind of primitive food cellar.

Graigue, Leigh, Rathmanna.

## TOGHERS AND ROADWAYS

A togher is a wooden trackway traversing boggy or wetland areas.

Ballybeg, Cloghmartin/ Galbertstown Lower, Leigh/ Longfordpass North/ Long-fordpass South (2), Moy-carkey.

*Ballymoreen Graveyard in 2009.*

## ENCLOSURES

These are defined by an earth or stone bank, generally circular or irregular, sometimes with a fosse (moat). Most are probably degraded ringforts.

Ballymoreen, Ballybeg, Ballymoreen/Parkstown, Borris, Coldfields/Rathmanna, Coolcroo, Fertiana, Graigue (2), Liskeveen/Parkstown, Monaraheen, Moycarkey, Parkstown (7), Rathcunikeen, Turtulla.

## EARTHWORKS

These are earthen structures which form no specific monument type.

Ballyhudda, Cloghmartin, Fertiana.

## ECCLESIASTICAL SITES

(From earliest times to A.D. 1700)

Ballymoreen, Borris, Galboola, Leigh, Moycarkey, Rathmanna, Turtulla (Kildarmody).

## HOLY WELLS

The tradition of venerating springs or pools has its origins in pre-Christian Ireland. These pagan sites were later Christianised and became Holy Wells. The pilgrimages to Wells, which were usually for penitential and healing purposes, followed a set pattern. After some preliminary prayers, usually five decades of the Rosary, the pilgrim would approach the Well, kneel and say some prayers then go clock-wise around the well reciting more prayers. The circuit or 'round' was made three times. The pilgrim would then drink some water or bless him/herself with it. Holy Wells are also associated with Pattern Days, usually the feast day of a local patron saint. Domhnach Cruim Duibh – Garland Sunday – First Sunday in August each year was the traditional Pattern Day in Moycarkcy parish.

Coolkennedy – Toberavocky = Tobar an Bhachaill = The Well of the Crozier.

Turtulla - Lady's Well - Assosiated with an annual Pattern.

Bishop's Well, near Killough Castle

Toberarockoge in the townland of Clohoge. Tobar Naomh Mochaomhóg = St. Mochaomhóg's Well

Lahardan – Holy Well.

## HOLY TREES

Holy Trees are often associated with holy wells. Usually a personal item, such as a piece of clothing, is tied to the branches, hence the name 'rag bushes'.

Lahardan – An Crann Beannaithe

Turtulla – Lady's Well.

## ROUND TOWER

These are tall slim pencil-shaped stone towers with a small doorway located twenty or so feet above ground level and a number of small windows at different levels; all had originally, pointed conical roofs. There were wooden floors at various levels within, reached presumably by means of wooden or rope ladders.

The precise function of these towers is uncertain; they were associated with monastic settlements and probably had several uses: - as bell-towers (Cloigtheach in the Irish Language), from which the hours were tolled; as secure places of refuge, when the adjoining monastery came under attack; as repositories for the monastic treasures in times of strife, and as look-out and early warning places.

Round Tower at Leigh – Burnt down by Viking invaders in 851 A.D.

## BURIAL GROUNDS

This was usually a burial ground for unbaptised babies, who were not permitted, at the time, to be buried in consecrated ground. Suicide victims and 'strangers' were also buried in these places as were famine victims of the 1840s.

Moycarkey.

## MEDIEVAL EARTH AND TIMBER CASTLES

These are of Anglo-Norman origin, constructed in order to control newly acquired territory, which had been granted to the Norman lords.

Borris, Lahardan, Moycarkey.

## MOATED SITES

These are usually square or rectangular areas, sometimes raised above the ground, enclosed by a wide often water-filled moat and with a wide causewayed entrance. These were constructed, from the late 13th century, by the Anglo Normans as fortified residences for lesser lords.

Curraheen, Fertiana, Lahardan, Moycarkey.

## RECTANGULAR ENCLOSURES

These are rectangular enclosures which cannot be more precisely classified at this time.

Ballydavid, Rathcunikeen, Borris, Garraun, Noard, Turtulla.

## CASTLE SITES

Most of the sites listed here come from the Ordnance Survey maps. Many have been totally destroyed leaving little surface remains.

Ballydavid, Ballymoreen, Fertiana, Parkstown.

## SETTLEMENTS

Settlements dating from the early medieval period to the 17th century

Borris (Medieval Borough), Galboola (Deserted Settlement), Leigh (Deserted Settlement), Moycarkey (Deserted Settlement).

## SHEELA-NA-GIGS

These are medieval carvings of naked female figures. They date from the 12th to the 16th centuries. They were used as a warning to the people against 'sins of the flesh'.

Leigh (on the Romanesque doorway), Moycarkey (on the south wall of the Tower House and was locally known as Cathleen Owen).

## MILLS

Archerstown – Water mill on the bank of the Poulaneigh River. The civil Survey (1654-6) indicates a 'Mill in repaire' in Archerstown. On the 1843 Ordnance Survey map it is indicated as being a flour mill.

Newbrook – Water mill also on Poulaneigh River.

Manor Mill (Byrne's) – Mill Road.

Lester's (formerly Shaw's) – Lady's Well. Tucking mill. Tucking is a Cornish term for the process in the woollen industry in which woven cloth was hammered and felted with water-driven "stocks".

Brady's Mill – Archerstown.

## WEIRS

These were mostly simple constructions associated with salmon and eel fishing. These were built across the river to capture the eels as they descended downstream towards the sea. The eels were stopped by a stone or timber wall which was built across the river at an angle. The eels moved along the face of the weir looking for a gap and would enter a box-like structure which prevented their escape. This also kept the eels alive until they were required.

Fertiana (5).

## TOWER HOUSES AND BAWNS

The majority of these were built and occupied between the 15th and mid-17th centuries as residences for both Gaelic and Old English families. They were three to five storeys high, sometimes with an attic and mostly rectangular in shape. These were constructed as defensive strongholds in which the lord, his family and retainers could live securely.

Archerstown, Ballybeg, Ballydavid, Borris (Blackcastle), Cabragh, Coolcroo, Forgestown , Grallagh, Liskeveen, Moycarkey, Shanballa.

## HOUSES

This refers to 17th and early 18th century houses. This period saw a gradual move away from the well defended but uncomfortable Tower Houses to more comfortable, better lit accommodation with an increased emphasis on privacy.

Archerstown, Ballybeg, Cloghmartin, Galbertstown Lower, Graigue.

## NATIONAL INVENTORY OF ARCHITECTURAL HERITAGE

Sites listed from Moycarkey-Borris Parish

Archerstown House, Ballydavid House, Cabragh Castle, Glebe House, Laurel Lodge, Littleton Lodge, Liskeveen House, Maxfort House, Newbrook House, Parkstown House, Turtulla House.

SOURCES:

Archaeological Inventory of Co. Tipperary, Vol. 1 – North Tipperary

National Inventory of Architectural Heritage

Local History Notes – Daniel Maher, Liam Ó Donnchú.

# Talking with Dad

*Maria O'Keeffe*

**M**Y FATHER, Dick O'Keeffe, went to school in the 'Old School' at Pouldine in the 1960s. The classroom was a big, bare and dull room. It was heated by a turf stove. He travelled to school on foot and sometimes stopped into an orchard for apples. The school subjects at that time were English, Maths, Irish, History, Geography and Religion. The toilets were in a separate house at the back of the school. The names of the teachers were: Mr. Maher, Miss Treacy, Miss Butler and Miss Ryan. The Principal was Mr. Maher. School started at 9.30 a.m. and finished at 3.00p.m. You were punished if you talked, misbehaved, didn't have your homework done or you were left-handed. You were slapped with a belt, a ruler or the hand of the teacher.

*Dick O'Keeffe from his schooldays in Pouldine.*

I go to the 'New School' across the road from my father's school. The classroom is big, colourful and full of Art. It is heated by oil-fired central heating and is lovely and comfortable. I travel to school by car; some come on the school-bus and very few walk. In school we learn Maths, Irish, English, History, Geography, S.P.H.E., Science, P.E., Art and Craft, and Religion. The teachers are: Mr. Ó Donnchú, Mr. White, Ms. McCullagh, Mrs. Carroll, Mrs. Minchin, Mrs. Hayes, Ms. Brady, Ms. McGann and Ms. Horgan. The Principal is Mr. Donnchú, but he is retiring this year. The new Principal will be Mr. White. School starts at 9.25a.m. and finishes at 3.05p.m. Nowadays we don't get hit; we just get detention if we are really bold. I wouldn't like to go to school back in my father's time, because almost everything was different then.

*Maria O'Keeffe, Maxfort. Sixth Class pupil 2008-'09.*

*Confirmation Class:- 1985-'86*

*Back row: Isabel Coman, Mary Teresa Butler, Brian Delahunty, Eugene Dunne, Caroline Lambe, Joanne Maher, Yvonne Shaw, Miriam Mooney, Martina Loughnane, Anne Barry, Breda Kane, Catherine Barrett. Middle row: Norma Stapleton, James Moriarty, Denis Costello, Cyril Stapleton, Johnny Flanagan, Gerard O'Dwyer, Nollaig Ryan, Treasa Murphy, Cora Delaney. Front row: Agnes Kane, Séamus Concagh, Daniel Maher, Bridget Ryan, Tara Coman, Elaine Mooney, Janette Butler, Tracy Browne.*

*First Communion 1991*

*Front row: John Leahy, Claire Kirwan, Ann-Marie Dixon, Neasa O' Donoghue, Aileen Ryan, Aisling Crowe, Fiona Flanagan, (Gaile) Breda Kirwan, AnnMarie O'Dwyer, Thomas O'Dwyer. 2nd Row: Mrs Mary Minchin, Mrs Jane Gleeson, Sean O'Dwyer, Colette Fogarty, Ann Marie Dempsey, Elaine Roche, Jackie O'Halloran, Dolores Purcell, Siobhán McGuire, Catherine Burke, Darragh McGuire, Fr. Richard Ryan P.P. Back row: Michael Spillane (Gaile) John O'Meara (Gaile) John McLoughlin, Martin Kane, Conor Butler, Shane Dunne, Eoghan O'Sullivan, John Shorley (Gaile), Liam Shanahan, David Shorley (Gaile).*

*First Communion Class year – 2001*

*Back row: Stephen Fitzpatrick, Tommy Nonan, Jamie Costello, Conor Hayes, Stephen Lyons, William O'Dwyer, James Shanahan (Gaile). Front row: Niamh Butler, Michelle-Rose Ryan, Melissa Morris, Maryese Noonan, Nora Connolly, Antonia McGrath, Ciara Shorley (Gaile).*

# A Local
# History Timeline

| | |
|---|---|
| 580 | Liathmore Monastery at Two Mile Borris founded by St. Mochaomhóg. |
| 851 | Liathmore Monastery burned by Viking invaders. |
| 1057 | The O'Fogarty Lord of Éile killed by the O'Briens. |
| 1111 | Synod of Rathbreasail, near Thurles – creation of the dioceses. |
| 1169 | Anglo Normans arrive in Ireland. |
| 1174 | Anglo Normans defeated at Thurles by Dómhnall Mór Ó Brian. |
| 1180 | Holy Cross Abbey founded by Dómhnall Mór Ó Brian. |
| C.1182 | Kilcooly Abbey founded by Dómhnall Mór Ó Brian. |
| 1185 | Prince John grants lands in Tipperary to Theobald Walter (Butler). |
| 1190 | Anglo Normans settle at Two Mile Borris. |
| 1192 | Anglo Normans defeated at Thurles by Dómnall Mfir Ó Brian. |
| 1194 | Death of Dómhnall Mór Ó Brian. |
| 1200 | Building of Motte and Bailey defences at Thurles. |
| 1206 | Death of Theobald Walter. |
| 1300 | Carmelites Order come to Thurles (site of Cathedral of the Assumption). |
| 1304 | At Moycarkey manor, there were 39 English tenants and only 9 Irish. This manor was overwhelmingly English and had no betaghs. A common name among the English here is Samlesbury, from Lancashire. |
| 1324 | 20 March – Around 200 of the Irish and wrongdoers of Thurles were killed by Robert Caunteton. |
| 1328 | James Butler made 1st Earl of Ormond. |
| 1329 | July 19th, At Thurles Brian O'Brien defeated allies of William de Burgh, Earl of Ulster |
| 1331 | May 2nd – "at Thurles, William Hackett with others of the neighbourhood, killed around 50 of the men of Brian O'Brien..... William was himself killed". |
| 1350 | Plague, The Black Deat.h |
| 1356-7 | Murage grant – to raise taxes to build town wall in Thurles. |
| 1450 | Bridge Castle built in Thurles. |
| 1480 | Archbishop John Cantwell reconstructed the castle of Killough. |
| 1530 | Suppression of religious houses. |
| 1547 | Inquisition at Clonmel on Thursday before the Annunciation of the B.V.M., in the first year of Edward VI (March 24, 1547) ...Thomas O'Hogan of Thulres, Kern, stole a horse at Ballyherke. Walter Mores of Ballincassy, Kern, stole a cow of Malachy O'Donill, husbandman, at Thurles. Theobald Owre Butler, of Ballyvody, horseman, stole 18 cows at the late Monastery of Holycross. John Cantwell of Cowlkippe, horseman, at the Oldtown of Mockarke stole a cow three spears and a "fallaing" (Irish Cloak). |

| | |
|---|---|
| 1571 | Indenture dated 28th January, between Sir Thomas Butler, Earl of Ormond, and James Cantwell of the old town of Mokayrk in County Tipperary, witnesses that the Earl grants to Cantwell the town or village of Garren Ro in Ellyogirty, Co. Tipperary, excepting the game for a period of 21 years. |
| 1572 | Indenture dated July 26, 1572, between Sir Thomas Butler, Earl of Ormond, and Donyll Oge O'Trehy of the Ballybeg Alias Littletown, Co. Tipperary, physician, witnesses that said Earl, grants said town of Ballybeg with the castle, meases, lands etc., thereto belonging, reserving to himself all game,to have and to hold to said Donyll, his executors and assigns, for a term of 21 years at annual rent of 8L., a poundage hog, a summer sheep and 6 watch hens, with a moiety of all heriots, strays and profits of courts. |
| 1578 | Thomas Butler, Earl of Ormond, General of the Army of Munster, etc, in consideration of 200 marks, Irish, paid by William Archer of Rathfern, alias Archerstown, Co. Tipperary, and in performance of certain conventions made between the Earl's Father and Walters grandfather, grants to Walter all his lands, tenements and hereditaments in Rathfern, alias Archerstown, Garranvullin, Ballyovin, Corballi, Drehednekilli, Cnokcarballi, Rathgarrowe, Rathcoill, Galbollie, Rathlawrace, Shanclone, Nemoinkkin, Garranhallie, Garrankeapagh, and Thurles. To hold to use of said Walter and his heirs, male, lawfully begotten of the Earl, his heirs and assigns, as of his manor of Thurles, and for lack of such heirs to the use of the heirs of the earl forever. Paying from time to time the rents, services and burden accustomed to repair and suppling one horse solider as often necessary for the service of the Queen in Munster only. |
| 1619 | Death of Viscount Thurles, leaving Lady Thurles a widow. |
| 1620 | Lady Thurles marries George Mathew. |
| 1636 | Jerome Alexander purchases Kilcooly from Ormond. |
| | Death of George Mathew. |
| 1649 | Aug -1650 May – Cromwell in Ireland. |
| 1650 | Towns in Tipperary surrender. |
| | Ormond leaves Ireland. |
| | April – Oliver Cromwell and his forces pass through Moycarkey on their way to attack Clonmel. |
| 1653 | Lady Thurles appeals to Cromwellians to leave her in possession of property. |
| 1673 | Death of Lady Thurles aged 86. |
| 1684 | Franciscan Order established in Thurles. |
| 1688 | Death of James Butler 1st Duke of Ormond. |
| 1690 | July-August – Rev Rowland Davies in and about Thurles. |
| 1690 | August 5th – Holycross plundered by troops of General James Douglas. |
| 1695 | Fr. Edward Comerford on being appointed Archbishop remains in Thurles. |
| 1699 | Death of Theobald Mathew of Thurles. |
| 1704 | Parish priests registered pursuant to Act of Irish Parliament. Rahelty and Seyne -James Boyton( Rahelty). Thurles – Edward Comerford (Thurles). Muckarky, Ballymurreene, Borresleagh and Gaile – Francis Ryan (Muckarky). Holycross and Templebeg – Edward Leahy (Cistercian, Holycross). |
| c.1750 | Death of the last Cistercian monk in Holycross Abbey. |
| 1759 | Dublin Cork Roadway constructed. |
| 1786 | St. Mary's Church, Littleton built. |
| 1787 | Ursuline Order arrive in Thurles. |

| 1798 | United Irishmen Rebellion. Battle of Tubberadora. |
|---|---|
| 1816 | Christian Brothers established in Thurles. |
| 1820 | Construction of St. Mary's Church, Thurles. |
| 1824 | Julia Kavanagh author, born in Thurles – died 1877 in France. |
| 1827 | "Mining Company of Ireland" begins coal mining in Ballingarry. |
| 1829-1832 | St. Peter in Chains Church, Moycarkey built. |
| 1830 | Improvement in road systems Thurles – Newport and Thurles-Nenagh. |
| 1837 | St. Patrick's College, Thurles opened. |
| 1838 | County Tipperary divided into North Riding and South Riding. |

1838 Oct 24th – Charles O'Keeffe agent for Valentine Maher, Turtulla shot dead at Brewery Gate, Kickham Street, opposite Eliogarty Road (College Lane).

Fever Hospital (Later Thurles District Hospital) erected.

1840 Building of the Thurles Workhouse began. Mr. Denis Leahy, brother of Archbishop Leahy, contactor.

1841 Railway line from Dublin laid as far as Thurles.

Death of Lady Elizabeth Mathew last of the direct line.

1842 Thurles Workhouse opened.

1845 Arrival of potato blight in Ireland.

Danial O'Connel's Monster Repeal Meeting at Knockroe, Moycarkey.

1847 Moycarkey N.S. opened at Pouldine. Littleton N.S. opened.

1848 July – Uprising in Ballingarry.

August 5th – Arrest of William Smith O'Brien at Thurles Railway Station.

Saturday 29th July – Outbreak of Insurrection; Attack on Widow Cormack's House, The Commons, Ballingarry.

Major General McDonald, with four companies of the 74th Regiment of Highlanders, three field pieces, a squadron of the 8th Hussars, 250 rank and file of the 43rd Regiment of Foot, a company of Sappers and Miners, a company of the 60th Rifles, with forty cars loaded with ammunition, baggage, etc. arrived in Thurles and formed an encampment on the demense of Turtulla, the residence of Mr N. Maher, M.P. All is quiet here. The military band plays during parade, which makes it a quite joyous scene. Boyton's Hotel was searched on Tuesday at midnight for Smith O'Brien. Women's rooms, cupboards and every nook where you could put an infant underwent the ordeal. Business totally suspended in the town; farming operations unattended to; men's mind torn by anxiety. The government proclamation offering a reward of £500 for capture of Mr. O'Brien have been torn down or covered with mud and gutter.

(Dublin Evening Post)

1849 Bianconi's Car service between Thurles and Clonmel, passing Pouldine Cross, discontinued.

1850 Thursday, 22nd August – First Catholic Synod held in Ireland since the "Reformation"; held in St. Patrick's College, Thurles.

*Turtulla 1848*

| | |
|---|---|
| 1856 | Sadliers Bank ceases in Thurles, much consternation and panic ensues. |
| 1858 | May 11th – Cormack brothers, Daniel and William housed at Nenagh Gaol for the murder of John Ellis, Dovea, Thurles. |
| 1865 | Foundation stone of Thurles Cathedral laid. |
| 1867 | March. Excitement in Thurles and neighbouring locality over Fenian activity. |
| 1871 | Birth of Joseph Shanahan in Glankeen, Borrisoleigh (later Bishop Shanahan, Nigeria). |
| 1872 | Presentation Sisters arrive in Ballingarry. |
| 1875 | Charles Bianconi died, on Sept 22nd, at Longfield House, Boherlahan. |
| | Thomas William Croke appointed Archbishop of Cashel and Emly. |
| 1878 | Mercy Sisters arrive in Borrisoleigh. |
| | T.K. Dwyer, Ballyvinane, wins Irish Open Mile Championship. |
| 1879 | June 21st – Cathedral of the Assumption consecrated in Thurles. |
| | Charles Joseph Kickams "Knocknagow", or "The Homes of Tipperary," published. |
| 1880 | July 1st, Thurles - Clonmel Railway Line opened. |
| 1882 | Funeral of Charles Kickham passes Pouldine Cross on its way to Mullinahone. |
| 1884 | Nov 1st – Gaelic Athletic Association - Foundation meeting in Hayes' Hotel Thurles. |
| | Two locals present John Butler, Ballyhudda, Tim Dwyer, Ballyvinane. |
| 1885 | Nov 1st – Moycarkey G.A.A Club founded. |
| 1888 | April 1st – Thurles, representing Tipperary, wins first All Ireland Hurling title. Hurlers from the parish of Moycarkey Borris were well represented. |
| 1889 | Stanwix Home built in Kickham Street, Thurles. This charity was founded by Miss Emma Stanwix who left a sum of money to build alms-houses and a hospital for females aged over sixty years. The work was carried out by Mr. J. Kiernan, Talbot Street, Dublin, at a cost of about £2,500. The building was designed by Mr. Albert E. Murrray, Dawson Street Dublin. |
| | Moycarkey, Tipperary Senior Hurling Champions. Tom O'Grady – Captain. |
| | Moycarkey Hall opened. Rev. John Bourke P.P. |
| 1891 | Oct 6th – Death of Charles Stewart Parnell. |
| 1892 | Franciscan presence in Thurles ends. |
| 1898 | Centenary Co-op Ballyduff founded. |
| 1899 | Horse and Jockey – All Ireland Hurling Champions. Tim Condon, Captain. |
| 1900 | Two Mile Borris win All Ireland Hurling Final. Ned Hayes, Captain. |
| | New School at Gaile opened. |
| 1902 | July – Death of Archbishop Thomas Croke. |
| 1903 | Two Mile Borris, Tipperary Senior Hurling Champions. Ned Hayes-Captain. |
| | June 29th – The townland of Tubberadora becomes part of the parish of Boherlahan-Dualla. Prior to this date it was in the parish of Moycarkey. |

*Tipperary's first handball win – All-Ireland Junior Doubles Final 1926 (l.-r.): Tom O'Keeffe, James 'Shelly' McCarthy and Fr. Philip Fogarty.*

| | |
|---|---|
| 1904 | New Handball Alley at Horse and Jockey completed in eighteen days in July. This was the first use of cement in the locality. |
| 1905 | Two Mile Borris, Tipperary Senior Hurling Champions. Ned Hayes- Captain. |
| 1909 | Pallottine Order established in Thurles. |
| | "Tipperary Star" Newspaper founded. |
| 1910 | Dec. – General Election, great excitement in Thurles between candidates Hackett and O'Dwyer "Exciting Day in Thurles but nobody killed". |
| 1912 | Tenants in Thurles able to buy their houses. |
| 1916 | Easter Rebellion. |
| 1917 | Aug. 15th – Raid on Molloys Hardware Thurles for arms and explosives . |
| 1919 | Jan. 21st – Soloheadbeg Ambush and start of War of Independence. |
| 1919 | June – District Inspector Hunt killed in Thurles. |
| 1920 | Jan 18th – Attack on Drombane barracks. |
| 1920 | Jan 20th – Policeman killed in Thurles. Reprisals – The Sacking of Thurles. |
| 1920 | July 12th – Attack on Rearcross Barracks. |
| 1920 | November 1st – Littleton Barracks captured and burned. Reprisals in Thurles. |
| 1926 | Moycarkey Borris, Tipperary Senior Hurling Champions. John Joe Hayes – Captain. |
| 1927 | St. Mochaomhóg's Monastery at Leigh, Two-Mile Borris declared a National Monument |
| 1928 | Handball. Local players Tom O'Keeffe and Jimmy 'Shelly' McCarthy win All Ireland Junior Softball titles. |
| 1932 | Moycarkey Borris, Tipperary Senior Hurling Champions. Phil Purcell – Captain. |
| 1933 | Nov 25th – Taoiseach Éamonn de Valera cuts the first sod of Thurles Sugar Factory. The factory was formally opened by Mr Seán McEntee, Minister for Finance on Nov. 25th 1934  Moycarkey Borris, Tipperary Senior Hurling Champions. Phil Purcell – Captain. |
| 1934 | Seán Treacy Pipe Band founded at Shine's Hall, Pouldine. |
| | G.A.A Golden Jubilee Celebrations in Thurles. |
| | Moycarkey Borris, Tipperary Senior Hurling Champions. Phil Purcell - Captain. |
| | Horse and Jockey Handball Alley roofed and new lighting system installed costing £800. |
| 1935 | Edmund Gorman publishes – Records of Moycarkey and Two Mile Borris, with some Fireside Stories. |
| 1936 | Coolcroo Athletic Club formed. |
| 1937 | Moycarkey Borris, Tipperary Senior Hurling Champions. Paddy Ryan - Captain. |

*1899 – Horse and Jockey All-Ireland Champions – 1999*
*Back row: Kevin Moran, Brian Moran, Aidan Ryan, Conan O'Hara. Front row: Eoin O'Dwyer, Thomas Quinn, Larry Power, James Doran, Eamonn Flanagan, Colm Skeahn, Cilian O'Hara, Rory Ryan, Aidan Healy, Sinéad O'Hara, Eoin Ryan.*

*Horse and Jockey Centenary Committee 1999*
*Front row (l.-r.): Mary Fahey, Tommy Gleeson, Tom Mullins, Jimmy Tobin, Joe Bourke, Tommy Maher, Eamon Barry. Middle row (l.-r.): Concepta O'Keeffe, Billy Molumby, Jim Burke, T.K. Dwyer, Mick Roche, Jack Bergin, Seán Barry, Jim Scott, Liam Ó Donnchú. Back row (l.-r.): Harry Ryan, Dan Bergin, Michael Bourke, Eamon Donnelly, Henry Bourke, Joe Tobin, John O'Keeffe, Bart Howard.*

*Fr. John McGrath (Mullinahone), Paul O'Neill, Tipperary G.A.A. Chairman, Liam Hennessy, Jim Scott, Liam Ó Donnchú at the Jockey Centenary Celebrations.*

*Harry Ryan, Seamus King, Sam Melbourne and Mattie Connolly at the Centenary Celebrations at Horse & Jockey.*

*Horse & Jockey Team from the early days of the G.A.A.*

| | |
|---|---|
| 1939 | Sept 3rd – Start of Second World War. |
| | Sept 4th – Larry Slattery, Littleton – First Prisoner of War in World War II. |
| | Sept 9th – Blackouts. |
| 1940 | Moycarkey Borris, Tipperary Senior Hurling Champions. Tom Kennedy - Captain. |
| 1941 | Feb. – Government to re-open Slieveardagh coal mines. |
| | May – Outbreak of Foot and Mouth disease. |
| 1944 | Turtulla Estate sold to Thurles Golf Club. Purchase price £6,100. |
| 1945 | End of Second World War. |
| 1946 | Turf Development Board changed its name to Bord na Móna. |
| | Moycarkey Borris Athletic Club formed. |
| 1948 | Paddy Fahy, Coolcroo A.C., represents Ireland at the Olympic Games in London. |
| | Full production by Bord na Móna at Littleton bog. |
| 1949 | New glass back wall added to the Handball Alley at Horse and Jockey. This along with other improvements cost £400. Contractor – Oliver Croke, Thurles |
| | Paddy Fahy, Coolcroo A.C., a member of Irish Team that wins Bronze medals at the International Cross Country Championships. |
| 1949-51 | Turnpike Ball Alley built. |
| 1951 | Eamonn Donnelly represents Ireland at the International Cross Country Championships |
| 1952 | Local Muintir na Tíre guild founded. |
| 1953 | May 7th – Killough Limestone Quarry opened. |
| 1954 | Shrine to Our Lady at Turnpike opened. |
| | Galbertstown G.A.A club formed. 1960 was its final year to field a team. |
| | August – Moycarkey Legion of Mary first meeting. |
| 1955 | February – Moycarkey I.C.A. founded. First meeting held in Pouldine School. |
| 1958 | Handball. Local players Michael Shanahan and Thomas Doheny win All Ireland Junior Hardball Doubles. |
| 1959 | Feb.18th – Death of Archbishop Jeremiah Kinane. |
| 1960 | Archbishop Thomas Morris appointed Archbishop of Cashel and Emly. |
| | December – Muintir na Tíre Hall, Littleton opened. |
| 1961 | It was decided at the Moycarkey-Borris GAA convention that one team would represent the parish of Moycarkey-Borris. |
| 1963 | Ballydavid House, Littleton, demolished. |
| 1963 | Sept 9th – Last passenger train passes through Horse and Jockey. |
| 1967 | Last freight train passes through Horse and Jockey. |
| 1968 | Railway Bridge at Horse and Jockey removed. |

*Paddy Fahey, Hollyford and Coolcroo, winning in Dublin.*

| | |
|---|---|
| 1969 | Moycarkey G.A.A purchase grounds on the Thurles Road in Littleton. |
| | Nuala Bowe, Moycarkey Borris A.C. represents Ireland at the International Cross Country Championships. |
| 1970 | Moycarkey N.S, new school opened at Pouldine. |
| | Nuala Bowe, Moycarkey Borris A.C. represents Ireland at the International Cross Country Championships. |
| 1971 | Restoration of Holycross Abbey begins. |
| | St. Kevins Soccer Club formed. |
| | General Richard Mulcahy buried in Ballymoreen Graveyard. |
| 1974 | Ladies Football Foundation Meeting at Hayes' Hotel, Thurles. Dermot Shanahan, Sally and Ann Clohessy present. |
| | Moycarkey Borris Ladies Gaelic Football club formed. |
| 1975 | October – Restoration of Holycross Abbey completed. |
| 1977 | Church of Our Lady and St. Kevin, Littleton, consecrated . |
| | Moycarkey Borris win the Senior Scór All Ireland Set Dancing Competition . |
| 1977 | Aug 1st – Moycarkey-Borris Camogie Club formed. |
| 1978 | Sept. 24th – Fr. Robert Harkin C.C. died, aged 42 years. R.I.P. |
| 1979 | January – Paddy Maher (Best) memorial unveiled in Moycarkey old Graveyard. |
| 1980 | Feb 17th – Michael Webb and his son discover the Derrynaflan Hoard. |
| | Bord na Móna opens a Briquette Factory at Littleton. |
| 1982 | Moycarkey Borris, Tipperary and Munster Club – Senior Hurling Champions. Jack Bergin – Captain. |
| 1983 | Horse and Jockey Handball club's new 40/20 court opened. |
| 1984 | Moycarkey Borris G.A.A story launched. |
| | Centenary All Ireland Hurling Finals in Thurles . |
| | Moycarkey Borris, Tipperary Senior Hurling Champions. Jack Bergin - Captain. |
| 1985 | In December the appointment was announced of Dr. Dermot Clifford as Co-Adjutor Archbishop of Cashel & Emly. |
| 1986 | Liathmore Cheese starts production at the Hayes farm, Two Mile Borris. |
| | March 9th – Episcopal ordination of Dr. Dermot Clifford. |
| 1987 | Aisling Ryan, Moycarkey, represents Ireland in the European Junior Track and Field Championships. |
| 1988 | Sept. 12th – Archbishop Dermot Clifford installed as Archbishop of Cashel and Emly |
| | Aisling Ryan, Moycarkey, sets current Tipperary records for 3,000m (9 min. 22.33 sec.), 5,000m (16 min. 21sec.) and 10,000m (33 min. 37.4 sec.). |
| 1989 | Thurles Sugar Factory closes. |
| | Late Bronze Age sword found in Littleton Bog. |
| 1993 | Cabragh Wetlands opened. |
| | New Stand Erected at Moycarkey Borris G.A.A field in Littleton. |
| 1994 | November – Lár na Páirce officially opened by President Mary Robinson. |
| 1995 | Famine Museum opened at St. Mary's, Thurles. |
| 1997 | Jan. 16th – Death of Archbishop Thomas Morris. |
| 1999 | Tipperay Institute opens in Thurles. It was then called T.R.B.D.I. – Tipperary Rural and Business Development Institute. |
| | Centenary of 1899 All Ireland victory celebrated and memorial erected at Horse and Jockey. |

*School Year – Sixth Class 2008-'09*

Back row: Maria Kinane, Leah Murphy, Patricia Hayes, Michael Flanagan, Ann Connolly, Kathryn Connolly, Rachel Byrne. Middle row: Thomas Mernagh, Pádraig Kirwan, Maria O'Keeffe, Seán Darmody, Martha Kirwan, Liam Ó Donnchú (Principal). Front row: Shauna Fitzpatrick, Nora Donoghue, Aaron Hayes, Jack Kiely, Kieren Hennessy, Conor Ryan, Nicole O'Brien. Absent from photo: Lorna O'Regan, Darragh Ryan, Eimear Martin, Aoife Maher.

*School Year – Senior Infants and First Class 1985-'86*

Back row: Sean Carey, John Paul Shanahan, Frank Molloy, Mark Leahy, Mrs. Mary Minchin, Tom Higgins, Patrick Shanahan, Enda Callanan. 3rd Row: Marie Delaney, Claire Skehan, Helena Power, —, Linda Dee, Linda Power, Bríd Ryan, Erin Ryan, Claire O'Mahony. 2nd row: Marie Cummins, Susan Leahy, Ann Harrington, Claire Hogan, Caroline Roche, Pamela Quigley, Niamh Ryan, Ria O'Gorman, Catriona Ryan, Marie Webster. Front row: George Webster, Michael Minchin, Claire Dee, Colin Ryan, Siobhán Nagle, Sinéad O'Mahony, Jason Roche, Lorraine Dunne.

2000        Millennium monuments unveiled at Moycarkey and Littleton villages.

Centenary of 1900 All Ireland victory celebrated and memorial erected at Two Mile Borris.

Tomás Coman, Coldfields, represents Ireland at the Olympic Games in Sydney.

Tomás Coman sets current Tipperary record for 400m (45.84 sec.).

2002        April. Last in-take of milk at Centenary Co-Op Ballyduff.

2003        Two Mile Borris/ St. Kevin's F.C Grounds - New Hill Park opened.

2005        Thurles Co-op merges with Centenary co-op. The new co-op, known as Centenary Thurles Co-operative Society Ltd., will have a combined milk pool of 94.5 million litres (21m gallons).

2006        Oct. 2nd – The Source Arts centre opened in Thurles.

2007        Horse and Jockey Hotel opened.

2008        Mr. Noel Dempsey T.D., Minister for Transport, (Mon. 8th December) officially opened the M8 Cullahill to Cashel road project. Almost 16,000 vehicles will be removed from the bypassed towns and villages daily.

2009        Feb. 14th – Floodlighting at Semple Stadium, Thurles.

August 9th – Borris/St. Kevin's F.C., Official opening of 'All Weather 'pitch.

September 5th – Moycarkey Borris G.A.A. Club win All-Ireland Hurling 'Sevens'.

October 27th – Thurles native, Richard Quirke, announces plans for a development at Two-Mile-Borris encompassing a Casino, Hotel, Racecourse, Concert Arena etc. Complex to be known as 'The Tipperary Venue'.

*Willie Shanahan on holidays from America outside Shine's shop, Pouldine.*

*Littleton's main street long ago.*

**_Green Flag presentation by An Taisce 2009_**
_Holding the flag are School Principal Liam Ó Donnchú and Mrs. Fionnuala Hayes (right), Green Flag co-ordinator with pupils Nicole O'Brien and Brian Maher._

_**Céilí Mór, Lá na Pádraig 2009,
with Michael Cooney, Irish dancing coach.**_

# Register for Girls
# Moycarkey National School
## 1866 to 2008

| Date of Entrance | Pupils Name in Full | Residence | Date of Entrance | Pupils Name in Full | Residence |
|---|---|---|---|---|---|
| Nov 1866 | Shanahan Julia | Horse & Jockey | May 1871 | Moloney Brid | Coolkennedy |
| Jan 1864 | Mary Stokes | Moycarkey | July 1871 | Hanrahan Ellen | Galboola |
| Jan 1867 | Maher Margaret | Saltsquarter | Sept 1871 | Currivan Joanna | Liskeveen |
| April 1867 | Molumby Mary | Moycarkey | April 1871 | Mackey Maria | Curraheen |
| April 1867 | Molumby Anne | Moycarkey | Sept 1871 | Gleeson Anne | Curraheen |
| May 1868 | Maher Joanna | Galboola | Nov 1870 | Wilson Kate | Ballymoreen |
| Sept 1867 | Molumby Kate | Graigue | Nov 1870 | Broderick Mary | Maxfort |
| Feb 1868 | Mara Ellen | Pouldine | June 1870 | Benson Maggie | Turtulla |
| April 1869 | Ryan Joanna | Kilmealan | Nov 1870 | Ryan Kate | Coolkip |
| May 1867 | Mara Kate | Graigue | Nov 1870 | Ryan Maggie | Coolkip |
| March 1868 | Ryan Julia | Graigue | Nov 1871 | Molumby Brid | Maxfort |
| April 1868 | Maher Mary | Forgestown | Sept 1871 | Heffernan Ellen | Liskeveen |
| April 1868 | Maher Kate | Forgestown | Jan 1872 | Moloney Maggie | Graigue |
| May 1868 | Bourke Anne | Graigue | April 1872 | Shanahan Ellen | Horse & Jockey |
| May 1868 | Mara Hannah | Pouldine | April 1873 | Gleeson Kate | Curriheen |
| Jan 1872 | Moloney Maggie | Coolkennedy | April 1872 | Molumby Ellen | Rosevilla |
| April 1869 | Maher Hanora | Galboola | April 1874 | Molumby Anne | Rosevilla |
| Feb 1870 | Ryan Mary | Graigue | July 1873 | Delaney Antonia | Curriheen |
| April 1870 | Bourke Ellen | Graigue | April 1872 | Kerwin Ellen | Ballytarsna |
| Jan 1867 | Brien Eliza | Moycarkey | April 1872 | Maher Ellen | Galboola |
| Nov 1870 | Hunt Kate | Kylenoe | Oct 1874 | Broderick Alice | Maxfort |
| Nov 1870 | Hunt Bridget | Kylenoe | April 1872 | Fogarty Fanny | Killough |
| Jan 1871 | Hunt Hannah | Kylenoe | Oct 1874 | Maher Kate | Killough |
| April 1868 | Mansergh Mary | Grallagh | Jan 1874 | Kearney Mary | Dromgower |
| April 1873 | Hogan Joanna | Maxfort | May 1872 | Cassen Maggie | Newbrook |
| April 1871 | Leahy Mary | Moycarkey | Oct 1873 | Wilson Annie | Ballymoreen |
| May 1871 | Maher Ellen | Galboola | May 1872 | Ryan Maggie | Pouldine |
| July 1873 | Molumby Anne | Graigue | June 1872 | Kerwin Brid | Ballytarsna |
| Sept 1871 | Gleeson Anne | Drombo | April 1874 | Ryan Joanna | Pouldine |
| May 1871 | Gleeson Kate | Drombo | July 1872 | Grady Mary | Archerstown |
| May 1871 | Murphy Ellen | Drombo | July 1872 | Glasheen Brid | Curraheen |
| May 1871 | Delaney Mary | Curraheen | April 1874 | Dwyer Mary | Knockroe |

| Date of Entrance | Pupils Name in Full | Residence | Date of Entrance | Pupils Name in Full | Residence |
|---|---|---|---|---|---|
| July 1872 | Grady Ellen | Archerstown | May 1876 | Mason Maggie | Pouldine |
| July 1873 | Currivan Mary | Liskeveen | April 1875 | Molumby Agnes | Rosevilla |
| Sept 1872 | Spillane Maggie | Drombo | May 1876 | Mara Margaret | Pouldine |
| Sept 1872 | Gleeson Brid | Curraheen | May 1875 | Hanrahan Kate | Galboola |
| Nov 1872 | Keating Ellen | Knockroe | May 1875 | Grant Brid | Coolkip |
| July 1870 | Moloney Sarah | Graigue | Nov 1875 | O'Keeffe Mary | Horse & Jockey |
| Nov 1872 | Shanahan Jane | Maxfort | May 1875 | O'Keeffe Mary | Horse & Jockey |
| Nov 1872 | Shanahan Mary | Maxfort | May 1875 | Mara Mary | Coolkip |
| Jan 1873 | Gleeson Mary | Drombo | Nov 1875 | Dwyer Ellen | Graigue |
| Jan 1873 | Brien Maggie | Moycarkey | May 1875 | Mara Mary | Moycarkey |
| Jan 1873 | Heffernan Mary | Galboola | May 1876 | Ryan Ellen | Pouldine |
| Jan 1873 | Moloney Joanna | Graigue | April 1876 | Mackey Joanna | Curriheen |
| Jan 1873 | Bourkie Kate | Graigue | May 1876 | Gleeson Maggie | Horse & Jockey |
| Mar 1873 | Bourke Mary | Knockroe | July 1875 | Fitzgerald Mary | Horse & Jokcey |
| Mary 1873 | Tobin Maggie | Grallagh | April 1876 | Grady Alice | Graigue |
| Mary 1873 | Coady Kate | Pouldine | Sept 1875 | Grady Ellen | Turtulla |
| April 1874 | Bourke Margaret | Graigue | Sept 1875 | Grady Bridget | Turtulla |
| Oct 1874 | Brien Nanno | Moycarkey | April 1877 | Fitzgerald Maggie | Graigue |
| Oct 1873 | Cummins Bridget | Coolkennedy | Sept 1875 | Hanrahan Joanna | Galboola |
| Apr 1874 | Sullivan Mary | Horse & Jockey | Oct 1875 | Mason Mary | Pouldine |
| Nov 1872 | Ènglish Kate | Horse & Jockey | Nov 1875 | Spillane Maggie | Drombo |
| Jun 1873 | Gleeson Mary | Ballytarsna | Nov 1875 | Fanning Kate | Coolkip |
| April 1874 | Fitzgerald Joanna | Graigue | Nov 1875 | Smith Maggie | Drombo |
| Jun 1873 | Maher Catherine | Saltsquarter | Oct 1876 | Butler Mary | Parkstown |
| Oct 1874 | Hogan Anne | Coolkip | Feb 1876 | Wilson Mary | Ballymoreen |
| April 1874 | Stapleton Kate | Coolkennedy | June 1877 | Mara Ellen | Graigue |
| June 1873 | Banon Mary | Kilenoo | April 1876 | Butler Kate | Parkstown |
| Oct 1874 | Maher Maggie | Forgestown | May 1879 | Molloy Mary | Moycarkey |
| Oct 1874 | Grady Mary | Graigue | June 1877 | Gleeson Maria | Drombo |
| Nov 1875 | Brien Ellen | Moycarkey | May 1876 | O'Keeffe Anne | Horse & Jockey |
| Oct 1874 | Mackey Ellen | Curraheen | Mar 1878 | Cahill Mary | Maxfort |
| Jan 1874 | Cormack Kate | Knockroe | May 1876 | Keating Brid | Knockroe |
| Jan 1874 | Keating Maria | Knockroe | May 1876 | Maher Maggie | Maxfort |
| Mar 1874 | Ryan Mary | Horse & Jockey | Nov 1876 | Hannah Regan | Coolkennedy |
| Oct 1874 | Wilson Anne | Graigue | June 1876 | Gleeson Bridget | Drombo |
| Feb 1876 | Ryan Margaret | Pouldine | Mar 1878 | Gleeson Maggie | Drombo |
| May 1874 | Dwyer Brid | Knockroe | May | Mara Kate | Coolkip |
| April 1875 | Ryan Hanora | Galboola | June 1877 | Dwyer Mary | Parkstown |
| Jan 1874 | Carroll Maggie | Drombo | June 1877 | Wilson Ellen | Graigue |
| Jul 1874 | Kearney Anne | Dromgrower | June 1877 | Dwyer Mary | Graigue |
| July 1874 | Carroll Ellen | Drombo | Mar 1878 | Gleeson Maggie | Drombo |
| Feb 1875 | Wilson Jane | Graigue | Oct 1877 | Mara Kate | Coolkip |
| Feb 1875 | Bourke Ann | Graigue | Mar 1879 | Carrie Ellen | Knockroe |
| May 1876 | Maher Ellen | Killough | Jul 1877 | Regan Alice | Coolkennedy |
| May 1876 | Ellen Hanrahan | Newtown | Jul 1876 | Croake Anne | Grallagh |

| Date of Entrance | Pupils Name in Full | Residence | Date of Entrance | Pupils Name in Full | Residence |
|---|---|---|---|---|---|
| Jul 1876 | Lyons Brid | Turtulla | June 1880 | Maher Anne | Maxfort |
| | Brien Joanna | Moycarkey | April 1879 | Wilson Anne | Graigue |
| Jun 1878 | Moloney Kate | Graigue | May 1878 | Guilmartin Margaret | Cabra |
| May 1879 | Murphy Sarah | Drombo | May 1879 | Guilmartin Joanna | Cloughmartin |
| May 1879 | Murphy Mary | Drombo | June 1878 | Guilmartin Hanora | Cabra |
| May 1877 | Mara Joanna | Turtulla | June 1878 | Fahy Kate | Parkstown |
| Feb 1877 | Kenna Mary | Coolkennedy | June 1878 | Leahy Brid | Liskeveen |
| | Fanning Ellen | Turtulla | June 1878 | Fanning Ellen | Turtulla |
| Sept 1878 | Sullivan Kate | Parkstown | July 1878 | Maher Anne | Killough |
| Sept 1876 | Fanning Mary | Turtulla | Dec 1879 | Cawdy Mary | Horse & Jockey |
| Sept 1876 | Fanning Kate | Coolkip | May 1879 | Hall Catherine | Turtulla |
| Oct 1876 | Slattery Maria | Drombo | Feb 1880 | Butler Kate | Liskeveen |
| June 1878 | O'Keeffe Ellen | Horse & Jockey | Aug 1878 | Hall Anne | Turtulla |
| Jan 1877 | Skehan Ellen | Grallagh | Dec 1878 | Tobin Anne | Drombo |
| Jan 1877 | Mullins Susan | Grallagh | Apr 1880 | Maher Winifred | Forgestown |
| May 1877 | Barry Anne | Horse & Jockey | Mar 1879 | Bennet Mary | Forgestown |
| June 1877 | Molumby Maggie | Rosevilla | Apr 1880 | Delaney Ellen | Curriheen |
| June 1877 | Molumby Catherine | Rosevilla | May 1879 | Butler Mary | Grallagh |
| April 1877 | Slattery Brid | Killough | May 1879 | Dwyer Sarah | Knockroe |
| April 1877 | Slattery Joanna | Killough | June 1880 | Mara Catherine | Moycarkey |
| April 1873 | Kirwin Brid | Ballytarsna | May 1883 | O'Keeffe Kate | Horse & Jockey |
| April 1877 | Gleeson Brid | Ballytarsna | June 1879 | Hogan Johanna | Maxfort |
| May 1877 | Ryan Mary | Coolkip | Sept 1879 | Brien Catherine | Turtulla |
| May 1877 | Gleeson Mary | Ballytarsna | Oct 1879 | Walsh Mary | Coolkip |
| June 1878 | Gleeson Brid | Forgestown | Oct 1879 | Walsh Anne | Coolkip |
| April 1879 | Maher Mary | Turtulla | Oct 1879 | Spillane Alice | Coolkip |
| May 1877 | Currivan Kate | Liskeveen | Oct 1879 | Maher Joanna | Galboola |
| June 1880 | Dwyer Kate | Knockroe | Nov 1879 | Ryan Eliza | Liskeveen |
| May 1879 | O'Keeffe Anne | Horse & Jockey | Nov 1879 | Ryan Mary | Liskeveen |
| June 1878 | Brien Joanna | Graigue | Mar 1880 | Hogan Maggie | Coolkip |
| July 1880 | Croake Brid | Drombo | April 1880 | Hanrahan Joanna | Joanna |
| July 1880 | Bourke Maggie | Graigue | June 1880 | Maher Catherine | Galboola |
| Mar 1878 | Brien Brid | Moycarkey | Jan 1882 | Mara Joanna | Coolkip |
| Mar 1879 | Grady Ellen | Graigue | July 1880 | Maher Kate | Galboola |
| Jun 1877 | Gleeson Ellen | Ballytarsna | Aug 1880 | Spillane Ellen | Coolkip |
| June 1877 | Maher Mary | Graigue | Aug 1880 | Murphy Bridget | Drombo |
| July 1877 | Kerwin Kate | Ballytarsna | Oct 1880 | Tobin Kate | Drombo |
| July 1877 | Slattery Kate | Killough | Feb 1881 | Creed Ellen | Graigue |
| Aug 1877 | Keating Bridget | Coolkennedy | April 1881 | Ryan Anne | Horse & Jockey |
| Aug 1877 | Keating Anne | Coolkennedy | April 1881 | Ryan Brid | Horse & Jockey |
| Aug 1877 | Crede Ellen | Graigue | April 1881 | Ryan Maggie | Horse & Jockey |
| Sept 1877 | Maher Bridget | Killough | April 1881 | Molumby Margaret | Rosevilla |
| Sept 1877 | Delaney Anne | Curriheen | May 1884 | Maher Mary | Maxfort |
| Oct 1877 | Gleeson Maggie | Curriheen | May 1884 | Maher Maggie | Galbooly |
| Jun 1882 | Gleeson Ellen | Horse & Jockey | May 1881 | Dwyer Maggie | Parkstown |

*First Communion Class Year 2005*

Back row: Fr. Bourke, Mary Minchin, Deirdre Dunne, Bridget O'Gorman. 3rd row: Maria O'Keeffe, Eimear Martin, Ann Connolly, Kathryn Connolly, Patricia Hayes, Larry Cawley, Edward Murphy (Gaile), Aoife Maher, Michael Flanagan. 2nd row: Conor Ryan, Aaron Hayes, Pádraig Kirwan, Liam Meaney, Lorna O'Regan, Maria Kinane, Darragh Ryan, Jack Kiely, Mícheál Ryder. Front row: Thomas Mernagh, Laura Jane Stapleton, Nicole O'Brien, Martha Kirwan, Rachel Byrne, Shauna Fitzpatrick, Fíona Hanafin (Gaile), Hannah Ralph, Tomás Ryan (Gaile).

*-First Communion Class year – 2006*

Front row: Ruairí Martin, Gillian Fogarty, Emer Whelan, Michelle Carew, Kevin O'Regan, John Corbett. Middle row: Mark Cummins (Gaile), Darren Ryan, Brian Maher, David Shaw, Aaaron Ryan, Daniel Kavanagh. Back row: Fr. George Bourke P.P., Mrs Aileen Colton, Mrs Ann-Marie Carroll, Mrs Mary Minchin, Liam Ó Donnchú.

**First Communion Class Year – 2007**

*At Back: Mr Gerard Neville, Mrs Deirdre Dunne, Fr. Joe Tynan, Mrs Mary Minchin, Liam Ó Donnchú, Fr. George Bourke, Mrs Aileen Colton, Mrs. Ann-Marie Carroll. Back row: Jack O'Meara, Kath Flanagan, Philip Maher, Bríd Gleeson (Gaile), Seamus Telford. Middle row: Michael O'Callaghan, Olivia Hogan, Eoghan Hayes, Sinéad Cummins (Gaile), Kieran Dunne, Megan Lahart, Caolan O'Brien. Front row: Caolan Noonan, Deirdre Ryan, Victoria Donoghue, Nicola Doyle, Caithlin Donnelly, Fiona Kavanagh, Conor Harnett.*

**First Communion Class 2009**

*Back row: Fr. George Bourke, Bill O'Keeffe, Bill Maher, John Kirwan, Zach Jackson, Brendan Looby, Fr. Joe Tynan. Middle row: Mrs Fionnuala Hayes, Colin Hartigan, Dylan Shaw, Ben O'Dwyer, Patrick Doyle, Daniel Brown, Aidan Scott, Liam Ó Donnchú. Front row: Stephen Fitzpatrick, Lauren Cloonan, Heather Ryan, Linda Donoghue, Aoife Meagher, Seán Kavanagh.*

| Date of Entrance | Pupils Name in Full | Residence | Date of Entrance | Pupils Name in Full | Residence |
|---|---|---|---|---|---|
| Jun 1881 | Mara Joanna | Coolkip | Sept 1884 | Dwyer Maggie | Parkstown |
| Jun 1881 | Felle Hanora | Graigue | Feb 1885 | Hasset Eliza | Ballytarsna |
| Jul 1881 | Bourke Alice | Graigue | May 1885 | Slattery Kate | Drombo |
| Jul 1881 | Stokes Joanna | Coolkennedy | Nov 1886 | Bourke Kate | Graigue |
| May 1882 | Hanrahan Maggie | Galboola | June 1885 | Hackett Mary | Coolkip |
| Oct 1881 | Spillane Mary | Drombo | May 1887 | Fennessy Mary | Parkstown |
| Oct 1881 | Fahy Kate | Parkstown | May 1887 | Boyle Bridget | Moycarkey |
| Nov 1881 | Coady Kate | Horse & Jockey | May 1889 | Boyle Mary | Moycarkey |
| Nov 1881 | Wall Mary | Grallagh | May 1887 | Maher Ellen | Maxfort |
| Jan 1882 | Mackey Kate | Curriheen | Oct 1885 | Grant Mary | Coolkennedy |
| Jan 1882 | Dwyer Maggie | Parkstown | Oct 1885 | Baker Mary | Coolkennedy |
| Feb 1882 | Tobin Mary | Drombo | Nov 1889 | Tynan Johanna | Drombo |
| Feb 1882 | Butler Ellen | Liskeveen | Aug 1885 | Cormack Kate | Graigue |
| Feb. 1882 | Murphy Maggie | Drombo | Sept 1885 | Bourke Kate | Graigue |
| Jan 1882 | Ryan Maggie | Drombo | Nov 1885 | Maher Bridget | Forgestown |
| May 1884 | Bourke Eliza | Graigue | Jan 1885 | Cormack Ellen | Moycarkey |
| May 1884 | Costello Kate | Shanballa | Feb 1885 | Dwyer Joanna | Knockroe |
| June 1882 | Flanagan Anne | Graigue | Feb 1886 | Barry Maggie | Curriheen |
| May 1884 | Maher Maggie | Pouldine | April 1886 | O'Keeffe Ellen | Horse & Jockey |
| May 1884 | Maher Ellen | Forgestown | April 1886 | Cawdy Maggie | Horse & Jockey |
| Sept 1882 | Slattery Sarah | Drombo | May 1887 | Purcell Ellen | Knockroe |
| Jan 1883 | Tobin Kate | Drombo | May 1887 | Cormack Kate | Graigue |
| May 1884 | Hogan Joanna | Coolkip | May 1887 | Brien Mary | Knockroe |
| May 1884 | Hagan Minnie | Coolkip | May 1886 | Melbourne J. Harriet | Curriheen |
| Jun 1886 | Fogarty Maggie | Graigue | May 1889 | Brien Brid | Knockroe |
| May 1883 | Fanning Maggie | Coolkennedy | June 1886 | Heffernan Mary | Ballytarsna |
| May 1886 | Mara Joanna | Ballymoreen | Jul 1889 | Fennessy Alice | Parkstown |
| May 1883 | Molumby Teresa | Rosevilla | April 1887 | Fogarty Hannah | Graigue |
| May 1883 | Molumby Cieily | Rosevilla | May 1890 | Maher Mary A. | Pouldine |
| June 1883 | Gleeson Anne | Drombo | Sept 1886 | Grant Maggie | Coolkennedy |
| May 1884 | O'Keeffe Kate | Horse & Jockey | Sept 1886 | Cahill Johanna | Maxfort |
| May 1885 | Gleeson Kate | Horse & Jockey | May 1890 | Keating Bridget | Moycarkey |
| Jul 1883 | Maher Brid | Parkstown | May 1889 | Bourke Nanno | Graigue |
| Jul 1883 | Maher Maggie | Parkstown | May 1889 | Felle Mary | Killough |
| May 1885 | Cawdy Ellen | Horse & Jockey | June 1887 | Grant Kate | Coolkip |
| May 1886 | Fennessy Kate | Kilenoo | June 1887 | Molumby Elizabeth | Rosevilla |
| Oct 1883 | Whelan Lizzy | Galbooly | Sept 1887 | Tobin Ellen | Drombo |
| June 1883 | Keating Maggie | Moycarkey | Sept 1887 | Tobin Bridget | Drombo |
| May 1885 | Delaney Kate | Curriheen | Sept 1888 | Barry Kate | Curriheen |
| May 1885 | Costly Mary A. | Pouldine | Oct 1887 | Sullivan Maggie | Curriheen |
| May 1884 | Currivan Ellen | Parkstown | June 1889 | Cawdy Maggie | Horse & Jockey |
| June 1884 | Barry Maggie | Horse & Jockey | May 1890 | Boyleson Mary | Kilenoo |
| May 1885 | Corcoran Mary | Shanballa | Aug 1891 | Fogarty Joanna | Graigue |
| June 1886 | Costello Maggie | Shanballa | May 1890 | Fogarty Kate | Graigue |
| Nov 1886 | Gleeson Brid | Drombo | May 1890 | Purcell Mary | Knockroe |

| Date of Entrance | Pupils Name in Full | Residence | Date of Entrance | Pupils Name in Full | Residence |
|---|---|---|---|---|---|
| Jul 1892 | Boyle Maggie | Maxfort | Sept 1894 | Mockler Hanora | Curraheen |
| May 1890 | Cormack Kate | Knockroe | Sept 1895 | Ryan Mary | Forgestown |
| Aug 1891 | Gleeson Kate | Drombo | Aug 1896 | Buckley Joanna | Knockroe |
| May 1891 | Cahill Anne | Maxfort | June 1895 | Grady Maggie | Cabra |
| Aug 1891 | Dwyer Annie | Graigue | Sept 1894 | Cahill Ellen | Maxfort |
| June 1889 | Fogarty Statia | Graigue | Sept 1894 | Hogan Mary Ellen | Coolkip |
| Aug 1889 | Mockler Sarah | Curriheen | Sept 1894 | Fahy Joanna | Coolkip |
| May 1890 | Smyth Johanna | Knockroe | Aug 1893 | St. Clare Kathleen | Horse & Jockey |
| May 1890 | Fennessy Lizzie | Horse & Jockey | Sept 1894 | Hogan Sarah | Coolkip |
| May 1889 | Skehan Johanna | Ballymoreen | Aug 1896 | Fogarty Mary | Graigue |
| Aug 1891 | Cahill Maggie | Maxfort | June 1895 | Maher Joanna | Maxfort |
| Aug 1891 | Skehan Mary | Ballymoreen | June 1895 | Molloy Annie | Moycarkey |
| June 1890 | Gleeson Maggie | Drombo | Sept 1894 | Tobin Maggie | Drombo |
| June 1890 | Tobin Statia | Drombo | Sept 1894 | Shaw Hanora | Drombo |
| June 1890 | Molumby Louisa | Rosevilla | Aug 1896 | Fahy Sarah | Coolkip |
| June 1890 | Kenna Bridget | Moycarkey | Oct 1893 | Kearney Joanna | Graigue |
| June 1890 | Mason Janie | Cabra | Jan 1894 | Dee Kathleen | Littleton |
| Aug 1891 | Fennessy Bridget | Horse & Jockey | July 1897 | Toomey Mary | Forgestown |
| June 1890 | Grant Mary | Coolkip | Feb 1894 | Quinlan Annie | Graigue |
| May 1895 | Mason Mary | Cabra | May 1894 | Cuinningham Catherine | Kylenoe |
| Aug 1890 | Murphy Anne | Liskeveen | July 1898 | Mockler Mary | Curraheen |
| Sept 1894 | Addish Maggie | Liskeveen | Jun 1895 | Baker Bridget | Coolkennedy |
| Mar 1891 | Dwyer Bridget | Graigue | Aug 1896 | Cahill Bridget | Maxfort |
| Sept 1893 | Barry Sarah | Curraheen | July 1897 | Stokes Katie | Graigue |
| April 1891 | Kenna Ellie | Turtulla | Sept 1894 | Fanning Mary | Graigue |
| May 1891 | Tynan Ellen | Parkstown | Sept 1894 | Fanning Maggie | Graigue |
| Sept 1893 | Purcell Joanna | Knockroe | Aug 1896 | Grady Bridget | Graigue |
| Sept 1893 | Murphy Annie | Liskeveen | Aug 1896 | Grady Mary | Cloughmartin |
| June 1891 | Hayes Alice | Turtulla | June 1895 | Costello Joanna | Pouldine |
| Sept 1893 | Cormack Mary | Knockroe | Sept 1894 | Costello Bridget | Pouldine |
| Sept 1894 | Smyth Mary | Knockroe | Oct 1894 | Donnelly Joanna | Coolkip |
| June 1895 | Baker Kate | Coolkennedy | Nov 1894 | Fogarty Maggie | Coolkip |
| Sept 1894 | Quinlan Alice | Moycarkey | July 1897 | Callanan Mary | Turtulla |
| Sept 1893 | Buckley Mary J. | Knockroe | Mary 1895 | Harrington Catherine | Ballymoreen |
| May 1892 | Buckley Maggie | Knockroe | July 1898 | Purcell Katie | Knockroe |
| Oct 1893 | Baker Maggie | Coolkenedy | Feb 1897 | Callanan Helena | Parkstown |
| Oct 1893 | Callaghan Maggie | Turtulla | May 1895 | Fitzpatrick Ellie | Pouldine |
| June 1895 | Boyle Katie | Maxfort | May 1895 | Maher Maggie | Ballymoreen |
| Sept 1894 | Wilson Hannah | Ballymoreen | May 1895 | Dunphy Maggie | Graigue |
| Sept 1894 | Gleeson Joanna | Drombo | Aug 1896 | Baker Mary | Parkstown |
| Nov 1892 | Donnelly MaryAnne | Coolkip | July 1898 | Mockler Maggie | Curraheen |
| Nov 1892 | Fahy Mary | Coolkip | Mar 1898 | Cody Mary Anne | Curraheen |
| April 1893 | Ryan Kate | Curraheen | Sept 1895 | Grady Mary | Grawn |
| April 1893 | Ryan Anne | Curraheen | Sept 1895 | Fahy Annie | Coolkip |
| April 1893 | Ryan Hanora | Curraheen | Sept 1899 | Boyle Ellen | Maxfort |

| Date of Entrance | Pupils Name in Full | Residence | Date of Entrance | Pupils Name in Full | Residence |
|---|---|---|---|---|---|
| July 1897 | Skehan Kathleen | Ballymoreen | May 1899 | Tobin Maggie | Turtulla |
| Aug 1896 | Fogarty Joanna | Cabra | June 1899 | Lambe Bridget | Maxfort |
| April 1896 | Fogarty Mary | Cabra | June 1899 | Buckley Bridget | Pouldine |
| Sept 1900 | Fitzpatrick Maggie | Pouldine | Nov 1902 | Shanahan Ellen | Kylenoe |
| July 1897 | Quinlan Mary | Graigue | Nov 1902 | Carey Mary | Maxfort |
| May 1896 | Patterson Katie | Coolkennedy | June 1899 | Fitzpatrick Katie | Pouldine |
| July 1898 | Shanahan Katie | Kylenoe | Sept 1899 | Flynn Mary | Maxfort |
| June 1896 | St. Clair Hanora | Horse & Jockey | April 1900 | Gooney Mary | Ballytarsna |
| June 1896 | Boyleson Katie | Kylenoe | Nov 1902 | Wilson Janie | Graigue |
| July 1897 | Lyons Maggie | Turtulla | May 1900 | Dwyer Katie | Galboola |
| June 1896 | Maher Alice | Graigue | Nov 1902 | Callanan Alice | Turtulla |
| Sept 1896 | Patterson Julia | Coolkennedy | 1900 | Toomey Kathleen | Forgestown |
| Jan 1897 | Patterson Mary | Coolkennedy | | Loughnane Katie | Ballymoreen |
| April 1897 | Fanning Mary | Newtown | | Russell Bridget | Galboola |
| May 1897 | Fogarty Stasia | Graigue | 1901 | Shanahan Mary | Coolkip |
| May 1897 | Wilson Katie | Graigue | | Kerwick Annie | Coolkip |
| May 1897 | Barry Annie | Curraheen | | Grady Josephine | Cloughmartin |
| Mar 1897 | Dwyer Hanora | Forgestown | Nov 1902 | Dwyer Mary | Forgestown |
| Sept 1899 | Hogan Bridget | Coolkip | Nov 1902 | Ryan Lizzie | Curraheen |
| Sept 1899 | Baker Bridget | Parkstown | 1901 | Carey Joanna | Maxfort |
| July 1897 | Cahill Kathleen | Maxfort | | Coman Mary Bridget | Killough |
| Sept 1899 | Long Katie | Graigue | | Hogan Bridget | Coolkip |
| Sept 1900 | Shaw Mary | Drombo | 1902 | Ryan Mary | Graigue |
| Sept 1900 | Wilson Mary | Graigue | | Whelan Margaret | Parkstown |
| Sept 1897 | Murphy Mary | Grallagh | | Lambe Catherine | Maxfort |
| Sept 1899 | Hogan Ellen | Coolkip | | Cawdy Ellen | Parkstown |
| May 1898 | Corovan Mary | Drombo | | Toomey Josephine | Forgestown |
| May 1898 | Breen Bridget | Graigue | | Gooney Catherine | Ballytarsna |
| May 1898 | Murphy Helena | Grallagh | | Gooney Hanora | Ballytarnsa |
| May 1898 | Quinlan Joanna | Graigue | | Grady Joanna | Graigue |
| May 1898 | Lambe Annie | Maxfort | | Toomey Ellen | Forgestown |
| May 1898 | Ryan Bridget | Forgestown | | Shanahan Mary | Kylenoe |
| May 1898 | Ryan Mary | Forgestown | | Maher Ellen | Shanaclune |
| Sept 1900 | Toomey Bridget | Forgestown | | Wilson Hannah | Graigue |
| Sept 1900 | Toomey Stasia | Forgestown | | Coady Kathleen | Curraheen |
| Sept 1900 | Whelan Kate | Parkstown | | Shaw Catherine | Drombo |
| Sept 1900 | Fahy Anastatia | Coolkip | 1903 | Gorman Ellen | Crohogue |
| Sept 1900 | Burke Maggie | Maxfort | | Cummins Annie | Grallagh |
| May 1899 | Fanning Maggie | Newtown | | Callanan Bridget | Turtulla |
| May 1899 | Callanan Mary | Turtulla | | Ftizpatrick Bridget | Pouldine |
| May 1899 | Pyne Maggie | Coolkennedy | | Lambe Ellen | Maxfort |
| May 1899 | Cawdy Maggie | Parkstown | | Fahy Ellen | Coolkip |
| May 1899 | Cawdy Annie | Parkstown | | O'Brien Mary | Moycarkey |
| Nov 1902 | Skehan Bridget | Balymoreen | | Coman Ellen | Killough |
| Sept 1900 | Ryan Annie | Curraheen | 1904 | Heffernan Mary | Maxfort |

| Date of Entrance | Pupils Name in Full | Residence | Date of Entrance | Pupils Name in Full | Residence |
|---|---|---|---|---|---|
| | Moloney Katie | Graigue | | Bridget Fanning | Turtulla |
| | Mason Mary | Cloughmartin | 1908 | Mary Fanning | Turtulla |
| | Hunt Mary | Kylenoe | | Hanora O'Grady | Graigue |
| | Shanahan Annie, Agnes | Kylenoe | | Bridget Heffernan | Coolkip |
| | Shanahan Anastasia | Kylenoe | | Joanna Heffernan | Coolkip |
| | Dunne Mary | Forgestown | | Catherine O'Brien | Graigue |
| | Manning Mary | Ballymoreen | | Bridget McCarthy | Curraheen |
| | Heffernan Julia | Maxfort | | Kathleen Manning | Ballymoreen |
| | O'Brien Margaret | Moycarkey | | Maria Heffernan | Coolkip |
| | Coady Maggie | Horse & Jockey | | Mary Shanahan | Moycarkey |
| | O'Keeffe Kathleen, Mary | Horse & Jockey | | Bridget Gooney | Ballytarsna |
| | | | | Mary Maher | Shanaclune |
| | O'Grady Annie | Cloughmartin | | Josephine Benson | Turtulla |
| | Coman Kathleen | Killough | | Bridget Benson | Turtulla |
| | Patterson Lizzie | Cloughmartin | | Joanna Fitzpatrick | Pouldine |
| 1905 | Butler Mary | Killough | | Mary Hanly | Liskeveen |
| | Butler Bridget | Killough | | Winifred Doherty | Ballytarsna |
| | Shanahan Katie | Moycarkey | | Margaret Maher | Shanaclune |
| | Ryan Joanna | Kilmelan | | Alice O'Grady | Graigue |
| | Brien Mary | Two-Mile-Borris | | Margaret Moloney | Graigue |
| | | | | Elizabeth Fitzpatrick | Pouldine |
| | Toomey Hanora | Forgestown | | Lily Heney | Grallagh |
| | Hayes Catherine | Pouldine | | Bridget Heney | Grallagh |
| | Roache Mary | Grallagh | | Kathleen Buckley | Pouldine |
| | Hayes Joanna | Pouldine | | Catherine Fanning | Newtown |
| | Lonergan Mary | Colkip | | Mary Lambe | Maxfort |
| | Lonergan Catherine | Coolkip | | Jane Agatha Shanahan | |
| | O'Keeffe Kathleen | Thurles | | | Moycarkey |
| | Wilson Mary | Ballymoreen | | Mary McCarthy | Curraheen |
| | Dwyer Josephine | Curraheen | | Mary Hogan | Coolkip |
| 1906 | Ryan Delia | Graigue | | Catherine Connors | Grallagh |
| | Flynn Mary Ellen | Horse & Jockey | | Alice Ryan | Parkstown |
| | Fanning Ellen | Newtown | 1909 | Margaret Molumby | Moycarkey |
| | Shanahan Ellen | Maxfort | | Kathleen O'Keeffe | Horse & Jockey |
| | Butler Katie | Killough | | Mary Fitzgerald | Heathview |
| | Dunne Annie | Forgestown | | Catherine Fanning | Shanballa |
| | Maher Ellen | Parkstown | | Ellen Carey | Maxfort |
| | Hogan Anastasia | Coolkip | | Madaline Manning | Ballymoreen |
| | O'Brien Annie | Moycarkey | | Catherine Maher | Shanaclune |
| | Cahill Kathleen | Coolkip | | Ellen Fanning | Turtulla |
| | Mary O'Grady | Graigue | | Mary Butler | Turtulla |
| | Sarah Moloney | Graigue | | Mary Heney | Grallagh |
| | Mary Fitzpatrick | Parkstown | | Hanora Hogan | Coolkip |
| | Margaret Wilson | Graigue | | Bridget Taylor | Graigue |
| 1907 | Alice Dolan | Maxfort | | Joanna Fanning | Newtown |

*First Communion 1994*
*David Kinane, Damien Shanahan, Shane Barry, Seán Quirke, Dick O'Sullivan,*
*Carol Sweeney, Mairéad Dixon.*

*First Communion 1993*
*Back Row: Ms. Yvonne Grogan, Ms. Mary Minchin, James Ryan, Darren Maher, Rory Coote, Bill Collins, Brian Hogan, Brian Mullins, Joseph Dixon, Mrs. Jane Gleeson, Fr. Richard Ryan P.P. Front row: Siobhán O'Meara (Gaile N.S.), Mairéad Roberts, Nikita Purcell, Patricia O'Mahony, Lisa Cleary, Ann-Marie Molloy, Mary Jo Molloy, Naomi Dempsey.*

*James Kennedy,*
*Curraheen –*
*Confirmation Day,*
*Moycarkey.*

*School Tour 1983*
*Photograph taken at Roscrea Heritage Centre.*
Front row: Bill O'Sullivan, P.J. Butler, Patrick Dunne, Timothy Scott, Martin Flanagan, Denis Rayel, Cormac Cassidy, Declan O'Dwyer, Andreas Maher, Seamus Lahart. Middle row: Pat O'Brien, Irwin Bannon, Thomas O'Halloran, Damien Loughnane, Declan Hogan, Martin Campbell. Back row: Michael Cooney, Patrick O'Connell, Adrian Delahunty, Liam Ó Donnchú, Heritage Centre Guide, Thomas McCormack, Siobhán Bourke, Esther Ryan, Siobhán Hogan, Esther Butler, Martina Croke, Cristin O'Reilly, John McCormack.

*June 1983*
*– Ms. Bríd Ryan with*
*her pupils enjoying*
*the natural beauty of*
*the Slieve Blooms.*

| Date of Entrance | Pupils Name in Full | Residence | Date of Entrance | Pupils Name in Full | Residence |
|---|---|---|---|---|---|
| | Helena Meara | Clohogue | | Mary O'Brien | Graigue |
| 1910 | Mary Benson | Turtulla | | Margaret Costello | Graigue |
| | Bridget Heffernan | Ballymoreen | | Sarah Dwyer | Parkstown |
| | Alice Butler | Killough | | Kathleen Hanly | Liskeveen |
| | Mary Heffernan | Galboola | | Margaret Hackett | Grallagh |
| | Annie Murphy | Grallagh | | Bridget McGrath | Moycarkey |
| | Joanna Fanning | Galboola | 1915 | Margaret Boyle | Coolkennedy |
| | Mary Ryan | Parkstown | | Josephine Boyle | Coolkennedy |
| | Josephine O'Brien | Graigue | | Margaret Mary Hanly | |
| 1911 | Margaret Hayes | Pouldine | | | Liskeveen |
| | Ellen Heffernan | Maxfort | | Hannah O'Keeffe | Horse & Jockey |
| | Margaret Moloney | Maxfort | | Bridget O'Grady | Graigue |
| | Margaret Mary O'Grady | Graigue | | Ellen Shanahan | Pouldine |
| | Alice Carrie | Knockroe | | Mary Flanagan | Graigue |
| | Mary Fanning | Shanballa | | Mary Anne Gleeson | Drombo |
| | Bridget Maher | Shanaclune | | Margaret Sweeney | Graigue |
| | Mary Kate Taylor | Graigue | | Annie Wilson | Ballymoreen |
| | Bridget Grady | Parkstown | | Bridget Connors | Grallagh |
| 1912 | Mary Heffernan | Ballymoreen | | Christina Heffernan | Coolkip |
| | Elizabeth Toomey | Forgestown | | Mary Moloney | Graigue |
| | Catherine Dwyer | Parkstown | | Joanna Patterson | Graigue |
| | Catherine Heffernan | Coolkip | | Mary Burke | Graigue |
| | Kathleen McElroy | Grallagh | | Catherine Sheehan | Grallagh |
| | Bridget Hyde | Killough | 1916 | Joanna Heffernan | Galboola |
| | Kathleen Connors | Graigue | | Ellen Mary O'Grady | Cloughmartin |
| | Mary McElroy | Grallagh | | Catherine Ryan | Horse & Jockey |
| | Mary Costello | Graigue | | Margaret Gleeson | Curraheen |
| | Anastatia Shanahan | Pouldine | | Jane Manning | Ballymoreen |
| | Mary Corbett | Clohogue | | Mary Hogan | Coolkip |
| 1913 | Margaret Mary Coman | | | Joanna Fanning | Shanballa |
| | | Dromgower | | Bridget Ryan | Curraheen |
| | Ellen O'Grady | Graigue | | Catherine Shanahan | Maxfort |
| | Annie Connors | Curraheen | | Margaret Burke | Graigue |
| | Teresa Purcell | Galbertstown | | Hanora Hanley | Liskeveen |
| | Margaret McCarthy | Curraheen | 1917 | Annie Connolly | Moycarkey |
| | Mary Connors | Grallagh | | Catherine Molloy | Maxfort |
| | Anastatia Fitzpatrick | Pouldine | | Margaret Maher | Forgestown |
| | Kathleen Wilson | Ballymoreen | | Annie Maher | Forgestown |
| | Mary Kate Lambe | Parkstown | | Mary Maher | Forgestown |
| | Mary Hayes | Dromgower | | Catherine Maher | Forgestown |
| 1914 | Mary Donnelly | Forgestown | | Margaret Dempsey | Ballytarsna |
| | Mary Furlong | Horse & Jockey | | Ellen Maher | Forgestown |
| | Blanche Lanphier | Parkstown | | Ellen Wilson | Graigue |
| | Annie Fitzpatrick | Pouldine | | Eveleen Mullins | Grallagh |
| | Annie Wilson | Graigue | | Margaret Mullins | Grallagh |

| Date of Entrance | Pupils Name in Full | Residence | Date of Entrance | Pupils Name in Full | Residence |
|---|---|---|---|---|---|
| | Margaret Cawdy | Curraheen | | Margaret O'Keeffe | Parkstown |
| | Mary Connelly | Grallagh | | Catherine Buckley | Cloughmartin |
| 1918 | Bridget Fitzgerald | Heathview | | Jane Dwyer | Cabra |
| | Joanna Dwyer | Parkstown | | Joanna Donnelly | Forgestown |
| | Patience Maher | Forgestown | | Margaret Mary Taylor | Graigue |
| | Bridget Beary | Graigue | | Catherine Corbett | Grallagh |
| | Bridget Sweeney | Graigue | | | |
| | Catherine Ryan | Moycarkey | | Catherine Sweeney | Graigue |
| | Josephine Costello | Parkstown | | Mary Healy | Knockroe |
| | Mary Maher | Clohogue | 1922 | Bridget Dempsey | Ballytarsna |
| | Ellen Dempsey | Ballytarsna | | Mary Fogarty | Graigue |
| | Mary Heffernan | Newtown | | Bridget Maher | Clohogue |
| | Maureen O'Keeffe | Parkstown | | Catherine Foley | Parkstown |
| | Ellen Tobin | Grallagh | | Ellen Phelan | Galboola |
| | Winifred Coman | Dromgower | | Anstatia Donnelly | Forgestown |
| | Bridget Hanly | Liskeveen | | Ellen Heffernan | Galboola |
| | Margaret Mary Quinlan | Dualla | 1923 | Mary Quirke | Heathview |
| 1919 | Ellen Cantwell | Newtown | | Maureen Shanahan | Graigue |
| | Agnes Manning | Ballymoreen | | Mary Bridget O'Keeffe | Horse & Jockey |
| | Mary Ann O'Keeffe | Horse & Jockey | | Mary Brereton | Turtulla |
| | Anna-Marie Lanphier | Parkstown | | Mary Harris | Parkstown |
| | Margaret Maher | Clohogue | | Catherine Ryan | Grallagh |
| | Ellen Ryan | Moycarkey | | Sarah Delaney | Knockroe |
| | Alice Josephine Connolly | Grallagh | | Christina M. Smyth | Knockroe |
| | Elizabeth Connolly | Grallagh | | Josie Skehan | Graigue |
| | Josephine Mary Shanahan | Pouldine | | Alice Skehan | Graigue |
| | Ellen Ryan | Curraheen | | Maggie Skehan | Graigue |
| | Catherine Dwyer | Cabra | 1924 | Catherine O'Keeffe | Horse & Jockey |
| | Josephine Buckley | Cloughmartin | | Mary Kate Cantwell | Newtown |
| | Alice Dempsey | Ballytarsna | | Annie Maher | Maxfort |
| 1920 | Ellen O'Keeffe | Horse & Jockey | | Annie Buckley | Graigue |
| | Ellen Flanagan | Graigue | | Rosamind Kennedy | Galboola |
| | Margaret Fitzpatrick | Pouldine | | Mary Maher | Curraheen |
| | Ellen Dwyer | Cabra | | Annie Molloy | Moycarkey |
| | Ellen Gleeson | Curraheen | | Mary Maher | Galboola |
| | Mary Doherty | Ballytarsna | | Johanna Heffernan | Newtown |
| | Ellen Slattery | Ballytarsna | | Catherine, Jane Melbourne | Curraheen |
| | Ellen Mary O'Keeffe | Horse & Jockey | | Mary Dwyer | Cloughmartin |
| | Eileen O'Keeffe | Horse & Jockey | | Mary Armstrong | Maxfort |
| 1921 | Joanna Ryan | Moycarkey | 1925 | Elizabeth Maher | Liskeveen |
| | Mary Ryan | Curraheen | | Margaret Leahy | Galboola |
| | Josephine McCarthy | Maxfort | | Catherine Brien | Coolkennedy |
| | Annie Doherty | Ballytarsna | | Joanna Harris | Parkstown |
| | | | | Kate Brereton | Turtulla |

| Date of Entrance | Pupils Name in Full | Residence |
|---|---|---|
| | Catherine O'Keeffe | Parkstown |
| 1926 | Nora Flanagan | Graigue |
| | Mary Fanning | Graigue |
| | Mary Ryan | Knockroe |
| | Catherine Ryan | Knockroe |
| | Johanna Buckley | Graigue |
| | Mary Tynan | Curraheen |
| | Margaret Ryan | Coolkennedy |
| | Bridget Armstrong | Maxfort |
| | Sarah Regan | Coolkennedy |
| 1927 | Norah Bourke | Graigue |
| | Ellen Fahey | Turtulla |
| | Bridget Mary Gorman | Ballymoreen |
| | Katie Dunne | Cloughmartin |
| | Mary Buckley | Cloughmartin |
| | Margaret Grant | Coolkennedy |
| | Winifred Brien | Coolkennedy |
| | Catherine Buckley | Pouldine |
| | Josie Butler | Clohogue |
| | Ellen Teresa Maher | Galboola |
| | Mary Bridget Costello | Parkstown |
| | Bridget Maher | Clohogue |
| 1928 | Margaret Dwyer | Cloughmartin |
| | Christina Maher | Galboola |
| 1929 | Maureen Costello | Galboola |
| | Hannah Fogarty | Graigue |
| | Norah Armstrong | Maxfort |
| | Margaret M. Mackay | Maxfort |
| | Margaret Harris | Liskeveen |
| | Anne Brien | Coolkennedy |
| | Catherine Fitzpatrick | Parkstown |
| | Bridget Murphy | Maxfort |
| | Maureen Murphy | Maxfort |
| | Ellen Ryan | Knockroe |
| 1930 | Josephine Shanahan | Turtulla |
| | Ellen Maher | Turtulla |
| | Mary Gleeson | Killough |
| | Catherine Ryan | Knockroe |
| | Margaret Buckley | Cloughmartin |
| | Lily Kenny | Clohogue |
| | Kathleen Kenny | Clohogue |
| | Gretta Harte | Curraheen |
| | Margaret Gleeson | Killough |
| | Ellen Shanahan | Clohogue |
| 1931 | Joan O'Keeffe | Parkstown |

| Date of Entrance | Pupils Name in Full | Residence |
|---|---|---|
| | Mary Christina Mackay | Maxfort |
| | Mary Heffernan | Parkstown |
| | Joan Buckley | Pouldine |
| | Catherine Patricia O'Keeffe | Horse & Jockey |
| | Ellen Bourke | Graigue |
| | Mary Shanahan | Turtulla |
| | Teresa Costello | Graigue |
| 1932 | Philomena Maher | Turtulla |
| | Mary Elizabeth Myers | Dromgower |
| | Joanna Fanning | Ballytarsna |
| | Ellen Scott | Kylenoe |
| | Mary Gooney | Shanaclune |
| | Margaret Kinane | Pouldine |
| | Margaret Mary Meehan | Knockroe |
| | Margaret Mary Boilson | Kylenoe |
| 1933 | Margaret Costello | Parkstown |
| | Teresa Buckley | Cloughmartin |
| | Agnes Hayes | Dromgower |
| 1934 | Alice Carroll | Clohogue |
| | Patricia Maher | Galboola |
| | Mary Patricia Maher | Turtulla |
| | Josephine O'Keeffe | Parkstown |
| | Bridget Ryan | Grallagh |
| | Annie Leahy | Kylenoe |
| | Catherine Gooney | Shanaclune |
| | Teresa Armstrong | Moycarkey |
| | Sarah Burke | Graigue |
| | Catherine Stokes | Cloughmartin |
| | Winifred Carroll | Clohogue |
| 1935 | Catherine Costello | Pouldine |
| | Mary Ryan | Newtown |
| | Bridget Fanning | Ballytarsna |
| | Kathleen Shanahan | Liskeveen |
| | Marry Harris | Graigue |
| | Ellen Tynan | Curraheen |
| 1936 | Catherine Noonan | Coolkennedy |
| | Eliza Noonan | Coolkennedy |
| | Maryanne Scott | Kylenoe |
| | Rosaria O'Keeffe | Horse & Jockey |
| | Statia Harris | Graigue |
| | Catherine, Ann Boilson | Kylenoe |
| | Mary Kinane | Pouldine |
| 1937 | Ellen Regan | Coolkennedy |
| | Elizabeth Callanan | Parkstown |

| Date of Entrance | Pupils Name in Full | Residence | Date of Entrance | Pupils Name in Full | Residence |
|---|---|---|---|---|---|
| | Ellen Toomey | Forgestown | | Eileen Chute | Knockroe |
| | Mary Croke | Curraheen | | Catherine Stapleton | Curraheen |
| | Josephine Stapleton | Horse & jockey | | Mary C. Burke | Ballyhudda |
| | Bernadette Noonan | Coolkennedy | | Mary Buckley | Graigue |
| | Josephine Ryan | Kylenoe | | Carmel Scott | Kylenoe |
| | Ellen Fitzpatrick | Parkstown | | Mary Fanning | Cloughmartin |
| 1938 | Margaret Mary O'Grady | Clohogue | | Nora M. O'Grady | Cloughmartin |
| | Sarah Lyons | Turtulla | | Mary Ryan | Coolkennedy |
| | Bridget Mary Bourke | Ballyhudda | 1945 | Mary Hanley | Graigue |
| 1939 | Margaret Ní Cheoiréis | Knockroe | | Margaret Twomey | Aughnagomaun |
| | Eileen Tobin | Parkstown | | Catherine Wilson | Ballymoreen |
| | Phyllis Scott | Kylenoe | | Flora Wilson | Ballymoreen |
| | Anstatia Shanahan | Curraheen | | Clare C. Murphy | Moycarkey |
| | Margaret Fanning | Ballytarsna | | Catherine Philips | Curraheen |
| | Mary Boilson | Kylenoe | | Mary Shanahan | Pouldine |
| | Bridget Ann McGrath | Moycarkey | 1946 | Anne Scott | Kylenoe |
| | Elizabeth Kinane | Pouldine | | Mary Britton | Parkstown |
| 1940 | Pauline Murphy | Moycarkey | | Noreen Cleary | Liskeveen |
| | Bridget Gleeson | Drombo | | Eileen Buckley | Coolkennedy |
| | Bridget Tobin | Parkstown | | Sheila Fitzpatrick | Parkstown |
| | Mary Twomey | Forgestown | 1947 | Josephine Bourke | Curraheen |
| | Anne Gleeson | Drombo | | Kathleen Shanahan | Moycarkey |
| | Catherine McGrath | Moycarkey | | Bridget Ann Lanphier | Curraheen |
| 1941 | Kathleen Lanphier | Littleton | | Kathleen O'Connell | Coolkip |
| | Phyllis Butler | Turtulla | | Kathleen Fanning | Cloughmartin |
| | Maureen Ryan | Graigue | | Josephine O'Grady | Cloughmartin |
| | Margaret Fitzpatrick | Curraheen | | Mary O'Dwyer | Graigue |
| | Catherine Ryan | Grallagh | | Mary Maher | Coolkennedy |
| | Nancy Wilson | Ballymoreen | | Bernadette McElwee | Moycarkey |
| | Mary Wilson | Ballymoreen | | Phylis Ní Theimhneáin | Curraheen |
| | Mary Lambe | Curraheen | | Kathleen Reilly | Shanballa |
| | Mary Purcell | Galboola | | Mary Reilly | Shanballa |
| | Ann Boilson | Kylenoe | | Clare Reilly | Shanballa |
| | Bridget Ní Theimhneáin | Curraheen | 1948 | Elizabeth M. Shanahan | Curraheen |
| 1942 | Kathleen Barry | Horse & Jockey | | Kathleen Nolan | Aughnagomaun |
| | Josephine Barry | Horse & Jockey | | Margaret Britton | Parkstown |
| | Elizabeth Barry | Horse & Jockey | | Margaret Bourke | Graigue |
| 1943 | Mary McGrath | Moycarkey | 1949 | Mary Shanahan | Moycarkey |
| | Margaret Ryan | Coolkennedy | | Eileen Heffernan | Moycarkey |
| | Josephine Fanning | Cloughmartin | | Mary Heffernan | Moycarkey |
| | Margaret Croke | Curraheen | | A nne Maher | Drumgower |
| | Bridget Twomey | Aughnagomaun | | Elizabeth Twomey | Aughnagomaun |
| | Angela Boilson | Kylenoe | | Eileen Lanphier | Curraheen |
| | Mary Molloy | Moycarkey | | Margaret Heffernan | Parkstown |
| 1944 | Margaret Barry | Curraheen | | Mary Heffernan | Ballymoreen |

*Enjoying a Forest Walk
in Dundrum Woods
in September 2000.*

*School Tour to Tralee June 1999*

*Semple Stadium – Here We Come, May 2000*

*In the V.I.P. section.*

*Patricia Coman, Máire O'Regan, Rachel Bourke, Laura Cleary and Hannah McGrath
outside Semple Stadium in May 2000.*

*Conor Fanning, Thomas Quinn, Eoghan Nagle, Dick O'Sullivan, Shane Barry and
Seán Quirke outside Semple Stadium in May 2000.*

| Date of Entrance | Pupils Name in Full | Residence | Date of Entrance | Pupils Name in Full | Residence |
|---|---|---|---|---|---|
| | Josephine Britton | Parkstown | | Mary Shaw | Ashill |
| | Anne Murphy | Moycarkey | | Eileen O'Meara | Clohogue |
| 1950 | Nuala Bulfin | Horse & Jockey | | Mary Graydon | Knockroe |
| | Mary T. Hogan | Coolkip | 1955 | Mary O'Keeffe | Moycarkey |
| | Margaret M. Flanagan | Graigue | | Patricia Ryan | Knockroe |
| | Mary Kelly | Moycarkey | | Margaret Costello | Parkstown |
| | Bridget Skehan | Knockroe | | Margaret Skehan | Knockroe |
| | Mary Skehan | Knockroe | | Mary O'Connell | Ashill |
| | Mary A. Flynn | Graigue | | Agnes S. Nolan | Parkstown |
| 1951 | Carmel Heffernan | Ballymoreen | | Mary O'Meara | Clohogue |
| | Breda M. Dwyer | Graigue | | Margaret M. Hayes | Moycarkey |
| | Eileen Lyons | Graigue | | Anne Heffernan | Moycarkey |
| | Anastatia Moloney | Graigue | | Teresa Ryan | Knockroe |
| | Eileen Shanahan | Moycarkey | | Ann Ryan | Pouldine |
| | Josephine Costello | Parkstown | | Mary O'Regan | Coolkennedy |
| | Dymphna Shanahan | Pouldine | 1956 | Josephine Ryan | Knockroe |
| 1952 | Kathleen Kavanagh | Graigue | | Máire Nic Iobáin | Coolkennedy |
| | Teresa Kavanagh | Graigue | | Bridget Nic Tobáin | Coolkennedy |
| | Mary R. Fitzgerald | Forgestown | | Mary O'Dwyer | Parkstown |
| | Mary Cahill | Moycarkey | | Anne Hewitt | Ballytarsna |
| | Elizabeth Gleeson | Parkstown | | Breda M. Leahy | Parkstown |
| | Anastatia Twomey | Ballytarsna | | Anne Marie Murphy | Moycarkey |
| | Bridget M. Nolan | Parkstown | | Mary Murphy | Mocarkey |
| | Mary Cummins | Graigue | | Eileen Heffernan | Ballymoreen |
| | Margaret M. Nolan | Parkstown | | Mary O'Brien | Graigue |
| | Mary Walsh | Graigue | | Patricia Fell | Coolkennedy |
| | Sinéad Philips | Curraheen | | Phyllis Nolan | Parkstown |
| | Mary Hewitt | Ballytarsna | | Pauline Murphy | Moycarkey |
| | Mary Heffernan | Kylenoe | | Eileen O'Regan | Coolkennedy |
| 1953 | Ann-Marie Flanagan | Graigue | 1957 | Catriona Ryan | Graigue |
| | Eileen O'Dwyer | Graigue | | Mary Costello | Shanballa |
| | Carmel Coman | Galboola | | Catriona Heffernan | Curraheen |
| | Mary Philips | Curraheen | | Kathleen Costello | Liskeveen |
| | Mary Ryan | Knockroe | | Josephine Butler | Parkstown |
| | Mary McCormack | Curraheen | | Mary Dee | Curraheen |
| | Elizabeth Shanahan | Moycarkey | | Margaret Fitzgerald | Forgestown |
| | Eileen Butler | Parkstown | | Kathleen Fogarty | Pouldine |
| | Margaret Moloney | Graigue | | Mary T. Ryan | Pouldine |
| | Teresa Fell | Coolkennedy | | Eileen Maher | Saltsquarter |
| 1954 | Margaret O'Meara | Graigue | 1958 | Kathleen O'Meara | Clohogue |
| | Anne Heffernan | Ballymoreen | | Ann O'Regan | Knockroe |
| | Teresa O'Keeffe | Parkstown | | Mary Skehan | Graigue |
| | Nora Fell | Coolkennedy | | Eileen Cummins | Graigue |
| | Teresa Britton | Parkstown | | Eileen Shaw | Ashill |
| | Mary Ryan | Knockroe | | Mary Maher | Knockstowry |

| Date of Entrance | Pupils Name in Full | Residence | Date of Entrance | Pupils Name in Full | Residence |
|---|---|---|---|---|---|
| | Mary Morris | Ashill | | Mary Carrie | Knockroe |
| | Margaret Buckley | Graigue | | Bernadette Sheehy | Clohogue |
| | Anne Sheehy | Clohogue | | Mary O'Connell | Cloughmartin |
| | Eileen O'Regan | Coolkennedy | | Kathleen Cawley | |
| | Anne Quigley | Newtown | | Margaret Cawley | |
| | Elizabeth Graydon | Knockroe | 1963 | Bernadette MacLoughney | |
| | AnnMarie Lanfier | Curraheen | | | Coolkennedy |
| 1959 | Mary Butler | Parkstown | | Teresa Costello | Liskeveen |
| | Catherine Gleeson | Curraheen | | Geraldine Dee | Pouldine |
| | Bridget Heffernan | Curraheen | | Noreen Fogarty | Graigue |
| | Josephine O' Regan | Coolkennedy | | Bridget Ryan | Moycarkey |
| | Eileen McCormack | Curraheen | | Mary Hogan | Coolkip |
| | Angela Maher | Coolkennedy | | Dennise Lanphier | Curraheen |
| | Mary T. Fogarty | Pouldine | 1964 | Concepta O'Keeffe | Parkstown |
| | Kathleen Morris | Ashill | | Teresa Dee | Pouldine |
| | Margaret Costello | Knockroe | | Ann Shaw | Ashill |
| | Phyllis Graydon | Knockroe | | Marie Callanan | Parkstown |
| | Margaret M. O'Brien | Graigue | | Una Coman | Newtown |
| | Frances Skehan | Graigue | | Catherine Butler | Knockroe |
| | Mary Sheehy | Clohogue | 1965 | Josephine Graydon | Knockroe |
| | Mary Moloney | Graigue | | Lucy O'Keeffe | Parkstown |
| | Mary Dwyer | Newtown | | Bridget Costello | Liskeveen |
| | Bridget M. Ryan | Pouldine | | Josephine A. Leahy | Kylenoe |
| | Margaret Ní Mhaolcamadh | Galboola | | Bridget A. Kirwan | Graigue |
| 1960 | Bridget Ryan | Graigue | | Abherghil Nic Ghothraidh | |
| | Mary Costello | Liskeveen | | | Ballymoreen |
| | Mary Leahy | Kylenoe | | Bridget Kirwan | Moycarkey |
| | Margaret Leahy | Kylenoe | | Mary T. Fogarty | Graigue |
| | Catherine Shaw | Ashill | 1966 | Pauline O' Regan | Knockroe |
| 1961 | Kathleen Sweeney | Graigue | | Mary Ní Labhradha | Forgestown |
| | Anne M. Callanan | Parkstown | | Caroline Nic Gothraidh | Ballymoreen |
| | Teresa Lanphier | Curraheen | | Teresa Coman | Newtown |
| | Alice Regan | Ballymoreen | | Sheila Flanagan | Curraheen |
| | Helen Regan | Ballymoreen | | Nora Shaw | Curraheen |
| | Ann Ryan | Moycarkey | | Ann Brennan | Pouldine |
| | Annette Lanphier | Curraheen | | Mary Flanagan | Graigue |
| | Nuala Heffernan | Graigue | 1967 | Catherine Skehan | Graigue |
| 1962 | Geraldine O'Brien | Graigue | | Doreen Cullagh | Knockroe |
| | Bernadette Lanphier | Curraheen | | Breda Fahey | Graigue |
| | Bridget Shaw | Ashill | | Martha Kirwan | Graigue |
| | Josephine Coman | Newtown | | Angela Shaw | Ashill |
| | Rita Dee | Pouldine | | Bridget Lanphier | Curraheen |
| | Monica MacLoughney | Coolkennedy | | Geraldine Lanphier | Curraheen |
| | Josephine O'Halloran | Graigue | | Mary O'Keeffe | Curraheen |
| | Mary E. Ryan | Kylenoe | | Kathleen Leahy | Kylenoe |

| Date of Entrance | Pupils Name in Full | Residence |
|---|---|---|
| | Geraldine Coman | Newtown |
| | Margaret McCormack | Dromgower |
| | Mary S. McCormack | Dromgower |
| 1968 | Margaret Flanagan | Graigue |
| | Breda Regan | Ballymoreen |
| | Mary Scott | Kylenoe |
| | Kathleen Fanning | Newtown |
| | Mary Cummins | Graigue |
| 1969 | Elizabeth Sheehy | Clohogue |
| | Eileen Lanphier | Curraheen |
| | Geraldine Costello | Liskeveen |
| | Ester Kirwan | Moycarkey |
| | Deirdre Heaney | Graigue |
| | Kathleen M. Stapleton | Curraheen |
| | Josephine M. Stapleton | Curraheen |
| | Mary Coonan | Galboola |
| | Dolores Cummins | Graigue |
| 1970 | Anstatia M. O'Halloran | Graigue |
| | Evelyn Fogarty | Graigue |
| | Christine Croke | Dromgower |
| | Angela C. Lanphier | Curraheen |
| 1971 | Martina Scott | Kylenoe |
| | Mary Dunne | Ballymoreen |
| | Kathleen Doyle | |
| | Breda A. Cummins | Graigue |
| | Dolores Coman | Newtown |
| | Dolores Croke | Curraheen |
| | Helen Lahart | Newtown |
| | Frances Fanning | Newtown |
| | Elizabeth McCormack | Dromgower |
| | Catríona Cooney | Galboola |
| | Katherine Flanagan | Forgestown |
| | Mary P. Kirwan | Moycarkey |
| | Blanche Lanphier | Curraheen |
| | Josephine Lanphier | Curraheen |
| 1972 | Eileen Kelly | Moycarkey |
| | Catherine Cummins | Graigue |
| | Josephine Shaw | Ashill |
| | Nora Doyle | Shanballa |
| 1973 | Ella Cooney | Galboola |
| | Helen Ryan | Ballymoreen |
| | Martina Regan | Ballymoreen |
| | Linda Shaw | Curraheen |
| | Caroline Dunne | Cloughmartin |
| | Catriona Loughnane | Dromgower |

| Date of Entrance | Pupils Name in Full | Residence |
|---|---|---|
| | Mary Loughnane | Dromgower |
| | Mary Doyle | |
| 1974 | Deirdre Rayel | Ballymoreen |
| | Michelle Kelly | Moycarkey |
| | Kathleen Fahey | Graigue |
| | Teresa Cummins | Graigue |
| | Elaine Higgins | Knockroe |
| | Majella Dunne | Ballymoreen |
| 1975 | Karen Meaney | Kylenoe |
| | Kathleen S. Meaney | Kylenoe |
| | Stephaine Ivors | Galboola |
| | Mary Fahey | Graigue |
| | Siobhán Hogan | Coolkennedy |
| | Esther Ryan | Newtown |
| | Siobhán Burke | Coolkennedy |
| | Niamh Cassidy | Knockroe |
| | Esther Butler | Parkstown |
| | Eileen Flanagan | Forgestown |
| | Martina Croke | Curraheen |
| | Teresa Doyle | |
| 1976 | Michelle Delahunty | Curraheen |
| | Angela O'Reilly | |
| | Christine O'Reilly | |
| | Noreen O'Reilly | |
| | Margaret O'Reilly | |
| | Helen Delaney | |
| | Catherine Brennan | Turtulla |
| | Geraldine Lahart | Newtown |
| | Maria Maher | Coolkennedy |
| | Elizabeth Cummins | Graigue |
| | Sharon Croke | Curraheen |
| | Siobhán O'Reilly | Graigue |
| | Susan O'Reilly | Graigue |
| | Christine O'Reilly | Graigue |
| | Vanessa O'Reilly | Graigue |
| | Ellen Flanagan | Curraheen |
| | Bridget Cawley | |
| 1977 | Mairéad Cooney | Galboola |
| | Josephine Connors | |
| | Mary Connors | |
| | Josephine McCormack | Curraheen |
| | Teresa Ryan | Horse & Jockey |
| | Margaret O'Halloran | Graigue |
| | Mary O'Halloran | Graigue |
| | Joanne Maher | Coolkennedy |

| Date of Entrance | Pupils Name in Full | Residence | Date of Entrance | Pupils Name in Full | Residence |
|---|---|---|---|---|---|
| | Isabel Coman | Shanballa | | Mary Ryan | Knockroe |
| | Eimear Bannon | Ballymoreen | | Chanelle Shanahan | Curraheen |
| | Yvonne Shaw | Curraheen | | Teresa Walsh | Heathview |
| | Janette Shaw | Curraheen | | Majella Fitzgerald | Forgestown |
| | Catriona Burke | Kylenoe | | Julie Harrington | Dromgower |
| | Susanne Heaphy | Graigue | | Jenny Harrington | Dromgower |
| | Catherine Burke | Coolkennedy | 1982 | Ciara McCormack | Curraheen |
| | Mairéad Burke | Maxfort | | Deborrah Colvin | Horse & Jockey |
| | AnnMarie Shanahan | Curraheen | | Breda Coman | Shanballa |
| | Cora Delahunty | Rathinch | | Pauline Coman | Shanballa |
| | Norma Stapleton | Horse & Jockey | | Fionnuala Concagh | Knockroe |
| | Catherine Barrett | Knocknanuss | | Catherine Harrington | Dromgower |
| | Helena O'Keeffe | Horse & Jockey | | Catherine Stapleton | Parkstown |
| | Martina Loughnane | Pouldine | | Alma Delaney | Rathinch |
| | Ann Barry | Horse & Jockey | | Fiona McCullagh | Shanballa |
| 1978 | Mary Teresa Butler | Parkstown | | Caroline Abbott | Shanballa |
| | Bridget Ryan | Knockroe | | Maria O'Brien | Pouldine |
| | Mary Ivors | Newtown | | Debbie Quigley | Turtulla |
| | Miriam Mooney | Ashfield | | Andrea Murphy | Kylenoe |
| | Nollaig Ryan | Newtown | | Dervla Fitzgerald | Forgestown |
| | Caroline Lambe | Grallagh | | Debbie Quigley | Turtulla |
| | Ann Doyle | | | Linda Power | Graigue |
| | Maura Ann, O'Connell | Ashill | | Barbara Dunne | Ballymoreen |
| 1979 | Bridget O'Reilly | | | Oonagh Nagle | Pouldine |
| | Margaret Gleeson | Curraheen | | Ann-Marie McGuire | Liskeveen |
| | Janette Butler | Curraheen | | Claire Skehan | Parkstown |
| | Elaine Mooney | Ashfield | 1983 | Sandra McCormack | Kylenoe |
| | Tracy A. Browne | Curraheen | | Clare O'Mahony | Knockroe |
| | Tara Coman | Shanballa | | Marie Delaney | Rathinch |
| | Phylis Abbott | Shanballa | | Marguerite Minchin | Littleton |
| | RoseMarie Lanphier | Curraheen | | Marie Webster | Graigue |
| | Bridget Kane | Liskeveen | | Nicola Kavanagh | Maxfort |
| | Agnes Kane | Liskeveen | | Linda Hanley | Pouldine |
| 1980 | Catherine O'Reilly | | | Mary Callanan | Curraheen |
| | Catherine Britton | Liskeveen | | Bríd Ryan | Graigue |
| | Agnes Britton | Liskeveen | | Ruth O'Gorman | Thurles |
| | Olivia O'Brien | Dromgower | | Fiona Sinclair | Knockroe |
| | Louise Delaney | Rathinch | | Christine Sinclair | Knockroe |
| | Caroline Stapleton | Maxfort | | Clare Molloy | Thurles |
| | Fiona O'Mahoney | Knockroe | | Bridget Ryan | Graigue |
| | Ann Butler | Parkstown | | Bridget Lanphier | Curaheen |
| | Valerie Lanphier | Curraheen | | Lisa Magnier | Killough |
| | Helen McCormack | Curraheen | | Caroline Ryan | Galboola |
| 1981 | Catherine O'Sullivan | Kilmealon | | Helena Power | Graigue |
| | Catherine Moriarty | Newtown | 1984 | Anne M. Kelly | Curraheen |

# First Summer of the New Millennium – June 2000

*This photograph was taken in the first summer of the new millennium – June 2000.*

Back row: Eoghan Nagle, Thomas Quinn, Laura Cleary, Rachel Bourke, Máire O'Regan, Marie Carey, Hannah McGrath, Anita Bannon, Marie Kirwan, Felicity Dempsey, Conor Fanning, Shane Barry, Dick O'Sullivan, Tony Flanagan, Kevin Mullanney, Seán Quirke, Eoghan Ryan.

Fourth row: Margaret Mary McGrath, Sheena O'Dwyer, Laura Heffernan, Patricia Coman, Kilian O'Donoghue, Robbie Delaney, Conan O'Hara, William Foley, Karen Hogan, Ann Kirwan, Denis Roche, Noel Kinane, Martha Dempsey, Sarah Kinane, Christine Ryan, Rosaleen O'Keeffe, Conor Skehan, Sinéad O'Hara, Karen Mullins, Niall Barry, Brendan McCormack, Jack Harnett.

Third row: Ms. Catherine O'Keeffe, Ms. Lucy McGann, Mary Shorthall, Caitríona Delahunty, Jennifer Coote, Aisling Hogan, Ailish O'Keeffe, Anna Harnett, Laura Maher, Pat Molloy, Finbarr Hayes, Colm Skehan, Daniel O'Regan, Lorcan O'Hara, Rory Ryan, Cillian O'Shea, Ciarán O'Shea, Seamus Cummins, Jack Hassett, Peter Kinane, Adam Carew, Claire Singleton, Laura Kirwan, Stephen Kirwan, Katie Quirke, Andrea O'Regan, Mrs. Máire Sheehy, Ms. Ann-Marie Shanahan, Mr. Donie Shanahan, Liam Ó Donnchú (Principal).

Second row: Michelle Carew, Fern Freeman, Jamie Maher, Peadar Kinane, Richard O'Keeffe, Joey Coman, Conor Hayes, Corina Abbott, Timmy Ryan, Kieran Stapleton, Andrew Fogarty, Ryan Noonan, Ryan Hayes, Thomas Quigley, Christopher Byrne, Cathal Gleeson Fahey, Lesley O'Sullivan, Brian Butler, Laurie O'Sullivan, Edwina McGrath, Iain O'Brien, Jamie Barry, Michael Roche, Aisling O'Dwyer, Orlaith McCormack, Ciara Maher,

Front row: Mrs Mary Minchin, Gavin O'Brien, Niamh Butler, Jamie Costello, Aidan Fitzpatrick, Neil Hewitt, Ivan Chadwick, William O'Dwyer, Tommy Noonan, Aaron Flanagan, Tomás Ryan, David Ryan, Michelle Shepperd, Melissa Morris, Michelle Ryan, Nora Connolly, Marguerite McCormack, Antonia McGrath, Michaela Graham, Maryese Noonan, Shauna Flanagan, Marita Moloney, Karen Corbett, Eleanor Kiely, Marguerite Gooney, Sarah Abbott, Fr. Richard Ryan.

*Visiting St. Mary's Memorial Park - Oct 2007.*

*Taking a break outside The Source, Thurles – Oct 2007.*

*School Bus Driver Eamonn Ryan with School Principal Liam Ó Donnchú – Semple Stadium Tour – Oct. '07.*

*Seas Apart Project – Tipperary Institute. Pupils from Pouldine with teachers Mrs. Ann Marie Carroll and Mrs. Aileen Colton.*

| Date of Entrance | Pupils Name in Full | Residence |
|---|---|---|
| | Susan Kelly | Curraheen |
| | Ria O'Gorman | Thurles |
| | Catriona Ryan | Newtown |
| | Catherine Sheppard | Forgestown |
| | Sarah Sheppard | Forgestown |
| | Louise Shortall | Newtown |
| | Caroline Roche | Newtown |
| | Lorraine Dunne | Cloughmartin |
| | Ann Harrington | Pouldine |
| | Claire Hanly | Pouldine |
| | Siobhán Nagle | Pouldine |
| | Claire Hogan | Coolkip |
| | Marie Cummins | Graigue |
| | Sinéad O'Mahoney | Knockroe |
| | Niamh Ryan | Knockroe |
| | Pamela Quigley | Turtulla |
| | Susan Leahy | Ashill |
| | Kate O'Connell | Ashill |
| | Elaine Carey | Forgestown |
| 1985 | Anne Barrett | Knocknanuss |
| | Erin Ryan | Newtown |
| | Muireann O'Donoghue | Ballymoreen |
| | Janette Burke | Graigue |
| | Angela Cummins | Graigue |
| | Mary Magnier | Killough |
| | Lorainne Stapleton | Maxfort |
| | Siobhán Grace | Parkstown |
| | Catríona Murphy | Dromgower |
| | Máire Treasa Murphy | Dromgower |
| 1986 | Ann Ryan | Galboola |
| | Aisling Concagh | Knockroe |
| | Vanessa Purcell | Newtown |
| | Laura Cooney | Galboola |
| | Lyana Maguire | Liskeveen |
| | Katherine Ryan | Newtown |
| | Moira Skehan | Parkstown |
| 1987 | Laura English | Liskeveen |
| | Lesley Abbott | Curraheen |
| | Emma Delaney | Rathinch |
| | Mary Hannigan | Grallagh |
| | Elaine Nagle | Pouldine |
| | Emma Sweeney | Graigue |
| | Patricia Hanigan | Liskeveen |
| | Alma Mullins | Grallagh |
| | Marie McLoughlin | Liskeveen |

| Date of Entrance | Pupils Name in Full | Residence |
|---|---|---|
| | Imelda Britton | Kylenoe |
| | Christine Hannigan | Liskeveen |
| | Geraldine Hannigan | Liskeveen |
| | Sinéad McLoughlin | Liskeveen |
| 1988 | Eileen Looby | Grallagh |
| | Mairead Looby | Grallagh |
| | Rachel Keogh | Graigue |
| | Laura Cleary | Turtulla |
| | Sarah Looby | Grallagh |
| | Neasa O'Donoghue | Ballymoreen |
| | Jacqueline O'Halloran | Graigue |
| | Ann-Marie Dempsey | Littleton |
| | Susan Smyth | Maxfort |
| | Breda Kirwan | Moycarkey |
| | Claire Kirwan | Moycarkey |
| | Dolores Purcell | Newtown |
| | Aisling Crowe | Ballybeg |
| | Elaine Roche | Parkstown |
| | Catherine Burke | Ballyhudda |
| | Aileen Ryan | Newtown |
| | Siobhan Maguire | Liskeveen |
| | Ann-Marie Dwyer | Pouldine |
| | Ann-Marie Dixon | Knockroe |
| 1989 | Joanne Corcoran | Aughnagomaun |
| | Regina Fanning | Turtulla |
| | Caroline Fahey | Galboola |
| | Jacqueline Fahey | Galboola |
| | Tara Quigley | Turtulla |
| | Evlyn Roberts | Thurles |
| 1990 | Louise Fahey | Galboola |
| | Tracey McCarthy | Galboola |
| | Collette Fogarty | Ballymoreen |
| | Noreen Quinn | Graigue |
| | Rose Mary Fanning | Turtulla |
| | Sinéad O'Regan | Knockroe |
| | Catherine Moloney | Graigue |
| | Una Moloney | Graigue |
| | Rebecca Keogh | Graigue |
| | Mary Hayes | DerryHogan |
| 1991 | Elizabeth Cleary | Knockroe |
| | Naomi Dempsey | Shanbally |
| | Patricia O'Mahoney | Knockroe |
| | Nikita Purcell | Galboola |
| | Ann-Marie Molloy | Knockroe |
| | Mary-Jo Molloy | Knockroe |

| Date of Entrance | Pupils Name in Full | Residence |
|---|---|---|
| | Máiread Roberts | Thurles |
| | Siobhan Roche | Parkstown |
| | Megan Quigley | Turtulla |
| | Carol Sweeney | Graigue |
| | Clare Carey | Forgestown |
| | Sarah Cummins | Graigue |
| | Majella Delaney | Rathinch |
| | Mairead Dixon | Knockroe |
| | Karen Freeman | Curraheen |
| | Mary Shortall | Galboola |
| | Ellen Butler | Parkstown |
| 1992 | Christine Ryan | Newtown |
| | Máire O'Regan | Knockroe |
| | Olivia Purcell | Galboola |
| | Patricia Coman | Galboola |
| | Hannah McGrath | Moycarkey |
| | Marie Carey | Forgestown |
| | Laura Cleary | Knockroe |
| | Rosaleen O'Keeffe | Maxfort |
| | Felicity Dempsey | Shanbally |
| | Anita Bannon | Ballymoreen |
| | Rachel Bourke | Graigue |
| | Marie Kirwan | Moycarkey |
| | Lisa Cleary | Knockroe |
| | Caroline Cahill | Liskeveen |
| 1993 | Shannon Hayes | Derryhogan |
| | Caitríona Delahunty | Drombo |
| | Sinéad O'Hara | Dromgower |
| | Karen Mullins | Grallagh |
| | Marie Kiely | Thurles |
| | Ann Kirwan | Moycarkey |
| | Karen Hogan | Coolkip |
| | Julie Cahill | Liskeveen |
| 1994 | Martha Dempsey | Shanballa |
| | Laura Heffernan | Ballybeg |
| | Sarah Kinane | Kevinsfort |
| | Margaret Mary McGrath | Moycarkey |
| | Sheena O'Dwyer | Knockroe |
| 1995 | Aisling Hogan | Coolkip |
| | Anna Harnett | Parkstown |
| | Ailish O'Keeffe | Maxfort |
| | Laura Maher | Coolkennedy |
| | Katie Quirke | Pouldine |
| | Clare Singleton | Graigue |
| | Jennifer Coote | Knockroe |

| Date of Entrance | Pupils Name in Full | Residence |
|---|---|---|
| | Laura Kirwan | Moycarkey |
| 1996 | Megan Ryan | Coleagh, Ballinure |
| | Orlaith McCormack | Pouldine |
| | Aisling O'Dwyer | Galboola |
| | Helena Ryan | Graigue |
| | Andrea O'Regan | Coolkennedy |
| | Laurie O'Sullivan | Turtulla |
| | Leslie O'Sullivan | Turtulla |
| | Edwina McGrath | Moycarkey |
| 1997 | Ciara Maher | Coolkennedy |
| | Marguerite Gooney | Ashill |
| | Eleanor Kiely | Liskeveen |
| | Karen Corbett | Shanballa |
| | Michelle Carew | Galboola |
| | Fern Freeman | Galboola |
| | Shauna Flanagan | Graigue |
| | Corina Abbott | Shanballa |
| | Marita Moloney | Pouldine |
| 1998/'99 | Michaela Graham | Littleton |
| | Nora Connolly | Archerstown |
| | Niamh Butler | Parkstown |
| | Antonia McGrath | Moycarkey |
| | Melissa Morris | Curraheen |
| | Michelle Rose Ryan | Graigue |
| | Maryese Noonan | Cloughmartin |
| | Michelle Sheppard | Aughnamonaun |
| | Marguerite McCormack | Pouldine |
| 2000 | Sarah Abbott | Shanballa |
| | Áine Hayes | Derryhogan |
| | Shauna Noonan | Cloughmartin |
| | Clare Hassett | Archerstown |
| | Micheala O'Meara | Pouldine |
| 2001 | Maria O'Keeffe | Maxfort |
| | Maria Kinane | Parkstown |
| | Leah Murphy | Thurles |
| | Aoife Maher | Kylenoe |
| | Nicole O'Brien | Beakstown |
| | Shauna Fitzpatrick | Cloughmartin |
| | Ann Connolly | Archerstown |
| | Catherine Connolly | Archerstown |
| | Rachel Byrne | Moycarkey |
| | Martha Kirwan | Moycarkey |
| | Patricia Hayes | Leigh |
| | Vanessa Cawley | Holycross |

| Date of Entrance | Pupils Name in Full | Residence |
|---|---|---|
| | Eimear Martin | Curraheen |
| | Sophie Thomas | Liskeveen |
| | Lorna O'Regan | Coolkennedy |
| 2002 | Karen Skehan | Horse & Jockey |
| | Naomi Cawley | Holycross |
| | Eimear Whelan | Kylenoe |
| | Gilian Fogarty | Parkstown |
| | Ann-Marie Carew | Galboola |
| | Róisín Mogridge | Thurles |
| | Klara Martin | Curraheen |
| 2003 | Megan Lahart | Ballybeg |
| | Caitlin Donnelly | Aughnagomaun |
| | Sinéad Cummins | Graigue |
| | Olivia Hogan | Knocknanuss |
| | Deirdre Ryan | Augnnagomaun |
| | Fiona Kavanagh | Pouldine |
| | Emma Dalton | Parkstown |
| 2004 | Holly Tobin | Parkstown |
| | Megan Donovan | Ballybeg |
| | Niamh Meaney | Ballybeg |
| | Saoirse O'Meara | Pouldine |
| | Claire Ryan | Aughnagomaun |
| | Rachel Dowling | Galboola |
| | Maeve Ryder | Thurles |
| | Lauren Albery | Shanballa |
| | Laura, Jane Stapleton | Pouldine |
| 2005 | Heather Ryan | Parkstown |
| | Aoife Meagher | Pouldine |
| | Lauren Cloonan | Ballynonty |
| | Laura Maher | Horse & Jockey |
| | Linda Donoghue | Ballybeg |
| | Donna Marie Cawley | Two-Mile-Borris |
| | Kathleen Donoghue | Ballybeg |
| | Nora Donoghue | Ballybeg |
| | Victoria Donoghue | Ballybeg |
| | Kat Flanagan | Graigue |
| | Nicola Doyle | Turtulla |

| Date of Entrance | Pupils Name in Full | Residence |
|---|---|---|
| 2006 | Kate Marie Looby | Aughnagomaun |
| | Amy Cummins | Killough |
| | Aoife Walsh | Clongour, Thurles |
| | Zoe O'Meara | Pouldine |
| | Deirdre Fogarty | Knocknanuss |
| | Emma Dowling | Galboola |
| | Megan O'Donoghue | Ballybeg |
| | Emily Murphy | Thurles |
| | Siobhán Hennessy | Holycross |
| | Ciara Darmody | Curraheen |
| | Cait Darmody | Curraheen |
| 2007 | Roseanna Toohey | Curraheen |
| | Sorcha Tobin | Littleton |
| | Clarisee Tobin | Littleton |
| | Kaylee Stonestreet | Thurles |
| | Lauryn O' Sullivan | Shanballa |
| | Aisling Maher | Ballymoreen |
| | Kelly-Ann Glleece | Ballinure |
| | Queva O'Meara | Pouldine |
| | Chloe O'Connell | Cloughmartin |
| | Marie Kennedy | Ballybeg |
| | Róisín Donnelly | Aughnagomaun |
| | Amy Cloonan | Ballynonty |
| 2008 | Sophie Ely | Newhill |
| | Catherine Fogarty | Knocknanuss |
| | Joan O'Keeffe | Horse & Jockey |
| | Ciara Coffey | Moycarkey |
| | Chloe Cummins | Killough |
| | Rebecca Hogan | Knocknanuss |
| | Gráinne Stapleton | Horse & Jockey |
| | Emma O'Sullivan | Shanballa |
| | Michelle Flanagan | Graigue |
| | Lizzy Freeman | Rahelty |
| | Eve Dardis | Cloughmartin |
| | Chelsie Hartigan | Piercetown |
| | Rachel Freeman Nash | Liskeveen |
| | Ciara Freeman Nash | Liskeveen |

# Register for Boys
# Moycarkey National School
## 1867 to 2008

| Date of Entrance | Pupils Name in Full | Residence | Date of Entrance | Pupils Name in Full | Residence |
|---|---|---|---|---|---|
| 1-1867 | William Davy | Newtown | 7-1871 | Thomas Fahy | Parkstown |
| 1-1866 | Denis Shanahan | Horse & Jockey | 7-1871 | William Hogan | Coolkip |
| 1-1868 | James Ryan | Pouldine | 10-1873 | Richard English | Horse & Jockey |
| 1-1867 | Pat Grady | Graigue | 1-1875 | Laurence Barry | Horse & Jockey |
| 4-1869 | John Molloy | Pouldine | 10-1871 | Philip Fitzgerald | Graigue |
| 5-1866 | Pat Moloney | Coolkennedy | 12-1871 | Pat Gleeson | Ballytarsna |
| 5-1868 | Tim Maher | Saltzquarter | 2-1871 | Jer. Fitzgerald | Graigue |
| 5-1868 | James Fitzgerald | Graigue | 10-1873 | William Mara | Pouldine |
| 6-1865 | John Stokes | Moycarkey | 10-1873 | Andrew Moloney | Coolkennedy |
| 8-1868 | James Grady | Graigue | 1-1872 | Michael Kerwin | Ballytarsna |
| 12 –1868 | Richard Delaney | Forgestown | 4-1874 | Edmond Molumby | Moycarkey |
| 4 -1869 | John Brien | Moycarkey | 5-1872 | Denis Skehan | Coolkennedy |
| 1-1869 | William Molloy | Pouldine | 4-1872 | James O'Brien | Moycarkey |
| 5-1869 | John Molumby | Moycarkey | 10-1873 | John Maher | Galboolo |
| 6-1869 | James Purcell | Killough | 10-1873 | Laurence Russell | Curriheen |
| 1-1869 | Denis Mara | Pouldine | 7-1874 | John Hogan | Coolkip |
| 9-1869 | William Mara | Graigue | 4-1874 | Michael Ryan | Pouldine |
| 6-1870 | James Maher | Forgestown | 5-1872 | Richard Mackey | Curriheen |
| 7-1869 | Michael Hahesey | Forgestown | 5-1872 | Stephen Stapleton | Coolkennedy |
| 9-1870 | Philip Grady | Graigue | 10-1873 | Pat Regan | Coolkennedy |
| 9-1870 | Thos Molloy | Pouldine | 6-1872 | Richard Glasheen | Curraheen |
| 9-1870 | John Barry | Horse & Jockey | 6-1872 | John Kerwin | Ballytarsna |
| 10-1873 | Michael Barry | Horse & Jockey | 12-1874 | Philip Mara | Graigue |
| 2-1871 | Pierce Maher | Saltzquarter | 8-1872 | Martin Benson | Turtulla |
| 2-1871 | Edmond Mara | Graigue | 9-1872 | Michael Maher | Galboola |
| 10-1873 | Cody James | Pouldine | 10-1872 | Joseph Cussen | Coolkennedy |
| 10-1873 | Pat Hunt | Kylenoe | 10-1872 | Maurice Keating | Knockroe |
| 5-1871 | John Cass | Newtown | 10-1872 | Pat Mackey | Curriheen |
| 10-1873 | Michael Gleeson | Drombo | 11-1872 | Pat Ryan | Graigue |
| 5-1871 | Thos. Sullivan | Curraheen | 11-1872 | Michael Ryan | Graigue |
| 5-1871 | William Currivan | Liskeveen | 11-1872 | Thomas Grady | Graigue |
| 10-1873 | John Bourke | Knockroe | 11-1872 | Pat Shanahan | Maxfort |

| Date of Entrance | Pupils Name in Full | Residence | Date of Entrance | Pupils Name in Full | Residence |
|---|---|---|---|---|---|
| 11-1872 | William Fitzgerald | Horse & Jockey | 4-1876 | Martin Gleeson | Forgestown |
| 11-1872 | Thomas Fitzgerald | Horse & Jockey | 4-1876 | Daniel Maher | Forgestown |
| 1-1873 | Henry Maher | Galboola | 4-1877 | James Carrie | Coolkennedy |
| 1-1873 | Martin Delaney | Rahinch | 4-1876 | Edmond Mara | Coolkip |
| 12-1874 | Michael Shanahan | Moycarkey | 6-1877 | James English | Horse & Jockey |
| 1-1873 | Daniel Wilson | Ballymoreen | 5-1876 | Thomas Grant | Coolkip |
| 1-1873 | John Ryan | Kilmailhane | 5-1875 | Edmond Cahill | Maxfort |
| 1-1873 | John Mannin | Ballymoreen | 6-1875 | John Delaney | Curriheen |
| 1-1873 | Thomas Gleeson | Drombo | 5-1876 | Joseph Mara | Graigue |
| 1-1874 | Eamonn Dwyer | Parkstown | 10-1878 | James Bourke | Knockroe |
| 1-1873 | John Gleeson | Ballytarsna | 9-1875 | Timothy Grady | Turtulla |
| 2-1873 | Pat Quinlan | Pouldine | 6-1878 | Richard Keeffe | Horse & Jockey |
| 3-1873 | Daniel Dwyer | Coolkennedy | 9-1875 | William Grady | Turtulla |
| 7-1875 | Pat Cody | Pouldine | 9-1875 | Thomas Leahy | Liskeveen |
| 7-1874 | Thomas Heffernan | Galboola | 9-1875 | Andrew Leahy | Liskeveen |
| 6-1880 | John Felle | Graigue | 9-1875 | John Leahy | Liskeveen |
| 6-1873 | John Carrie | Coolkennedy | 10-1875 | John Russell | Galboola |
| 9-1873 | Matthew Farrington | Littleton | 6-1878 | Daniel Mara | Ballymoreen |
| 5-1876 | Michael Bourke | Knockroe | 10-1875 | James Spillane | Drombo |
| 9-1875 | John Bourke | Graigiue | 10-1875 | Pat Spillane | Drombo |
| 11-1873 | Edmond Bourke | Knockroe | 10-1875 | Thomas Connors | Curriheen |
| 24-11-1873 | Davy Corcoran | Walshtown | 1-1878 | John Shanahan | Maxfort |
| 7-1885 | James Molloy | Pouldine | 23-2-1876 | Pat Kerwin | Turtulla |
| 12-1873 | Nicholas Tobin | Grallagh | 5-2-1875 | John Russell | Curriheen |
| 12-1873 | Edmond Maher | Galboola | 3-5-1875 | Walter Bourke | Graigue |
| 1-1873 | James Ryan | Grallagh | 17-1-1880 | Denis O'Keeffe | Horse & Jockey |
| 1-1874 | John Pollard | Grallagh | 9-6-1877 | John Dwyer | Graigue |
| 2-1874 | Martin Dwyer | Knockroe | 13-3-1877 | Stephen Keating | Knockroe |
| 4-1875 | Thomas Gleeson | Curriheen | 15-6-1878 | William Maher | Forgestown |
| 3-1875 | Thomas Cummins | Coolkennedy | 15-6-1878 | Edmond Grady | Turtulla |
| 4-1874 | William Wilson | Graigue | 13-8-1877 | John Stapleton | Coolkennedy |
| 4-1875 | Thady Regan | Coolkennedy | 10-5-1879 | Thomas Gleeson | Drombo |
| 1-1874 | Pierce Maher | Galboola | 9-8-1879 | William Gleeson | Drombo |
| 7-1874 | Cornelius Sweeney | Graigue | 10-1875 | James Croake | Grallagh |
| 7-1874 | James Kerwin | Coolkennedy | 18-7-1876 | John Lyons | Turtulla |
| 5-1878 | Cornelius Barry | Horse & Jockey | 5-9-1876 | David Mara | Archerstown |
| 12-7-1876 | Martin Brien | Turtulla | 5-9-1876 | Thomas Fanning | Turtulla |
| 9-1874 | Michael Farrington | Littleton | 5-9-1876 | John Brien | Turtulla |
| 9-1874 | Edmond Bourke | Knockroe | 5-9-1876 | Martin Fanning | Turtulla |
| 14-10-1874 | James Carroll | Horse & Jockey | 6-9-1876 | James Mara | Turtulla |
| 10-1874 | James Byrne | Cluchmartin | -4-1877 | John Maher | Turtulla |
| 11-1874 | Timothy Delaney | Rahinch | 12-9-1876 | Martin Brien | Turtulla |
| 1-1875 | Edmond Byrne | Cabra | 11-9-1876 | Pat Heffernan | Coolkip |
| 4-1876 | Pierce Maher (jnr) | Galboola | 19-9-1876 | John Currivan | Liskeveen |
| 10-1876 | Martin Sullivan | Kylenoe | 20-9-1876 | John Felle | Graigue |

| Date of Entrance | Pupils Name in Full | Residence | Date of Entrance | Pupils Name in Full | Residence |
|---|---|---|---|---|---|
| 18-2-1877 | Tade Leahy | Liskeveen | 26-4-1881 | James Mara | Graigue |
| 25-9-1876 | William Fanning | Coolkip | 6-4-1880 | Edmond Caudy | Parkstown |
| 25-9-1876 | Thomas Brierton | Turtulla | 13-10-79 | Patrick Felle | Graigue |
| 3-10-1877 | Michael Fitzgerald | Parkstown | 1-12-1879 | Michael Hackett | Coolkip |
| 13-11-1876 | Nicholas Felle | Graigue | 23-2-1880 | Michael Sullivan | Curriheen |
| 27-2-1875 | Daniel Mullins | Grallagh | 22-1-1883 | Joseph Mason | Pouldine |
| 9-4-1877 | John Kerwin | Ballytarsna | 18-5-1880 | Pat Maher | Turtulla |
| 9-4-1877 | Pat Kerwin | Ballytarsna | 29-5-1882 | Pat Costello | Shanballa |
| 9-4-1877 | James Kerwin | Ballytarsna | 15-5-1882 | Michael Gleeson | Forgestown |
| 7-5-1877 | John Heffernan | Ballytarsna | 16-5-1882 | James Mara | Graigue |
| 17-1-1880 | John Cormack | Graigue | 5-6-1880 | John Breen | Moycarkey |
| 7-5-1877 | John Manning | Ballymoreen | 22-6-1880 | Denis Regan | Coolkennedy |
| 29-5-1875 | Con Gleeson | Drombo | 20-7-1880 | Pat Clarke | Horse & Jockey |
| 29-5-1877 | Nicholas Felle | Graigue | 20-7-1880 | Martin Grant | Coolkennedy |
| 29-5-1877 | James Croake | Drombo | 20-7-1880 | John Grant | Coolkennedy |
| 18-6-1877 | Pat Hackett | Maxfort | 13-7-1880 | Pat Baker | Coolkennedy |
| 19-6-1877 | Nicholas Hogan | Coolkip | 26-7-1880 | John Bennett | Forgestown |
| 5-6-1880 | John Sullivan | Kylenoe | 2-7-1881 | Thomas Barry | Horse & Jockey |
| 8-5-1878 | Thomas Butler | Turtulla | 10-8-1880 | Pat Gleeson | Horse & Jockey |
| 18-6-1875 | Jer Regan | Coolkennedy | 13-9-1880 | Thomas Fanning | Turtulla |
| 10-5-1879 | John Grant | Coolkip | 17-9-1880 | William Melbourne | Curriheen |
| 18-6-1877 | John Croake | Drombo | 11-9-1880 | Richard Melbourne | Curriheen |
| 9-7-1875 | Martin Grant | Coolkennnedy | 29-9-1883 | Thomas Cahill | Maxfort |
| 9-8-1879 | John Maloney | Graigue | 4-1882 | Stephen Sullivan | Parkstown |
| 13-8-1877 | Michael Kenna | Turtulla | -4-1882 | Pat Gleeson | Horse & Jockey |
| 6-4-1880 | John Cahill | Maxfort | 1-2-1881 | Sam Melbourne | Curriheen |
| 5-6-1880 | Thomas Molloy | Moycarkey | 7-2-1881 | William Maher | Galboola |
| 5-6-1880 | Con Gleeson (Dan) | Drombo | 6-3-1881 | James Butler | Liskeveen |
| 22-5-1878 | Con Gleeson (Con) | Drombo | 9-5-1881 | Thomas Maher | Galboola |
| 22-5-1878 | Michael Guilmartin | Cabra | 15-5-1882 | Martin Delaney | Curriheen |
| 10-6-1878 | James Sullivan | Kylenoe | 17-5-1884 | J. Joseph O'Keeffe | Horse & Jockey |
| 26-6 1881 | William Carrie | Knockroe | 29-7-1882 | Pat Dwyer | Horse & Jockey |
| 1-7-1878 | John Caudy | Horse & Jockey | 15-5-1882 | John Maher | Forgestown |
| 18-8-1879 | Thomas Stokes | Knockroe | 15-5-1882 | Pat Baker | Coolkennedy |
| 29-7-1878 | James Maher | Turtulla | 15-5-1882 | John Brien | Moycarkey |
| 30-9-1878 | Pat Felle | Graigue | 29-7-1882 | Thomas Corcoran | Shanballa |
| 13-3-1880 | Andy Moloney | Coolkennedy | 29-7-1882 | Edmond Dwyer | Graigue |
| 28-4-1879 | James Dwyer | Graigue | 29-7-1882 | Charles Melbourne | Curriheen |
| 5-5-1879 | James Butler | Grallagh | 3-10- 1881 | Pat Maher | Galboolo |
| 13-5-1879 | Michael Gleeson | Forgestown | 27-9-1881 | Michael Hackett | Maxfort |
| 26-5-1879 | Edmond Grant | Coolkip | 29-7-1882 | Edmond Barry | Curriheen |
| 2-6-1879 | John Gilmartin | Cluchmartin | 21-11-1881 | Michael Wall | Grallagh |
| 2-6-1879 | Stephen Sullivan | Parkstown | 21-11-1881 | John Wall | Grallagh |
| 3-6-1879 | William Farrington | Littleton | 19-5-1883 | James O'Keeffe | Horse & Jockey |
| 16-6-1879 | Thomas Ryan | Graigue | 10-1884 | John Butler | Liskeveen |

*Participants in Scór na bPáistí 1999*

*Back row: Clare Carey, Carol Sweeney, David Maher, Eoghan Nagle, Gerry McGuire, Paul Singleton, David Kinane, Mícheál Heffernan. Front row: Maria Carey, Anita Bannon, Rachel Bourke, Siobhán Roche, Máiréad Dixon, Felicity Dempsey. In front: Patricia Coman, Maria Kirwan.*

*Scór na bPáistí 2006*

*Back row: Maria Kinane, Patricia Hayes, Lorna O'Regan, Michaela O'Meara, Rachel Byrne, Martha Kirwan, Emma Dalton, Kathryn Connolly, Ann Connolly. Front row: Jamie Costello, Nora Connolly, Melissa Morris, Michaela Grahan, Seán Dalton, William O'Dwyer, Niamh Butler.*

*Planting a Beech Tree in February 1988*

*Included are: Mairéad and Ann-Marie Dixon, Jenny Harrington, Oonagh Nagle, Channelle Shanahan, Liam Ó Donnchú, Susan Smyth, Julie Harrington, Maria O'Brien, Olivia O'Brien, Claire O'Mahony, Mrs Mary O'Regan, Robert Nagle, Fíona O'Mahony, Michael O'Regan, Enda Callanan, Sinead O'Regan, Mark Shanahan, Eoghan, Neasa and Muireann O'Donoghue, Ann Harrington, Siobhán Nagle, David O'Dwyer, Damien Shanahan, Pamela Quigley and Cyril Smyth.*

*Moycarkey N.S. Credit Union Table Quiz Team 2009*
*Back row: Kieren Hennessy, Kat Flanagan, Maria Kinane, Seán Darmody. Front row: Shane Maher, Claire Ryan, Mícheál Foley, Aaron Hayes.*

*School Quiz Team 1994*
*Martin Shortall, Moira Skehan, John Harrington, Paul Dempsey.*

*Book Week –*
*Prizewinners*
*1993-'94*

*Back row:*
*Vanessa Purcell,*
*Lyana Maguire.*
*Front row:*
*Aidan Bourke,*
*Frank Roche,*
*Paul Dempsey.*

| Date of Entrance | Pupils Name in Full | Residence | Date of Entrance | Pupils Name in Full | Residence |
|---|---|---|---|---|---|
| -5-1884 | John Grant | Coolkennedy | 10-8-1884 | John Gleeson | Drombo |
| -5-1883 | Dan Corcoran | Shanballa | -8-1885 | Michael Grant | Coolkip |
| -10-1882 | Thomas Hanrahan | Glaboola | 10-8-1884 | Costello William | Shanballa |
| -7-1882 | William Wilson | Ballymoreen | -8-1884 | James Tynan | Drombo |
| 4-12-1882 | Cornelius Lyons | Turtulla | 31-8-1885 | Thomas (H) Ryan | Galboola |
| 11-4-1883 | William Con Gleeson | Drombo | 24-8-1885 | Robert Phelan | Galboola |
| 16-4-1883 | Edmond Grady | Graigue | 7-9-1885 | Thomas Phelan | Galboola |
| -5-1884 | Thomas Costly | Pouldine | 24-8-1885 | John Grady | Archerstown |
| 16-4-1883 | John Heffernan | Parkstown | 21-9-1885 | Pat Stapleton | Coolkennedy |
| -5-1885 | Dan Gleeson | Drombo | 14-5-1887 | Jeremiah Fogarty | Graigue |
| 1-1885 | Thady Felle | Graigue | 5-1887 | John Hogan | Coolkip |
| -7-1883 | Edmond Maher | Maxfort | -4-1886 | Denis Brien | Newtown |
| -1-1885 | Denis Maher | Maxfort | -4-1886 | James Brien | Newtown |
| -1-1885 | Simon Baker | Coolkennedy | 6-8-1889 | John Maher | Maxfort |
| -7-1883 | Pat Maher | Galboola | 14-5-1887 | Thomas Purcell | Knockroe |
| -1-1885 | Dan Regan | Coolkennedy | 14-5-87 | Michael Dwyer | Graigue |
| -1-1885 | John Spillane | Drombo | 24-5-1890 | James Costello | Pouldine |
| -9-1883 | William O'Brien | Horse & Jockey | 11-1-1887 | Thomas Dwyer | Knockroe |
| -5-1885 | Thomas Hogan | Coolkip | 9-3-1887 | William Hogan | Coolkip |
| -1-1884 | Walter Stapleton | Coolkennedy | 18-4-1887 | Pat Currivan | Liskeveen |
| -7-1886 | John O'Keeffe | Horse & Jockey | 16-5-1887 | Kieran Costello | Shanballa |
| -6-1886 | Michael Keating | Moycarkey | 16-5-1887 | Wiliam Costello | Shanballa |
| -6-1886 | Pat Cormack | Graigue | 30-5-1887 | Edmond Cormack | Graigue |
| -5-1885 | Pat Maher | Pouldine | 3-5-1887 | John Gleeson | Drombo |
| -6-86 | Pat Molloy | Moycarkey | 13-6-1887 | John Brien | Knockroe |
| -7-1886 | William Molloy | Moycarkey | 3-11-1887 | Thomas Fennessy | Parkstown |
| -4-1884 | William Grady | Archestown | 23-11-1887 | John Gleeson | Drombo |
| -5-89 | Pat Barry | Horse & Jockey | 6-3-1888 | Andrew Hickey | Moycarkey |
| -6-1886 | Andy Fogarty | Graigue | 10-4-1888 | Pierce Maher | Galboola |
| -6-1884 | Denis English | Horse & Jockey | 16-4-1888 | Thomas Carrigan | Ballymoreen |
| -5-1885 | Andy Regan | Coolkennedy | 24-5-1890 | Michael Boyle | Maxfort |
| -8-1884 | Pat Cahill | Maxfort | 7-5-1888 | Dan Hogan | Forgestown |
| -4-1887 | John Gleeson | Drombo | 7-5-1888 | Thomas Shanahan | Horse & Jockey |
| 8-1-1885 | William Stokes | Littleton | 21-5-1888 | Michael Hogan | Forgestown |
| 27-4-85 | James Cummins | Littleton | 10-7-1888 | John O'Donnell | Fethards |
| 6-1891 | William Lyons | Turtulla | 12-11-1888 | Michael McGrath | Galboola |
| 14-5-1887 | Thomas Dwyer | Graigue | 1-8-1891 | Laurence Maher | Forgestown |
| 25-5-1884 | Thomas Cormack | Graigue | 24-5-1890 | James Barry | Horse & Jockey |
| 11-1891 | Denis Grant | Turtulla | 24-5-1890 | James Caudy | Horse & Jockey |
| 1-6-1885 | Henry Ryan | Galboola | 10-5-1889 | Joseph Barry | Horse & Jockey |
| 1-6-1885 | Pat Ryan | Galboola | 1-8-1891 | Michael Cawdy | Horse & Jockey |
| -6-1885 | James Hackett | Coolkip | 17-6-1889 | Denis Maher | Galboola |
| -6-1885 | Richard Hackett | Coolkip | 17-6-1889 | William Ryan | Galboola |
| -6-1885 | Edmond Ryan | Galboola | 1-8-1891 | Pat Cawdy | Horse & Jockey |
| -6-1885 | Thomas Ryan | Galboola | 15-7-1889 | Thomas Hogan | Forgestown |

| Date of Entrance | Pupils Name in Full | Residence | Date of Entrance | Pupils Name in Full | Residence |
|---|---|---|---|---|---|
| 1-8-1891 | Edmond Hogan | Coolkip | 27-6-1889 | William Hogan | Coolkip |
| 1-8-1891 | William Addish | Liskeveen | 18-7-1892 | Patrick Maher | Galboola |
| 1-8-1891 | Matthew Addish | Liskeveen | 26-9-1889 | Daniel Barry | Curraheen |
| 1-8-1891 | Timothy Barry | Horse & Jockey | 3-10-1892 | Patrick Maher | Turtulla |
| 5-5-1890 | Patrick Fogarty | Graigue | 14-11-1892 | Thomas Donnelly | Coolkip |
| 5-5-1889 | James Skehan | Ballymoreen | 22-11-1892 | John Fogarty | Coolkip |
| 5-5-1889 | Pat Skehan | Ballymoreen | 12-12-1892 | Edmond Fahy | Coolkip |
| 1-8-1889 | Daniel Wilson | Ballymoreen | 12-12-1892 | John Fahy | Coolkip |
| 12-5-1889 | James Heffernan | Parkstown | 30-1-1893 | William Brereton | Turtulla |
| 1-8-1891 | John Wilson | Ballymoreen | 6-3-1893 | Michael Murphy | Curraheen |
| 1-8-1891 | Pat Maher | Maxfort | -9-1893 | John Ryan | Curraheen |
| 1-8-1891 | Michael Maher | Maxfort | 1-8-1896 | Patrick Addish | Liskeveen |
| 3-6-1889 | John Tynan | Drombo | 1-8-1896 | James Baker | Parkstown |
| 9-7-1892 | Michael Tobin | Drombo | 1-8-1896 | Thomas Skehan | Ballymoreen |
| 1-8-1891 | Pat Murphy | Liskeveen | 1-5-1893 | Thomas Manning | Maxfort |
| 16-6-1890 | Andy Mason | Cabra | 1-5-1893 | Denis Manning | Maxfort |
| 9-7-1892 | Maurice Maher | Pouldine | 3-5-1889 | Michael Manning | Maxfort |
| 29-9-1890 | Andrew Gorman | Littleton | 15-5-1889 | Joseph Fitzpatrick | Pouldine |
| 9-7-1892 | William Baker | Parkstown | 22-9-1894 | Richard St Clare | Horse & Jockey |
| 9-7-1892 | James Maher | Maxfort | 5-6-1893 | Jeremiah Maher | Galboola |
| 11-5-18991 | Michael Callaghan | Turtulla | 29-6-1895 | Robert St.Clair | Horse & Jockey |
| 13-5-1891 | Michael Fanning | Turtulla | 29-6-1895 | Martin Hogan | Coolkip |
| 18-5-1891 | William Hayes | Turtulla | 1-8-1896 | Daniel Purcell | Knockroe |
| 23-6-1889 | Maurice Maher | Pouldine | 1-8-1896 | James Molloy | Moycarkey |
| 19-5-1891 | Thomas Lyons | Turtulla | 14-11-1889 | Timothy Doyle | Graigue |
| 19-5-1891 | Thomas Kenna | Turtulla | 29-6-1895 | William Callanan | Turtulla |
| 25-5-1891 | David Murphy | Grallagh | 20-3-1894 | Patrick Tobin | Ballymoreen |
| 25-5-1897 | Daniel Murphy | Grallagh | 29-6-1895 | Martin Boyleson | Kylenoe |
| 1-6-1891 | John Maher | Galboola | 1-8-1896 | James Boyleson | Kylenoe |
| 3-6-1891 | Daniel Muleahy | Turtulla | 1-8-1896 | John Barry | Curraheen |
| 1-7-1891 | John Connell | Galboola | 30-7-1898 | John Quinlan | Moycarkey |
| 6-7-1889 | Laurence Fitzpatrick | Pouldine | 1-8-1896 | Richard Smith | Knockroe |
| 10-7-1891 | John Byrne | Turtulla | 29-6-1895 | Joseph Grant | Coolkip |
| 21-7-1891 | Joseph Lyons | Turtulla | 23-7-1894 | Thomas Kirwan | Ballytarsna |
| 4-11-1889 | Pat Maher | Turtulla | 3-9-1894 | Michael Butler | Turtulla |
| 12-1-1892 | Pat Cormack | Turtulla | 1-8-1896 | Michael Tynan | Drombo |
| 25-4-1889 | Michael Purcell | Knockroe | 10-9-1894 | Patrick Byrne | Turtulla |
| 9-5-1889 | James Cahill | Maxfort | 10-9-1894 | Robert Byrne | Turtulla |
| 9-5-1889 | John Costello | Pouldine | 10-9-1894 | Thomas Byrne | Turtulla |
| 9-5-1889 | David Quinlan | Moycarkey | 29-10-1894 | Daniel Donnelly | Coolkip |
| 9-5-1892 | Richard Buckley | Knockroe | 29-10-1894 | John Donnelly | Coolkip |
| 10-5-1892 | Philip Cleary | Shanballa | 29-10 1894 | James Donnelly | Coolkip |
| 9-1893 | Bernard Lyons | Turtulla | 29-10 1894 | John Tobin | Turtulla |
| 30-5-1889 | Robert Mockler | Curraheen | 5-11-1894 | Daniel Fogarty | Coolkilp |
| 27-6-1889 | Patrick Hogan | Coolkip | 1-8-1896 | Cornelius Callaghan | Turtulla |

| Date of Entrance | Pupils Name in Full | Residence | Date of Entrance | Pupils Name in Full | Residence |
|---|---|---|---|---|---|
| 15-1-1895 | John Lalor | Thurles | 1-9-1900 | Timothy Shanahan | Graigue |
| -3-1895 | Daniel Norton | Graine | 16-5-1899 | William Toohey | Thurles |
| 6-5-1895 | Thomas Fogarty | Cabra | 25-5-1899 | Thomas Kerwick | Maxfort |
| 31-7-1897 | William Skehan | Ballymoreen | 1-9-1900 | William Donnelly | Coolkip |
| 1-8-1896 | William Callaghan | Parkstown | 29-5-1894 | Thomas Quinlan | Graigue |
| 1-8-1896 | Daniel Fanning | Graigue | 29-5-1894 | Joseph Quinlan | Killough |
| 6-5-1894 | Thomas St Clair | Moycarkey | 29-11-1902 | James Maher | Ballymoreen |
| 1-8-1896 | Patrick Hogan | Coolkip | 29-11-1902 | Thomas Murphy | Curraheen |
| 1-8-1896 | John Tobin | Drombo | 5-6-1902 | Thomas Dunne | Maxfort |
| 31-7-1897 | Patrick Donnelly | Coolkip | 29-11-1902 | John Skehan | Ballymoreen |
| 30-7-1898 | John Murphy | Curraheen | 29-11-1902 | William Costello | Pouldine |
| 1-8-1896 | Michael Donnelly | Coolkip | 29-11-1902 | Martin Shanahan | Kylenoe |
| 31-7-1897 | Thomas Baker | Knockroe | 12-9-1980 | Patrick Purcell | Knockroe |
| 2-9-1899 | Edmond Molloy | Moycarkey | 29-11-1902 | John Purcell | Knockroe |
| -9-1899 | John Molloy | Moycarkey | 1-9-1900 | Patrick Coady | Curraheen |
| 1-8-1896 | Thomas Byrne | Cloughmartin | 1-9-1900 | Michael Joseph Bourke | Maxfort |
| 4-7-1895 | James Byrne | Cloughmartin | 1-9-1900 | Patrick Tobin | Curraheen |
| 15-7-1895 | Michael Mooney | Maxfort | 29-11-1902 | Timothy Grady | Cloughmartin |
| 9-9-1895 | Patrick Tobin | Turtulla | 30-4-1900 | Thomas Loughnane | Ballymoreen |
| 20-4-1896 | Thomas Ryan | Thurles | 30-4-1900 | Thomas Daly | Ballymoreen |
| 14-1-1901 | Michael Patterson | Graigue | 3-5-1900 | Michael Kennedy | Thurles |
| -3-1904 | William Patterson | Coolkennedy | 3-5-1900 | Patrick Kennedy | Thurles |
| 8-6-1896 | Philip Maher | Galboola | 19-3-1904 | Richard Donnelly | Coolkip |
| 30-7-1898 | William Grady | Cloughmartin | 19-3-1904 | John Whelan | Parkstown |
| 2-9-1899 | James Murphy | Curraheen | 29-11-1902 | Martin Cawdy | Parkstown |
| -9-1899 | John Toomey | Forgestown | 5-5-1899 | Thomas Fahy | Coolkip |
| -9-1899 | Philip Maher | Turtulla | 15-10-1904 | John Fanning | Newtown |
| 2-9-1899 | Thomas Tobin | Turtulla | 29-11-1902 | Thomas Hogan | Coolkip |
| 2-9-1899 | Michael Shanahan | Kylenoe | 29-11-1902 | James Ryan | Graigue |
| 2-9-1899 | John Addish | Liskeveen | 29-11-1902 | Walter Ryan | Graigue |
| 13-9-1897 | John Murphy | Grallagh | 15-10-1904 | Cornelius Fanning | Newtown |
| 2-9-1899 | William Murphy | Grallagh | 19-3-1904 | Daniel Shaw | Drombo |
| 2-9-1899 | John Buckley | Knockroe | 19-3-1904 | Philip Pyne | Coolkennedy |
| 2-9-1899 | Edmond Callaghan | Turtulla | 19-3-1904 | Michael Wilson | Graigue |
| 1-9-1900 | Patrick Grady | Cloughmartin | 29-11-1902 | William Ryan | Forgestwon |
| 23-5-1898 | Patrick Carroll | Galboola | 15-10-1904 | John O'Brien | Moycarkey |
| 15-10-1904 | Lawrence Molloy | Moycarkey | 19-3-1904 | Peter Coman | Killough |
| 2-9-1899 | Matthew Lambe | Maxfort | 29-11-1902 | James Coady | Curraheen |
| 30-7-1898 | Martin Coady | Curraheen | 11-11-1905 | Michael Fitzpatrick | Pouldine |
| 6-9-1898 | John Joseph Coman | Thurles | 15-10-1904 | William Moloney | Graigue |
| 7-9-1898 | Edmond Shanahan | Horse & Jockey | 15-10-1904 | George Patterson | Graigue |
| 19-9-1898 | John Maher | Newbrook | 21-5 1901 | Patrick Patterson | Graigue |
| 23-9-1898 | Martin Maher | Ashfield | 15-10-1904 | Patrick Murphy | Grallagh |
| 16-11-1898 | Thomas Lonergan | Coolkip | 9-7-1901 | Chritopher Maher | Ballymoreen |
| 1-9-1900 | Daniel Pyne | Coolkennedy | 2-10-1901 | William Whitelegge | Ballymoreen |

| Date of Entrance | Pupils Name in Full | Residence | Date of Entrance | Pupils Name in Full | Residence |
|---|---|---|---|---|---|
| 11-11 1905 | John Moloney | Graigue | 10-9-1906 | David Shaw | Drombo |
| 6-5-1902 | Thomas Butler | Turtulla | 11-9-1906 | Joseph Flynn | Horse & Jockey |
| 6-5-1902 | Matthew Butler | Turtulla | 12-1906 | Richard Connors | Grrallagh |
| 11-11-1905 | James Dunne | Maxfort | 12-3-1907 | Patrick Quinlan | Graigue |
| 11-11-1905 | William O'Brien | Moycarkey | 4-1907 | James Maher | Ashfield |
| 29-9-1906 | Edmond Donnelly | Coolkip | 25-7-1908 | Patrick Lambe | Maxfort |
| 15-10-1904 | Daniel Lambe | Maxfort | 5-1907 | Thomas Shanahan | Coolkip |
| 11-1905 | Joseph Molloy | Moycarkey | 31-8-1907 | James Heffernan | Coolkip |
| 29-9-1906 | Thomas Pyne | Coolkennedy | 31-8-1907 | Thomas Heffernan | Coolkip |
| 11-11-1905 | Michael Buckley | Knockroe | –7-1908 | Denis Carey | Maxfort |
| 11-11-1905 | Michael Molloy | Moycarkey | –7-1908 | Michael Taylor | Graigue |
| 15-10-1904 | Charles McCarthy | Curraheen | 5-1907 | Patrick Gooney | Ballytarsna |
| 17-2-1903 | James Gorman | Clohogue | 30-7- 1910 | Patrick Shanahan | Maxfort |
| 24-2-1903 | Patrick Mackey | Maxfort | 31-7-1909 | Daniel Coman | Drumgrower |
| 11-1905 | Patrick Ryan | Graigue | 31-7-1909 | William Taylor | Graigue |
| 29-9-1906 | Thomas Fanning | Newtown | 31-7-1909 | James Hayes | Drumgower |
| 11-11-1905 | Martin Quinlan | Graigue | –7-1910 | Richard Heffernan | Maxfort |
| 7-9-1903 | Thomas Mahony | Curraheen | –3-1908 | Roger Hanly | Liskeveen |
| 11-11-1905 | William Heffernan | Maxfort | –4-1908 | Martin Doherty | Ballytarsna |
| 20-5-1904 | John Lonergan | Coolkip | –4-1908 | Lawrence Doherty | Ballytarsna |
| 11-11-1905 | Thomas Maher | Galboola | –7-1910 | James O'Brien | Moycarkey |
| 31-8-1907 | Thomas Shanahan | Moycarkey | –7-1909 | William Fanning | Shanballa |
| 29-9-1906 | Denis Donnelly | Coolkip | –7-1909 | John Fanning | Shanballa |
| -11-1905 | Thomas Mockler | Curraheen | –7-1909 | William Costello | Parkstown |
| -9-1906 | Edmond Skehan | Ballymoreen | –7-1910 | James Wilson | Graigue |
| -11-1905 | James Purcell | Knockroe | –7-1910 | James McCarthy | Curraheen |
| -11-1905 | James Hogan | Coolkip | –7-1910 | Timothy Connors | Grallagh |
| -8-1907 | Edmond Moloney | Graigue | 30-7-1910 | William Connors | Grallagh |
| -8-1907 | Martin O'Grady | Cloughmartin | –7-1910 | Patrick Hanly | Liskeveen |
| -8-1907 | Michael Cawdy | Parkstown | -10-1908 | James Ryan | Parkstown |
| -9-1906 | John McCarthy | Curraheen | -11-1908 | Thomas Ryan | Galboola |
| -8-1907 | Edmond Cawdy | Parkstown | 25-1-1909 | Joseph O'Keeffe | Horse & Jockey |
| -8-1907 | John Carey | Maxfort | 1-2-1909 | David O'Keeffe | Horse & Jockey |
| –9-1906 | Patrick Carey | Maxfort | 30-7-1910 | John Shanahan | Kylenoe |
| -7-1905 | Patrick Lonergan | Coolkip | 30-7-1910 | Denis Toomey | Forgestown |
| -7-1905 | Michael Lonergan | Coolkip | 1-7-1912 | Patrick Heffernan | Coolkip |
| –8-1907 | Martin Costello | Pouldine | 1-7-1911 | Edmond Heffernan | Coolkip |
| -8-1907 | Michael Skehan | Ballymoreen | 1-7-1911 | John Benson | Turtulla |
| -8-1907 | Patrick Buckley | Pouldine | 26-7-1913 | Patrick Shanahan | Moycarkey |
| -8-1907 | Edmond Shanahan | Kylenoe | 30-7-1910 | Edmond O'Grady | Graigue |
| –8-1907 | Michael O'Grady | Cloughmartin | 1-7-1911 | William Wilson | Graigue |
| -8-1907 | John Lambe | Maxfort | 30-7-1910 | James O'Keeffe | Horse & Jockey |
| -8-1907 | John Butler | Turtulla | 1-7-1911 | Patrick Costello | Parkstown |
| -8-1907 | Thomas Toomey | Forgestown | 1-7-1912 | Jeremiah Costello | Parkstown |
| -8-1907 | William Wilson | Ballymoreen | 1-7-1912 | Michael Fanning | Newtown |

*Taking a break – Disco June 2009*

*Back row: Rachel Byrne, Seán Darmody, Nicole O'Brien, Eimear Martin, Leah Murphy, Pádraig Kirwan, Maria Kinane, Jack Kiely, Kathryn Connolly, Conor Ryan, Kieren Hennessy, Michael Flanagan, Thomas Mernagh, Aaron Hayes. Front row: Ann Connolly, Patricia Hayes, Martha Kirwan.*

*Cór na n-Óg – May 1995*
*Múinteoir – Ms. Yvonne Grogan*

*Back row: Tracey McCarthy, Louise Fahey, Sarah Looby, Aidan Bourke, Emma Sweeney, Jackie O'Halloran, Elaine Roche. Centre row: Lesley Abbott, Dolores Purcell, Ann-Marie Dempsey, Breda Kirwan, Collette Fogarty, Elaine Nagle, Siobhán McGuire. Front row: Rick Quigley, Neasa O'Donoghue, Emma Delaney, Clare Kirwan, Ann-Marie Dixon, Noel O'Dwyer. Missing from photo: Aileen Ryan.*

| Date of Entrance | Pupils Name in Full | Residence | Date of Entrance | Pupils Name in Full | Residence |
|---|---|---|---|---|---|
| | John Murphy | Maxfort, Moycarkey | | William Shanahan | Drombo |
| | | | | Michael Shanahan | Drombo |
| | Patrick Murphy | Maxfort, Moycarkey | | Matthew Fanning | Ballytarsna |
| | | | | Walter Stapleton | Horse & Jockey |
| 1935 | Ronald O'Connor | Ballymoreen | | Diarmuid Molloy | Moycarkey |
| | Terence O'Connor | Ballymoreen | | Patrick Purcell | Pouldine |
| | Martin Fitzpatrick | Parkstown | | Timothy Bourke | Ballyhudda |
| | Kevin Maher | Turtulla | | James Mooney | Parkstown |
| | Thomas Boilson | Kylenoe | | Michael Mooney | Parkstown |
| | John Armstrong | Moycarkey | | Martin Boilson | Kylenoe |
| | Nicholas Stokes | Cloughmartin | 1941 | Anthony Lanphier | Parkstown |
| | Joseph Murphy | Moycarkey | | Lawrence Lanphier | Parkstown |
| | William Harris | Graigue | | Anthony Lambe | Moycarkey (Maxfort) |
| | Maurice Noonan | Coolkennedy | | | |
| 1936 | Philip Carroll | Clohogue | | John Barry | Grallagh |
| | Patrick Ryan | Kylenoe | | Eamonn Barry | Grallagh |
| | James Stapleton | Horse & Jockey | | Rodger Lambe | Curraheen |
| | James Normoyle | Ballymoreen | | Timothy Carroll | Clohogue |
| | James Noonan | Coolkennedy | | Daniel Casey | Curraheen |
| 1937 | Patrick Joseph Stokes | Cloughmartin | | Joseph Lanphier | Parkstown |
| | John Ryan | Newtown | 1942 | Thomas Barry | Horse & Jockey |
| | Daniel Ryan | Newtown | | Joseph Noonan | Coolkennedy |
| | Eamonn Fitzgerald | Horse & Jockey | | John Ryan | Grallagh |
| | Patrick Fanning | Ballytarsna | | Gerard Croke | Curraheen |
| | William Tynan | Curraheen | | Patrick Harris | Kylenoe |
| | Joseph Croke | Curraheen | | James Scott | Kylenoe |
| | Patrick Croke | Curraheen | | Joseph Ryan | Curraheen |
| | Patrick Toomey | Forgestown | 1943 | Thomas Twomey | Aughnagomaun |
| | James Tobin | Parkstown | | Ailbe Murphy | Moycarkey |
| | Joseph Kavanagh | Killough | | Seamus Bourke | Ballyhudda |
| 1938 | Thomas Carroll | Clohogue | | Joseph Carroll | Clohogue |
| | James Fanning | Cloughmartin | | Daniel Wilson | Ballymoreen |
| | Tomas McGrath | Curraheen | | Thomas Cormack | Curraheen |
| | Conor MacSweeney | Graigue | | Martin Murphy | Moycarkey |
| | Timothy Maher | Graigue | 1944 | John Fitzpatrick | Parkstown |
| 1939 | Thomas Noonan | Coolkennedy | | Thomas Chute | Knockroe |
| | John Fanning | Coughmartin | | Christopher Molloy | Moycarkey |
| | Diarmuid Shanahan | Liskeveen | | Thomas Lambe | Curraheen |
| | Patrick Burke | Ballyhudda | | Patrick McGrath | Moycarkey |
| | James Hackett | Coolkennedy | | Kevin Barry | Grallagh |
| | Michael Armstrong | Moycarkey | | William Boilson | Kylenoe |
| | Pádraig MacFheorais | Knockroe | | Thomas Ryan | Coolkennedy |
| | Tomás Purcell | Pouldine | | Denis Ryan | Coolkennedy |
| | Peter Purcell | Pouldine | | Patrick Mooney | Parkstown |
| 1940 | Thomas Murphy | Moycarkey | | Patrick S. Maher | Dromgrower |

St. Patrick banished snakes
from Ireland – but we brought one
back to the St. Patrick's Day Parade
at Littleton in 2005.

*Tree planting ceremony in memory of Harry Ryan, R.I.P., Galboola*
*– member of North Tipperary County Council.*
*Liam Ó Donnchú – School Principal – addresses the gathering in Spring 2006.*

*Pupils: Niamh Butler, Michelle Rose Ryan, William O'Dwyer and Conor Hayes watch proceedings as*
*Ms. Siobhán Geraghty North Tipperary Heritage Officer plants the tree. Also included is John Carroll*
*M.C.C. and at back is Seamus Ryan (Harry's Brother).*

| Date of Entrance | Pupils Name in Full | Residence | Date of Entrance | Pupils Name in Full | Residence |
|---|---|---|---|---|---|
| 1945 | Denis Twomey | Aughnagomaun | | Patrick McCormack | Curraheen |
| | John Twomey | Aughnagomaun | | Denis O'Meara | Coolkennedy |
| | Andrew Phillips | Curraheen | 1950 | Martin Hogan | Coolkip |
| | Patrick Bourke | Maxfort | | Francis Phillips | Grallagh |
| | James McGrath | Moycarkey | | Philip Fitzgerald | Graigue |
| | Nicholas Hogan | Coolkip | | Daniel Butler | Parkstown |
| | Patrick S. Hogan | Coolkip | | George Croke | Curraheen |
| | John Hogan | Coolkip | | Henry Maher | Cooklennedy |
| | Daniel Mooney | Parkstown | | John Walsh | Graigue |
| | Thomas Dalton | Galboola | | Patrick O'Connell | Coolkip |
| | Michael Dalton | Galboola | | Michael Fanning | Cloughmartin |
| | Walter Dalton | Galboola | 1951 | Richard Buckley | Cloughmartin |
| | Oliver Croke | Curraheen | | John O'Grady | Cloughmartin |
| | James Chute | Knockroe | | John McCormack | Curraheen |
| | Robert F. Stapleton | Horse & Jockey | | Martin Hewitt | Aughnagomaun |
| | Eoin Maher | Dromgrower | | Andrew Moloney | Graigue |
| | Paul Boilson | Kylenoe | | Robert Lanphier | Curraheen |
| | Philip O'Dwyer | Graigue | | Patrick Heffernan | Graigue |
| | Patrick Philips | Curraheen | | William Britton | Parkstown |
| | Agustine Buckley | Coolkennedy | | John Coman | Galboola |
| 1947 | James McCormack | Curraheen | | Thomas O'Connell | Ashill |
| | Michael Lambe | Curraheen | 1952 | Eamonn Shanahan | Curraheen |
| | James Fitzgerald | Forgestown | | Gerard Buckley | Cloughmartin |
| | Richard Fitzgerald | Forgestown | | Patrick Joseph Ryan | Pouldine |
| | John McGrath | Moycarkey | | Patrick Lambe | Curraheen |
| | John S. Daly | Curraheen | | John Dalton | Galboola |
| | William Mooney | Parkstown | | Michael Twomey | Ballytarsna |
| | Michael O'Connell | Coolkip | | John Buckley | Graigue |
| | Thomas Britton | Parkstown | | Patrick Costello | Parkstown |
| | Charles Ryan | Knockroe | | George Buckley | Cloughmartin |
| | Patrick Barry | Grallagh | | John Lamphier | Curraheen |
| 1948 | Thomas Buckley | Coolkennedy | | Daniel Fitzpatrick | Pouldine |
| | Robert Gleeson | Parkstown | | Edward Buckley | Pouldine |
| | Christopher Philips | Curraheen | 1953 | Thomas Ryan | Pouldine |
| | Kieran Philips | Curraheen | | James Costello | Liskeveen |
| | Patrick Buckley | Graigue | | John Gleeson | Liskeveen |
| | Brendan Hogan | Coolkip | | James Nolan | Curraheen |
| | Patrick Shanahan | Pouldine | | Patrick Costello | Shanballa |
| | Michael Dwyer | Graigue | | Daniel Shaw | Coolkip |
| | James Butler | Parkstown | | Daniel Pine | Knockroe |
| 1949 | William ⁔ | Knockroe | | James Graydon | Knockroe |
| | Jo⁔ | Parkstown | | John O'Brien | Graigue |
| | ⁔rady | Cloughmartin | | Patrick Buckley | Pouldine |
| | ⁔ Flanagan | Graigue | | Daniel O' Regan | Coolkennedy |
| | John Mooney | Parkstown | | Joseph Fell | Coolkennedy |

*LEFT: Jack and Anna Harnett, Parkstown, past pupils of the school, entertained the gathering.*

*BELOW: School pupils dance "a set" during the celebration.*

**Members of the Board of Management and the Ryan Family.**
*Back row: Liam Ó Donnchú, Mrs. Kathleen Kirwan, Mr. Christy Mooney, Fr. Paudie Moloughney, Mr. Tom Quinn, Mrs. Margaret O'Dwyer, Mr. Robert White. Front row: Fr. George Bourke P.P., Sr. Anna, Sr. Colette, Fr. Tom Ryan, Sr. Catarina, Fr. Danny O'Gorman C.C.*

**School staff with the Ryan Family.**
*Back row: Liam Ó Donnchú, Mrs Ann-Marie Carroll, Ms. Lucy Gann, Mrs. Mary Minchin, Mr. Robert White, Mrs. Aileen Colton, Mrs. Fionnuala Hayes. Front row: Fr. George Bourke P.P., Sr. Anna, Sr. Colette, Fr. Tom Ryan, Sr. Catarina, Fr. Danny O'Gorman C.C.*

## Moycarkey N.S., Pouldine, June 9th 2009

Back row: Nora Donoghue, Ann-Marie Carew, Gillian Fogarty, Maria Kinane, Ann Connolly, Maria O'Keeffe, Keith Melbourne, Seán Darmody, Kieren Hennessy, Aaron Hayes, Micheál Foley, Pádraig Kirwan, Tomás Darmody, Michael Flanagan, Rachel Byrne, Martha Kirwan, Olivia Hogan, Caitlin Donnelly, Patricia Hayes, Kathryn Connolly, Leah Murphy.

Fifth row: Liam Ó Donnchú (Principal) Ms. Siobhán Hoare, Ms. Jacqueline O'Meara, Ms. Sarah Horgan, Mr. Donie Shanahan Mr. Robert White, Ruairí Martin, David Shaw, Naomi Cawley, Daniel Kavanagh, Emer Whelan, Conor Ryan, Jack Kiely, Ryan White, Aaron Ryan, Darren Ryan, Brian Maher, Kevin O'Regan, Thomas Mernagh, Nicola Doyle, Nicole O'Brien, Shauna Fitzpatrick, Deirdre Ryan, Megan Lahart, Michael O'Callaghan, Dean O'connor, Alex Murphy, Jack O'Meara, Mrs Catherine Walsh, Fr. George Bourke P.P. Ms. Elaine Brady, Mr. Pádraig Fahey.

Fourth row: Mrs. Ann-Marie Carroll, Mrs. Mary Minchin, Robert O'Donoghue, Emily Murphy, Linda Donoghue, Aoife Meagher, Lauren Cloonan, Heather Ryan, Aidan Scott, Seamus Telford, Caolan Noonan, Victoria Donoghue, Kat Flanagan, Eoghan Hayes, Conor Harnett, Kieran Dunne, Fiona Kavanagh, Clarisse Tobin, Saoirse O'Meara, Claire Ryan, Aaron Cawley, Killian Ryan, Adam Condon, Cáit Darmody, Shane Maher, Jonathan Ely, Niamh Meaney, Holly Tobin, Ciarán Kirwan, Rachel Dowling.

Third row: Anthony Doyle, Zoe O'Meara, John Kirwan, Daniel Browne, Ben O'Dwyer, Sean Kavanagh, Patrick Doyle, Dylan Shaw, Brendan Looby, Bill Maher, Colin Hartigan, Bill O'Keeffe, Zachary Jackson, Brian O'Callaghan, Dean O'Brien, Noah Minchin, Kieran Carew, John Coffey, Amy Cummins, Deirdre Fogarty, Kate Looby, Emma Dowling, Megan O'Donoghue, Jack Fahey, Mrs. Fionnuala Hayes, Ms. Lucy McGann, Ms. Fiona McCullagh.

Second row: Adam O'Dwyer, Lauren O'Sullivan, James Shanahan, Conor Clohessy, David Doyle, Ciara Coffey, Seán Flanagan, James Webster, Joe Maher, Catherine Fogarty, Gráinne Stapleton, Joey Ryan, Ivan Cawley, Joan O'Keeffe, Thomas O'Donoghue, Adam Costello, Conor O'Grady, Rian Martin, Kelly-Ann Gilleece, Maria Kennedy, Róisín Donnelly, Evan Tobin, Jack Corcoran, Aisling Maher, Conor Dunne, Thomas Whelan, Kaylee Stonestreet, Amy Cloonan, Queva O'Meara.

Front row: Dean O'Donoghue, Emma O'Sullivan, Neil Maxwell, Adam Ryan, Michelle Flanagan, Cloe Cummins, Luke Fell, Rebecca Hogan, Kristian Ryan, Caleb Butler, Sophie Ely, Eve Dardis, Tristan McCormack Ryan, Ben Ely, Jack Fahey.

**Right:**
*Ciaran Dunne,
Eoghan Hayes,
Conor Harnett,
Alex Murphy.*

**Above:**
*Shane Maher,
Cillian Ryan,
Caolan Noonan,
Caolan O'Brien.*

**Left:**
*Once upon
a time . . .*

| Date of Entrance | Pupils Name in Full | Residence | Date of Entrance | Pupils Name in Full | Residence |
|---|---|---|---|---|---|
| | Daniel O'Regan | Knockroe | | Kieran O'Grady | Curraheen |
| | Ian O'Brien | Beakstown | | Loughlin Walsh Doherty | Thurles |
| | Pat Molloy | Knockroe | 2001 | Aaron Hayes | Knockroe |
| 1996 | Peadar Kinane | Kevinsfort | | Micheál Ryder | Thurles |
| | Jack Hassett | Archerstown | | Conor Ryan | Newtown |
| | Adam Carew | Galboola | | Pádraig Kirwan | Moycarkey |
| | Finbarr Hayes | DerryHogan | | Michael Flanagan | Graigue |
| | Stephen Kirwan | Moycarkey | | Liam Meaney | Thurles |
| | Niall Hewitt | Knockroe | | Thomas Mernagh | Moycarkey |
| | Thomas Quigley | Turtulla | | Darragh Ryan | Thurles |
| | Cathal Gleeson, Fahey | Galboola | 2002 | Keith Melbourne | Curraheen |
| | Brian Butler | Parkstown | | David Shaw | Horse & Jockey |
| | Ryan Noonan | Cloughmartin | | Mark Cummins | Moycarkey |
| | Ryan Hayes | Thurles | | Aaron Ryan | Turtulla |
| | Patrick Sinnott | Thurles | | John Corbett | Shanballa |
| 1997 | Jamie Maher | Ballymoreen | | Michael O'Sullivan | Thurles |
| | Timmy Ryan | Maxfort | | Jamie McCarthy | Thurles |
| | Andrew Fogarty | Parkstown | | Kevin O'Regan | Coolkennedy |
| | Cristopher Byrne | Moycarkey | | Darren Ryan | Newtown |
| | Richard O'Keeffe | Maxfort | | Ruairí Martin | Ballybeg |
| | Joey Coman | Galboola | | Brian Maher | Coolkennedy |
| | Thomas Noonan | Cloughmartin | | Daniel Kavanagh | Pouldine |
| | Aidan Fitzpatrick | Cloughmartin | 2003 | Merriman Mogridge | Thurles |
| 1998 | Jamie Costello | Lahardan | | Cody Jackson | Littleton |
| | William O'Dwyer | Moycarkey | | Conor Hartnett | Parkstown |
| | Ivan Chadfield | Turtulla | | Philip Maher | Kylenoe |
| | Conor Hayes | Leigh | | Eoghan Hayes | Leigh |
| 1999 | Seán Cawley | Two-Mile - Borris | | Seamus Telford | Littleton |
| | | | | Alexander Murphy | Thurles |
| | Aaron Flanagan | Graigue | | Kieran Dunne | Forgestown |
| | Tomás Ryan | Cooleagh | | Jack O'Meara | Pouldine |
| | David Ryan | Thurles | | Michael O'Callaghan | Turtulla |
| | Gavin O'Brien | Beakstown | | Caolan Noonan | Cloughmartin |
| 2000 | Jack O'Dwyer | Galboola | | Caolan O'Brien | Thurles |
| | David O'Shea | Thurles | | Seán Dalton | Parkstown |
| | Rory O'Regan | Coolkennedy | 2004 | Ciarán Kirwan | Moycarkey |
| | Patrick Maher | Ballymoreen | | Michael Dalton | Parkstown |
| | David O'Dwyer | Moycarkey | | Jonathan Ely | Newhill |
| | Ian O'Dwyer | Moycarkey | | Eamonn Martin | Ballybeg |
| | Patrick ˙ elan | Kylenoe | | Adam Condon | Liskeveen |
| | ˡᵃ ˌelan | Kylenoe | | Shane Maher | Coolkennedy |
| | ˏ Moloney | Graigue | | Killian Ryan | Thurles |
| | ˏˏˏ an L ˏns | Turtulla | | Jack Kiely | Liskeveen |
| | Stephen Lyons | Turtulla | | Neil Albery | Shanbally |
| | Andrew Dunne | Forgestown | 2005 | John Kirwan | Moycarkey |

| Date of Entrance | Pupils Name in Full | Residence |
|---|---|---|
| | Bill Maher | Coolkennedy |
| | Colin Hartigan | Piercetown |
| | Aidan Scott | Kylenoe |
| | Daniel Brown | Shanbally |
| | Stephen Fitzpatrick | Cloughmartin |
| | Seán Kavanagh | Pouldine |
| | Zachary Jackson | Littleton |
| | Bill O'Keeffe | Horse & Jockey |
| | Dylan Shaw | Horse & Jockey |
| | Ben O'Dwyer | Ballymoreen |
| | Feidhlim Ryder | Thurles |
| | Brendan Looby | Augnagomaun |
| | Oisín Copeland | Thurles |
| | Paddy Donoghue | Ballybeg |
| | Seán Cawley | Ashill |
| 2006 | Robert O'Donoghue | Turtulla |
| | Anthony Doyle | Turtulla |
| | Noah Minchin | Dromgower |
| | Dean O'Brien | Beakstown |
| | Brian O'Callaghan | Turtulla |
| | Jack Fahey | Graigue |
| | Dylan Stapleton | Pouldine |
| | Kieran Carew | Galboola |
| | John Coffey | Moycarkey |
| | Aaron Cawley | Ashill |
| | Ryan White | Parkstown |
| | Tomás Darmody | Curraheen |
| | Kieren Hennessy | Holycross |
| | Seán Darmody | Curraheen |
| 2007 | Micheál Foley | Ballinure |
| | Dean O'Connor | Lanespark |

| Date of Entrance | Pupils Name in Full | Residence |
|---|---|---|
| | Patrick Doyle | Turtulla |
| | James Shanahan | Thurles |
| | Adam O'Dwyer | Ballymoreen |
| | Conor Clohessy | Ballymoreen |
| | Evan Tobin | Horse & Jockey |
| | David Doyle | Turtulla |
| | Thomas Whelan | Moycarkey |
| | Conor O'Grady | Grallagh |
| | Conor Dunne | Forgestown |
| | Adam Costello | Graigue |
| | Rian Martin | Ballybeg |
| | Jack Corcoran | Tonagha |
| | Emmett Condon | Liskeveen |
| 2008 | Joey Ryan | Aughnagomaun |
| | Ben Ely | Newhill |
| | Jack Fahey | Graigue |
| | Niall Maxwell | Liskeveen |
| | Tristan McCormack | Ryan Liskeveen |
| | Thomas O'Donoghue | Ballybeg |
| | Joe Maher | Coolkennedy |
| | Seán Flanagan | Forgestown |
| | Adam Ryan | Pouldine |
| | Caleb Butler | Thurles |
| | Kristian Ryan | Liskeveen |
| | James Webster | Thurles |
| | Luke Fell | Knockroe |
| | Dean O'Donoghue | Turtulla |
| | Paul Freeman Nash | Liskeveen |
| | Nathan Dorney | Archerstown |
| | Ivan Cawley | Ashill |

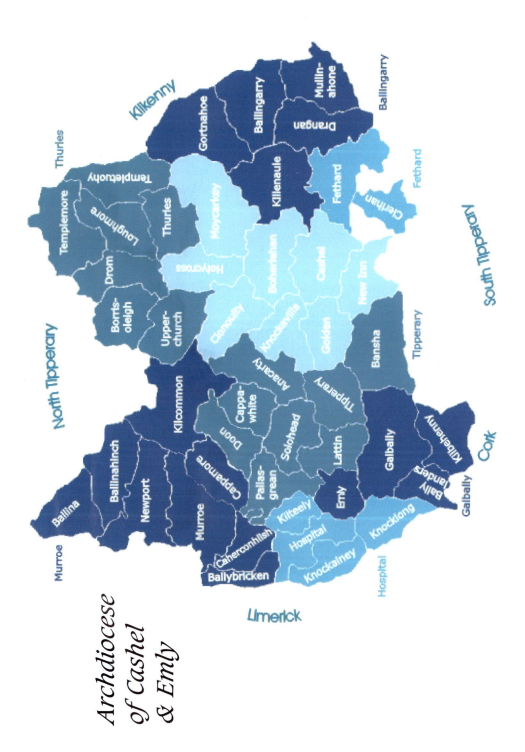

*Archdiocese of Cashel & Emly*

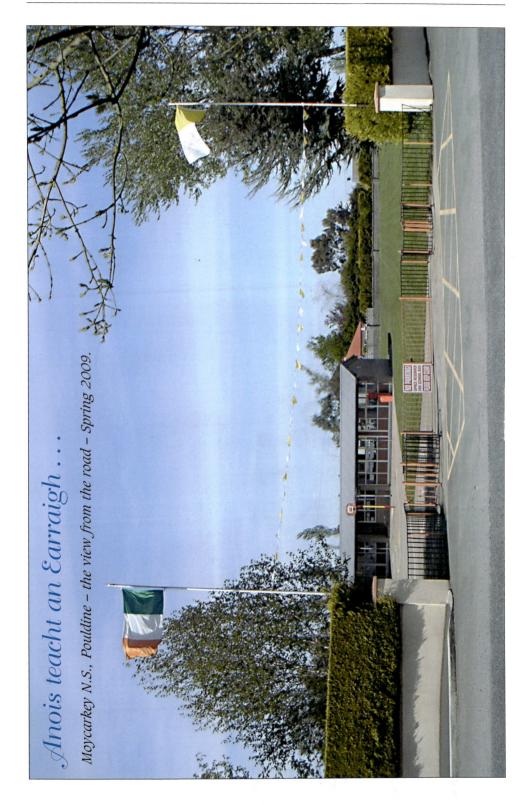

*Anois teacht an Earraigh . . . .*

Moycarkey N.S., Pouldine – the view from the road – Spring 2009.

# Sponsorship List

1. AIB Bank, Thurles
2. Allianz Insurance Co.
3. Amber Petroleum, Horse and Jockey
4. Carvery Restaurant, Thurles Shopping Centre
5. Centenary Thurles Co-Op
6. Christy and Catherine Mooney, Ashfield, Littleton
7. Copymore Ltd., Urlingford, Co. Kilkenny
8. Darmody Fencing Ltd., Ballyerk, Two Mile Borris
9. De Ja Sports Sales, Kilmeague, Naas, Co. Kildare
10. Donal and Mairéad O'Regan, Knockroe
11. Ed. And Michelle Donnelly, Aughnagomaun
12. Eileen Flanagan, Eileen's Cleaning Service, Galboola, Littleton
13. Eurogene AI Services, Cahir
14. F.B.D. Insurance, Thurles
15. Folens Publishing Company, Tallaght, Dublin
16. Frank Roche & Sons Ltd., Thurles
17. Gerald Stakelum Ltd., Parnell St., Thurles
18. Glasheen's Coaches, Holycross
19. Gleeson Quarries, Laffansbridge
20. Gleeson Steel & Engineering, Gortnahoe
21. Hennessy's Hackney & Bus Hire, Littleton
22. Horse and Jockey Hotel
23. J.J. Fogarty Ltd., Horse and Jockey
24. Jackson Electrical Services, 20 McDonagh Tce., Littleton
25. Joe Delaney, Lawnmowers, Ballygammane, Thurles
26. Joe O'Sullivan, Taxi & Bus Services, Littleton
27. John & Margaret Hogan, Coolkip
28. John Egan, Civil Engineer, Dovea, Templemore
29. John O'Keeffe, Car Sales – Horse and Jockey
30. Kevin Darmody Ltd., Thurles Retail Park, Stradavoher, Thurles
31. Lár na Páirce, Tipperary G.A.A. Merchandise Shop, Thurles
32. Liam & Mary O'Brien, Pouldine
33. Lycon Auto Spares Ltd., Thurles
34. Magh Coirce Montessori, Moycarkey Village
35. Michael and Mary Roche, Horse and Jockey
36. Michael Lowry T.D., Abbey Road, Thurles

37. Moycarkey – Coolcroo Athletic Club
38. Moycarkey N.S. Board of Management
39. Moycarkey National School Parents' Council
40. Moycarkey-Borris G.A.A. Club
41. Noel Ely Haulage, Newhill, Two Mile Borris
42. P.B.F. Contracting Ltd., T/A Pat Fahey, Graigue
43. Pat & Mary Bourke, Maxfort
44. Pat Ely, Centra Supermarkets, Kickham St. and The Mall, Thurles
45. Pat Maher, Industrial & Domestic Plumbing, Coolkennedy, Thurles
46. Pat Ryan, Senator Windows
47. Re:Charge Cartridges, Friar St., Thurles
48. Rev. George Bourke P.P., Moycarkey
49. Roadmaster Caravans Ltd., Johnstown, Co. Kilkenny
50. Ronayne Hardware, Thurles
51. Ryan Architectural Solutions, 29 Liberty Square, Thurles
52. Seamus Hanafin, Thurles Retail Park, Stradavoher, Thurles
53. Sean Treacy Pipe Band, Moycarkey Borris
54. Semple Stadium, Dúrlas Éile
55. Sheppard Opticians, Liberty Sq., Thurles
56. Stakelums Hardware, Thurles
57. The O'Hara Family, Pouldine
58. The O'Regan Family, Coolkennedy
59. The Pike, Kickham St., Thurles
60. Thurles Bouncing Castles, Metal Bridge, Upperchurch
61. Thurles Credit Union
62. Tom Maher, Maher Insurance Brokers, Thurles
63. Two Mile Borris/St. Kevin's F.C.
64. W. Fitzgibbon Furniture Store, Mitchel St., Thurles
65. Wallace Travel – Coach Hire, Rosegreen, Cashel

*Míle Buíochas to all our sponsors.*